A BIBLICAL TEXT AND I
The Survival of Jonah in W

This book charts the mutations of a particularly buoyant sliver of biblical text – the book of Jonah – as it latches onto Christian and Jewish motifs and anxieties, passes through highbrow and lowbrow culture, and finally becomes something of a scavenger among the ruins, as, in its most resourceful move to date, it begins to live off the demise of faith. Written at a point between Cultural Studies, Jewish Studies, Literature, and Art, this book is concerned with those versions of the biblical that escape proper disciplinary boundaries: it shifts the focus from 'Main-stream' to 'Backwater' interpretation. It is less a navigation of interpretative history and more an interrogation of larger political/cultural issues: anti-Judaism in Biblical Studies, the secularisation of the Bible, and the projection of the Bible as credulous ingénu, naïve Other to our savvy post-Enlightenment selves.

YVONNE SHERWOOD is Lecturer in Biblical Studies and Jewish Studies at the University of Glasgow, having completed degrees in English Literature, Biblical Studies and Jewish Studies and a British Academy Postdoctoral Fellowship in Biblical Studies. She has published articles in *Imprimatur*, *Semeia*, and *Biblical Interpretation*, has written for the Feminist Companion series (Sheffield Academic Press) and is the author of *The Prostitute and the Prophet* (1996). She currently chairs the 'Reading, Theory and the Bible' section at the Society of Biblical Literature.

A BIBLICAL TEXT AND ITS AFTERLIVES

The Survival of Jonah in Western Culture

YVONNE SHERWOOD

University of Glasgow

CAMBRIDGE
UNIVERSITY PRESS

CAMBRIDGE UNIVERSITY PRESS
Cambridge, New York, Melbourne, Madrid, Cape Town, Singapore,
São Paulo, Delhi, Dubai, Tokyo

Cambridge University Press
The Edinburgh Building, Cambridge CB2 8RU, UK

Published in the United States of America by Cambridge University Press, New York

www.cambridge.org
Information on this title: www.cambridge.org/9780521795616

First published 2000

A catalogue record for this publication is available from the British Library

ISBN 978-0-521-79174-8 Hardback
ISBN 978-0-521-79561-6 Paperback

Transferred to digital printing 2009

In memory of Robert Carroll

Contents

Illustrations

Acknowledgements

This book was conceived in the luxury of a year's scholarship at the Oxford Centre for Hebrew and Jewish Studies, and a British Academy Postdoctoral Fellowship gave it time to swell prodigiously – and then to be slimmed down to a more manageable size. The voices, influences, and friendships it relies on are legion, but here are some of the ones that particularly come to mind. So, thanks to Jeremy Schonfield for helping me get the ball rolling and keeping a considerate eye on Jonah's progress and to Philip Alexander, David Gunn, Amy-Jill Levine, and Stephen Moore for offering enthusiasm and feedback at crucial points. Many thanks to Tina Pippin for directing me to the *Northern Exposure* sequence, and to Tim Beal for sending me a copy of the video, complete with local advertising. This book would also be poorer visually and anecdotally without the help of Anne Datta at the British Museum, who supplied the nineteenth-century cetology diagrams and who put me onto *The Ocean Almanac*. Thanks also to the staff at the Warburg and Courtauld Institutes for helping me to rummage through the history of Jonah in art, to Ezra Golombok and Patrick Curran for hunting down stray illustrations, to Kevin Taylor at Cambridge University Press for taking the manuscript on, and to Jean Field for tidying it up for its public debut.

Since the completion of this book marks the transition from Oxford and London to Scotland I would like to thank the friends and colleagues who have made my time down south such a pleasurable one. Thanks especially to Tod Linafelt and Rebecca Nelson Linafelt for being neighbours in Oxford and hosts in Washington D.C., to Sarah Pearce and Julie Clague for generous gifts of beer, to Richard Hulme for never forgetting to ask how the book was going, and to my sister Alison who, with typical wit, greeted the completion of the second book with the immortal line: 'Good, I can have

matching book-ends now.' Particular thanks to friends and colleagues at the Roehampton Institute – but especially to Beverley
Clack, John Jarick, David Tombs, Brook Pearson and Matt
O'Donnell – for making it such a difficult place to leave. Above all,
thanks to the person who shelters behind that wonderful euphemism
the 'person without whom' – Richard Davie – who has lived through
two books now, and endured/enjoyed everything from the animated
pub conversations to the tedium of compiling bibliographies.

Finally, it is with great sadness, but also immense gratitude, that I
dedicate this book to the memory of Robert Carroll. Ever since I
first met Robert in the early nineteen-nineties, he has been a
constant source of friendship and support: he always found time to
involve himself in my work, and, as usual, was one of the main
contributors to this book (we regularly corresponded about Jonah
and he sent me copies of the Wolf Mankowitz play and the Abeshaus
painting). In the field of British and international Biblical Studies he
was a unique, larger-than-life character – not least because of his
breadth of reading, and his commitment to challenging the discipline
from outside its 'proper' borders – and his sudden death earlier this
year has left a great hole in the field, and in so many of our lives. I
will miss his wry humour, I will miss our recent drinking sessions as
colleagues here at Glasgow, and I will miss showing him the final
version of the book.

I hope he would have approved.

Introduction

Marvellous excess and monstrous mutations: on dishing up and spinning (out) biblical words

> Interdisciplinary work, so much discussed these days, is not about confronting already constituted disciplines (none of which, in fact, is willing to let itself go). To do something interdisciplinary it's not enough to choose a 'subject' (a theme) and gather around it two or three sciences. Interdisciplinarity consists in creating a new subject that belongs to no-one.
>
> (Roland Barthes)[1]

According to the rabbis, when God gave humankind Torah he gave it in the form of wheat for us to make flour from it, and flax for us to make a garment from it: Torah is the raw material, to be ground, woven, and spun (out). Inevitably, as time passed, the grindings, stitchings, and weavings of the word became more and more elaborate, the cloths more exotic and fabulous, the recipes more complex. No longer satisfied with bread and cotton, readers revelled in the meta-textual equivalent of exquisite satins, Paisley patterns, Chicken Marengo, wild mushroom fricassee. The ur-words were cooked up/ stitched together with contemporary buzz-words, fashions, anxieties, desires, to dish up the text in appetising ways.

This book offers a glimpse into the tailor's shop and gourmet restaurant that is the interpretative history of the book of Jonah. It watches readers as they spin out meaning, engage in careful exegetical stitch-work, and cook up ever more spicy and appealing recipes. It takes in all kinds of readings: reading as maverick and unconventional as Zandra Rhodes designs, and as repetitive and uncreative as a rationing cookbook, or *How to Do Things with Spam*. Above all, it looks at how the book has been stitched up (and closed

---

[1] Translated quotation by J. Clifford in *Writing Culture: The Poetics and Politics of Ethnography* (ed. J. Clifford and G. E. Marcus; Berkeley: University of California Press, 1984), p. 1, from R. Barthes, 'Jeunes Chercheurs', in *Le bruissement de la langue* (Paris: Seuil, 1984), pp. 97–103 (no page cited by Clifford).

down) by a reading in poor taste, a reading that habitually pairs
Jonah with Jewishness, and it aims to unpick that reading and start
reading again.

So to the interpretative menu or bill of fare. The book is divided
into three sections (starter, entrée, and dessert). The first section
('The Mainstream') takes in the staple diet of Jonah readings: those
served up in the Mainstream scholarly and Christian tradition from
the first to the twentieth century. The second course ('Backwaters
and underbellies') is appropriately by far the largest, meatiest, most
substantial portion of the book, and looks at alternative serving
suggestions, the way the text is dished up in independent *bijoux* little
eating establishments: medieval poetry, Netherlandish art, Jewish
interpretation, and other hidden cultural corners and sidestreet
cafés. To finish, I stir these new ingredients into the book of Jonah,
and so cook up a 'new' interpretation, which is also a kind of hash,
or jambalaya – a combination of insights from biblical scholarship
mixed with older, more piquant, marginal readings. In 'Regurgitating Jonah' I self-consciously stir up the text, swell it, fatten it,
inject it with new reading idioms: I take this perennial biblical
chestnut, turn it into purée, and serve it up, Terence Conran
fashion, with char-grilled peppers and *pommes de terre*.

Thus I am also stirring up the order and priorities of traditional
biblical studies, where the detailed discussion of the biblical text and
its setting in a specific historical context has been the main (and
indeed pretty much the only) course. Where popular non-scholarly
sources have featured, they have been featured as a pinch of cultural
spice (the odd quote from *Moby Dick*, the odd allusion to Aldous
Huxley, no more) and they have only been admitted at the point
where they cohere, or seem to cohere, with the largely sustained
official interpretation. In this study, interpretation comes first,
indeed interpretation overwhelms my text, as if to demonstrate how
it also overwhelms, eclipses, *and always precedes* the biblical 'original'.
My premise is that biblical texts are literally sustained by interpretation, and the volume, ubiquity, and tenacity of interpretation make
it impossible to dream that we can take the text back, through some
kind of seductive academic striptease, to a pure and naked original
state. The corollary to the rabbis' statement is that though the
biblical text can always be re-deflected, it can never be recovered.
For how can flour be turned back into wheat, how can cloth be
turned back into flax, and how can the cooked be made raw again?

The book of Jonah has been selected as my guinea-pig text for several reasons. Firstly, this is a book with which most readers will be – at least vaguely – familiar: most people know Jonah, as the Qur'an knows him, as the 'man in the fish', but there is much left to discover, for popular memory remembers little of the framing command to go to Nineveh, the flight to Tarshish, and wonderful details such as the sackcloth-wearing cattle, the shivering ship, the fabulously growing *qiqayon* plant and the plant-smiting 'warrior' worm. Secondly, this is a tiny text that is virtually capsising under the weight of interpretation: though measuring no more than forty inches square in my edition, the book of Jonah has generated literally acres of visual and verbal glosses, and has demonstrated an extraordinary capacity for cultural survival – surviving in spite of, and in some cases (as I will go on to show) living off, the energy of the demise of faith in the Judaeo-Christian[2] West. Thirdly, because it demonstrates the extreme divergence between Mainstream/scholarly/Christian and Jewish/popular readings, the book of Jonah obligingly concentrates all the issues raised in recent work on Biblical Studies/Cultural Studies: issues about the separation of a loose cultural surplus from proper scholarly activity, and questions concerning which (if any) interpretative trajectories have the right to define, and contain the text.[3] Fourthly, and this point is intrinsically related to the last, since professional interpretation has orbited so obsessively around the motif of 'Jonah the Jew', the book of Jonah provides a graphic opening into a discussion of what can be called the 'colonisation' of the 'Old Testament' by a Christian logic that all too often sinks back into an essentially supersessionist reflex. Fifthly, since Jonah is by general consensus an odd-man-out in the Old Testament/Hebrew

---

2 The difficulties of the term 'Judaeo-Christian' will be discussed later in the book (see pp. 72–4; 79–87).

3 For a sampling of recent work on the Bible and Cultural Studies see A. Bach, *Women, Seduction and Betrayal in Biblical Narrative* (Cambridge: Cambridge University Press, 1997); R. Boer, *Knockin' on Heaven's Door* (London and New York: Routledge, 1999); S. D. Moore, *God's Gym: Divine Male Bodies of the Bible* (New York: Routledge, 1996); T. Pippin, *Apocalyptic Bodies: The Biblical End of the World in Text and Image* (London and New York: Routledge, 1999); J. C. Exum and S. D. Moore (eds.), *Biblical Studies/Cultural Studies: The Third Sheffield Colloquium* (Sheffield: Sheffield Academic Press, 1998); S. D. Moore (ed.), *In Search of the Present: The Bible through Cultural Studies* (Semeia; Atlanta: Scholar's Press, forthcoming). Other studies focusing on the text's afterlife or reception history include J. F. A. Sawyer, *The Fifth Gospel: Isaiah in the History of Christianity* (Cambridge: Cambridge University Press, 1996); M. E. Stone and T. A. Bergren, *Biblical Figures Outside the Bible* (Harrisburg: Trinity Press International, 1998); and J. L. Kugel, *The Bible As it Was* (Cambridge, Mass.: Harvard University Press, 1997), although the latter two volumes concentrate on early biblical interpretation.

Bible[4] canon, fitting neither into the Prophets, nor, more specifically the Book of the Twelve,[5] it is the ideal book for raising the question of what we mean by (and can possibly entertain in the context of) the 'biblical', and what expectations scholars and general readers alike project onto a biblical book. The scholarly reflex that tends on the one hand to acknowledge Jonah as something of a mutant biblical branch – the 'last and strangest blossom on an ancient literary stem'[6] – and on the other, to retrieve the book as a purely conventional specimen of the biblical, bears further investigation, for it suggests that a certain homogenisation, standardisation, and sacralisation (as well as Christianisation) instinctively attends our readings of biblical literature. Sixthly, and finally, since Jonah has been regarded as a 'GCSE-level', childish story (and on this, at least, popular and scholarly interpretation seem to agree), this is the ideal text to challenge our modern projections of 'primitive' and particularly 'primitive biblical' literature, without necessarily relapsing into the hyperbole that assumes that the high moral/cultural value of the Bible finds a corollary in (or can even be substituted by) a superlative aesthetic. While scholars promote the myth of a school-teacherly text, chalking out an all-too-simple lesson about 'loving your enemies' on the blackboard, and post-Enlightenment, popular interpretation plays in the seeming abyss between a knowing 'now' and a naïve, mythical 'then' (when people could *believe* in a man-swallowing fish), the book of Jonah is busy crafting newness from twisted elements of tradition, creating intricate labyrinths of pun, and so interrogating any sense of a naïve text, coming to us from the religious childhood of consciousness.

If it is the task of criticism to mimic, in some sense, its subject,[7]

---

[4] The term Old Testament/Hebrew Bible is an attempt to do justice to the fact that the book does double duty as sacred text for both Christians and Jews. Though the term Hebrew Bible is not ideal – not to say tautologous – it is the term generally adopted in Biblical Studies to replace the problematic term 'Old Testament' and is the term that I shall be using throughout this book.

[5] In the Hebrew Bible there are four prophetic books: three 'Major' Prophets – Isaiah, Jeremiah and Ezekiel – and the 'Book of the Twelve', the collection of the twelve so-called Minor Prophets. The Minor Prophets are Hosea, Joel, Amos, Obadiah, Jonah, Micah, Nahum, Habakkuk, Zephaniah, Haggai, Zechariah, and Malachi (though they shuffle out in slightly different order in the Jewish and Christian canon).

[6] G. von Rad, cited without reference in K. Koch, *The Prophets*. II. *The Babylonian and Persian Periods* (trans. M. Kohl; London, SCM, 1983), p. 184.

[7] Of course in these postmodern/poststructuralist times we are supposed to have broken with ideas like mimesis and realism, and yet even the most self-consciously text-creating of critics finds it hard to transcend the belief that there should be some sense of (twisted) analogue in

then this book is not a 'proper' academic book, just as Jonah is not a proper biblical text. It is not 'original', or at least it foregrounds its reliance on the already-written: like Jonah it works on the basis that knowledge and meaning are *agglutinative*, and that new products can be made by bringing together existing traditions and recombining them. To this end, biblical commentary, Jewish midrash, the thirteenth-century poem *Patience*, sixteenth-century Netherlandish art, and the contemporary TV series *Northern Exposure* all meet and jostle between the same covers, and strange meetings between, say, Zygmunt Bauman and Old Testament biblical commentary, or between Michel Foucault and John Calvin, mimic the strange meetings between Jonah and the rest of the canon (as it seems so very different to a book like Deuteronomy, and so out of place at a summit meeting of the members of the Book of the Twelve). And insofar as it brings together subjects that are usually segregated – Biblical Studies, Jewish Studies, English and American Literature, Literary and Cultural Theory – this book falls into the catch-all category of a 'multidisciplinary' or 'interdisciplinary' work, or – to use a less official term also used of Melville's *Moby Dick* – an 'intellectual chowder'.[8] However, rather than reconciling myself like Barthes to creating a new (free-floating) subject that belongs to no one, I am concerned to *confront* already-established disciplines on the basis that one discipline can provocatively destabilise and expose the myopia of another. Thus Biblical Studies (specifically Old Testament Studies) is challenged head on by Jewish Studies, and nudged by literary and popular culture into engagement with a culture where 'God' is no longer a given; and conversely, Biblical Studies challenges literary/popular culture's rather naïve projections of the 'biblical' as a holistic, undifferentiated mass, defined by something of an inferiority complex in relation to the 'Scientific'.

Crossing disciplinary boundaries inevitably raises questions of how we legitimate 'proper' academic work and how we transfer

our relations with the text. So, for example, Stephen Moore writes: 'Rather than take a jackhammer to the concrete, parabolic language of the Gospels, replacing graphic images with abstract categories, I prefer to respond to a pictographic text pictographically, to a narrative text narratively, producing a critical text that is a postmodern analogue of the premodern text that it purports to read' (S. D. Moore, *Mark and Luke in Poststructuralist Perspectives: Jesus Begins to Write* (New Haven: Yale University Press, 1992), p. xviii).

8 The phrase, meant as a term of disparagement, was used by one Evert Duycknick, in an early review of *Moby Dick*. An extract from the review can be found in H. Melville, *Moby Dick* (A Norton Critical Edition; ed. H. Hayford and H. Parker; New York: W. W. Norton, 1967), p. 613.

criteria of propriety and permissibility between different sections of the university. As an English Literature graduate who has spent the last ten years with at least one, if not both, feet in the field of Biblical Studies, I find myself still in conflict with the pervasive positivism that permeates the discipline, and I find myself reacting against the tendency to take a literary text and convert it into a thesis – and so project the author of Hebrew Bible texts as proto-Christian or Proto-*Aufklärer*. Like Adorno, I believe that 'knowledge comes to us through a network of prejudices, opinions, innervations, self-corrections, presuppositions and exaggerations' and that 'Every thought [and every reading] which is not idle bears branded on it the impossibility of its full legitimation',[9] but I find that whereas a sense of the fundamentally experimental character of interpretation pervaded every corridor of the English Literature department, such beliefs in Biblical Studies tend to confine one to a small coterie of interpreters who crouch at the corners of the discipline under the catch-all umbrella of the 'postmodern'. I find myself straining against a system where we are encouraged to represent our conclusions like mathematical calculations and always show our working, or to progress slowly and stealthily towards a seemingly inevitable conclusion, weighed down by footnotes that we wear like concrete shoes. And I find myself pressing against the centripetal disciplinary pressures that encourage readers to situate their own new observations at just the right spot between the proper (the unique) and propriety (participation in the collective), and at just the right degree of remove from the comforting flanks of received opinion. Such an environment creates little space for the idea that thought can have an antithetical function and be valuable precisely because of 'its distance from the continuity of the familiar';[10] or that thought should have an 'element of exaggeration, of over-shooting the object, of self-detachment from the weight of the factual'.[11] But it is precisely such volatility that pervades our biblical text. With its extravagantly experimental narrative conditions, its big city, big fish, and big triffid-like plant, and its 'what ifs' or 'perhapses',[12] the book

---

[9] T. Adorno, *Minima Moralia* (trans. E. F. N. Jephcott; London: Verso, 1999), pp. 80–1.

[10] *Ibid.*, p. 80.

[11] *Ibid.*, pp. 126–7.

[12] Adorno argues that a certain 'volatility of thought' is intrinsic to philosophy (*Minima Moralia*, p. 127) and Nietzsche famously claimed that thought is characterised by the ability to say 'perhaps' (cited in J. Derrida, *Archive Fever: A Freudian Impression* (trans. E. Peronowitz; Chicago: University of Chicago Press, 1996), p. 49).

of Jonah gives the distinct impression of deliberately detaching itself from the continuity of the familiar. I have no particular desire to bring the 'furious harmony of reasonable people'[13] crashing down on my head, but cannot help but feel that the best way to read and explore a book like this is by imitating its own strategies of *stretching*.

A note on footnotes

The text that wanders beyond the safe confines of a disciplinary home is constantly traumatised by anxieties about its weight: is it too 'thin', too cursory, or too dense and allusive? In an attempt to imagine – at every turn – a reader who is a specialist in the particular area under discussion, and a reader who is not at all, I have tended to put necessary explanations (together with modifications and apologetic, for specialists) down below, in footnotes. If footnotes in mono-disciplinary(?) academic works act, as Anthony Grafton suggests, as an 'impregnably armoured bottom, like a tank' or as proof of guild membership (like the certificates on a dentist's wall),[14] these footnotes serve the additional function of contextualising any allusive comments and explaining any specialist terms. Most importantly, they allow the plot of the book to progress quite crisply, without stopping for explanation at every turn.

But not without cost. Sadly, these footnotes and explanations undermine that wonderful sense of mutual flattery that authors and readers can establish with one another, as I assume that you, the polymath reader, 'know' *Sir Gawain and the Green Knight* and the *Pirke de Rabbi Eliezer* and Hebrew and Middle English and sixteenth-century Netherlandish art, and as you admire the cavalier familiarity with which I deal with different areas of knowledge. Personally, I think it's worth the sacrifice. My aim above all is that the book should be complete in itself, understandable in itself, for non-specialist readers (though I have, where possible, also suggested further reading and further lines of enquiry in footnotes). I have also used Hebrew as sparingly as possible, but where I have, I have given the Hebrew script and a very rough English transliteration, rather than the conventional transliteration code, because this has always struck me as a highly cryptic sub-language which manages to be both more difficult to read than Hebrew for the Hebrew-reader and,

---

13 Adorno, *Minima Moralia*, p. 69.
14 A. Grafton, *The Footnote: A Curious History* (London: Faber and Faber, 1997), pp. 56, 9.

at the same time, about as indecipherable as Hebrew to the non-specialist. I have also used the verse-numbering of the English translations rather than the Hebrew (the only difference between them is at the end of Jonah chapter 1 and throughout chapter 2, where 1.17 (English) is 2.1 (Hebrew), 2.1 (English) is 2.2 (Hebrew) and so on, until the two texts join again at 3.1). God, who appears in the book of Jonah both under the specific name for the God of Israel, Yhwh, and the more generic term Elohim (or God) is referred to interchangeably as God or Yhwh throughout.

It goes without saying, I guess, that the academic caveats and disclaimers that traditionally foreground the limits of knowledge and the inevitable incompleteness of the book become particularly relevant in this kind of work.

CHAPTER I

The Mainstream

Then Jonah stepped into the book of himself – and into the world of sermons, literature, historical anachronism, tall tales and fables, Christian fulminations against the Jews, and cautionary tales for Victorian children . . .[1]

As the American poet Hart Crane indecorously puts it, interpreters have 'widely ruminated' on Jonah's 'travels in the snare':

> how he was stuck there, was reformed,
> forgiven also –
> and belched back as a word to grace us all.[2]

This chapter is an attempt to navigate the breadth and scope of Mainstream Christian and scholarly ruminations/navigations, and to construct what Foucault might term an archaeology/genealogy of interpretation.[3] New interpretations in biblical studies have always involved some kind of excavation of the past, which tend to be respectful to venerated scholarly figures, even while their purpose is to critique their readings, reduce them to rubble, and so clear the ground for a new construction. Archaeologies/genealogies of inter-

---

[1] N. Rosen, 'Justice for Jonah, or a Bible Bartleby', in D. Rosenberg (ed.), *Congregation: Contemporary Writers Read the Jewish Bible* (New York: Harcourt Brace Jovanovich, 1987), pp. 222–31 (223).

[2] H. Crane, 'After Jonah', in D. Curzon (ed.), *Modern Poems on the Bible: An Anthology* (Philadelphia and Jerusalem: Jewish Publication Society, 1994), p. 336. The poem was not published by Crane but can be found in M. Simon (ed.), *The Poems of Hart Crane* (New York: Liveright, 1987), pp. 19–20. An editorial note alongside the poem reads 'Composed c. 1922–26'.

[3] Foucault borrows the term 'genealogy' from Nietzsche, and 'archaeology' from Kant. His archaeologies/genealogies are concerned with tracing how our current conceptual universe – comprised of givens such as punishment, 'madness', sexuality, man – comes to congeal in the way it does. To sample the most famous examples of Foucault's histories, or de-compositions of the present, see, for example, M. Foucault, *Madness and Civilisation: A History of Insanity in the Age of Reason* (London: Tavistock, 1971) or *The History of Sexuality* 1: *An Introduction* (New York: Pantheon, 1978).

9

pretation, in contrast, take the spotlight off the autonomous subject, the transcendent scholar-hero, and occupy themselves with exposing how knowledge is sociologically situated and ideologically constructed, and how the traces of the dead make themselves heard in the voices of the living.[4] My purpose here is to show how the book of Jonah (as a sample of a biblical text) has been skewed by so much more than independent acts of genius, and to probe the sources, contexts, voices, and hauntings that converge in the solid tangible norm of Jonah commentaries. It's an attempt to decompose, and critique, contemporary critical 'knowledge'; to construct what Foucault might term a 'history of the (interpretative) present'.[5]

The story told will paradoxically be a story both of radical deviation and of endless repetition. On one level, the body of the text of Jonah undergoes bizarre and unpredictable mutations to form four very different meta-stories. Indeed, if it were possible somehow to scrutinise the book of Jonah in a cultureless, timeless zone of objectivity (to get into that ideal textual lab that scholars still yearn to inhabit), it would be impossible to predict the curious pathways that interpretation would take, and the strange chemical reactions between text and culture that would ensue. Looking at the text cold, for example, one might expect the man-eating fish to function as the book's 'monster' – not that Jonah would become, in a phrase that J. J. Cohen coins in his book *Monster Theory*, 'monsterised'.[6] Yet the site of monstrosity shifts dramatically in the history of reading, locating itself variously in the body of the fish, the interiorised monster within, the dangerous populace and, most persistently, the (national) body of the Jew. Yet even as readings undergo such dramatic shifts and mutations, they also show an equal and opposite tendency towards preserving themselves, cloning themselves, repeating themselves *ad nauseam*. The body of interpretation is both dramatically evolutionary and rather prone to sclerosis, as readings wear out a groove in the critical imagination.

Fortunately, at least from the perspective of information management, Mainstream Christian and scholarly readings seem to oblig-

---

[4] S. Greenblatt, *Shakespearean Negotiations: The Circulation of Social Energy in Renaissance England* (Oxford: Clarendon Press, 1988), p. 1.

[5] M. Foucault, *Discipline and Punish: The Birth of the Prison* (trans. A. Sheridan; Harmondsworth: Penguin, 1991), p. 31.

[6] J. J. Cohen (ed.), *Monster Theory: Reading Culture* (Minneapolis: University of Minnesota Press, 1996).

ingly collect themselves into four main clusters, meta-stories, or heaps. The four roughly hewn, and roughly chronological, piles are:

Jonah and the Fathers: Jonah and Jesus as typological twins (a study of the early Christian analogy between the exit from the fish and the resurrection – or the 'belching' and the 'grace', as Crane might put it);

Jonah the Jew: the evolution of a biblical character (tracing a negative Jonah stereotype, from Augustine and Luther through to the Enlightenment);

Divine disciplinary devices – or the book of Jonah as a tractate on producing docile disciple-bodies (a study of the dire red-letter warnings of the book of Jonah, as expounded in the sonorous, Reformation sermons of John Calvin and John Hooper);

Cataloguing the monstrous: Jonah and the 'cani cacharis' (an investigation of what happens when the book of Jonah begins to sense the *Origin of Species* creeping up behind it and threatening its credibility).

For the moment (at least for the first half of this chapter), I will let the four stories remain in their four discrete heaps. But in the second half I plan to abandon the purely academic decorum that keeps them apart, and to permit these segregated words to infiltrate, attack and deconstruct one another.

I. JONAH AND THE FATHERS: JONAH AND JESUS AS TYPOLOGICAL TWINS

The strong reader, whose readings will matter to others as well as himself, is thus placed in the dilemmas of the revisionist, who wishes to find his own original relation to truth, whether in texts or reality (which he treats as texts anyway), but also wishes to open received texts to his own sufferings . . . [Harold Bloom][7]

To the healthy and pure internal eye [Christ] is everywhere. [Augustine][8]

If the strong reader is the reader whose 'readings will matter to others as well as himself' and who wishes to open received texts to

---

[7] H. Bloom, *A Map of Misreading* (Oxford: Oxford University Press, 1990), pp. 3–4.
[8] Augustine, *On Christian Doctrine* (trans. D. W. Robertson, Jr.; New York: Bobbs-Merrill, 1958), p. 13.

his own 'truth' and his own 'sufferings', then the ultimate strong reader in the Christian tradition is the Jesus figure himself. And it is Jesus (or, that is, 'Jesus' as constructed by the narrators Matthew and Luke) who begins the book of Jonah's strange semiotic journey by posing a seductive and enigmatic riddle about the 'sign of Jonah'. In essence the saying, given in reply to the Pharisees' and Sadducees' request for a sign, is: 'An evil and adulterous generation seeks for a sign, but no sign shall be given to it except the sign of Jonah' – but the metaphorical connection between Jesus and the sign of Jonah seems to require some solid 'ground' or rationale to stand on. Matthew 12 and Luke 11 unravel the puzzle in different interpretative glosses: Luke 11.29–30 explains: 'for as Jonah became a sign to the men of Nineveh, so will the Son of Man be to this generation', while Matthew 12.38–40 adds: 'For as Jonah was three days and nights in the belly of the whale, so will the Son of Man be three days and nights in the heart of the earth.' Matthew takes the analogy in the direction of the whale-tomb and (fiddling the maths a bit) equates Jonah's 'three days' in the fish to Christ's 'three days' in the grave; Luke sees Jonah as a (proto)type of Jesus on the basis that both are teachers of the truth. The syn-opsis blurs, the glosses deviate, the significance of Jonah bifurcates, becomes fuzzy. Then focus is restored, the two diffractory gospel lenses reconverge in Jesus's declaration: 'The men of Nineveh shall rise upon the judgement with this generation, and shall condemn it; for they repented at the preaching of Jonah, and behold, one greater than Jonah is here' (Matthew 12.41; Luke 11.32).

Two points can be noted about this, the first (unscheduled) stop on the Jonah narrative's long interpretative journey through Christian history. Firstly, the interpretation given by the Christ-figure is an unexpected detour, a tantalising, riddling, circuitous explanation. As a marginal comment in the *Douai Old Testament* (1610) puts it: 'who could have thought that Jonas had been a figure of our saviour's death and resurrection unless himself had so expounded it?'[9] The reading, which seems so over-creative and audacious, is legitimated by its origin in the mouth of Christ, at the source and guarantee of Christian orthodoxy. Secondly, from its very earliest inception, the interpretation splits, bifurcates, multiplies, and mutates. The eye that sees Christ everywhere actually sends the text out of focus, splits it –

---

[9] Cited in R. H. Bowers, *The Legend of Jonah* (The Hague: Martinus Nijhoff, 1971), p. 39.

by seeing two Jesuses, two different connections to Jesus's life. Paradoxically it is the very riddling, tangential quality of the logion that ensures its generative capacity, its potential for spawning co-metaphors and enlisting readers in the obsessive hunt to run the elusive sign to ground. (Contemporary scholars remain obsessed with tracing the point of the sign – the point of origin, and the conceptual point. They track it down to the sayings source Q, but Q is quizzical, questioning, about which meaning is original (Matthew's, Luke's, or neither?); finally despairing, they officially label the saying a 'riddle' or a *Rätselspruch*,[10] and put it in that drawer of cryptic, biblical texts, for the special use of supervisors and doctoral students.)[11]

The split between Matthew and Luke is like the initial splitting of a cell, that leads to infinite multiplication and the production of a whole body of texts. Between the Church Fathers and the medieval period, typology expands exponentially, and the interpretative lens that sees double in the gospels begins to see a kaleidoscope of Christs – little Jesuses everywhere. If it was, as the author of Galatians claims, for freedom that Christ set us free (Galatians 5.1) then Jesus's own strong reading of the book of Jonah sets the early Christian reader loose in interpretative freedom. The Jesus-Jonah New-Old analogy provides plenty of room for manoeuvre and plenty of space in which the book of Jonah can re-live, move, and have its (marvellously expansive) being. The whole text, under Christ's authority, becomes a prooftext for the New Testament, and the constituent elements – Ninevites, whales, storms, prophets, sailors – are re-sorted to form a version of the gospel narrative. And yet Jonah is not, like Isaiah, a grandiose 'fifth gospel' (whose lines and

---

[10] J. Schniewind, *Das Evangelium nach Matthäus* (Göttingen: Vanderhoeck and Ruprecht, 1950), p. 162. Similar statements of (official) bewilderment include W. G. Kümmel's declaration that 'it is hardly possible to discover a certain interpretation' (W. G. Kümmel, *Promise and Fulfilment* (London: SCM, 1957), p. 68) and Norman Perrin's statement that 'we do not know what Jesus and his contemporaries would have understood by the phrase "the sign of Jonah"' (N. Perrin, *Rediscovering the Teaching of Jesus* (London: SCM, 1967), p. 194).

[11] Famous suggested solutions include: the sign of Jonah is a pun on *Johanon* and an allusion to John the Baptist (B. W. Bacon); it is a sign of the dove and the Holy Spirit (Pierre Bonnard); Jonah is a symbol of the messenger authorised by deliverance from death (Joachim Jeremias); and Jonah is a sign of one who comes to Nineveh to preach from a distant country, just as the Son of Man comes down from heaven (Bultmann). For a discussion of these solutions, and others, see A. K. M. Adam, 'The Sign of Jonah: A Fish-Eye View', *Semeia* 51 (1990), pp. 177–91 (185). For a recent discussion of the alternatives and a new solution see S. Chow, *The Sign of Jonah Reconsidered: A Study of its Meaning in the Gospel Traditions* (Stockholm: Almqvist and Wiksell, 1995).

images have long ago been integrated into the body of the New Testament),[12] but a strange, cartoonish little proto-gospel, attached to the gospels by one strange little thread of analogy, reflecting the New Testament as in a cracked little mirror, very cryptically and darkly. Like Danny de Vito and Arnold Schwarzenegger in the Hollywood movie *Twins*, Jonah and Jesus show little overt resemblance. Indeed, the sign of Jonah logion can be seen as a kind of interpretative dare – defying the reader to compare the careers and significance of Jesus on the one hand and this most quirky of Old Testament prophets on the other.

The challenge gives rise to a multiplicity of answers – a sprawling web of interpretations, a 'space full of stories' as Italo Calvino might put it, where 'you can move in all [mutually irreconcilable] directions'.[13] The Jesus–Jonah equation spawns a saturation of stories, 'like a forest that extends in all directions and is so thick that it does not allow light to pass',[14] a rich dense welter of material that grounds the analogy ten fathoms deep and that elaborates it in every conceivable, and inconceivable, direction. As the Patristic specialist Yves-Marie Duval puts it (in the introduction to his 748-page digest of this material), the texts 'multiply and fragment', resist academic cataloguing and rationalisation, and dissolve into 'a dust of disparate opinions', as interpreters subvert one another and a single author chases the analogy in mutually exclusive directions.[15] As the text-wheat is ground, it produces handfuls of flour, or handfuls of dust, that slip through the fingers when you try and hold them in your hand.

So that is what I'm gathering here – just some strands of the web, or handfuls of dust, to give a sense of how significances ricochet across a potentially infinite interpretative space. For if the gospels, looking at the significance of Jonah, see double, producing an image of Jesus in the tomb, and Jesus standing up and teaching, looking at the text through the cumulative readings of the Fathers is like putting on thick bi- or tri-focal spectacles. For Jerome, for example, Jonah is like Christ because Christ fled the heavens to come to Tarshish, that is, 'the sea of this world', and Jonah in flight is a sign

[12] For a discussion of Isaiah as fifth gospel, see J. F. A. Sawyer, *The Fifth Gospel: Isaiah in the History of Christianity* (Cambridge: Cambridge University Press, 1996).
[13] I. Calvino, *If On a Winter's Night a Traveller* (London: Picador, 1982), p. 88.
[14] *Ibid.*, p. 88.
[15] Y.-M. Duval, *Le Livre de Jonas dans la littérature chrétienne grecque et latine: sources et influence du commentaire sur Jonas de saint Jérôme* (Paris: Etudes Augustiniennes, 1973), p. 608.

of the incarnate Christ, who 'abandons his father's house and country, and becomes flesh'.[16] Jerome looks at Jonah sleeping in the hold of the ship and sees Jesus asleep on the storm-tossed lake (thus Jonah 1.5 mutates into Mark 4.35–41, Matthew 8.23–17, and Luke 8.22–5).[17] Pseudo-Chrysostom, looking at the same sleeping prophet, sees the Christ-foetus curled in the womb of the virgin,[18] and Ambrose of Milan and Cyril of Alexandria see the sleeping Jonah as a laid-out Christ-corpse, a sign of Jesus in a death-stupor in the tomb.[19] The semiotic twinning of Jonah and Jesus acts as a huge magnet that realigns all the actors, like so many iron filings, around it, subordinating them to the climatic drama of the passion and resurrection. As Old Testament images and words are hooked up to the New Testament Word, interpretation forms a fabulously tangled network, in which bit-part actors such as ships, sailors, waves, and fish, play numerous (mutually deconstructing) parts. In this huge proto-Passion Play, the ship functions as the Church, *or* Humanity, *or* the Synagogue, snatched from ruin by Jonah's vicarious sacrifice.[20] The sailors become variously the Apostles, steering the ship of the church (and sleeping in Christ's hour of need), *or* the Roman authorities who condemn Christ to death, *or* the Jews who oppose Christ, *or* Pontius Pilate, washing his hands of Jesus-Jonah's death, and asking (in so many words): 'Let us not perish for this man's life, and lay not on us innocent blood' (thus Jonah 1.14 mutates into Matthew 27.24, and the water sloshing around the sailors becomes the water in which Pilate washes his hands).[21] The storm, meanwhile, becomes the affliction of humanity, *or* the turbulence caused by sin, *or* a sign of the storms that shipwreck Peter and Paul,[22] *or* the malevolent works of the devil who infiltrated the heart of Judas (a

---

[16] Jerome, *In Ionam* 1.3a, in J. Migne (ed.), *Patrologia Latina* (221 vols., Paris 1844–1963; henceforth *PL*), xxv, 1122 B–D, cited in Duval, *Le livre de Jonas*, p. 342. For a similar reading of flight as incarnation, see Maximus the Confessor, *Quaestio 64 ad Thalassium* in *Patrologia Graeca* (161 vols., Paris, 1857–1945, henceforth *PG*), xc, 697 D, cited in Duval, *Le Livre de Jonas*, p. 604.

[17] Jerome, *In Mattheum* 9, 24–5 (*PL* xxvi, 53 C–D), cited in Duval, *Le Livre de Jonas*, pp. 350–1. A similar reading can be found in Tertullian, *De Baptismo* 12, 6–7, see Duval, *Le Livre de Jonas*, p. 606.

[18] Pseudo-Chrysostom, *Quod Mari* c. 22, cited in Duval, *Le Livre de Jonas*, p. 464.

[19] Both readings are discussed by Duval, *Le Livre de Jonas*, p. 606.

[20] See *ibid.*, p. 604.

[21] Jerome *In Ionam* 1.14 in *PL* xxv, 1129 D, cited in Duval, *Le Livre de Jonas*, p. 21.

[22] See for example, Hilaire de Poitiers, *Tractatus in Psalmum* 68.5, in A. Zingerlé (ed.), *Corpus Christianorum Ecclesiasticorum Latinorum*; Vienna, xxii, pp. 316–17, cited in Duval, *Le Livre de Jonas*, p. 462.

figure here played by one of the sailors)[23] and made him throw his 'Jesus's overboard. The 'healthy' eye that looks to Christ, in the process, sends a single image skidding across the retina, splits infinitely malleable signifiers into lots and lots of tiny Jesuses, blurs the text as through a cataract or stigmatism. And as the book is fashioned into a roughly hewn New Testament template, the 'Nine-vites' become, indelibly, 'the gentiles', or as St Bede put it, 'the splendid; the Church ornate with the glory of all virtue' ('Ecclesiam decore virtutem ornatam')[24] and polemical capital is made out of the fact that the 120,000 Ninevites exceed the number of the twelve tribes of Israel[25] or that gentile repentance shames the Jews by showing how 'credit praeputium et circumcisio permanet infidelis' ('the foreskin believes; but circumcision remains faithless').[26] This is the first time, of many, that we will see this text entangled with anti-Judaism and the polemic of supersession, of the rhetoric of size and the dwarfing of the Jew. But crucially, at this stage of the interpreta-tive game (a game which will have very sinister consequences), Jonah himself is not Jewish, though anti-Semitic asides insinuate themselves between every line.

Though interpretation splays out in multiple directions, the lines intersect at the (compulsively repeated) point of the cross: X marks the spot. Indeed, adapting the rabbis' statement about Torah, it seems as if Old Testament words proffer themselves as so much raw material, from which the resourceful interpreter can make endless replicas of the tomb and the cross. Demonstrating the ingenuity of this DIY, recycling exegesis, Augustine breaks down the wood of Noah's ark to make a crucifix, then re-uses the ark as the body of Christ (with doors in the side where the soldier's spear goes through), and then refashions the same wood into a tomb from which the resurrected Christ exits.[27] Similarly, in Jonah, the resour-ceful cross and tomb replicate themselves throughout the text, hook themselves onto any loophole, insert themselves audaciously into

---

[23] Peter Chrysologus, *Sermon* 37 (*PL* LVII, 304 C), cited in Duval, *Le Livre de Jonas*, p. 606.

[24] Bede, *In Matt. Evangelium Expositio* IV (*PL* XCII, 64), cited in Bowers, *The Legend*, p. 40.

[25] Jerome *In Ionam* 4.10–11 in *PL* XXV, 1152, cited in Duval, *Le Livre de Jonas*, p. 463.

[26] Jerome, *In Ionam*, in P. Antin (ed.), *St Jerome's In Ionam* (Sources Chrétiennes 43; Paris: Les Editions du Cerf, 1956), p. 95.

[27] Augustine, *De Civitate Dei* XV. 24, trans. D. B. Zema and G. G. Walsh, *The City of God* II (The Fathers of the Church; Washington, 1952), pp. 447–9. For a fascinating discussion of the changing shape of the ark in early Christian writings, see N. Cohn, *Noah's Flood: The Genesis Story in Western Thought* (New Haven and London: Yale University Press, 1996), pp. 23–31.

every gap and every word. Christ's death and resurrection are inscribed in Jonah's sleep and waking, in his self-sacrifice and descent overboard, and even, in one interpretation, in the lines of his psalm. According to Hesychius of Jerusalem, every line of Jonah's psalm can be paired up with a moment in the passion narrative. Jonah's appeal to God to hear his cry (2.2) trembles with Jesus's cry from the cross; Jonah's testimony 'When my soul fainted within me, I remembered the Lord' (2.7) anticipates the line 'Into your hands I commit my spirit'; Jonah's pledge to carry out what he has vowed (2.9) is pregnant with Jesus's commitment to universal salvation; and his reference to those who (in a rather loose translation) 'keep vain lies and thus forfeit mercy' (2.8) is an allusion to the Jews who guarded 'his' corpse in vain and who then lied that it had been stolen (another fragment of anti-Jewish rhetoric that has not yet assumed monstrous proportions).[28]

As the text becomes a gigantic and accommodating receptacle for Christ's truth and Christ's sufferings, Jonah's outline begins to melt; he loses his own voice and script and outline and becomes a ventriloquist for Christ. And as the Old Testament narrative is chomped and consumed by the New, emphasis is redistributed, and elements of the Old Testament text are lost. What disappears, specifically, is any sense of Jonah's resistance to God. As his 'flight' slides into 'incarnation', a gesture of rebellion is converted to one of submission; as the storm scene is engulfed by the gospel version, we lose any sense of the storm as an act of divine discipline and punishment. The narrative is drained of all residual friction between the prophet and deity because, as Jesus-twin, Jonah becomes a mere extension of the father's will, and the showdown between God and prophet is replaced with the more conventional showdown of dualistic theology – the battle between Christ and the devil, alias hell, alias the fish. Rather like the snake in Eden, the fish is swelled and fattened by theology until it assumes monstrous, devilish proportions. Pulling open the jaws of the Matthean whale-tomb analogy as far as it will go, interpretation turns the fish into a monstrous conglomerate of all the enemies, swallowers and consumers of humankind. The fish is the Devil 'the author of all

---

[28] Hesychius of Jerusalem, *Capita Ionae prophetae* (*PG* xciii, c. 1353 B–C), cited in Duval, *Le livre de Jonas*, pp. 449–50. Compare the ingenuity with which the rabbinic midrash the *Pirke de Rabbi Eliezer* takes Jonah's psalm in a different direction and matches each line to an element from Israel's history. See chapter 2, p. 110.

transgression',[29] Time (that consumes all things), the Carnal Nature, that destroyed the First Adam, and, of course, a huge bodily incarnation of Death and Hell. As hell's jaws, in religious iconography, expand outwards, and develop a monstrous body to match (see fig. 1), so Jonah's fish, conversely, contracts into the jaws of hell.[30] Inside are not intestines, debris, half-digested ships (as in later, more fabulous reconstructions) but languishing lost souls, held in the clutches of death. Strengthened by New Testament associations, empowered by Christian theology, the muscular Jonah-Jesus hybrid defeats the Devil, conquers Time, overcomes the Carnal Nature, triumphs over Death and so becomes, as one early poem puts it, a triumphant

> sign hereafter of the Lord –
> A witness . . .
> Not of destruction but of death's repulse[31]

On early Christian sarcophagi, Jonah features as the ultimate icon of death's defeat, far outflanking other (lesser) heroes, such as Shadrach, Meshach, and Abednego in the fiery furnace.[32] The heroic pairing of an emergent Jonah and an emergent Christ can still be seen – as it were frozen in stained glass – for example at Lincoln College Oxford, or Cologne Cathedral. A sixteenth-century window at St Janskerk, Gouda (designed at the behest of the Gouda fishmongers) depicts Jonah stepping from a virtually inanimate, cave-like fish as cleanly as if stepping from a car ferry, while his speech-bubble banner proclaims 'Behold one greater than Jonah is here!' (fig. 2). The cleanness of the exit signifies another significant loss from the Old Testament original: a loss of earthiness, for according to the Hebrew, Jonah is not simply 'cast out', as the

---

[29] Irenaeus, *Against Heresies* III.xx.i in A. Roberts and J. Donaldson (eds.), *The Anti-Nicene Fathers* 1 (Buffalo: The Christian Literature Publishing Company, 1885), pp. 315–567 (450), cited in Adam, 'The Sign of Jonah', p. 183.

[30] For a description of hell's evolution, and of the monstrous bodies and faces attached to the 'jaws of hell' in the middle ages, see A. K. Turner, *The History of Hell* (London: Robert Hale, 1993).

[31] Anon., 'A Strain of Jonah the Prophet', in Roberts and Donaldson (eds.), *The Anti-Nicene Fathers*, III, pp. 150–2, cited in Adam, 'The Sign of Jonah', p. 183.

[32] In this case the visual leads the verbal, and iconography sets the agenda for the written interpretations that follow. For a discussion of the close relationship between Jonah iconography and contemporary literary interpretations, see L. Réau, *Iconographie de l'art chrétien. II. Iconographie de la Bible. Ancien Testament* (Paris: Presses Universitaires de France, 1956).

Septuagint hygienically puts it, but is vomited, regurgitated, or as the *Good News Bible* puts it, 'spewed'.

In the strange interpretative alchemy that converts the book of Jonah into a mini proto-gospel, much is lost, but something is gained. What is lost is a sense of the messiness/untidiness of the text – both the literal messiness (the embodied, grotesque nature of the book) and the conceptual messiness (the clash between Yhwh and his prophet, which leads to all kinds of disjunctions and paradoxes). But what is gained, at least from Jonah's perspective, is an exemplary character, an immaculate prophetic c.v., for Jonah comes off rather well from his association with the Christ-figure. Hanging out in such superlative company has a good influence on the prophet, and adjectives and gestures seen as typical of Jesus rub off typologically on him. In a gesture that is repeated even in contemporary Christian readings, Jonah's name, meaning 'dove', effects a smooth conceptual flight path between the Old and New Testaments; Jerome muses: 'Jonah signifies our Lord, that is to say a dove', or the 'sad one . . . since the Holy Ghost descends in the form of a dove, or since He sorrows for our sins, and weeps for Jerusalem so that we might be cleansed'.[33] As Old Testament dove, or compassionate one, Jonah evolves into precisely the kind of character that early Christian leaders want to associate themselves with. The Irish abbot Columba, who was expelled from Burgundy in 610 by Theodoric II for having been over-critical of the king's penchant for concubines, exploited the fact that his name also fortuitously meant 'dove' in Latin, and extrapolated a whole rhetoric of self-promotion from the connection. 'Thus', he wrote, 'I am cast into the sea in the manner of Jonah' and entreated his followers to 'Pray that the rowing of the blessed whale recall me, so that the safe concealor may restore me, *your Jonah*, to his wished-for home.'[34] The same nexus of Jesus and Jonah and ecclesiastical office is enshrined in a stained glass window in Cologne cathedral, where Jonah slides effortlessly from the jaws of a kind of fish-serpent-dragon hybrid and raises his hands in a sign of blessing

---

[33] Jerome, cited in Bowers, *The Legend*, p. 27.

[34] Cited in Bowers, *ibid.*, p. 42; my italics. If subsequent legends are to be believed, the analogy between Columba and Jonah did not stop there. Adomnán of Iona reports how, when living on Iona, the 'great saint' warned a brother who was sailing to Tiree about the danger of a 'great whale'. The brother ignored his advice and encountered, and narrowly escaped from, 'a whale of extraordinary size, which rose up like a mountain above the water, its jaws open to show an array of teeth' (R. Sharpe (trans.), *Adomnán's Life of St Columba* (London: 1995), pp. 125–6).

while on a neighbouring panel a prelate-like Christ figure makes the sign of peace (fig. 3). (This tendency to associate oneself with Jonah, to have one's photograph taken with the prophet, is in stark contrast to later interpretation, which only invokes Jonah as comic Other, the antithesis to true obedience, and the butt of sermon jokes.)

What is fascinating about early Christian interpretation, particularly in the light of readings that will be uncoiled later in this chapter, is the force of resistance to recalcitrant elements in Jonah the text, and Jonah the character, that would potentially subvert Jonah hagiography. When Jonah's deviance from God's command to go to Nineveh is acknowledged, it is instantly remedied with strong drafts of apologetic: Jerome describes how 'Jonah acts thus as a patriot, not so much that he hates the Ninevites, as that he does not want to destroy his own people' – poignantly, Jonah avoids his mission because he 'despairs of the safety of Israel'.[35] Jerome, peering into the mechanisms of Jonah's psyche, sees a man who feels that speaking a word to the Ninevites would be like speaking a word against the Israelites, a man who justifiably refuses to curse the people of God (just like Balaam in Numbers 22–4). Thus Jonah becomes a nationalist in a *positive* sense, and stands among the noblest heroes in the biblical hall of fame. In his passion for his people he is like Moses, who pleads for the builders of the golden calf, and argues that if they die then he dies also (Exodus 32.32). And, as the New Testament continues to spill into and cross-fertilise the Old, he is like Paul in his zeal for 'his brethren, his kinsmen by race', whom he considers to be the rightful owners of 'the sonship, the glory, the covenants, the giving of the law, the worship and the promises' (Romans 9.4). Most dramatically, he is like Jesus – but Jesus in moments where he slips into nationalism, or is plagued by doubt. Jonah is equated with a Christ who briefly feels his confidence in the divine plan waning ('Father take this cup of suffering away from me') and who, in certain fervently nationalistic (and repressed) moments, advises his disciples not to preach in pagan cities, and refuses to give the children's bread to 'the dogs' (Mark 7.27). Radically, in the strong readings of Cyril of Alexandria and Jerome, Jonah and Jesus are joined not only by compassion and sacrifice but by nationalism, a passionate zeal for Israel, and a sense of alienation from the Father's plan.

[35] Jerome, cited in Bowers, *The Legend*, p. 27.

If watertight categories were abandoned, and this reading were allowed to seep into the reading below, it would pollute it, muddy it, destroy its clarity. For the reading that follows is absolutely dependent on maintaining clear and well-defined boundaries between universalist Christianity and separatist Judaism.

2. JONAH THE JEW: THE EVOLUTION OF A BIBLICAL CHARACTER[36]

The modern construction of the Jew and the establishing of a coherent Jewish identity may be said to have begun with the construction of modernity. . . [Nochlin][37]

No vital force comes into the figure unless a man breathes into it all the hate or all of the love of which he is capable. The stronger the love, or the stronger the hate, the more life-like is the figure produced. For hate as well as love can write a life of Jesus [or Jonah] . . . [Schweitzer][38]

It is always possible to bind together a considerable number of people in love, so long as there are other people left over to receive manifestations of their aggressiveness. [Freud][39]

---

[36] For other critiques of anti-Semitism in Jonah studies see E. Bickerman, 'Les deux erreurs du prophète Jonas', *Revue d'histoire et de philosophie religieuses* 45 (1965), pp. 232–64; and F. W. Golka, 'Jonaexegese und Antijudaismus', *Kirche und Israel* 1 (1986), pp. 51–61. André and Pierre-Emmanuel Lacocque criticise the 'cheap theological anti-Semitism' that casts Jonah as a 'petty stiff-necked Jew' but at the same time do not exactly disentangle themselves from Jewish and Christian stereotypes: one of their conclusions is that 'Voicing doubt as to God's justice and equanimity may appear more "Jewish" and pleading for it more "Christian"' and that 'perhaps the book of Jonah takes us to the very heart of the Jewish-Christian problem' (A. Lacocque and P.-E. Lacocque, *The Jonah Complex* (Atlanta: John Knox, 1981), pp. xv, 99). The view that the book reports a showdown between Jews and gentiles is also discussed by R. E. Clements, *The Purpose of the Book of Jonah* (Vetus Testamentum Supplement 28; 1975), pp. 16–28 and by S. D. F. Goitein, 'Some Observations on Jonah', *Journal of the Palestine Oriental Society* 17 (1937), pp. 63–77, and the negative characterisation of Jonah the Jew has been questioned by A. D. Cohen, 'The Tragedy of Jonah', *Judaism* 21 (1972), pp. 164–75, and, in passing, by Ezekiel Kaufmann, who resists the characterisation of Jonah as a 'narrow-minded zealot' (*The Religion of Israel: From its Beginnings to the Babylonian Exile* (trans. and abridged M. Greenberg; London: Allen and Unwin, 1961), p. 285). The fact that the myth is still very much intact despite these critiques (many of which are journals that are considered peripheral to Mainstream biblical scholarship) testifies to the durability of the motif of 'Jonah the Jew'.

[37] L. Nochlin, 'Starting with the Self: Jewish Identity and Its Representation', in L. Nochlin and T. Garb (eds.), *The Jew in the Text: Modernity and the Construction of Identity* (London: Thames and Hudson, 1995), pp. 7–19 (10).

[38] A. Schweitzer, *The Quest of the Historiacal Jesus: A Critical Study of Its Progress from Reimarus to Wrede* (trans. W. Montgomery; London: Adam and Charles Black, 1910), p. 4.

[39] S. Freud, *Civilization and its Discontents* (trans. J. Strachey; New York: Norton, 1961), p. 61.

As early Christian interpreters join together in panegyric to the Jonah-Christ, a single dissident voice pipes up. For Augustine, Jonah is a sign of Jesus *and* the embodiment of 'carnal' fleshy Israel, a staunch *opponent* of the divine universalistic campaign, going counter-flow to the spirit of the Christian gospel. Schizophrenically, for Augustine Jonah remains a Christ-figure, overwhelmed by the Jew-waves that crash over him, frothing 'Crucify Him, Crucify Him' – and yet he is also, himself, the embodiment of the Jew. At this point, the emphatically Jewish Jonah is still a foetus, struggling to emerge from a strong reading current that pulls in entirely the opposite direction, trying to shake off the idea of the Jonah-Christ – but eventually, he will become strong enough to militate against, and topple, his nicer better half.[40]

Jonah the Jew has a long incubation period: he does not appear again until Luther goes to Augustine to prepare his lectures on Jonah. But by now Jonah the Jew has had several centuries to grow, and, while the tensions are still apparent, Jekyll-Jonah is beginning to be overwhelmed by Jonah-Hyde. In Luther, Jonah is the dove who is 'a prototype of the Holy Spirit and his office, the Gospel'[41] *and* an embodiment of the begrudging Jewish spirit summed up in Psalm 79.6: 'Pour out your anger on the nations who do not know you and on the kingdoms that do not call on your name'.[42] In the belly of the fish he is a symbol of Christ in the tomb *but* he also retains 'a Jewish, carnal, idea of God' as the 'exclusive' property of Israel.[43] Jonah's characterisation pulls in two directions, which for Luther are self-consciously pulled together in the paradox 'in death we are in life'. In Luther's sermon this oft-repeated phrase means both:

(a) in the depths of the tomb/fish, we discover resurrection through Christ;

and

(b) in the midst of dying Judaism, a new Christian organism springs forth.

As the weak Jonah is reborn in the whale's belly (as a sign of Jesus and the sinner who depends on him) so Christianity emerges from the murky Jewish depths of the Old Testament tradition. And by

---

[40] Augustine's reading of Jonah can be found in *Epistulae* 102, 6 (35), and is discussed by Duval, *Le Livre de Jonas*, p. 515.

[41] M. Luther, 'Lectures on Jonah', in H. C. Oswald (ed.), *Minor Prophets* II: *Jonah, Habakkuk* (Luther's Works 19; Saint Louis: Concordia, 1974), p. 97.

[42] *Ibid.*, p. 93.   [43] *Ibid.*, p. 50.

preaching to the gentiles, Jonah becomes a kind of twisted pioneer – 'the first to make Judaism contemptible and superfluous'.[44]

In Luther's reading Jonah no longer orbits the realm of christological superlatives but is emphatically grounded in the realm of the 'weakness of the flesh'.[45] The Reformer has no patience with the Church Fathers' 'silly deference' to the prophets, which, he snaps, they took to 'such extremes that they even preferred to violate Holy Scripture, to force it and stretch it, before they would admit that the saints were sinners'.[46] As defender of the text, Luther rebukes those who have manipulated and forced the poor defenceless words against their will – and then stretches those same beautifully elastic words and letters into equally magnificent shapes. The meaning he replicates across the text (with an equally creative use of New Testament intertexts as the Fathers) is not the cross, nor the drama of Christ's defeat of the devil, but the drama of the anachronisation and invalidation of Judaism by the advent of Christ. This meaning, once discovered, is found under every stone and in every textual crevice. The supersessionist drama of the humiliation of the Jew is performed in the exchange between the ungodly Hebrew and the godly sailors in which (to borrow a pinch of New Testament rhetoric) 'the most pious becomes the basest and the first becomes last'. The superiority of the gentiles is illuminated, in Bede-like hyperbole, by the Ninevites, who act like 'saints' and shine forth as 'pure angels' of God. Allegedly, as Jonah unwittingly invalidates his own tradition, so he condemns his own race – who are quite clearly the referent for the psalm's cryptic allusion to 'those who observe lying vanities and forsake mercy' (Jonah 2.7). Thus just as earlier he began to ventriloquise the voice of Christ on the cross, so he now slips into the voice of the author of *The Jews and Their Lies*.

The interpretative move that scripts Jonah the Jew with a harsh denunciation of Judaism may lack a certain psychological plausibility, but yet more creative interpolations are to come. For at the end of the text, in a rather surprising denouement, Luther flips over the leaves of the *qiqayon* plant to reveal a 'poor crucified [Christ] Worm' crawling underneath. The *qiqayon* is a hybrid, or grafting of two other plants: Judaism, 'a real wild plant',[47] and the fruitless fig tree of Mark 11.12–14, 20–5 and Matthew 21.18–22 replanted in Old Testament soil, and the fertile soil of Luther's imagination. And the

---

[44] *Ibid.*, p. 94.   [45] *Ibid.*, p. 27.   [46] *Ibid.*, p. 45.   [47] *Ibid.*, p. 103.

absence of fruit on the *qiqayon* is significant: it shows that the *qiqayon*, which is the fig-tree, which is Judaism, is fruitless, and therefore entirely deserving of God's curse. Luther gets abundant exegetical fruit out of the plant's fruitlessness, and the 'Worm' becomes 'Christ and his Gospel' (for does not Christ himself declare in Psalm 22.6 that he is a worm and no man?). The climax of the book becomes a surreal drama of supersession in which the wild and fruitless plant of Judaism is assiduously nibbled away at by the angry, hungry Christ-worm.[48]

Like the Fathers, Luther finds his single interpretative schema (the withering of Judaism) and in promoting it tends to flatten out or ignore all recalcitrant elements in the text. But lest I do the same and make my reading of Luther too univocal, I want to point out a strange counter-current in his sermons – an acknowledgement of the curiousness and cruelty of the Old Testament text. Even as he maligns the prophet, Luther notes how 'poor Jonah has to suffer many deaths',[49] and how God 'plays' with life and death as if they were 'trivial playthings'[50] and 'toys with Jonah' in the episode of the plant and the worm.[51] Thus he suggests – despite and indeed contrary to his own polemic – that Jonah, rather like the poor text abused by early Christian readings, is somehow a victim of over-manipulative handling by the Father. As he disrupts his diatribe with empathy for Jonah, the divine plaything, so he muses on the seeming absurdities of the book. Scratching his chin, sucking his pen, he observes that 'Sackcloth is a strange clothing for beasts of burden'[52] and reasons that since a five-word sermon would have been a ludicrous thing, the taciturn 'forty days and Nineveh will be over-thrown' must be a sermon summary – something like 'He preached on sin' or 'He preached on the mass'. Having not yet learnt the demure reticence of later (more professional) commentators, the Reformers quite freely express their befuddlement and dissatis-faction with biblical texts: they class epistles as 'strawy', confess that the prophets often have a queer way of talking, and protest that the book of Revelation should be prosecuted under the trade descrip-

---

[48] In yet another interpretation of the *qiqayon* episode (this tree is inexhaustible) the sequence mingles with Acts 10.11ff. In this New-Old mangled drama, Jonah-Peter is exhorted to avoid preaching to Cornelius/the gentiles/the Ninevites, but Peter accepts and Jonah resists, and so is dwarfed by the pious Ninevites.

[49] Luther, 'Lectures', p. 40.

[50] *Ibid.*, p. 82.   [51] *Ibid.*, p. 94.   [52] *Ibid.*, p. 24.

tions act, for are not revelations meant to be *revealing?*[53] Although in this case Luther displaces his uneasiness about the book of Jonah onto a doubting alter-ego, or questioner, whom he then promptly squashes, he does release a niggling set of questions into the interpretative arena – where later, unsupervised, they will cause much mischief.

In a key shift, or mutation, in interpretation, Luther establishes a spirit of antagonism between Jonah the book and Jonah the character: while Jonah represents the envy and jealousy of Jewishness, the book, speaking in a different idiom, inveighs against those who 'rely on law' and 'snub the gospel of grace'.[54] And this sense of a text militating against its central protagonist extends into the so-called modern period, where it is academicised, translated into the idioms of rationalism, stripped of bizarre life-forms like the Christ-worm, or the *qiqayon*-fig-tree, and set up as the most muscular of strong readings. If Jonah the Jew is conceived by Augustine, and begins to toddle in Luther, in the Enlightenment he becomes a fully grown, fully delineated persona. And now he is a man, the Jewish Jonah has the power to floor – indeed fatally wound – his older, more saintly brother: in an appropriately biblical twist of fortune, the younger brother usurps the birthright of the elder, the elder disappears from the page, and we hear not another squeak from the Jonah-Christ.

Scanning scholarly tomes on Jonah from the late eighteenth to the early twentieth centuries, we can see the character of Jonah materialise right before our eyes. (In this brief survey the film will be run at super-high speed, the page of history turned quickly as in a Victorian/Edwardian 'flick-book', where the quick flick of the pages creates the impression of a living character or image.) In 1782, the biblical scholar J. D. Michaelis muses that 'Der Sinn der Fabel fällt genug in die Augen' ('the meaning of the fable hits you right between the eyes') and concludes that the book is written as an attack upon 'the Israelite people's hate and envy towards all the other nations of the earth'.[55] One year later, virtually the same meaning hits his student Eichhorn right between the eyes: the book

[53] Luther's complaint that the prophets have a queer way of talking is cited by G. von Rad, *Old Testament Theology* II: *The Theology of Israel's Prophetic Traditions* (trans. D. M. G. Stalker; London: SCM Press, 1975), p. 33. His complaint that Revelation 'should be revealing' is cited by F. F. Bruce, *The Canon of Scripture* (Glasgow: Chapter House, 1988), p. 244.
[54] Luther, 'Lectures', p. 81.
[55] J. D. Michaelis, *Deutsche Übersetzung des Alten Testaments mit Anmerkungen für Ungelehrte* (Göttingen: Vanderhoeck and Ruprecht, 1782), p. 106.

is obviously a 'didactic fable' designed to teach the Jews that the 'despised heathen' excel them in 'generosity and goodness of heart'.[56] (Later, reflecting fawningly on these giants of interpretation in 1841, P. Friedrichsen sees the fortuitous agreement as vindication of the reading, as well as a testimony to Eichhorn and Michaelis's 'great sagacity' and 'excellent learning': awed, he also concurs that the book is transparently about the 'naked exposure of Jewish prejudice'.)[57] In 1866 C. F. Keil sees Jonah as a typical prophet in that he embodies in his speech and actions the crimes of a people – in this case 'die fleischlichen Juden' – just as Jeremiah and Ezekiel make themselves and their clothing into visual aids.[58] Keil sees the repentance of Nineveh as the advent of *das messianische Reich*; Bruno Bauer describes how the book dramatises the ancient struggle between 'der particularen, verstockten Gesinnung' ('the stubborn, particularist, principle') and the emergent 'question of universalism'.[59] In 1860 Otto Bleek defines the central question of the book of Jonah as 'ob es recht sei gegen alle anderen Völker schon als solche eine feindselige Gesinnung zu hegen' ('whether it is right for the Jews to entertain such a hostile mindset towards all other nations')[60] – so locating the so-called *Judenfrage* at the heart of the Old Testament text.

By the mid-nineteenth century the interpretative paradigm has firmly shifted – and set. The iconic moment of the text has moved from Jonah's emergence from the fish-tomb to Jonah looking out over Nineveh and glowering over God's act of forgiveness; the dominant paradigm has become (Christian) universalism versus (Jewish) particularism; the dominant intertext has become Romans 3.29, proclaiming that God is not the God of the Jews only but of the gentiles also. The site of monstrosity has shifted from the fish (as

---

[56] J. G. Eichhorn, *Einleitung ins Alte Testament* (Leipzig: 1783), p. 334.

[57] P. Friedrichsen, *Kritische Übersicht der Verschiedenen Ansichten von dem Buch Jonas* (Leipzig: 1841), p. 113.

[58] Keil's reading is quoted (without referencing) by Friedrichsen, *Kritische Übersicht*, p. 172. Addressing the question why Jonah is placed with the Prophets, rather than with the Writings, Keil writes: 'Die Geschichte des Jonas stellt das Betragen der Juden in Gegensatz gegen die heidnischen Völker dar. Jonas vertritt durch seine Person das judische Volk, und bildet in seinen Reden unde Handlungen die Gesinnung unde Handlungsweise desselben ab. So wird oft in der Person der Propheten das Volk angebildet, z.B. Jer. 13, Eze. 4.12.'

[59] B. Bauer, *Die Religion des Alt Testament in der geschictlichen Entwickelung ihrer Principien dargestellt* (Berlin: 1838), p. 301.

[60] O. Bleek, *Einleitung in das Alt Testament* (1860), p. 574 . Bleek is cited in Bickerman, 'Les deux erreurs', p. 248, n. 61.

devil, hell, death incarnate) to the body of the Jew, the monstrous Other in whom the boundaries between the personal and national bodies blur. It is no coincidence that, as the modern European novel begins to emerge (with its detailed inventories of 'character'), Jonah is typified by a whole range of adjectives, becoming, among other things, proud, vicious, superstitious, and brimful of hate and envy (a sprawling chain of negatives that go well beyond the adjectives used by the taciturn biblical narrator). And, rather like the figure of the historical Jesus, famously exposed by Albert Schweitzer, the figure of the historical Jonah reflects back – as it were in negative – an epoch's image of itself. As 'Jesus', according to Schweitzer, becomes the scholar's idealised self-reflection and 'ally in the struggle against the tyranny of dogma',[61] so the Jewish 'historical Jonah' becomes iconic of all the tyrannical dogma and narrowness that the Enlightened scholar must by definition resist. Just as the 'yawning gaps'[62] in the gospels' portrayal of Jesus are filled by love- and hate-inspired portraits, so Jonah is fleshed out (in a very un-lifelike way) and over-written with all the passion of hate. If you look up Voltaire's entry for *juifs* in the *Dictionnaire Philosophique* you find that they are 'an ignorant and barbarous people, who have long united the most sordid avarice with the most detestable superstition and the most invincible hatred for every people by whom they are tolerated and enriched';[63] if you look in the *Grosses Vollständiges Universal Lexicon* of 1735, you find Jews described as 'slaughterers of Christian children', crucifiers of Christ, who have been rightly rejected by civilised society for 'almost 1,700 years'; and if you look at emergent Bible dictionary entries you find that a bemused Jonah attracts to himself precisely the same litany of characteristics, as he passes through the eighteenth and nineteenth centuries. Jonah is clearly created in the image of the stigmatised European shtetl Jew: conversely, the Author separates out as his compassionate, benevolent, and rational alter-ego. The unnamed (hence universalised?) Author is praised for his visionary qualities and his capacity to read the signs of the times – qualities that allow him to usurp Jonah (the anti-prophet) as the true prophetic voice of the text. A. Krahmer talks of 'unser Verfasser und anderer *aufgeklärter*

---

61 Schweitzer, *The Quest of the Historical Jesus*, p. 4.
62 *Ibid.*, p. 5.
63 Voltaire, 'Juifs', *Dictionnaire Philosophique* XLI, cited in R. S. Wistrich, *Antisemitism: The Longest Hatred* (London: Methuen, 1991), p. 45.

Juden' ('our author and other *Enlightened* Jews');[64] Tom Paine takes
the logic one stage further and reasons that the book is a satire on
Jewish institutions written not by a singularly advanced Jew, but by a
gentile.[65] As Michaelis, elsewhere, styled Moses as an enlightened
liberator in the Montesquieu mould,[66] so the author of Jonah is
styled as a liberal intellectual and biblical scholar. Thus 'our author',
unnamed, effectively becomes a universalised displacement of a
universalistic 'us', our ambassador, or our representative, in the
recalcitrant and foreign world of the Old Testament text.

Thus Enlightenment interpretation of the book of Jonah becomes
a textbook example of how the Other becomes monsterised, dehumanised, and how the 'normative categories of . . . national
identity, and ethnicity slide together like the imbricated circles of a
Venn diagram, abjecting from the centre that which becomes the
monster'.[67] At the centre is the singularly enlightened author
(liberal, benevolent, and flatteringly before his time) – a displacement of the Enlightenment critic – at best literally a gentile *Aufklärer*
and, at the very worst, a kind of biblical Nathan the Wise. And on
the periphery lies Jonah the retrogressive Jew, with his xenophobic
tendencies and monstrous psyche. The assured, Hegelian dialectic
subjects one cultural body to another, naturalises the subjugation of
slave-Jew to master-gentile. And in the process it seems that the
gentile obtains the natural right to manage Jewish scriptural territory, to appropriate the Jew's cultural body, in ways that will be
explored more fully at the end of this chapter (the book is 'our book',
says Friedrichsen, *unser Buch*).[68]

---

[64] A. W. Krahmer, *Historische-kritische Untersuchung über das Buch Jonas* (Cassel: 1839), p. 13, cited
in Friedrichsen, p. 181; my italics.

[65] Paine reasons 'as the book of Jonah, so far from treating of the affairs of the Jews, says
nothing upon [the book's authorship], but treats altogether of the Gentiles, it is more
probable that it is a book of the Gentiles than of the Jews; and that it has been written as a
fable, to expose the nonsense and satirise the vicious and malignant character of a Bible
prophet, or a predicting priest' (T. Paine, *The Theological Works of Thomas Paine* (Boston: The
Advocates of Common Sense, 1834), p. 119).

[66] Following the spirit of Montesquieu's *The Spirit of the Laws* (1748), Michaelis cast Moses as
'proposing moderate reforms of an Enlightenment cast, aimed towards leniency of
punishment, alleviation of the conditions of slavery, defence of the rights of women,
protection of the status of strangers, magnanimity to the conquered' (cited in E. Manuel,
The Broken Staff: Judaism Through Christian Eyes (Cambridge, Mass.: Harvard University Press,
1992), p. 259).

[67] J. J. Cohen, *Monster Theory*, p. 11.

[68] Friedrichsen, *Kritische Übersicht*, p. 39.

If early Christian interpretation diffracts the text, kaleidoscopically, uncontrollably, through myriad different eyes, modern interpretation brings the text back into a single focus. But the problem, evidently, is that the focus is myopic, in a way that makes Michaelis's claim that the reading hit him right between the eyes seem acutely ironic ('allegorised, abstracted and reified', writes Garb, 'the Jew marks the blind-spot of the text, even as "he" is projected as its non-seeing narrative focus').[69] Through the figure of Jonah the Jew all the recent critiques that have been applied to modernity (and that have begun to make the slogan *Sapare Aude* ('Dare to Know') ring rather tinny and hollow) begin to stream into unsuspecting Old Testament Studies. As historians of anti-Semitism have shown, the ebullient Enlightenment sense of shaking oneself free from 'self-incurred tutelage'[70] is somewhat shaken by the realisation that the secular break with Christian mythology is also a reinscription of Christian mythology, and that even Voltaire (he who so famously cackled at a God who was born of a girl, died on a gibbet, and could be eaten in a morsel of paste) is dependent on a Christian legacy for his anti-Semitic rhetoric.[71] Similarly, critical Biblical Studies, for all its disavowals of the pre-critical past, is also its meek inheritor, and a clear line of continuity can be traced between Augustine's description of Jonah as an embodiment of 'carnal Judaism', Luther's idea that Jonah had a 'Jewish, carnal idea of God',[72] and modern sketches of Jonah as a representative of *die fleishlichen Juden*. As Tamar Garb has so eloquently put it in a radical critique of 'universalist' sectarianism:

The secularising and universalising dream [of the Enlightenment] whilst purporting to be inclusive and democratising, resembled the proselytising ethos of the Christian missionaries in a fundamental way. It was premised on an eradication of difference that was by no means reciprocal. There was no negotiation of a new shared culture for Christians and Jews, involving a give and take, a symbiosis or universal respect. Rather Jews were expected

---

69 T. Garb, 'Modernity, Identity, Textuality', in Nochlin and Garb (eds.), *The Jew in the Text*, pp. 20–30 (20).
70 I am referring, of course, to Kant's famous 'motto of Enlightenment' (I. Kant, *What is Enlightenment?* (trans. and ed. L. W. Beck; Chicago: Chicago University Press, 1955), p. 286).
71 As the historian Arthur Herzberg argues, Voltaire was both a bridge to, and break with, the past, and became the 'vital link, the man who skipped over the Christian centuries and provided a new, international, secular anti-Jewish rhetoric' (A. Herzberg, *The French Enlightenment and the Jews* (New York: 1968), p. 313). For a brief discussion of modern secular anti-Semitism see also Wistrich, *Antisemitism*, pp. 43–53.
72 Luther, 'Lectures', p. 50.

to discard their cultural specificity for a more 'rational', 'modern', 'universal' identity and thereby enter into the 'common culture of man'.[73]

Since Old Testament scholarship and Christian theology also partake of a modernity that 'practises moral parochialism under the mask of promoting universal ethics'[74] then they must also share in the fallout from the post-modern critique. They too are guilty of a 'tendency to essentialise Self and Other', of creating 'grand schemata of cultural (or theological) history that cloak themselves in the rhetoric of scientific authority but appear in retrospect as ludicrously speculative':[75] they too are implicated in the abstraction and critique of Europe's others, and so they too must be contaminated by this realisation, and the realisation that 'our ways of making the Other are ways of making ourselves'.[76] 'Universalism' is a dangerous term: the 'abstract motto'[77] is too roomy to be useful, and, by its own self-definition, it stops us hunting for the logic of exclusion that so often lies within its all-too-expansive folds. As an ideal of humanity, it is prone to postulate a non-ideal, particularistic Other, and so 'incorporate in its very centre its opposite'.[78] Totalising discourses always leave a residue, an antithesis, and, as Adorno and Horkheimer acutely put it, 'from the outset there has always been an intimate link between anti-Semitism and totality'.[79] The irony is that it is with the rise of modernity and the nation-state that anti-Semitism becomes strongest, condemning the Jew precisely on the basis of his particularism and 'nationalism'.[80]

[73] Garb, 'Modernity, Identity, Textuality', p. 24.

[74] Z. Bauman, *Postmodern Ethics* (Oxford: Blackwell, 1995), p. 14.

[75] J. Boyarin, 'The Other Within and the Other Without', in *Storm from Paradise: The Politics of Jewish Memory* (Minneapolis: University of Minnesota Press, 1992), pp. 77–98 (79).

[76] J. Fabian, 'Presence and Representation: The Other and Anthropological Writing', *Critical Inquiry* 16 (1989), pp. 753–72 (756).

[77] E. Balibar, 'Racism as Universalism', in *Masses, Classes and Ideas: Studies on Politics and Philosophy Before and After Marx* (trans. J. Swenson; London and New York: Routledge, 1994), pp. 191–204 (204). Balibar's essay is a fabulously counter-intuitive critique of 'universalism' that reads universalism through Derrida and Hegel, and comes to a rest, of sorts, in the assertion that we cannot 'effectively face racism' with the 'abstract motto of universality' (p. 204).

[78] Balibar, 'Racism as Universalism', p. 197.

[79] M. Horkheimer and T. Adorno, *Dialectic of Enlightenment* (New York: Seabury Press, 1972), p. 172.

[80] Jonathan Boyarin, for example, argues that 'so long as Jews were useful to Christian Europe as an object lesson of the degradation of the unredeemed soul, some level of Jewish existence was tolerated even when Jews were murdered wholesale; but when the legitimating notion of universal individual redemption gave way to the territorial, this-earthly dream of collective progress through the defined nation-state, there was eventually no room for the Jews at all' (Boyarin, *Storm from Paradise*, p. 19).

Polemicised, polarised, and diffracted through Enlightenment values, the book of Jonah becomes a tract for the times, an exhortation to Jews to abandon superstition and exclusivity and to claim what Heinrich Heine termed their 'admission ticket to western culture'.[81] As a type of the exclusivist, separatist ghetto Jew, Jonah is given a simple ultimatum by a proto-Christian God – to modernise, progress, or be thrown overboard. Yet anxieties about the retrogressive role of the Jew and fantasies of the Jew's expulsion are not the only factors at work in critical re-stagings of this text. For at the heart of Old Testament study in its infancy, and integrally caught up with social stigmatising of the Jew, is a profound anxiety about the status, and content, of the Old Testament. The Old Testament is a compendium of cannibalism, folly, and error (Voltaire), an exhausted child's primer torn out of our hands by the coming of Christ (Lessing), a document that fumes with anger and xenophobia (just like the Jews) and that is 'marked by enmity towards all peoples and [that] therefore evokes the enmity of all' (Kant).[82] Bound up with images of the primitive, the savage, the childish, it is the dark hinterland of its purer better sequel, the foreign country in need of civilisation, colonisation. At best the 'statutory' Old Testament foregrounds in childish stutters, or as in a mirror darkly, the 'universal human reality' and the 'pure moral religion' of the New – at worst (as Schleiermacher was to put it in the nineteenth century) it displays a restrictive monotheism that 'by its limitation of the love of Jehovah to the race of Abraham displays a lingering affinity with fetishism'.[83] The sense of revulsion with this canonical fossil reaches its logical culmination in Harnack's suggestion that the Old Testament (now not merely the Old but the Exhausted, Paralysed, Infirm Testament, given to senile mutterings) be forcibly retired, or merely printed after the New, as an appendix.[84] The forum for this radical proposal,

---

81 Heinrich Heine, cited in Manuel, *The Broken Staff*, p. 294.
82 G. E. Lessing, *The Education of the Human Race* (1777), in H. Chadwick (ed.), *Lessing's Theological Writings* (Stanford: 1957), p. 91. The critique that Voltaire applied to the whole Bible, accusing it of 'contradictions, follies and horrors', was, in the more moderate critique of the *Aufklärers*, concentrated solely on the Old Testament.
83 F. Schleiermacher, *The Christian Faith* (ed. H. R. Mackintosh and J. S. Stewart; Philadelphia: Fortress, 1976; 1st edn 1830), pp. 37–8.
84 Harnack wrote: 'To reject the Old Testament in the second century was an error which the great church rightly rejected; to retain it in the sixteenth was a fate which the Reformation was still unable to escape; but to preserve it during the nineteenth century and beyond as a canonical document for Protestantism is the result of religious and churchly paralysis' (A. von Harnack, *Marcion: Das Evangelium vom Fremden Gott* (Darmstadt: Wissenschaftliche

appropriately, was called *Marcion: Das Evangelium vom Fremden Gott.*
Thus Harnack aligned himself with the second-century gnostic,
Marcion, who drew a firm distinction between the Unknown God,
revealed in Christ, and the raving, arbitrary, vengeful, *fremd,*
uncanny God of the Old Testament.

In an Enlightenment context in which the Jew and the Old
(Jewish) Testament become the objects of intense anxiety, Jonah, as
text and character, is caught up in an intense psychomachia of
supersession. The Old Testament (now so much darker and so much
more needing of illumination) is interpreted in the light of the New,
just as it is in early Christian readings, but now the relationship is
more ingenious, more twisted, more subtle. The book of Jonah is still
seen as a trailer for the main film, the support act before the curtain
of the New Testament goes up, but now Jonah anticipates Christ not
by being like him, but by becoming his antithesis, the hard-hearted
Jew. The Old Testament text is salvaged from disdain by joining the
Aufklärers in their resistance to the Old, the Jewish, the Anachronistic,
and the voice of the (singularly Enlightened) Author and the (sweetly
proto-Christian) deity, speak, together, in the cultured rationalist
idiom of the *Aufklärer/philosophe.* Thus the book of Jonah becomes a
progressive proto-gospel, a biblicised socio-political tract, a Christian
outpost in the Old Testament, a righteous stowaway, compliantly
critiquing Old-ness from the heart of an Old Testament text. And
this particular reading, this particular cut of the textual cloth, is
hemmed down tightly, stitched and re-stitched – it is perennially in
fashion, and tortuously difficult to unpick.

3. DIVINE DISCIPLINARY DEVICES: OR THE BOOK OF JONAH AS A TRACTATE ON PRODUCING DOCILE DISCIPLE-BODIES

I'd like to go back on myself now to the Reformation, for during the
sixteenth century interpretation splits, and we need to pick up the
thread of another trajectory. Even as Luther, following Augustine, is
busy displacing monstrosity onto the Jewish Other, other Reformation theologians are using Jonah as a book about the monster within
either the Self or the state. In this section, I plan to listen in on two
Reformation sermons, one by John Calvin, the other by the English

Buchgesellschaft, 1960, 1st edn 1924), p. 217, cited in and trans. F. Watson, *Text and Truth:
Redefining Biblical Theology* (Edinburgh: T. & T. Clark, 1997)), p. 143. I am grateful to Francis
Watson for letting me read his discussion of Harnack prior to publication.

Protestant John Hooper, both of which clamp the text and subordinate it neither to Jonah-Christ and the point of the cross, nor to
Jonah-the-Jew and anti-Jewish rhetoric, but to a blood-curdling,
tortured rhetoric of boiled consciences, expelled dissidents, and
(highly effective) divine disciplinary devices.

Knocked out on John Calvin's anvil, the book of Jonah becomes
a heavy, sombre, brittle text, a sonorous warning addressed to any
would-be Jonahs, tempted to become 'fugitives from God's presence'[85] and to run away to their own personal Tarshishes. Though
no Judaeophile, Calvin is keen to throw the Jewish–gentile axiom
overboard. There is no idealisation of the 'gentiles': the sailors are
'hard and iron-hearted, like Cyclops';[86] Nineveh is luxury-, pride-,
and ambition-crammed (and very Catholic-looking) and the
strange sackcloth and ashes fiasco demonstrates nothing more than
the King's 'untrained' fumblings as a 'novice' disciple.[87] The Jews,
according to Calvin, are guilty of nothing worse than 'blending
things of no weight', of constructing interpretations light as air,
and of writing 'puerile' midrashic interpretations that 'indulge in
frigid trifles in divine things'.[88] (In the middle section of this book
you will have the opportunity to weigh up for yourself the heavy-
weight, bone-crushingly strong Calvinist reading against the
trifling, light bubbles of Jewish interpretation – as well as to assess
how Herman Melville's imagined encounter between Calvinism
and Jonah, in Father Mapple's sermon, compares with genuine
bona fide Calvinism.)

Whereas Luther and modern biblical scholars drive a wedge
between Jonah the person and Jonah the book, in Calvin's sermon
the two are conflated. The book becomes a first-person testimony
spoken by the prophet, a humble confession of wrongdoing by a
man who has been through the fires (or more specifically the bellies)
of divine correction. Invited (or forced?) up to the lectern to give
testimony, a trembling Jonah takes the stand. His voice is quaking,
submissive, monotone, like one lobotomised, and, like a reformed
alcoholic, or newly converted Christian, he uses his book as an

---

[85] J. Calvin, *Commentaries on the Twelve Minor Prophets* (trans. J. Owen; Edinburgh: Calvin
Translation Society, 1847), p. 71.

[86] *Ibid.*, p. 36.

[87] *Ibid.*, p. 110. Indeed, Calvin's main preoccupation in discussing the repentance scene is to
emphasise the superfluity of sackcloth and ashes and to condemn, by contrast, the vain
rituals of the Papists.

[88] *Ibid.*, p. 26.

inventory of his sins, evidence of a sinful, rebellious, former life. 'Accus[ing] himself in plain words',[89] he shows, by example, and the pain of his correction, how 'preposterous' it is to follow one's own fragile reasoning. As he reads out his story, he inserts lines of self-chastisement: when he gets to the part that tells how he spoke back to God and wished that he could die (Jonah 4.3) he raises his head, pauses, looks to Calvin for guidance, then condemns his 'disgraceful obstinacy'.[90] Limply, Jonah stands before the congregation as a visual aid, 'so that all may know that [God] is not to be trifled with, but that he ought to be obeyed as soon as he commands anything'.[91] But he is not the only illustration of this, the text's meaning, which, like the Fathers' cross, or Lutheran anti-Semitism, clones itself across the text. The message – the absolute futility of trying to go against (or read against) the tide – is also inscribed in the drama of the sailors frantically rowing, or literally 'digging', against the current, yet beaten back by the relentless pressure of God. And the storm, which terrifies even the most hardy and godless of men, is an example of the salvific efficacy of being 'disquieted by fear', an illustration of how 'since hardly any one of himself comes to God, we have need of goads; and God sharply pricks us, when he brings us to danger, so as to constrain us to tremble'.[92]

Goads and sharp pointed objects are in fact only two specimens from the Divine Father's box of disciplinary instruments. Lamenting, like Luther, the 'dull sophistry' of the Fathers, and their tendency to cocoon Jonah in apologetic, like a Christ-foetus in the fish-womb, Calvin spits that this *cavillating* is simply 'not to be endured',[93] and vows to take a far less mollycoddling approach. His readers must know that Jonah is a 'terrifying chronicle', albeit short on detail and requiring 'amplification' and 'illustration in a rhetorical manner'.[94] The amplification is amply supplied by lexis of boiling, torment, execution, slaying, pricking, binding, cutting, rigid handling, anguish, and howling, as Jonah's soul is brutally man- (or God)-handled in a strikingly corporal lexis of torture. Jonah is 'boiled with grief',[95] 'enclosed within narrow bounds',[96] 'heavily chastised',[97] 'heavily pressed, and rigidly handled by God'.[98] The thinly meta-phorical curtain parts to reveal all the horrors of the medieval

---

[89] *Ibid.*, p. 118.   [90] *Ibid.*, p. 142.   [91] *Ibid.*, p. 59.   [92] *Ibid.*, p. 36.
[93] *Ibid.*, pp. 131, 142. Jerome in particular is singled out for condemnation as a 'cavillator'.
[94] *Ibid.*, p. 142.   [95] *Ibid.*, p. 71.   [96] *Ibid.*, p. 74.   [97] *Ibid.*, p. 128.
[98] *Ibid.*, p. 74.

torture chamber: boiling in oil, binding in iron shackles, pinning the victim down with heavy weights across his body. And the torture – as all effective torture must be – is swelled by superlatives, and practised without respite. In the torture-chamber/fish-belly Jonah squeaks his suspicion that God does not intend to 'slay him at once' but plans to 'expose him to innumerable deaths'.[99] His intuition is correct: as the early Christian reading stutteringly repeats the drama of the Passion, in scene after scene, so Calvin compulsively re-stages the scene of Jonah's 'virtual death'. The prophet 'dies' in the bowels of the ship, in the storm, in the depths of the sea, and in the bowels of the fish and endures (in a continual chain of images of interminability) 'continual uneasiness', 'continual execution', and 'continual torments'.[100] Consigned to an awful virtual death by superlatives, Jonah is knocked out by hyperbole and denied the relative pleasure of death as release. Calvin is constantly emphasising that Jonah's death is virtual – in the sense that it is death, but not quite, and in the sense that it is (at least technically) an internal, metaphorical death. But the point is that this type of death is worse than anything that can be imagined, that it is a 'fate worse than a hundred deaths'.[101] In an attempt to evoke the immensity of the horror, Calvin simply stacks up words like 'execution' and 'torment', adds the intensifiers 'one hundredfold' or 'interminable', and lets them hang there, repeating themselves *ad nauseam* on the edge of the awful unspeakable abyss. The result is something as graphic as Christian martyr texts, but, since the torturer is God, these are martyr texts with a twist. The motif of a God armed with oil, knives, fire and heavy weights may be an obvious Calvinism, but it is also a disturbingly apt transposition of God who arranges exquisite torments in fishes' bellies, and who, in chapter 4, switches the sun on, turns up the heat, and trains it on Jonah, with the air of an interrogator switching on an interrogation lamp. Thus Calvin teases out and expands on a vein in the biblical text that is rarely mined (for obvious reasons, not least those of good taste): the thrice-repeated emphasis on fear, the sailor's terror, the seemingly relentless assault on Jonah using the storm, the fish, and the sun, the sadistically short-lived provision of shade, and the prophet's twice-uttered plea for death, since death would clearly be better than life (Jonah 4.3, 9).

---

[99] *Ibid.*, p. 71.   [100] *Ibid.*, p. 7.   [101] *Ibid.*, pp. 71–2.

As the most Calvinist of Calvinist deities stands over him, knife glinting in his hand, Jonah's role is not to complain 'contumeliously', not to writhe or twist (for that only increases pain), but to submit to being 'tamed and subdued'.[102] Jonah's psalm (which has already served as a condemnation of Jewishness, or an Old Testament pre-scripting of Christ's words on the cross) here becomes testimony of a soul 'tossed here and there by temptations', 'agitated with great trouble and hard contests', yet emerging subdued, triumphant and, above all, *quiet*. Jonah does not 'pour forth vain howlings' like the unbeliever, but 'strenuously conquers' his soul, without screaming out.[103] The line 'my soul fainted within me' (Jonah 2.7), translated by Calvin as 'my soul infolded itself', suggests that the pressure bearing down upon the embodied soul is such that the soul almost implodes under its weight. Boiled with grief, pricked, heated until his soul or conscience melts, the racked subject collapses, near-dead, exhausted, emptied – and so triumphant. His ego lanced, his self emptied, he begins to murmur the Calvinist catechism: 'we are all more indulgent to ourselves than we ought to be';[104] the 'wit of man cannot be trusted, for it is the workshop of all errors';[105] and, most emphatically 'God must not be deprived of his supreme power'.[106]

If the punishment that the soul undergoes is brutally corporal, it is also revealing where that punishment takes place. For Calvin describes the belly of the fish in three ways: conventionally as 'hell or the grave', surprisingly as 'a tribunal' (to which Jonah is 'drawn . . . as it were by force'),[107] and more strangely still as 'a hospital'.[108] A hellish vocabulary of boiling, torment, pricking and execution collides strangely with the salve of salvation, the tender ministrations of care, and the reassuring sense that pain is for one's own good. On one metaphorical level we are invited to feel the graphically hellish fire in which Jonah's conscience is 'boiled'; on another, we are invited to imagine that, within the scrubbed white walls of the fish-belly, his body is 'as safe as if walking on land'.[109] In Calvin's *Institutes* the Word of God is described as a nurse, gently administering the right draft of revelation for the right time, adapting the dose to the needs of each generation. Now here, the belly of the fish becomes a

---

[102] *Ibid.*, p. 128.   [103] *Ibid.*, p. 74.   [104] *Ibid.*, p. 32.   [105] *Ibid.*, p. 32.
[106] *Ibid.*, p. 54.   [107] *Ibid.*, p. 71.
[108] Later the fish will become a different kind of public building, a synagogue (see the discussion of the rabbinic midrash *The Pirke de Rabbi Eliezer*, in chapter 2, p. 109).
[109] Calvin, *Commentaries*, p. 73.

place of healing, of tender ministrations, where the divine torturer becomes the divine surgeon (what appeared to be a knife was really a scalpel all the time). Jonah's torture is also treatment, his imprisonment is also care, his pain is part of a solicitous and corrective re-education programme. Through his sufferings, Jonah learns to internalise self-discipline, to pummel his own soul, and, as Calvin tellingly puts it, to *'carry within his heart his own executioner'*.[110]

It is evidently high time that Calvin was introduced to the Foucault of *Discipline and Punish* and vice versa. For both authors seem to be wandering in and out of the same nexus of institutions – the prison, the hospital, and the court/tribunal[111] – and both are struggling (albeit in rather different ways) with the production of the self-policing soul and 'docile bodies'. Foucault famously argues that the end of the eighteenth century in Europe saw a major transition from a system of punishment written graphically in flesh and blood, anger and revenge, to a more solicitous regime, in which 'the body was directly touched as little as possible, and then only to reach something other than the body itself'.[112] This new regime, instigated by social reformers, took as its key motifs *scrutiny/observance* (epitomised in Bentham's Panopticon), *diagnosis*, and the idea that 'the expiation that once rained down on the body must be replaced by a punishment that acts in depth on the heart, the will, the inclinations'.[113] Discipline was committed to cure: to the internalisation of self-preserving, rather than self-serving, mechanisms in the (docile) body of the individual subject. And punishment was now habitually accompanied by the theoretical disavowal 'do not imagine that the sentences that we judges pass are activated by the desire to punish; they are intended to correct, reclaim, cure'.[114] Though punishment was still, by definition, corporal (what would a non-corporal punishment look like?, Foucault asks), it was rhetorically

---

[110] *Ibid.*, p. 73 (my italics).
[111] Foucault also deals with the school, which is not present in Calvin, but which becomes more prominent as modern interpreters attempt to extrapolate the book's disciplinary programme. For a discussion of the curriculum taught by the book of Jonah, and the examination set, see pp. 60–4.
[112] Foucault, *Discipline and Punish*, p. 11.
[113] *Ibid.*, p. 16. For a discussion of the omniscient deity as panopticon, see S. D. Moore, *Mark and Luke in Poststructuralist Perspectives: Jesus Begins to Write* (New Haven: Yale University Press, 1992), pp. 129–44.
[114] Foucault, *Discipline and Punish*, p. 10.
[115] *Ibid.*, p. 16.

detached from its own corporeality.[115] In a characteristically modern aporia, the body of the condemned was watched over by the figure of the doctor, alleviator of pain, agent of welfare, who juxtaposed himself to the (almost effaced) figure of the executioner.[116]

Calvin's treatment of Jonah both resonates with and stymies this scheme, appearing to fall on both sides of the divide at once. On one level punishment is graphically and overtly written in the language of the body – of torture, boiling, pricking, and compression – and is portrayed as the rightful revenge of the divine monarch upon the presumptuous subject. The God-King is rightly furious at one who has attempted to 'deprive him of his supreme power'[117] and Jonah's hundredfold punishment is, at least metaphorically, as angry and bloodily excessive as that of Damiens the Regicide (another dissident against the king, whose body – ripped by pincers, drawn, quartered, tortured with boiling lead and wax – forms Foucault's iconic example of an unreconstituted justice system). But even as Jonah falls foul of the anger of the God-King, God also takes on the compensatory roles of solicitous doctor, and fair and reluctant judge. The textual events that are interpreted as Jonah's hundredfold execution are also interpreted as the divine disciplinarian drawing him, '*as it were* by force', to a tribunal, and as the divine surgeon-doctor bringing him to the hospital, island of care and refuge of safety (from the Self). Cruelty and care collide in the same text: the 'force' is merely seeming, the execution metaphorical. And as in modern dissimulating depictions of punishment, the focus of the seemingly corporal exercise is really, emphatically the heart, the thoughts, the will, the inclinations, the soul. Torture is really a metaphorical means to an end: the aim of the operation/sentence is to render external constraints superfluous. Through his sufferings, Jonah learns to be a self-disciplined, docile disciple-body, who carries around his own conveniently portable internal executioner.

And this phrase, this idea of 'carrying in one's heart one's own executioner', nicely puts its finger on the tensions in Calvin. On one hand the internalisation of discipline suggests an affinity between the Protestant reformer and social reformers of the eighteenth and nineteenth centuries, but on the other, it is still alloyed with a violent rhetoric of torture, discipline, and execution – a violent rhetoric

[116] *Ibid.*, p. 11.   [117] *Ibid.*, p. 54.

that would cause Jeremy Bentham and his fellow humanitarians to wince. Just as Calvin and the Reformers are precariously perched between the medieval period and the modern,[118] so Calvin seems to straddle both epochs of Foucault's punitive history. As Foucault raises difficult questions for Calvin and his readers, so Calvin hurls a question back. To what extent does a humane, internalised system of discipline and punishment draw on earlier discourses of the taming of the soul, or what is the *theological* history of internalised discipline?[119]

In Calvin's reading, Jonah's body – both the cowering body of the prophet, and the naughty textual body – present themselves as a cautionary tale, a testimony to the horror of dissidence and the pain of correction. Monstrosity is relocated to the individual soul and discipline is focused on Jonah's body as a figure for the Calvinist Christian subject. But, as if to demonstrate that the Reformation is not a single ideological product, 'exported across the Channel and installed in England by Luther, Calvin and Co. Ltd',[120] the social-political chemistry of the English Reformation bubbles through the book of Jonah to produce a very different text. In John Hooper's sermons, preached in 1550 before King Edward VI, the site of monstrosity relocates to the monstrous populace and the Catholic Church, and the focus of discipline is not the individual body, but the body politic.[121]

Whereas Calvin's dominant metaphor is the tossing of the individual conscience, the key image in John Hooper's Lenten sermon series is the storm-tossed ship of state. The iconic textual moment is not Jonah's agonised capitulation in the fish-belly hospital, but Jonah

---

[118] See E. Troeltsch, *Protestantism and Progress: A Historical Study of the Relation of Protestantism to the Modern World* (trans. W. Montgomery; London: Williams and Norgate, 1912); and T. George, *Theology of the Reformers* (Nashville: Broadman Press, 1988), pp. 15–16.

[119] Since Foucault is not here to answer the question, we can only guess what that answer might be. Certainly he wants to claim that there is a difference between the soul represented by Christian theology, 'born in sin and subject to punishment', and the modern soul 'born rather out of methods of punishment, supervision and constraint' (*Discipline and Punish*, p. 29). Yet, while I appreciate the neat rhetorical twist, frankly the distinction is not clear to me. 'Souls' and 'consciences' have always been those most elusive parts of the human anatomy, un-locatable, un-extractable by dissection – and have always been created by (theological) discourse. And what kind of discourse actualises a 'soul', if not one of (eternal) reward and punishment and (divine) supervision and constraint?

[120] C. Haigh, *English Reformations: Religion, Politics and Society under the Tudors* (Oxford: Clarendon Press, 1993), p. 13.

[121] A more detailed discussion of the sermons and the historical context that gives rise to them can be found in Y. M. Sherwood, 'Rocking the Boat: Jonah and the New Historicism', *Biblical Interpretation* 6.1 (1998), pp. 364–402 (379–88).

1.15. The expulsion from the ship is the iconic moment – read as the expulsion of dissidents from the ship of state. Thus, warns Hooper, if we find that 'our poor ship of the commonwealth is so tossed that she can hardly sail above the water',[122] it is because of the pernicious Jonasses rocking the boat.

'Jonasses' for Hooper is a fairly ample and flexible category. It includes Catholic bishops, dishonest merchants, exploiting lawyers, 'whosoever is offended by this message',[123] and those who say 'Let the Bible in English [and] the preacher of God's word be cast into the sea, and so shall follow quietness, for it was never well since preaching began.'[124] But by far the most dominant, all-subsuming category of Jonasses is 'as manye as be in this realme that neglect or pervert their appoynted vocacyon'.[125] Although Jonasses can be found among the mercantile and upper classes, they are found, most commonly, among the people – a force Hooper elsewhere refers to as a 'many-headed monster',[126] a veritable Hydra. In its natural state and habitat this amorphous creature desires to 'live without subjection and all manner of laws, except such as please himself', whispers Hooper, putting down his fieldglasses, and speaking to the camera.[127] The animal is naturally 'recidivus, hurtful and danger-ous', and if left to its own devices will convert (itself) to treason, murder, and even regicide. Eyes burning, Hooper prophetically points to devilish insurrection and the collapse of all order:

> For do the Kinge and Magistrate what he can, the people will never be content. Many of them live on idleness and will not labour, and in case they cannot have what they would they convert themselves to sedition and treason and care no more to kill and oppresse theyre lawful King and magistrates than the devil cared to kill Adam in Paradise.[128]

Hooper and the book of Jonah advocate a zero-tolerance policy, as befits dissidents and devils. 'Can you live quietly with so many Jonasses? Nay then, throw them into the sea.'[129]

---

[122] J. Hooper, *An Oversighte and Deliberacioun uppon the Holy Prophet Jonas: Made, and Uttered before the Kinges Majesty, and His Most Honorable Councell* (Lent 1550), in S. Carr (ed.), *Early Writings of John Hooper Lord Bishop of Gloucester and Worcester* (Cambridge: The Parker Society, 1843), pp. 435–558 (468).

[123] *Ibid.*, p. 468.   [124] *Ibid.*, p. 472.   [125] *Ibid.*, p. 461.

[126] Hooper, cited in Haigh, *English Reformations*, p. 181.

[127] Hooper, 'Annotations in the Thirteenth Chapter of Romans', in C. Nevinson (ed.), *Later Writings of Bishop Hooper* (Cambridge: Cambridge University Press, 1852), pp. 94–116 (103).

[128] Hooper, *Jonas*, p. 461.

[129] *Ibid.*, p. 480.

Rather like the reading of Jonah the monstrous Jew, Hooper's sermon deflects attention from the gigantic fish to the spectre of the huge social monster behind the text. And whereas in Calvin's reading Jonah's individual body is operated on in the fish-belly hospital, here Jonah becomes a cancer in the body politic, leading to the tossing and sweating of the traumatised ship of state. In the context of social unrest, instability in the monarchy, and rumours of rebellion, the book of Jonah becomes a book that magnifies social danger, and that then recommends appropriately uncompromising treatment – swift lancing of the cancer, throwing dissidents overboard. The lesson of the text (like the lesson instilled into Calvin's trembling Jonah) is quite simply, for fear of death by drowning, 'Don't rock the boat'.

Thus Hooper's Bible, represented in microcosm through the book of Jonah, styles itself as a harsh magistrate and disciplinarian, as brittle and weighty as Calvin's God. It is a sceptre of iron, not a 'rod of willow to be bowed with every man's finger',[130] a book that is not soft on crime and that teaches uncompromisingly that even in the face of mistreatment '[The people] should call unto the Lord for redresse of their thynges, and not redress it themselves.'[131] Hooper is preaching at a time when the future of Protestantism is precariously tied up with the health of the sickly twelve-year-old King and his Protector the Earl of Warwick (who has recently risen to power by making ominous-sounding promises to various Catholic leaders) – a time when, as the astute political commentator Paget observed in 1549, 'the use of the old religion is forbidden by law, and the use of the new is not yet printed in the stomachs of eleven of twelve parts of the realm'.[132] Only seven years previously, a law has been passed forbidding 'women, artificers, prentices, journeymen, and servingmen of the degrees of yeomen or under'[133] from reading the newly disseminated, translated, English Bible, for fear that it is a Pandora's

---

[130] *Ibid.*, p. 436.   [131] *Ibid.*, p. 464.

[132] J. Strype, *Ecclesiastical Memorials* II (Oxford: Oxford University Press, 1822), p. 431, cited in Haigh, *English Reformations*, p. 175.

[133] S. E. Lehmberg, *The Latter Parliaments of Henry VIII, 1536–1547* (Cambridge: Cambridge University Press, 1977), pp. 186–7, cited in Haigh, *English Reformations*, p. 161. The exclusion of about 90 per cent of the population from Bible reading is nicely illustrated by a note on the flyleaf of a copy of Virgil's History: 'At Oxford, the year 1546, brought down to Saintbury by John Darbye, price 14d, when I keep Mr Latimer's sheep. I bought this book when the Testament was abrogated, that shepherds may not read it. I pray God amend that blindness. Writ by Robert Williams, keeping sheep upon Saintbury Hill, 1546' (cited in Haigh, *English Reformations*, p. 161).

box, capable of unleashing social insurrection; and now a series of social rebellions in the previous summer is stoking fears that dissociation from the Catholic Church is leading to other less desirable forms of social Protest. In this context Hooper promotes the Protestant Bible as a book well able to instil political quietism, fear, and subjection in the King's subjects. Addressing the young King and his chancellors, rather than the many-headed monster direct, he paints a perfect Althusserian[134] picture of the power of religion to produce law-abiding citizens.

Both Calvin and Hooper squeeze images of pain and punishment from the book of Jonah and clamp the text in the interpretative pincers of fear. The book becomes a tractate about the production of docile bodies: a book able to induce effective (self-)government, through the internalisation of a sense of the 'internal executioner', or a sceptre of iron, able to enforce ruthless and effective management of the body politic or ship of state. Whether the lesson of the text is externally or internally administered, that lesson is essentially 'Submit or else' – or else you will be boiled in grief/internally executed/subject to innumerable deaths/thrown overboard/executed/expelled. But neither Hooper or Calvin, I think, offers such a terrifying and spectacular threat as another Tudor preacher, the Catholic martyr John Fisher, who in 1509 tells how 'if Jonah had not remembered God he would have been digested and voyded out from hym [i.e. the whale] in a manner of dunge'.[135]

Perhaps the Protestants, ultimately, simply lacked imagination.

4. CATALOGUING THE MONSTROUS: JONAH AND THE *CANI CACHARIS* (OR A CONCLUDING SCIENTIFIC POSTSCRIPT)

[In 1857] my father was engaged to deliver a long series of lectures on maritime natural history throughout the north and centre of England. These lectures were an entire novelty; nothing like them had been offered to the provincial public before; and the fact that the newly invented maritime aquarium was the fashionable toy of the moment added to their attraction. [E. Gosse][136]

[134] See Althusser's description of religion in 'Ideological State Apparatuses', in L. Althusser, *Lenin and Philosophy and Other Essays* (trans. B. Brewster; London: New Left Books, 1971), pp. 160–5.

[135] John Fisher, Bishop of Rochester, 'Sermon Seven', in *Seven Penitential Psalms* (1509), cited in Bowers, *The Legend*, p. 73.

[136] E. Gosse, *Father and Son* (Harmondsworth: Penguin, 1972; 1st edn 1907), pp. 54–5.

A lady – when I was just four [in 1853] – rather injudiciously showed me a large print of the human skeleton, saying 'There, you don't know what that is, do you?' Upon which, immediately and very archly, I replied 'Isn't it a man with the meat off?' . . . I had often watched my Father, while he soaked the flesh off fishes and small mammals. If I venture to repeat this trifle, it is only to point out that the system on which I was being educated deprived all things, human life among the rest, of their mystery. The 'bare-grinning skeleton of death' was to me merely a prepared specimen of that featherless plantigrade vertebrate, *homo sapiens.* [E. Gosse][137]

We should believe that the most apparently bizarre forms . . . belong necessarily and essentially to the universal plan of being. [Darwin][138]

In 1860 the book of Jonah (formerly employed as magistrate and disciplinary sceptre of iron) becomes, rather curiously, a biblicised biology. In the Reverend E. D. Pusey's *The Minor Prophets, with a Commentary, Explanatory and Practical,*[139] the bulk of the commentator's attention is transferred from the body of the text (a quirky difficult narrative) to the body of the fish (a far more analysable structure) which is laid out like a neatly labelled exhibit in a museum of natural history. Though commentators as early as the Church Fathers have worried about the plausibility of fish-surviving men and men-swallowing fish, Pusey's commentary (written one year after the publication of *The Origin of Species*) is a distinctively obsessive quest for classification, discovery, and specificity. Like a fossil retrieved from the past, Jonah 1.17 is laid out by the naturalist, and, using modern "works of zoology"[140] and calculations based on the size of jaw bones, the commentator-scientist tries to measure, calculate and identify the species (cf. fig. 4).

For a long time the natural world had been a pliant and passive ally of the Bible, proffering various relics, fossils, and evidences as corroborations of the Word. The natural world and the Bible had amicably merged in 'diluvialism' – the theory that mountains, rocks, oceans all testified to a global flood, that had traumatised the once eggshell-smooth surface of the earth – and this theory was still being taught at Oxford as late as the 1820s.[141] Outsize, monstrous

---

[137] *Ibid.*, p. 23.
[138] J. B. Robinet, *Considérations philosophiques sur la gradation naturelle des formes de l'être* (Paris: 1768), p. 198.
[139] E. D. Pusey, 'Jonah', in *The Minor Prophets with a Commentary, Explanatory and Practical* (London: Walter Smith and Innes, 1860), pp. 247–87.
[140] *Ibid.*, p. 258.
[141] For a discussion of the complicity and clashes between the Bible, palaeontology and geology see N. Cohn, *Noah's Flood.*

skeletons were interpreted not as 'dinosaurs' (the word was not invented until 1841) but as the remains of beasts who had perished in the Deluge; similarly a skeleton discovered by one Johann Jakob Scheuchzer in 1725 was instantly and excitedly presented as *homo-diluvi-testis*, 'Man who witnessed the flood' (later he would sadly have to be more prosaically re-labelled as a 'giant salamander of the Miocene epoch').[142] Scheuchzer had earlier published a pamphlet entitled *Piscium Querelae et Vindicae* ('Complaints and Claims of the Fishes' [1708]), in which fossilised fish declare, in remarkably proficient Latin, 'We, the swimmers, voiceless though we are . . . bear irrefutable witness to the universal inundation.'[143]

But by 1860 fishy relics were no longer being so compliant, and would no longer simply burble their support. In a transition that has become over-familiar, and hence over-simplified, the 1800s saw a violent upheaval, every bit as dramatic as the upheaval imagined for the universal flood, in which the idea that the sacred and the scientific formed an eggshell-smooth continuum was irrevocably smashed. Palaeontology, geology, Lyell, Wollaston, Agassiz, Darwin gradually demolished the complicity between the earth-sciences and the sacred 'records', making the biblical spectacle of a man-swallowing fish look increasingly like primitive, pre-scientific fanta-sising. Whereas previous readers had relocated the site of the text's monstrosity (from fish, to Jew, to populace, to rebellious soul), scholars of the Victorian era had to concentrate on explicating the 'monster', and grafting it onto the real world of 'descriptive exacti-tude'.[144] In a world in which scientific discourse was gaining the upper hand, critics had to close the gap between a childish lexis of big fish, big plant, and a big city, and the real world, the world of observable fact, meticulously examined, and described in the 'smooth, neutralised and faithful words' of academic discourse.[145] Feeling the pressure, various commentators changed the fish's body into a more believable structure: a ship called *The Great Fish*, an inn called *At the Sign of the Big Fish*, where Jonah booked in for three days

---

[142] As a posthumous consolation to Scheuchzer, however, the species was named *Andrias Scheuchzeri*.

[143] These are the 'claims'. The 'complaints' are (i) that ancient humans caused the primordial flood, and (ii) that modern humans compounded their crime by misinterpreting the poor fossilised fish as mere lumps of stone.

[144] M. Foucault, *The Order of Things: An Archaeology of the Human Sciences* (New York: Vintage, 1994, 1st edn 1970), p. 159.

[145] *Ibid.*, p. 131.

and three nights, or, more wonderfully yet, a bathing establishment or swimming pool.[146] (There is a world of difference, incidentally, between this building and Calvin's fish-belly hospital, or the fish-belly synagogue that puts in an appearance later in this book. For whereas the 'hospital' and the 'synagogue' are rhetorical flourishes, the inn is a literal, carefully erected construction, an expression of the need to *accommodate* the sceptical scientific mind, to create facilities for it to *stay* in the biblical text, by booking it into conducive, comfortable, persuasively solid surroundings, five-star rational accommodation, with swimming pool.)

It is in this context that Edward Pusey's clinical scrutiny of the book of Jonah, as if it were a specimen in an aquarium, makes its own kind of very particular sense. Gone is the mystery of Jonah and the whale, the awesome fascination with 'death' in a fish's belly: Pusey is more concerned with dissecting the Hebrew word דָּג (*dag*, fish), and the shell cracks open to yield a vast ocean of sea-creatures, a volume of marine biology. Pusey takes the cryptically identified 'fish', defined only by its big-ness and its prophet-swallowing potential, to a zoology textbook and concludes, in an erudite burst of Latin and German, that candidates for identity are:

(a) the white shark, or *cani cacharis*, which according to *Blumenbarch* is 'found the size of 10, 000 lbs., with horses whole in its stomach';

(b) the *lamia* also called *Carcharias* (in whose stomach a man in armour was once found);

(c) the fish that the Germans called the *Menschen-Fresser* (i.e. the 'People-Eater');

(d) the sea-calf (the size of an ox, reported to have swallowed whole reindeer).[147]

The language of mathematics is also invoked: if 'in all modern works of zoology, thirty feet is given as the length of a shark's body', and 'if the length of the body is 11 times the length of half its lower jaw' this would mean a jaw of 'nearly 6 ft in its semicircular extent, teeth measuring four and a half inches and a throat of eight or ten feet wide'.[148] The zoological cataloguing and calculation is reinforced by reports of, for example, a shark who swallowed a sailor in the Mediterranean in 1758, but who 'cast out' the sailor when shot by

---

[146] For an inventory of some of these bizarre suggestions, see Friedrichsen, *Kritische Übersicht*, pp. 25 and 292; Pusey, 'Jonah', pp. 247–53.

[147] Pusey, 'Jonah', pp. 257–8.

[148] *Ibid.*, p. 258.

the captain, or the fish cast up on the shores of Marseilles in the sixteenth century, which weighed 4,000 lbs. and had a whole man in its stomach.[149] (These tales are stripped of any air of fictionality by giving the date, weight, and precise geographical location, and mentioning, for the benefit of any sceptics in the audience, that the sailor-swallowing Mediterranean fish was stuffed and exhibited all over Europe.)

By stuffing their fish and exhibiting it, the eighteenth-century discoverers transformed it from seaman's tale to *bona fide* museum exhibit – which is precisely what Pusey does for the fish in the book of Jonah. What may appear to be mythicality and quaintness in the biblical text, a mark of the text's primitiveness, is translated into the language of modernity, as a member of a recognised and tabulated species *and* as a scientifically calculated equation. The seemingly unbelievable becomes simply the unknown quantity in an algebraic equation (thus the mysteries of the Bible become calculable) where the possibility of a fish swallowing a man becomes x and:

$$x = \frac{\text{the jawsize of a shark} = \text{body length}}{11}$$

Alternatively, the seemingly excessive and unnatural (hence mythical) creature is rehabilitated from monster to member of a species or class of cetaceans, a creature no more primitive and fantastic than those catalogued by Darwin on his voyage to the Galapagos Islands.

Indeed if you place Pusey's dissection of Jonah's fish alongside the first edition of Darwin's *Origin of Species* some curious cross-fertilisations begin to emerge. The *Origin* is exactly the same kind of diagram-less prosy biology as Pusey's text, and seems, from a late twentieth-century perspective, a peculiar combination of Graeco-Latin species-labelling (of Umbelliferous and Compositous plants, Brachiopod shells, phosphatic nodules, azoic rocks, and sessile cerripedes), anecdotal science, and rather quaint-seeming calculation. Testing the ability of seeds to disseminate themselves, Darwin floats 94 dried plants on sea water, finds that 18/94 plants with ripe fruit float, multiplies this by the average rate of the several Atlantic currents (as given in *Johnston's Physical Atlas*) and concludes that, 'on this average, the seeds of 14/100 plants belonging to one country

---

[149] *Ibid.*, p. 258.

might be floated across 924 miles of sea to another country'.[150] He discusses whales, sharks, and fish as classes, based on analogical comparison 'between the body and fin-like limbs';[151] as diagrams, for example the *teleostan* fish in Pectet's *Palaeontology*;[152] and as skeletons, the discovery or non-discovery of which can tell us whether whales were present in the secondary or tertiary period.[153] In this period of scientific ferment, even the largest creatures were demythologised. Edmund Gosse (whose father was a contemporary of Lyell, Wollaston, and Darwin) remembers seeing a whale 'brought to our front door on a truck'.[154]

The story of Jonah and the *cani cacharis* (while probably less mythologically compelling than Jonah and the whale) marks, in a huge quasi-scientific gloss, anxieties about the Bible, as whales become skeletons in textbooks, and science becomes the new lexis of power. Ever evolving, ever committed to survival, the biblical text shapes itself in response to cultural anxiety, to new dominant energies in the pursuit of knowledge which threaten to bypass it as an anachronism. As the Protestant Word in the Reformation offers reassurance against social disintegration, and the Enlightenment Old Testament shores itself up against accusations of irrationality, so the Word in the 1860s legitimates itself by deflecting the new discourse of power through it, reconnecting itself to the new ciphers of knowledge by punctuating words with numbers, and by taking on the Graeco-Latin-based idiom of biology. As Jonah in the 1780s counters fears about an uncivilised Old Testament by transforming itself into a benign work of universalism, speaking in the same idiom as the *philosophes*, so an 1860 production of the book counters anxieties about its primitiveness by packaging its wisdom in the instantly recognisable, up-to-the-minute language of zoology, and by talking about Jonah's fish as a fossil, to prevent the book itself becoming fossilised.

A commentary which begins with a huge quasi-scientific gloss, problematises any simplistic historical sense of a nineteenth-century battle between Bible/Creation and Science/Evolution. The Bible resists and assimilates scientific alien bodies – it refuses the subjection of faith to fact *and* appropriates the discourse of factuality to

---

[150] C. Darwin, *On the Origin of Species: A Facsimile of the First Edition With an Introduction by Ernst Mayr* (Cambridge, Mass.: Harvard University Press, 1964), p. 360.
[151] *Ibid.*, p. 428. [152] *Ibid.*, p. 305. [153] *Ibid.*, p. 303.
[154] Gosse, *Father and Son*, pp. 164–5.

itself. Although Pusey invokes his capacious catalogue of possible species as 'facts' to 'shame those who speak of the miracle of Jonah's preservation in the fish as a thing less credible than any of God's other miraculous doings',[155] he proves the validity of the fish not by appealing to miraculous doings and the un- or super-natural, but by showing the book to be an integral part of the natural world of biological 'fact'. The mystery of the fish is no longer a mystery, precisely because it is transformed into a solvable mathematical problem, or a species that can be identified if you look hard enough through contemporary zoological catalogues.

'All the forms of life, ancient and recent', writes Darwin, 'make together one grand system'.[156] Pusey's reading seems to be struggling to insist that the (ancient) Bible is part of this grand system, and to naturalise the biblical text as an integral part of our *natural* history. The fish in some sense, I think, represents the biblical text – as a strange body that does not fit into modern symbolic structures. But as Darwin draws lines of connection between ancient and modern species, and creates a rationale even for seemingly aberrant life-forms, so this reading reinforces lines of connection between ancient and modern bodies (of thought), and grafts the biblical text onto the new wisdom of contemporary culture.

5. TAKING STOCK: SURVIVALS, HAUNTINGS, JONAH AND (STANLEY) FISH, AND THE CHRISTIAN COLONISATION OF THE BOOK OF JONAH

(a) Jonah and (Stanley) Fish, or how the figure of Jonah rotates through one-hundred-and-eighty degrees

Like the author of the book of Jonah, I can't resist a pun, and so can't resist playing with the famous double act 'Jonah and the Fish', substituting Jonah's aquatic, scaly companion with the iconic figure-head of 'reader-response', the president of the so-called *Reader's Liberation Movement*.[157] In one sense the move is a tired one: the Fish

---

155 Pusey, 'Jonah', p. 258.

156 Darwin, *Origin of Species*, p. 344.

157 The idea of the revolt of the reader and the Reader's Liberation Movement comes from Terry Eagleton's spoof on reader-response in T. Eagleton, 'The Revolt of the Reader', *New Literary History* 13 (1982), pp. 439–52. This is also not the first time that Jonah has been paired with Stanley Fish: A. K. M. Adam has very effectively beaten me to it in 'The Sign of Jonah: A Fish-Eye View'.

now floats belly-up on the surface of the postmodern aquarium displaced by bigger, brighter, more exotic specimens – and many biblical scholars, visitors to the wild postmodern fairground, have already brought home a (gold)Fish as one of the tamest souvenirs. And yet, since Jonah criticism seems to suggest that the discipline's self-assurance about its own objectivity still stands largely unassailed, one more theoretical volley (using the bulky polemic of relativism and subjectivity, rather than a more subtly honed tool) is perhaps not entirely out of place.

Certainly the aesthetics are hard to resist, for Jonah criticism provides a beautiful set of prooftexts for Fish. Even the most epistemologically assured reader, moving through the historically kaleidoscoped readings catalogued in this chapter, must experience something of a sense of interpretative vertigo or sea-sickness. And were I to remove the arbitrary barriers that separate the readings into four neat chunks, they would all look at each other in bemusement and then start arguing vociferously. From their places in sections 2 and 3 respectively, Luther and Calvin are already busy shouting abusive names like 'wanton sophist' and 'cavillator' back at the Church Fathers cowering in section 1, and taking them to task for their cotton-wool apologetics. Similarly, the Enlightenment biblical scholars, though by instinct more restrained and polite, would feel a professional compulsion to shout down Chrysostom's equation between a nationalistic, doubting Christ and a nationalistic, doubting Jonah, since this would do fatal damage to the contrast between Christian universalism and Jewish nationalism, on which their argument depends. The cacophony that results makes it extremely difficult to continue to subscribe to the reading myth of the ever-rich text, that, like the fabulous porridge pot of fairytale, or the magic jars of meal and cruses of oil that last forever in the books of Kings (see 1 Kings 17.8–16; 2 Kings 4.2–7), manages to generate more and more substance, ever new readings. Even the most credulous of readers must begin to suspect that if all these readings are somehow *in* the text, in essence, then the 48-verse book of Jonah must be an immensely rich concentrate. Even side by side, safely cordoned off from one another, the different readings compliantly foreground textual plasticity. For, depending on your vantage point, your politics, and your churchmanship, the expulsion from the fish can mean both the resurrection and the purgation of the rebellious Jonasses, and the Ninevites can be superlative gentiles or a sign of clownish Catholics.

Frankly, I can think of no better prooftext for a Fishy fore-grounding of the role of the reader than a text that, between the early Christian period and critical biblical studies, manages to rotate in meaning *through one-hundred-and-eighty degrees*. For Jonah, as shape-shifter and riven signifier, completely at odds with himself, functions as both a Christ-figure and, if not exactly the antichrist, as the Jew as the antithesis of a benevolent Christianity. Whereas the Church Fathers (busy scribbling anti-Gnostic tracts such as Tertullian's *Against Marcion*) see Jonah as a type and sign of Christ, a neo-Marcionite tendency in post-Enlightenment criticism leads scholars to read Jonah as the absolute antithesis of the Christ figure. The neat geometry of the turn (from Jonah-Christ to Jonah-Jew) mirrors, in a perfect diagrammatic arc, the logical and symmetrical theoretical turn from the foregrounding of text, to reader. Fascinatingly the only common rubric that makes all these readings 'Christian' is that the text must have *some* relationship to Christ and the New Testament – the rules about how that relationship is to be worked out are entirely fluid. In early readings the book achieves Christian relevance by acting out familiar New Testament scenes in (what seem to the modern eye) lumpish and rather hammed up allegories; in Enlight-enment readings it must defend its own status by becoming an outpost of proto-Christian *concepts* in a retrogressive Old Testament. Seismic shifts in Jonah's personality and signification reflect Christianity's own shifts in identity in relation to the Old Testament and the figure of the Jew. And it seems that 'Christianity' – defining itself, in different contexts, as anti-Gnostic, neo-Gnostic, and taking on different significations in response to different cultural pressures/conversations – is itself an entity whose voices and manifestations are legion. In the context of the book of Jonah 'Christianity' defines its dominant meaning, variously, as the internalisation of discipline in the storm-tossed soul; as social discipline (submitting to one's 'apoynted vocacyon'); as a natural (reasonable) religion consonant with Enlightenment/scientific values; or as the supersession of the exhausted religion of the Jews. Each reading selects a singularly illustrative narrative moment which it then abstracts, magnifies to billboard proportions and plasters a lesson over, as it were in red paint. For the Church Fathers the key moment is the expulsion/resurrection and the message ALL MEANING CULMINATES IN CHRIST; for the Enlightenment critics the revealing moment is Jonah fuming over a repentant Nineveh and the lesson is REJECT ANACHRONISM;

SUSPECT THE JEW. For Calvin, the key moment is the lancing of Jonah's ego in the fish-belly hospital and the attendant lesson is SUBMIT TO GOD; for Hooper the iconic image is the storm-tossed ship of state and the lesson – DON'T ROCK THE BOAT.

Despite popular condensations of 'what Stanley Fish says' (or said) there is nothing monolithic about a book like *Is There a Text in This Class?*, and reading it again, alongside these re-performances of Jonah, sparks off all kinds of provocative associations.[158] Fish's study of the gushy, euphoric homiletics of Lancelot Andrewes resonates with my reading of the Fathers – in both texts Christ releases the writer into a free associative freedom, so that all roads lead to Christ and 'every but is an and, every however an also, and every transition is nothing more than the opportunity to take a breath'.[159] This gallery of readings amply demonstrates the capacity of readers to hammer all howevers into alsos and to subordinate recalcitrant textual elements to a monologic reading of the text. Similarly, Fish's discussion of 'significant absences', and their infinite potential for generating vast exegetical capital,[160] resonates with Luther's reading of the *qiqayon* and the way in which the unmentioned fruit is converted to significant fruitlessness, which in turn is converted to an allegorical condemnation of the Jews. If readers, as Fish reminds us, provide not only the meaning of a text, but its illocutionary force and the tone in which it is to be read, this nicely glosses our readers' predilection for supplying a sense of the book's tone and the book's

---

158 When I first read *Is There a Text?* I was a callow undergraduate in an English Literature department, and I read it as a euphoric manifesto for 'reader-response'. Revisiting it, from a different disciplinary address in a department of Theology and Religion, it now seems to be a book that is very much about Christianity. Fish spends fifteen pages dissecting a sermon of Lancelot Andrewes and discusses, among other things, how Christ emerges in Samson Agonistes, and how divine providence asserts itself in the interpretative framework of the baseball player Pat Kelly. The fact that I had never noticed before how religion-saturated *Is There a Text?* is, seems to triumphantly confirm the Fishy thesis that 'what anyone sees is not independent of his (or in this case her) verbal and mental categories (and disciplinary preoccupations) but is in fact a product of them' (S. Fish, *Is There a Text in This Class?: The Authority of Interpretive Communities* (Cambridge, Mass.: Harvard University Press, 1980), p. 271).

159 Fish, *Is There a Text?* pp. 181–96 (193). The study of Andrewes is called 'Structuralist Homiletics', in a play on Jonathan Culler's 'Structuralist Poetics'. Provocatively Fish is making an equation between the anti-humanism of structuralism, in which the subject is eliminated in favour of discursive systems which 'speak it', and the belief that the Christian subject is not a maker of meaning, but is 'found', and 'spoken' by Christ.

160 The context is a discussion of the interpretative history of Milton's 'Samson Agonistes', in which critics have claimed that 'Samson Agonistes is about Christ because he is nowhere mentioned' (*Is There a Text?*, pp. 272–4).

Author. Calvin's Jonah is to be performed in a trembling contrite voice, the Jonah of modern biblical criticism speaks in the authoritative, rational tones of the *Aufklärer*, Hooper's Jonah rants and threatens – all readings come with an implied tone and stage directions, as well as with a pre-packaged message.

Yet reader-response theory is a roughly hewn tool for exploring the intricate relations between text and society. It tends to replace (at least by implication) an autonomous Author with an autonomous Reader and to imply a relatively free, unencumbered reading subject, who is constrained only by her membership of an 'interpretative community'. Interpretative communities sound rather vague and sinister to me these days, rather like Masonic clubs. In the world of Biblical Studies they are often reductively interpreted as religious communities so that readings can be simply and mechanistically dismissed as manifestations of the reader's Protestantism, agnosticism, Jewishness, atheism, and so on.[161] Since it is a fair assumption that Pusey, Eichhorn, Augustine, Calvin, Luther, *et al.* are all Christian, to point to the Christ-centredness of their readings is not to say very much. But what invites analysis is the radically different shapes the 'Word' takes as it shapes itself, and accommodates itself, to different intellectual and social environments.

Hovering in the background of this study, but not yet explicitly visible, are some assumptions gleaned from Cultural Studies and particularly New Historicism. The New Historicisms (and here I am using the term quite generally) dissolve the autonomy of both the writing and the speaking subject, proclaiming that the 'freely self-creating and world-creating Individual of so-called bourgeois humanism is – at least in theory – now defunct'.[162] The New Historicism is a response to (and in a sense an inversion of) New Criticism in which texts are not seen as self-contained objects of value, hermetically sealed off from the world, but as 'part of human life, society and historical realities of power, authority and

---

[161] Actually, this is probably only a return to the 'interpretative community's' religious roots. For, according to Samuel Weber, Fish's phrase comes from Josiah Royce's *Problem of Christianity*, where it is used in reference to the Christian interpretative community that shaped the Christian story under the authority of the figure of Jesus. See S. Weber, 'Introduction to Demarcating the Disciplines', in *Glyph Textual Studies* 1 (Minneapolis: University of Minnesota Press, 1986), p. xi, cited in V. Cunningham, *In the Reading Gaol: Postmodernity, Texts and History* (Oxford: Blackwell, 1994), p. 405, n. 14.

[162] L. A. Montrose, 'Professing the Renaissance: The Poetics and Politics of Culture', in H. Aram Veeser (ed.), *The New Historicism* (London: Routledge, 1989), pp. 15–36 (21).

resistance'.[163] Similarly the writing or interpreting subject is seen (after Foucault) as one who is subject to the influence of external forces, and authors/interpreters become 'cultural artefact[s]'[164] rather than creators *ex nihilo* who bequeath the text to the world. In a move that can be applied as much to the way that we interpret and package texts as to how we write them, New Historicism confronts the myth that 'whole cultures possess their shared emotions, stories and dreams only because a professional caste invented them and parcelled them out'[165] and breaks down the perceived wall between 'literary symbolism and symbolic structures operative elsewhere'.[166] It dissolves the neat demarcations between present and past, and problematises the ideal of a butter-wouldn't-melt-in-your-mouth objectivism by demystifying history as 'not merely a chronicle of the past, but . . . a pragmatic weapon for explaining the present and controlling the future'.[167] From a defamiliarising New Historicist perspective, histories are stories that we tell ourselves about ourselves, stories that define us 'in relation to hostile others (despised and feared Indians, Jews, Blacks) and disciplinary power (the King, Religion, Masculinity)', stories that strategically select documents and data and interpret and plot them as 'Romance, Comedy, Tragedy, and Satire'.[168] And the act of emplotment is never innocent: by placing events which have no inherent structure into a coherent narrative, the historian gives it an ideological and moral structure, (promoting, for example, 'Anarchism, Conservatism, Radicalism or Liberalism').[169]

Though rubbing culture's nose in the mud of politics (as Edward Said puts it) can be a messy business,[170] the process is a vital one for

---

[163] J. N. Cox and L. J. Reynolds, *New Historical Literary Study: Essays on Reproducing Texts, Representing History* (Princeton: Princeton University Press, 1993), p. 1.

[164] S. Greenblatt, *Renaissance Self-Fashioning: From More to Shakespeare* (Chicago and London: University of Chicago Press, 1980), p. 3 (citing C. Geertz, *The Interpretation of Cultures: Selected Essays* (London: Fontana, 1973)).

[165] Greenblatt, *Shakespearean Negotiations*, p. 4.

[166] Greenblatt, *Renaissance Self-Fashioning*, p. 3.

[167] H. Aram Veeser, *The New Historicism Reader* (London: Routledge, 1984), p. 11.

[168] Veeser, *The New Historicism*, p. xiii.

[169] H. White, *Metahistory: The Historical Imagination in Nineteenth Century Europe* (London: Johns Hopkins Press, 1973), p. x.

[170] E. W. Said, *Orientalism: Western Conceptions of the Orient* (Harmondsworth: Penguin, 1995; 1st edn 1978), p. 13. Because Said makes it clear that ideological/postcolonial criticism is not about introducing a sense of context, so much as politicising and contaminating the sense of context which has long surrounded and shrouded textual studies, his comments are worth quoting in full. He writes: 'Most humanistic scholars are, I think, perfectly happy with the notion that texts exist in contexts, that there is such a thing as intertextuality, that

writers in Biblical Studies. For, more than any other Western cultural artefact, the Bible is perceived as occupying a transcendent zone, and as speaking an eternal message directed to 'the unchanging transhistorical core of the human'.[171] In discussions of 'the Bible' and 'Power', the Bible is habitually assumed to be the ally of social institutions and social hierarchies, dispensing power downwards, as it were from on high. Little attention has been given, to date, to the way in which the Bible and biblical texts are themselves caught in a network of power relations, reforming themselves under the impact of what Stephen Greenblatt would (loosely) term 'social anxiety and social desire'.

Certainly the influences that spill into the readings catalogued here are far more extensive than those that could be summarised in the views, biographies, and religious dispositions of 'Eichhorn', 'Michaelis', 'Hooper', 'Pusey' as discrete authorial entities (the *Dictionary of National Biography* is of limited use here). In the 1550s (a period of perceived social instability and doubts about the ability of the Protestant Bible to replace the Church as agent of control) the book of Jonah becomes an idealised picture of dissident forces being pitched overboard and turbulent social storms calmed, aided by a strict and uncompromising Protestant Word. In Germany in the 1780s the book first learns to speak in the sweet tones of reason, to internalise *die Judenfrage* and to expel the retrogressive ghetto-Jew. In 1860 a fish's body is covered with mathematical calculations and inscribed with the zoological idiom of the *Origin of Species*. These readings suggest a curious textual-social chemistry bubbling away: a complex chain reaction that cannot be explained by individual quirks, or anti-Semitic 'interpretative communities'. For there is

the pressures of conventions, predecessors and rhetorical styles limit what Walter Benjamin once called the "overtaxing of the productive person in the name of creativity" in which the poet is believed to have his own and out of his pure mind, to have brought forth his work. Yet there is a reluctance to allow that political, institutional, and ideological constraints act in the same manner on the individual author. A humanist will believe it to be an interesting fact to any interpreter of Balzac that he was influenced in the *Comédie Humaine* by the conflict between Geoffroy Saint-Hilaire and Cuvier, but the same sort of pressure on Balzac of deeply reactionary monarchism is felt in some way to demean his literary "genius" and therefore to be less worth serious study. Similarly . . . philosophers will conduct their discussions of Locke, Hume, and empiricism without ever taking into account that there is an explicit connection in these classic writers between their "philosophic" doctrines and racial theory, justifications of slavery, or arguments for colonial exploitation.'

[171] J. Hawthorn, *Cunning Passages: New Historicism, Cultural Materialism and Marxism in the Contemporary Literary Debate* (London: Arnold, 1996), p. 71.

something very apt and canny about the way in which the text mutates, chameleon-like, into a rod of discipline, an anti-Jewish tract, and a biblicised biology. Ever-expansive, ever committed to survival, the Word absorbs social anxieties (about social discipline, a retrogressive Old Testament, a Bible superseded by science), processes and answers them and gives back to society an ideal view of itself (all dissidents purged; a rational Bible; a scientifically plausible, naturalised text). Thus the edges of 'The Bible' dissolve, the text itself becomes a subjected entity, drawing new lifeblood from different social contexts, forever reshaping, reforming itself.

This picture of the evolutionary biblical text, the text that re-animates itself by grafting itself onto different ideological contexts, has the potential to undermine a different, more familiar story of 'biblical evolution'. For a common story told in Biblical Studies circles is the story of the Old Testament's gradual theological progress from primitive religion, embarrassing anthropomorphisms, polytheistic slips, towards ethical monotheism and universalism. These New-Testament-like sentiments reach their healthy evolutionary climax in Jonah, Ruth and Deutero-Isaiah, but are contrasted with a mutant, retrogressive strain, a falling off into the 'dark age' of narrow xenophobic post-exilic Judaism.[172] But the healthy, and indeed the dominant theological DNA strain finds its way into

---

[172] This evolutionary scheme, and the idea of the falling-off of post-exilic Judaism can be traced back to Julius Wellhausen and his predecessors; although, as John Barton has argued, issues of anti-Semitism in Wellhausen may not be as clear-cut as they would appear (see J. Barton, 'Wellhausen's *Prolegomena to the History of Israel*: Influences and Effects', in D. Smith-Christopher (ed.), *Text and Experience: Towards a Cultural Exegesis of the Bible* (Sheffield: Sheffield Academic Press, 1995), pp. 316–29). The legacy is clearly inscribed in many contemporary introductory texts: Anderson, for example, includes a section on 'The Weaknesses of Judaism', in his discussion of the post-exilic era, and argues that 'Devotion to the Torah easily lapsed into legalism . . . We have only to read the New Testament to become aware of this weakness within Judaism . . . Preoccupation with Torah seemed to stifle the spirit of prophecy' (B. W. Anderson, *Understanding the Old Testament* (Englewood Cliffs, N.J.: Prentice-Hall, 1986), p. 538). On the way in which Ruth becomes a 'universalist' companion-piece to Jonah, see, for example, G. A. F. Knight, *Ruth and Jonah: Introduction and Commentary* (London: SCM, 1960). Though the anti-Judaism tends to be less focused and overt, it still remains the shadow-side of a celebration of universalism, and Flanders, Crapp, and Smith, for example, see Ruth as an indictment of the exclusivity of the Jews: 'In this light the particularism of the Jews is shown to be shallow and selfish and a stance that should be surrendered to a more hospitable attitude toward those gentiles who desired to share blessings from Yahweh' (H. Jackson Flanders, *et al.*, *People of the Covenant: An Introduction to the Old Testament* (New York: The Ronald Press, 1973), p. 470). (I am grateful to Julia O'Brien for pointing out these examples in her article 'On Saying "No" to a Prophet', in J. Capel Anderson and J. L. Staley (eds.), *Taking It Personally: Autobiographical Biblical Criticism* (*Semeia* 72; Atlanta: Scholar's Press, 1995), pp. 111–21 (119).)

the New Testament, where it flourishes and becomes characteristically 'Christian'.

A New Historicist story of the evolutionary Bible may shake our
faith in this other story of evolution. For if our histories, even our
theological histories, are stories that we tell ourselves about ourselves, stories that define us 'in relation to hostile others (despised
and feared Indians, Jews, Blacks)', then we must begin to suspect an
evolutionary scheme that sees the Jewish as an aberration, and
climaxes in the Christian. When the Jewish question is enacted at
the heart of a biblical text, then we may suspect that our biblical
history, and its attendant theologies, have become 'a pragmatic
weapon for explaining the present and controlling the future'.[173] In
the strain to hear voices from the past, we may be listening in not on
Ancient Judaean ghosts, but on more recent voices – voices that
speak with a suspiciously strong European accent.

It is to the question of the haunting of the present, and indeed the
control of the future, that I now want to turn.

(b) How the traces of the dead make themselves heard in the voices of the living: the haunting of twentieth-century Jonah criticism

According to Stephen Greenblatt, 'The dead conspire to leave
textual traces of themselves, and those textual traces make themselves heard in the voices of the living.'[174] In Jonah commentary the
spectres of the past are particularly vocal, like screeching poltergeists
or wailing banshees. Of the four readings toured in this chapter, one
('Jonah the Jew') dominates, and one ('Jonah as a disciplinary tract')
survives. Two ('Jonah and the *cani cacharis*' and the early Christian
reading of the Jonah-Christ) have clearly slipped off the page
altogether.

First, an obituary to the two dead (or at least missing, presumed
dead) readings. A tour of twentieth-century commentary proves
conclusively that the Jonah-Christ figure has been killed off by his
evil twin Jonah the Jew, and that the dissection of the body of the *cani
cacharis/Menschen Fresser*, though the most recent reading, is (perhaps
for that reason) the most noticeably out of fashion. If, as Greenblatt

---

[173] Veeser, *The New Historicism Reader*, p. 11.
[174] Greenblatt, *Shakespearean Negotiations*, p. 1.

puts it, a certain 'minimal adaptability' is the key to survival[175] and readings linger on the basis of the survival of the fittest, a Darwinian reading has (appropriately) been ousted by a Darwinian mechanism of selection. Pusey's quasi-scientific ruminations on the species of the fish and the size of its teeth now seem to us childish 'old salt's tales'[176] – they cannot survive the changes in 'cultural value' and the body of the *cani cacharis* enters the twentieth century 'dead on arrival'. (These days, rather than trying to map the fish's bigness onto some naturally calibrated scale, critics tend to stress the fish's littleness, its minnow-like insignificance. The fish is but a textual red-herring[177] a 'one-verse wonder',[178] the sojourn in the fish's belly is a 'mere intermezzo':[179] the fish may indeed not be a verifiable species, but then again it is not *really* important, and only has a minor swim-on bit part.)

And yet, with the pointed exception of the fish, the tendency to graft the biblical text onto the 'natural' (that is, the scientifically and archaeologically verifiable) world still persists. As if in testimony to its survival, a recent article in the journal *Zeitschrift für die Alttestament-liche Wissenschaft* goes to great lengths (thirteen pages to be exact) to trace the Hebrew and botanical roots of Jonah's *qiqayon*. Just as Pusey, one hundred years before him, attempted to assess the prophet-swallowing potential of the *cani cacharis*, so Bernard Robinson, writing in 1985, attempts to compare the prophet-shading potential of the *ricinus communis*/the gourd/the ivy/the vine/the *Palma Christi* entwining the tendrils of biology and etymology to discuss the ricinus's 'erect stem and palmate leaves', and its capacity to grow (depending on which authority you read) to 'four metres or more', 'ten feet high', or 'between three and twelve feet'.[180] And as

---

[175] *Ibid.*, p. 7.

[176] E. Bickerman, *Four Strange Books of the Bible: Jonah, Daniel, Qoheleth, Esther* (New York: Schoken Books, 1967), p. 3.

[177] R. P. Carroll, 'Jonah as a Book of Ritual Responses', in K. Schunck and M. Augustin (eds.), *'Lasset uns Brücken bauen . . .': Collected Communications to the Fifteenth Congress of the International Organization for the Study of the Old Testament, Cambridge, 1995* (Frankfurt: Peter Lang, 1998), pp. 261–8 (268).

[178] G. Campbell Morgan, *The Minor Prophets* (1960), p. 69, cited in L. C. Allen, *Joel, Obadiah, Jonah and Micah* (London: Hodder and Stoughton, 1976), p. 192.

[179] Koch, *The Prophets*, II, p. 182.

[180] B. P. Robinson, 'Jonah's Qiqayon Plant', *Zeitschrift für die alttestamentliche Wissenschaft* 97 (1985), pp. 390–403 (399). The worm that nibbles the plant has also come in for some degree of scrutiny, though with less emphasis on scientific precision: Jack Sasson observes how translators have variously regarded the worm as 'larva', 'maggot', 'weevil', 'beetle' or 'centipede' (see J. Sasson, *Jonah* (The Anchor Bible; New York: Doubleday, 1990), p. 301).

Robinson sits in one corner of the scholarly laboratory, carefully doing chlorophyll tests on the leaves of the biblical text, musing over Zohary's *Plants of the Bible*, and reasoning that 'the withering of the plant because of the attack of the worm suggests a plant with a supple stem',[181] other scholars submit the claim that Nineveh was three days' walk across to various feasibility and time-and-motion studies. Taking a tape-measure or trundle-wheel around Nineveh's city limits, they aim to assess whether this is a reference to Nineveh's circumference or diameter. Scrawling his calculations across the whiteboard, Leslie Allen works out (in a very Pusey-like calculation) that, if 'an inscription of Sennacherib mentions that the circumference of [Nineveh] was 9,300 cubits, less than 3 miles' and then Sennacherib added '12,515 cubits', and if archaeological surveys 'suggest a circumference of 7 and a half miles', but 'the oblong area had on its widest axis a diameter of 3 miles'[182] – then regrettably we are still far short of the required fifty-mile diameter (assuming that a prophet walks at normal walking speed). The text can be proved not by division (the body size of a shark divided by eleven) but by a simple addition, in which the sum of the evidence must come to approximately fifty miles. Finding that all his calculating, digging and rummaging in archives thus far have only given him three, Allen finds the rest by trigonometry, or at least by the ingenious use of triangles, reasoning that maybe Nineveh means 'Nineveh' in the broadest sense and the area we are dealing with is actually an 'administrative triangle stretching from Khorsabad in the north to Nineveh and Nimrud in the east'.[183]

Thus, even while Pusey's carefully catalogued fish takes its last gasp on the beach of the twentieth century, the cult of the tape-measure, the mathematical scribblings, and the botany/biology cross-referencing survives. The textual body is submitted to classification, taxonomy, calculation, and so transformed into an object for *serious* study; exaggeration is quantified, the gap of incredulity measured, and so made manageable (Nineveh is precisely 47 miles too big; the *qiqayon* is improbable by about a couple of feet and a couple of days). Awed by the master-lexis of science, the biblical text still feels the embarrassment of its own childishness, its own wide-eyed innocence. The 'big plant' becomes a *ricinus communis*, and the

---

[181] Robinson, 'Jonah's Qiqayon Plant', p. 402.
[182] L. C. Allen, *Joel, Obadiah, Jonah and Micah*, pp. 221–2.
[183] *Ibid.*, pp. 221–2.

big three-days'-walk-across city becomes a mappable 'administrative triangle stretching from Khorsabad in the north to Nineveh and Nimrud in the east', and thus (big fish notwithstanding), we reach scientific *terra firma* – the reassuringly real world of academic precision.

So to the living readings. For if the Jonah-Christ equation and the story of Jonah and the *cani cacharis* are certifiably dead, the concept of Jonah as a disciplinary tract – a supremely strong reading – flexes its muscles and brandishes a cane. For many twentieth-century 'disciples' as for Calvin, Jonah is emphatically a book about learning to keep one's passions within due limits and about 'hold[ing] our [rebellious] thoughts captive'.[184] As Calvin describes how Jonah is 'tamed and subdued by so heavy a chastisement',[185] so E. M. Good celebrates the way in which Yhwh 'takes the ego out of Jonah' and makes him into an 'underling',[186] and H. W. Wolff smiles at the story of a 'dismally mulish prophet' and how 'God handles him'.[187] Yet, though criticism still quivers with a sense of God capable of ego-extraction and (rough?) handling, Wolff's and Good's descriptions are less violent, less knuckle-dusting than Calvin's. And, instead of taking Jonah to prison, to hospital, or to the torture chamber, these critics take Jonah to another ostensibly moderate, humane, and regimented disciplinary site (and another Foucauldian chapter) – the schoolhouse – (in fact Wolff specifically refers to Jonah as a hard-hearted *pupil*).[188] Like the remedial disciples in the Gospel of Mark, Jonah becomes the foil for the text's education programme: he is, as William Tyndale so wonderfully put it, 'but yet a young scholar, weak and rude'.[189] The disciplining of Jonah the errant prophet is coupled with the discipline of Jonah the misfit text: as pedagogy masquerading as story, narrative pared down to a point – the text-as-blackboard clearly 'demonstrates an important truth',[190] serves a utilitarian purpose, and so earns its place in the canon.

---

[184] Calvin, *Commentaries*, p. 128.

[185] *Ibid.*, p. 128.

[186] E. M. Good, 'Jonah: The Absurdity of God', in *Irony in the Old Testament* (London: SPCK, 1965), pp. 39–55 (47).

[187] H. W. Wolff, *Obadiah and Jonah* (trans. M. Kohl; Hermeneia; Minneapolis: Augsburg, 1988), p. 176.

[188] *Ibid.*, p. 183.

[189] From Tyndale's prologue to his translation of Jonah in D. Daniell (ed.), *Tyndale's Old Testament: Being the Pentateuch of 1530, Joshua to 2 Chronicles of 1537 and Jonah* (New Haven: Yale University Press, 1992), p. 631.

[190] L. C. Allen, *Joel, Obadiah, Jonah and Micah*, p. 177.

As the bell sounds and the book of Jonah separates out into a classroom, the text, the critic, Jonah, and the readers all take up their clearly demarcated places. Jonah, the unruly hard-hearted and hard-headed pupil, shuffles in and sits between Wolff and Good, for in the properly structured classroom things should be so arranged that 'an unruly and frivolous pupil should be placed between two who are well behaved and serious, a libertine either alone or between two pious pupils'.[191] The critics variously position themselves as exemplary children, monitors, prefects, and assistant teachers (deputies of the ultimate instructor, God himself).[192] And the book of Jonah obligingly proffers itself as a teaching text, a catechism, a 'means of correct training'. The old Peake's commentary frames the text – in chalked Edwardian copperplate – with captions such as 'Jonah vainly attempts to Evade the Mission to which God Appoints Him' (Jonah 1) and 'Jonah's Intolerance Rebuked and God's Mercy Vindicated' (Jonah 4),[193] while the *Good News Bible*, simplifying the book for a more junior class, uses the didactic captions 'Jonah disobeys the Lord' (Jonah 1) and 'Jonah obeys the Lord' (Jonah 3). Jack Sasson expounds the book as the story of the student Jonah's graduation from 'obstinacy' to 'submission', and Stuart (in his own words) helpfully 'boils down' the text to the essential warning 'Don't be like Jonah' (so resolutely distilling all the meaty and comic juices off, and reducing the text to its bare pedagogic bones).[194] The book contains all the classic components of an ideal Victorian teaching text:[195] the naughty strong-willed child who resists authority and is subjected to horrors, and a plot in

---

[191] Foucault, *Discipline and Punish*, p. 147, citing Jean Baptiste de la Salle's *Conduite des écoles chrétiennes*.

[192] This seems to be another instance of commentators zealously reinforcing what they perceive to be the ideology of the text (and in the process making a text that is arguably more stringent than the 'original'). In an earlier study, *The Prostitute and the Prophet*, I explored how commentators, like faithful henchmen, carry out the threats issued against the uncooperative woman in the text (Y. M. Sherwood, *The Prostitute and the Prophet: Hosea's Marriage in Literary-theoretical Perspective* (Sheffield: Sheffield Academic Press, 1996), p. 261). In this study, it seems that commentators are faithful assistant teachers, reinforcing what they see as the text's stern education programme.

[193] A. S. Peake, 'Jonah', in *Peake's Commentary on the Bible* (London: Nelson and Sons, 1919), pp. 556–8.

[194] D. Stuart, *Hosea–Jonah* (Word; Waco, Texas: Word Books, 1987), p. 434.

[195] For a fascinating discussion of the evolution of children's Bible stories, including the use of the Bible to reinforce parental discipline, see R. B. Bottigheimer, *The Bible for Children: From the Age of Gutenberg to the Present* (New Haven: Yale University Press, 1996). Bottigheimer's fascinating study explores some unlikely children's stories including Noah's drunkenness, the sacrifice of Isaac, Jael and Sisera and the rape and murder of the Levite's 'wife', but

which submission is coerced, indeed ensured, by a highly efficient system of snares, traps and swallowings. It reminds me of the parodic teaching-texts of Hilaire Belloc, in which children eat string, tell lies, run away, and die in ghastly ways, and learn, as their heads are detached from their bodies and roll off down the hill, that they should 'always keep a hold of nurse for fear of finding something worse' (is the lesson of Jonah, then, 'always keep a hold of God, for fear of encountering a worse "monster"'?). In my Disneyed and Sunday-schooled young brain, Jonah the rebellious prophet became entangled with Pinocchio the rebellious puppet, and the mixing (which was probably based on no more than Jonah's whale and Pinocchio's 'Monstro') proved to be intuitive. For both are on a moral quest to become a real boy (or a real prophet); both are lamentably wooden-headed, errant pupils who run away to Tarshish/Pleasure Island; but both inhabit a storyworld where the progress from naughtiness to obedience is absolutely ensured, where noses grow if you tell lies, and where whales and winds and consciences will retrieve you and deposit you on the pre-prescribed plot-line at the first sign that you are beginning to branch out into your own little subplot.[196]

So the book of Jonah is a lesson about obedience, submission, conscience (a lesson reinforced by Jiminey Cricket or Biblical Critic). For, at least as taught on the contemporary curriculum, the book congeals into a version of the nursery song that tells how 'God sent Jonah to Ninevy land' and how 'Jonah disobey my God command' and concludes, finger-waggingly: 'Children don't do that . . . (because) God got his eye on you.'[197] Glasses perched on their noses, leaning intimidatingly over the lectern, the critic-teachers inveigh against the stupidity, silliness, and hard-headedness of the pupil-prophet. Shaking his sage head over his stubborn pupil, Holbert

says nothing, unfortunately, about the various mutations and manipulations of the book of Jonah.

[196] The moral design of Pinocchio is very much a Disney addition. In Disney, Gepetto prays for a son, whereas in Collodi, he simply makes him; in Disney, the Blue Fairy puts the boy-puppet on a conscious quest to become a real boy, by learning to be 'brave, truthful and unselfish', whereas in Collodi, Pinocchio simply blunders about, has adventures, and discovers what he might become. The difference between the two versions provides a striking analogy with Jonah, suggesting the tantalising question, if we could get shake ourselves loose of the Disneyfying, moralising layer of scholarship, and Jonah's conscious education programme, what kind of story would Jonah then become?

[197] Slave song in C. Joyner (ed.), *Down By the Riverside* (Urbana: University of Illinois Press, 1984), pp. 163–4 (cited in Sasson, *Jonah*, p. 85).

laments that Jonah shows all the symptoms of a 'fox-hole' or 'fish-belly' religion and that the liturgical clichés 'turn to ashes in his mouth';[198] Wolff comments knowingly on his 'miscalculated flight';[199] while Stuart, shaking his fist, looking his pupils in the eyes, bellows, 'Jonah said "I have the right!" But he did not.'[200] As Jonah the prophet is coerced towards conformity, so the text is steered towards the norm, made to fit with a perceived biblical and prophetic standard. The misfit prophetic text, narrative without diatribe, odd-man-out in the canon, is urged to be more like Zechariah, Habakkuk, and its fellow-prophets (just as the pressure is on Jonah to be like Wolff, Good, the Author, and other good students). Fabulous accretions (kilos of blubbery flesh, plants that grow up overnight as on a speeded-up nature film, cattle in sack-cloth) are air-brushed out, superlatives kept under reasonable control, and the reader is encouraged to concentrate on the lesson and not to be distracted by humorous 'red-herrings'. Catching two pupil-readers at the back tittering over cattle in sackcloth, Mr Bewer insists that the phenomenon may *seem* 'somewhat humorous', but that 'the humour is due to a copyist . . . [who] repeated somewhat carelessly *and animals* from v. 7 after *men* in v. 8'[201] (thus a cause for laughter is converted into a cautionary instance of careless hand-writing). This ritual, the geography/history master insists, is a serious Persian mourning custom.[202] The book, emphatically, is no laughing matter.

On the contrary, it is a book full of evils and dangers and prophet-traps, and incriminations of the Jonah-figure. In the hands of the creative teacher-exegete, these multiply prodigiously. Jonah's re-peated use of the first-person pronoun underlines his selfishness[203] (this is surely the point at which Jonah's isolation in his own text

---

[198] J. C. Holbert, 'Deliverance Belongs to YHWH!: Satire in the Book of Jonah', *Journal for the Study of the Old Testament* 21 (1981), pp. 59–81 (73).

[199] Wolff, *Obadiah and Jonah*, p. 133

[200] Stuart, *Hosea–Jonah*, p. 510.

[201] J. A. Bewer, *Critical and Exegetical Commentary on Jonah* (International Critical Commentary; Edinburgh: T. & T. Clark, 1912), p. 54.

[202] Bewer, *Jonah*, p. 55. This argument, which has often been perpetuated in commentary, apparently depends on Herodotus (a suitably learned source). But if the class actually opens their copies of Herodotus, they find that the only relevant passages are in Book I, 140, where Herodotus refers to the Zoroastrian custom of exposing the dead to cows and dogs, and Book IX, 24, where the Persians cut the manes of their horses and mules as a sign of mourning.

[203] Wolff, *Obadiah and Jonah*, p. 55.

becomes most acute, when even his own 'I' testifies against him and convicts him of hubris). And as the Calvinist suppression of autonomy climaxes, so the threats to Jonah's life are compounded by intertexts. The dangers Jonah incurs in looking out over Nineveh are literally *petrifying* (if you bring in Genesis 19, that is): 'For when one thinks about what happens to Lot's wife, one may ask whether God will tolerate such inquisitive contemplation of divine judgement.'[204] (Thus Jonah is not to contemplate but to be contemplated; not to look, but to be scrutinised, by the omniscient, panopticon-deity with a monopoly on looking.)

A good pupil-prophet is evidently seen and not heard. When Jonah speaks uninvited the posse of teacher-critics instantly tell him to sit down and shut up: his protest in 4.2 is dismissed as a 'lame excuse' for disobedience[205] or as an irreverent 'attempt to limit the scope and intention of God's word'.[206] The hushed atmosphere of the classroom promotes quietism in the most literal sense. And as Jonah's speech is converted to silence, so his silence, ironically, is interpreted as speech. As if to show that traditional critics are just as happy lounging in the expansive freedom of white spaces, lacunae, and gaps as the postmodernists, the space at the end of the text (where Jonah, for his own reasons, does not answer God's rhetorical question) is interpreted as either a moment where Jonah bows the knee and acknowledges his error, *or* a moment where the reader and Jonah's education come to a climax in an exam. 'The reader has to carry away the question, think about it, and decide rightly', Wolff declares.[207]

Thus the reader comes away from many contemporary readings clutching a takeaway examination paper. As she scans it she realises that it contains two questions: (i) is Jonah's example to be imitated or resisted? and (ii) is God the God of the Jews only, or of the gentiles also? (Romans 3.29). The questions set are obviously rhetorical questions; the prescribed, coerced answers are respectively 'resisted' and 'gentiles also'. The lesson of the text, which so often merges with the coercively pedagogic slant, is that 'Israel has no monopoly of

---

204 G. von Rad, *God at Work in Israel* (trans. J. H. Marks; Nashville: Abingdon, 1980), p. 62.
205 P. Trudinger, 'Jonah: A Post-Exilic Verbal Cartoon?', *The Downside Review* (April 1989), pp. 142–3 (143).
206 Holbert, 'Deliverance Belongs to YHWH!', p. 75.
207 Wolff, *Obadiah and Jonah*, p. 175.

God's loving care.'[208] As the book is subjected to a 'discipline that organises [and hierarchises] analytical space',[209] it is made into a conventionally prophetic tirade, targeted at the seething Ezra-Nehemites, Jewish xenophobes, just visible off the edges of the page. And the point of the text is to set a skewed discursive essay title, with pre-prescribed answer: 'Compare and contrast the relative values of justice and mercy, universalism and xenophobia, with special reference to the Jews and the gentiles.'

At this point a chill wind blows through the commentary-classroom (the presence of ectoplasm, or just an ideological chill?). For, according to the strict education programme imposed on the book, the 'Jew–gentile confrontation' remains the 'central defining feature', or axiom.[210] The gentiles are 'more humane, more active, wiser, and also more devout' than the Jewish prophet;[211] 'The readiness of the people of Nineveh to repent [is] . . . a salutary lesson to the Jews, who [are] renowned for their stubbornness and lack of faith';[212] the '[gentile] sailors pray the prayer that Jonah would not pray';[213] thus 'the sailors rise in our estimation' but 'Jonah continues his inexorable descent'.[214] The rhetoric of super-session, displacement, hierarchisation inserts itself in every space and every line (just like the cross of the Fathers), and the sinking of Jonah proffers itself as a compliant cartoonish allegory of Judaism sinking in relevance, spluttering down to the sea-bed, while the proto-Christian gentiles float to the top. As the storm scene exposes 'Israel's prerogative' to 'bitter ridicule',[215] so the book as a whole exposes the 'untenability of the understanding of the ways of God that was then prevalent in Israel'[216] and 'calls into question Israel's beliefs and ministry in the world'.[217] Adjectives that characterise Jonah as the recalcitrant, lazy pupil slide into adjectives that conjure up the spectre of the Enlightenment/Lutheran legacy of Jonah the

---

[208] L. C. Allen, *Joel, Obadiah, Jonah and Micah*, p. 194.

[209] Foucault, *Discipline and Punish*, p. 143.

[210] L. C. Allen, *Joel, Obadiah, Jonah and Micah*, p. 190.

[211] Wolff, *Obadiah and Jonah*, p. 123.

[212] 'Jonah', in J. D. Douglas (ed.), *The New Bible Dictionary* (Leicester: IVP, 1962), pp. 652–4 (653).

[213] Stuart, *Hosea–Jonah*, p. 121.

[214] R. Payne, 'The Prophet Jonah: Reluctant Messenger and Intercessor', *Expository Times* 100 (1988), pp. 131–4 (134, n. 7).

[215] Wolff, *Obadiah and Jonah*, p. 119.

[216] Good, 'Jonah: The Absurdity of God', p. 54.

[217] Wolff, *Obadiah and Jonah*, p. 176.

Jew. Jonah is 'self-centred, lazy, hypocritical and altogether inferior to the wonderful pagans around him';[218] he is *revêche et têtu* ('cantankerous and bad-tempered'),[219] *Engherzig* (narrow-minded),[220] 'mulish',[221] 'good-for-nothing',[222] 'sinister',[223] 'petty',[224] 'ludicrous',[225] a 'bigot' who is 'eyeless with hate'.[226] He is an unappealing embodiment of *Fleischliche Gesinnung und niedrige Rachsucht* ('carnal mentality and base vindictiveness')[227] and *giftiger Hochmut* ('poisonous arrogance');[228] he is a mutant 'dove' who is less like a dove than a hawk.[229] 'Self-centred, self-righteous, and self-willed',[230] he is a 'type of the narrow, blind, prejudiced and fanatic Jews',[231] a *Judenspiegel*,[232] or as Kaiser unabashedly puts it (in 1973) *ein Bild des Judentums*,[233] who even as late as 1989 can be heard snarling: 'It's just like God to forgive these wretched Ninevites, these outsiders . . . Now we will have to welcome them as fellow-members in the

[218] Holbert, 'Deliverance Belongs to YHWH!', p. 70.

[219] A. Lods, *La religion d'Israël* (1939), p. 196, cited in C. A. Keller, 'Jonas. Le portrait d'un prophète', *Theologische Zeitschrift* 21 (1965), pp. 329–40 (329).

[220] W. Novack, *Die Kleinen Propheten* (1903), p. 196; J. Meinhold, *Einführung in das Alte Testament* (1919), p. 287, cited in Keller, 'Jonas', p. 329.

[221] von Rad, *God at Work in Israel*, p. 76.

[222] Wolff, *Obadiah and Jonah*, p. 109.

[223] G. von Rad, *The Message of the Prophets*, p. 257, cited in A. D. Cohen, 'The Tragedy of Jonah', p. 167.

[224] Holbert, 'Deliverance Belongs to YHWH!', p. 74.

[225] M. Burrows, 'The Literary Character of the Book of Jonah', in H. T. Frank and W. L. Reed (eds.), *Translating and Understanding the Old Testament: Essays in Honour of H. G. May* (Nashville: Abingdon Press, 1970), pp. 82–105 (86).

[226] A. D. Martin, cited without reference in Goitein, 'Some Observations on Jonah', p. 66.

[227] K. Kautzsch, *Biblische Theologie des Altes Testaments* (1911), p. 317, cited in Keller, 'Jonah', p. 329.

[228] C. H. Cornhill, *Einleitung in das Alte Testament* (1896), p. 187, cited in Keller, 'Jonah', p. 329.

[229] A. and P.-E. Lacocque, *Jonah: A Psycho-Religious Approach to the Prophet* (Columbia: University of South Carolina Press, 1990), p. 31.

[230] Burrows, 'The Literary Character of the Book of Jonah', p. 87.

[231] Bewer, *Jonah*, p. 64. Bewer's prestigious 1912 commentary is still recommended, without warning, in the introductory undergraduate Old Testament Guides series (see R. Salters, *Jonah and Lamentations* (Old Testament Guides; Sheffield: Sheffield Academic Press, 1994), p. 13, where Salters's only caveat is that the book is a 'bit dated now'). Jack Sasson, in contrast (but only in passing) points out that Bewer's 'notions are offensive' (Sasson, *Jonah*, p. 274).

[232] The phrase is taken from the title of a pamphlet published in 1909 by a Protestant pastor and cited by Bickerman, 'Les deux erreurs', p. 248. Bickerman gives the details as: K. Gerecke, *Biblischer Antisemitismus: Der Juden weltgeschichtlicher Charakter, Schuld und Ende in des Propheten Jonah Judenspiegel* (1909).

[233] O. Kaiser, 'Wirklichkeit, Möglichkeit und Vorurteil. Ein Beitrag zum Verständnis des Buches Jona', *Evangelische Theologie* 33 (1973), pp. 91–103 (102). (*Vorurteil*', 'prejudice', is an interesting title for this article, that rebounds on the writer somewhat.)

community of faith!'[234] He is a 'psychological and religious monster';[235] a representative of 'flinty-hearted Judaism' that had 'jealously sunk into itself';[236] a possessor of a 'hot Jewish heart'[237] that bursts open in fury; a man full of a 'bloodthirsty hope' for vengeance,[238] the incarnation (to put it mildly) of 'all that the author of this book means to reject'.[239]

Seeping through the strangely diverse designations of Jonah as lazy pupil, bungling peasant, bigot, and clown, bleeding beneath the professional, polite, critical veneer, are clearly barely metaphorised and deflected anti-Semitic designations. Jonah's 'bloodthirsty hope', poison-filled psyche, eyeless hatred, and religious monstrosity evoke a familiar welter of medieval mythologies: the Jew as murderer, monster, the dehumanised Other, 'eyeless' hence faceless, convicted of blood-lust and the blood-libel. Though the original text could barely have anticipated the comparison, Jonah has clearly mutated into a biblical Merchant of Venice. The venom of his heart (or the poison of his mind) congealing, Jonah 'feed[s] fat his ancient grudge', demands his pound of gentile flesh, booms 'I stand for judgement. Answer: shall I have it?' – to which the critics and the sweetly spoken proto-Christian text answer with a triumphant and resounding 'No', then break into a liltingly poetic apostrophe to the mercy that 'droppeth as the gentle dew from heaven'. Jonah, who once hung out with Jesus, has now become a Shylock-twin: both are a barely concealed eruption of medieval superstition, for, just like Jonah's 'bloodthirsty hope', Shylock's metaphorised 'grudge' that needs 'feeding' is but 'ritual murder at one remove'.[240] And, like 'Jonah', Shylock is a word-crammed agglomerative cultural space, stockpiled with adjectives: as if to prove it, Hazlitt defines Shylock as 'a decrepit old man, bent with age and ugly with mental deformity, grinning with deadly malice, with the venom of his heart congealed in the expression of his countenance, sullen, morose, gloomy,

---

[234] Trudinger, 'Jonah: A Post-Exilic Verbal Cartoon?', p. 143.

[235] von Rad, *God at Work*, p. 66. Compare Leslie Allen's exclamation: 'What religious monster is this?', *Joel, Obadiah, Jonah and Micah*, p. 229.

[236] Peake, 'Jonah', p. 556.

[237] Bewer, *Jonah*, p. 64.

[238] R. H. Pfeiffer, *Introduction to the Old Testament* (New York: Harper and Row, 1948), p. 588. Pfeiffer elaborates: 'The contemptible attitude of some Jews in the time of the author, represented by Jonah's bitter disappointment when Jehovah in his mercy failed to destroy Nineveh, is stigmatised in God's stinging rebuke to Jonah.'

[239] Good, 'Jonah: The Absurdity of God', p. 40.

[240] J. Gross, *Shylock: Four Hundred Years in the Life of a Legend* (London: Vintage, 1994), p. 17.

inflexible, brooding over one idea, that of his hatred, and fixed on one unalterable purpose, that of his revenge'.[241] While Jonah is in a similarly unflattering position, scholarship freezes its perception of him: 'We are *used* to seeing Jonah as haughty and prideful' comments Rosenberg;[242] even Jewish readers replicate him, complains Rosen (albeit without the 'anti-Semitic garnish'),[243] while Good relaxes into the polite peace that consensus produces, celebrating the 'remarkable unanimity . . . among biblical scholars (a notoriously quarrelsome lot) which might seem suspicious were it not so welcome'.[244] The repetition of the emphatically negative stereotype is not always done in consciousness of its emphatically 'Jewish' roots, but in this case 'innocence', as Graham Greene puts it in *The Quiet American*, is like a 'dumb leper who has lost his bell, wandering the world, meaning no harm'.

Now none of this is very subtle stuff. Instead of tracing ghosts, pale spectres, as they disappear around the corner, we seem to be working with poltergeists, who make their presence absolutely clear and all but leave calling-cards. Metacommentary is at its most interesting when it is subtle, when it works with a fine needle, teasing out hitherto unperceived ideological threads; in contrast this seems to be *Metacommentary for Beginners*. Yet there is a sense in which the evidence simply needs to be catalogued, in all its tedious monotony and self-revealing hysteria. Just as the first feminist biblical critics began with the texts of terror – the texts of female dismemberment,

---

[241] Cited in Gross, *Shylock*, p. 107.

[242] J. Rosenberg, 'Jonah and the Nakedness of Deeds', *Tikkun* 2.4 (1987), pp. 36–8 (36); my italics.

[243] Rosen, 'Jonah: Justice for Jonah, or a Bible Bartleby?', p. 224. This obviously raises the question why many contemporary Jewish interpreters repeat the excessively negative characterisation of Jonah, and the universalistic-xenophobic dichotomy by which he stands condemned. Norma Rosen 'guesses' at a reason: 'though such commentary makes Jews and a Jewish prophet look bad, it makes what Christian commentators call the "Old Testament God" look good. Vindictive judgment, wrath, devouring punishments are banished. In their place, mercy, pity, love. To which Jonah so perversely objects' (p. 224). John Miles also offers an explanation: 'Christians, jealous of the privilege of Israel which their own Scriptures (cf. Romans 9.11) oblige them to acknowledge, eulogize those few Jewish writings which minimize the privilege and, in so doing, disparage the enormous remainder, which celebrates it. Jews, resentful of a charge which is embarrassing, at least in its contemporary context, respond by relativizing the context. Fascinating in its way, this *pas de deux* is also painful to witness, doubly so because the real issue is never broached' (J. Miles, 'Laughing at the Bible: Jonah as Parody', in Y. T. Radday and A. Brenner (eds.), *On Humour and the Comic in the Hebrew Bible* (Sheffield: The Almond Press, 1990), pp. 203–15 (212–13)).

[244] Good, 'Jonah: The Absurdity of God', p. 39.

abuse, rape – that offered themselves as all-too garish and all-too-literal prooftexts of female victimisation, so a critique of anti-Judaism in biblical commentary needs to begin with the most obvious crimes and offences: the metaphor of the sinking (and potential drowning?) of the Jew and the rising of the gentile; the medieval mythologies that are too complacent, or un-self-knowing, to even bother with masks. Commentary, obligingly, proffers itself like a huge trail of footprints, leading to the cave of the 'psychological and religious monster'. No psychic talent is required to identify the ghosts and traces, no previous monster-hunting experience is required. Even the most casual acquaintance with contemporary commentary makes poring over the yellowing pages of Michaelis, Eichhorn, and Friedrichsen a most *unheimlich* experience, because, instead of the expected alien voices, you encounter familiar ghosts and dark familiars. According to the Polish poet Wislawa Szymborska, the historian of ideas can reasonably expect to feel god-like, omniscient, in relation to the dead, reading their letters 'like [a] helpless god', for they are 'poor' and 'blindfolded', and 'the most fervent of them gaze confidingly into our eyes' because 'their calculations tell them that there they'll find perfection'.[245] But here, the 'blindfolded' dead are looking across the abyss of the centuries towards their would-be redeemers, to find that we are still proudly sporting the same, now rather tattered, blindfold. Contemporary commentary preoccupies itself with tweaking details and reconsidering reconsiderations, without stopping to examine, critically, the ideology of the macrocosm within which it is doing its tweaking. And the result is that every element of Enlightened interpretation – the overt Jewishness of Jonah, the fear of the Old Testament, the idealised figure of the author – finds its cartoonish culmination in the present. The author continues his career as Jewish Jonah's proto-Christian antithesis, the classroom swot as opposed to the stubborn and hard-headed pupil: 'our author' is a liberal-minded pre-Christian Jew, a true ecumenical, who 'opens the door to a wider and more tolerant viewpoint';[246] a 'universalist' who opposes the 'arrogance' that accompanies 'chosenness'[247] and who writes

---

[245] W. Szymborska, 'The Letters of the Dead', in *View With a Grain of Sand: Selected Poems* (trans. S. Baraczak and C. Cavanagh; London: Harcourt Brace and Company, 1995), p. 71.

[246] J. Magonet, *Form and Meaning: Studies in the Literary Techniques of the Book of Jonah* (Sheffield: Almond Press, 1983), p. 95.

[247] *Ibid.*, p. 95. Jonathan Magonet, a Jewish writer, takes up the image of the author-as-

specifically to attack a group who 'believe that they hold the God of heaven and earth in their pocket'.[248] Writing in the tradition of Tom Paine, eager to make the prejudice absolutely clear, an interpreter writing in 1937 classes Jonah as that cultural anomaly, a 'singularly broad-minded Jew'.[249] (And as the phrase 'our author' implies, there is an above-average participation in the character of the author, who still shows considerable affinities to the idealised image of the liberal Christian churchman/academic.) As conventional prophetic texts are traditionally, Romantically, read as a cardiac print-out of the prophetic heart, so the book of Jonah becomes the expression of the writer's prophetic soul. As the 'flickering unrest' of Hosea and Jeremiah and the 'majestically rolling sentences of Isaiah' map the prophets 'inner emotions',[250] so Jonah the text charts the vacillations of the author's 'spiritual experience' or pilgrimage, his initial resistance to the 'disgusting' idea that 'God's love embraced alien people', and his recognition of the truth after he 'was lifted into the divine heart and shared the glory of its compassion'.[251] And as the Author settles down into lifetime, guaranteed employment as a projection of the universalist Christian Self, critics continue to agonise over the senile, muttering, Old Testament. More is clearly being dealt with in contemporary readings than the figure of Jonah the Jew, and Jonah is thrown overboard clutching sheaves of sodden Old Testament text. Pfeiffer imagines a Jonah who believes in 'the Jewish exclusivism of Nehemiah and the sanguinary apocalyptic dreams of Jehovah's extermination [*sic*] of the gentiles (Ezekiel 38–39, Joel, Obadiah, and the like)';[252] Otto Kaiser draws specific-ally on the language of Genesis 19 when he depicts a Jonah who longs for God to 'annihilate' his enemies with 'fire and sulphur'.[253] Thus Jonah, who goes down dreaming bloody dreams and clutching

---

universalist but at the same time questions the appropriation of universalism by Christian interpreters. In a later article he criticises the idea of the author as a 'pre-Christian Christian' (see Magonet, 'Jonah', in D. N. Freedman (ed.), *The Anchor Bible Dictionary* (New York and London: Doubleday, 1992), pp. 936–42 (941)).

248 Good, 'Jonah: The Absurdity of God', p. 54.
249 F. A. Malony, *Journal of the Transactions of the Victoria Institute* 69 (1937), p. 246, cited and reaffirmed by L. C. Allen, *Joel, Obadiah, Jonah and Micah*, p. 179.
250 H. Gunkel, 'The Prophets as Writers and Poets' (trans. J. L. Schaaf), in D. L. Petersen (ed.), *Prophecy in Israel* (Philadelphia: Fortress, 1987), pp. 22–73 (47).
251 H. H. Rowley, *The Missionary Message of the Old Testament* (lectures given in 1944 to the Baptist Missionary Society; London: The Carey Press, 1948), p. 68.
252 Pfeiffer, *Introduction to the Old Testament*, p. 589.
253 Kaiser, 'Wirklichkeit, Möglichkeit und Vorurteil', p. 102.

a soggy collection of quite specific file-cards, is a scapegoat for the Old Old Testament (in its darker, crueller, more nationalistic manifestations) *and* for the Old Old Testament God – for it is *Yhwh*, the exterminating Jehovah, who annihilates his enemies with fire and sulphur. Jonah internalises and personifies all of those texts and 'sanguine' manifestations of God that critics cannot quite stomach, yet also cannot bear to catalogue in their entirety – Ezekiel 38–39, Joel, Obadiah, 'and the like'. (The critique of the Old Testament God is only obliquely alluded to, while 'and the like' is an extremely compressed category, for as critics like Orlinsky and Soares-Prabhu have pointed out, there are 'literally, hundreds, not just tens and scores, of passages in the Hebrew Bible . . . that assert positively or at least reflect the relationship of God and Israel as being purely nationalistic'.)[254] The book of Jonah, like the book of Ruth and Deutero-Isaiah, is seen as part of a pure progressive golden core, an over-prioritised and overstretched slither of text, addressed to blood-thirsty xenophobes, clutching their copies of Ezra and Nehemiah, and invested with the weighty task of purging the Old Testament of its darker, more primitive self. Jonah is one of the few, idealised, would-be New books, testifying to how the Old Testament is already writhing internally, purging itself of its oldness, trying frantically, like Lady Macbeth, to wash their hands of 'damned [trouble] spots'.

Thus Jonah personifies all that the author, and indeed the Old Testament, always meant to reject (even though it never fully got around to it). And his survival, his overliving, testifies to the vibrant, cultural afterlives of biblical characters, animated by forces other than the biblical text. In a book that critiques the 'old-boy network that holds the Bible in thrall'[255] and that shifts the point of focus to the afterlife of female characters, the feminist biblical critic Alice Bach traces how Salomé's sensuous fleshy curves, as well as her name, are all supplied by culture. Jonah criticism supplies a different kind of 'flesh', a defining carnality, and 'Jonah' is a space defined by a frenzied collection of negatives. Jonah acts as a magnet for all antitheses of the Self (no discriminating criteria are applied) – thus

---

[254] H. M. Orlinsky, 'Nationalism-Universalism and Internationalism in Ancient Israel', in Frank and Reed, *Translating and Understanding the Old Testament*, pp. 206–36 (235). See also G. M. Soares-Prabhu, 'Laughing at Idols: The Dark Side of Biblical Monotheism (an Indian Reading of Isa. 44.9–20)', in F. Segovia and M. Tolbert (eds.), *Reading From This Place*. II. *Social Location and Biblical Interpretation in Global Perspective* (Minneapolis: Fortress, 1995), pp. 109–31.

[255] Bach, *Women, Seduction, and Betrayal in Biblical Narrative*, pp. 32–3.

Jonah is associated with bigotry and evil, and, more puzzlingly, with laziness, and membership of the lower/peasant classes. Reading commentary is like spying on a game of free-association, in which scholars pass round a list of attributes and a thesaurus, and each participant has to add a new adjective to the list (feeling the list of available words shrinking, some participants panic – floundering helplessly, Halperin and Friedman produce the phrase 'mantic bumpkin',[256] to the rather embarrassed silence of the other scholars).

Jonah's 'too too solid flesh' is, of course, only an illusion: he is just a cultural hologram, or, in Roland Barthes's terms, a textual effect conjured by *semes* (words, adjectives, fragments of typifying behaviour) which combine to create the illusion of substance.[257] Fattened by adjectives, solidified by scholarship, the established scholarly photofit of Jonah is transferred across to 'popular' culture. Jonah can regularly be spotted stomping through the pages of children's fiction: the Macmillan children's version depicts a livid, fist-shaking Jonah and the accompanying text reads '[Jonah] didn't care about the people of Nineveh. They weren't like the Israelites . . . They were different.'[258] (Meanwhile the 'Biblical Backgrounds' section in a 1971 edition of the RSV informs the curious Bible-consumer that: 'To the Jews who sometimes thought that God loved no one but them, the book of Jonah was a powerful lesson. No one can draw a circle around God's love.') A similar message is performed in Technicolor in the 1996 television series *Testament: The Animated Bible*[259] where a balding, hook-nosed Jonah is nicknamed 'Jonah the Moaner', besieged by a veritable posse of redemptive images (laughing children, rainbows, yellow butterflies), and described in the accompanying storybook as a 'bony', 'scraggy', and 'irritable' individual, much given to 'grunting', 'strutting', and 'exploding with scorn'.[260] In the Animated Bible version, Jonah's eyes, the key to his cartoon-soul, flash with fire (rather than love-

256 B. Halpern and R. E. Friedman, 'Composition and Paranomasia in the Book of Jonah', *Hebrew Annual Review* 4 (1980), pp. 79–92 (89).

257 See R. Barthes, *S/Z* (trans. R. Miller; London: Blackwell, 1990; 1st edn 1973), pp. 94–5. Barthes is emphatic that, although we often speak of characters as though they have a future, an unconscious, a soul, s/he is in fact only an effect of language, a conglomeration of attributes, for which the proper name is an 'instrument of exchange'.

258 C. Christian, *Jonah* (London: Macmillan, 1996), p. 38.

259 *Testament: The Animated Bible* was produced in Russia, Wales, and England, and was financed by the BBC (England) and S4C (Channel Four Wales) and Christmas Films (Russia). It was produced with the endorsement of The Bible Society.

260 *Testament: The Animated Bible* adapted by S. Humble-Jackson (London: Boxtree, 1996),

hearts or dollar-signs) as he contemplates the annihilation of Nineveh with sadistic pleasure (fig. 5). Somehow the forces that animate Jonah become so much clearer when animated. The naïve symbolic structures of cartoon lay bare the process of monsterisation that commentary so barely conceals, as it substitutes physical deformity for psychological deformity, and foregrounds the motif of deformation/defamation.

'What religious monster is this?' asks Leslie Allen,[261] and the question begs asking a second time, but this time taking the question mark more seriously (for Allen it is only a virtual question mark, the limp signifier of a rhetorical question). For monsters (from the Latin *monstrum*, to show/warn/reveal) reveal things and issue warnings, and lead us into the matrix of social, cultural relations that generate them. This monster, however, is primarily a *religious* monster – Allen is right on that account. So far I have suggested that Jonah is a critical anachronism, overliving in the present, but insofar as this story implies that Jonah only lingers because his character wore out a groove in the critical imagination, or because critics were not paying enough attention, it is misleading. The monstrous Jonah survives, indeed lives on and flourishes, because this reading of him, and of the text he inhabits, is so successful at enabling Christian theology to 'deal with' perennial tensions in its relations with Judaism. The two-dimensional stereotype of Jonah the Jew, when probed, leads into a multidimensional cultural-theological space, fraught with all the fissures and divisions of Western Christian culture's encounters with its Others. Others, disturbingly, are never entirely other, they always brush up against, contaminate, infiltrate the Self; they are exterior *and* indispensable, bound to the Self by a relation of 'conjunction and disjunction'.[262] In this sense the Jew is Christianity's quintessential Other, habitually tied to Christianity in the hyphenated hybrid 'the Judaeo-Christian', and yet, equally habitually, physically and conceptually ghettoised, segregated, anni-hilated, and expelled beyond Christian borders. If, as Jonathan Dollimore puts it, 'To be against (opposed to) is also to be against

---

pp. 127–50. Jonah clearly speaks in a lower-class Yorkshire accent, so demonstrating his lineage as something of a 'bumpkin'.

[261] L. C. Allen, *The Books of Joel, Obadiah, Jonah and Micah*, p. 229.

[262] M. de Certeau, *The Practice of Everyday Life* (trans. S. Rendall; Berkeley: University of California Press, 1984), p. 127.

(close up, in proximity to), or in other words, up against',[263] then Christianity is both against and intimately up against the Jew. The Jew stands at the origin of Christianity *and* represents the dangerous possibility of its denial; the Christian narrative of Self depends on 'him', and yet if 'he' retains his distinctiveness then that same narrative is under threat. The mythologised spectre of the Jew is both the vilified Christ-killer and the one to whom Christianity is in debt (the 'Gift' in a double Derridean sense of present and poison(er)). 'He' violates the vital boundary that separates believers from non-believers, for whereas 'ordinary heathens paved the road to Christianity's future, the Jews challenge its past and clouded its present'.[264] As Zygmunt Bauman argues, the Jew, for the Christian, becomes the ultimate site of frenzied logical incoherence, loaded with the 'awesome ambivalence of parricide and fratricide'.[265] It is something of an understatement to say that, like all monstrous projections of racial, social and political alterity, the 'Jew' represents a 'crisis' in binary thinking[266] – more accurate to say, as Bauman does, that he becomes the very image of 'mind-boggling and spine-chilling incongruity', the ultimate residue of the quest for order, the 'wasteyard onto which all the ambiguity squeezed out of the universe could be dumped'.[267]

Thus the intimate but sometimes claustrophobic stage of Jonah criticism opens out into a much wider conceptual world in its attempts to negotiate the question 'Just how other . . . is the Other?'[268] For a reading that assigns all the negative values to Jonah as character, and all the positive values to Jonah as text, demonstrates one – albeit rather simplistic – way of negotiating the aporia

---

[263] J. Dollimore, *Sexual Dissidence: Augustine to Wilde/Freud to Foucault* (Oxford: Clarendon, 1991), p. 229.

[264] Z. Bauman, 'Allosemitism: Premodern, Modern, Postmodern', in B. Cheyette and L. Marcus (eds.), *Modernity, Culture and 'the Jew'* (Cambridge: Polity, 1998), pp. 143–56 (148).

[265] *Ibid.*, p. 147. As Bauman elaborates, 'the Jews were the venerable ancestors of Christianity, who however refused to withdraw once Christianity was born and took over, and having overstayed their time and outlived their divine mission, continued to haunt the world as living fossils; and the Jews gave birth to Christ only to reject, denigrate and disown him'.

[266] For a discussion of the monster as a crisis of dichotomy, see J. J. Cohen, *Monster Theory*, p. 6.

[267] Bauman, 'Allosemitism', pp. 147–8. Bauman's brilliant study is an attempt to describe the particular forms that anti-Semitism takes in the context of modernity. His key thesis is that fear of the Jew is governed not by *heterophobia* so much as *proteophobia*: the Jew threatens because he stands against modernity's drive towards logical coherence, and comes to represent the impossibility of order.

[268] S. P. Mohanty, 'Us and Them: On the Philosophical Bases of Political Criticism', *Yale Journal of Criticism* 2.2 (1989), pp. 1–32 (5).

of Jew as ally and enemy, proto- and anti-Christian, and secures its ongoing relevance and appeal within a Christian ideological framework. The small stage of Jonah criticism demonstrates how Christianity links itself with *and* expels its Jewish Other, because its identity paradoxically depends on both annexing and expulsion. In this sense this book is about far more than the work of a few select scholars on forty-eight choice biblical verses: it illustrates the very necessary compulsion to read the text through very clear dichotomies (Jew–gentile; particular–universal) and so police the boundary between Christianity and Judaism.

The boundary is unpoliceable of course, the dichotomies unsustainable (you only have to touch them and they fall apart). Universalism has a distinctly particularistic edge, and saccharine-sweet mercy-speeches leave something of a nasty aftertaste. The critical condemnation of a fire-and brimstone-hungry Jonah displaces the critical violence that taunts/represses/humiliates him and that stages the sinking/supersession of the Jew – just as the mercy-speeches of the Christians of Belmont collide with the harsh treatment and forced conversion of Shylock. And if Jonah is at once ice-cold and flinty (Peake) and boiling fit to burst (Bewer) – just like his Shylock-twin, who has been played as choleric 'malignant, rapacious, vengeful, red-hot' (Henry James) and as phlegmatic 'sullen, morose, gloomy, inflexible' (Hazlitt)[269] – then Jonah-as-hologram begins to flicker, disintegrate, and expose the solid-seeming 'monster' as pure culture without substance. Like all monstrous aberrations, Jonah is too hot and too cold: the excess is what is important, not the temperature. Thus he is situated at the heart of the aporiae of anti-Jewish rhetoric in which 'Jews are too smart and innately incapable of genius . . . over-intellectual but over-emotional, hyper-rational but superstitious' for 'only mutually exclusive categories seem large enough to encompass the totality of Jewish iniquity'.[270] Prejudice exposes itself at the point where, in the attempt to locate the Other, it prods him with hyperbole and pushes him off the spectrum at both ends. The spectre of one who is at once too hot and too cold explodes the very binary system on which his existence depends.

Let us leave the Jew–Christian dichotomy hanging there, reeling

---

[269] For a history of performance and interpretation of *The Merchant of Venice*, see Gross, *Shylock*. Henry James is discussed on pp. 138–9, Hazlitt on p. 107.
[270] Nochlin, 'Starting with the Self', p. 7.

and decomposing, and turn our attention briefly to two distinctly twentieth-century Jonah mutations. *Jonah the clown* first makes his appearance in the mid-1960s when the text, now redrafted as satire, is performed on the scholarly comedy circuit (is this an attempt to mitigate the violence, I wonder, to dilute the polemical force with a touch of comedy?). Turning on what they call the 'harsh light of satire',[271] Wolff and Good put on a bit of a theological slapstick in which Jonah, bungling xenophobe, trips over the truth of Romans 3.29 to the appreciative hoots and cheers of the audience (thus, as Linda Nochlin observes, in a different context, 'once more irony puts Jewish figures in their place').[272] 'How the narrator laughs at the Hebrew who takes great pains to flee from his God, and in the process, and quite against his will, brings non-Israelites to believe in this God',[273] chuckles Wolff, while Good, having promised a piece on the 'absurdity of God', in fact revels in the absurdity of Jonah.[274] In 1981, a slicker comedian takes the mike, milking the text's puns, playing the pauses just right: 'The fish', pronounces Holbert, pausing, looking round the smoke-filled room, 'who is literally sick of the prophet's false piety' (pausing again, lips twitching, waiting) – 'throws up'.[275] The laughter and groans that circulate from the critical one-liner promptly dissipate, however, when the figure of *Jonah the Zionist* takes the stage, and the book shifts from satire to political manifesto. Following the establishment of the State of Israel, 'Jonah the Jew' begins to mutate into Jonah the Israeli. His debut is anticipated in 1956, in a comment that Jonah is a 'first class expansionist (Israel First)';[276] his presence is hinted at in observations that 'Jonah is an ardent nationalist, pro-Israel and anti-foreign',[277] but he only comes to the fore in Rosemary Radford

---

[271] Wolff, *Obadiah and Jonah*, p. 176.

[272] Nochlin, 'Starting with the Self', p. 12.

[273] Wolff, *Obadiah and Jonah*, p. 109.

[274] Good, 'Jonah: The Absurdity of God'. Good's reasons for shifting the site of absurdity are interesting: 'The alternative to Jonah's absurdity is the absurdity of God, and if the author's readers are not prepared to settle for the former, he offers no recourse but to the latter' (p. 55). There seems to be a certain anxiety in Good's reading that suggests that the humour or absurdity of this text, once unleashed, would be no respecter of divine persons.

[275] Holbert, 'Deliverance Belongs to YHWH!', p. 74.

[276] J. D. Smart, 'The Book of Jonah: Introduction and Exegesis', in G. A. Buttrick, T. S. Kepler, H. G. May, *et al.* (eds.), *The Interpreter's Bible* VI (Nashville: Abingdon, 1956), pp. 875–94 (876).

[277] Stuart, *Hosea–Jonah*, p. 431. Stuart adds the qualification 'anti-Assyrian', but I'm not sure if this reminder that we are talking about an ancient context actually negates the contemporary resonances of 'pro-Israel and anti-foreign'.

Ruether's and H. J. Ruether's 1989 production *The Wrath of Jonah*.[278]
The ideological geography of the book is clearly laid out on the
opening page where a map entitled 'Territories captured by Israel in
1948 and 1949' is placed opposite God's question to Jonah: 'Should I
not pity Nineveh, that great city, in which there are more than a
hundred and twenty thousand persons?' (but no cattle, interestingly,
presumably because cattle would inject too much levity into the
proceedings). The backdrop for the performance is Palestine (for the
directors see the establishment of Israel as a misguided political act,
contravening the spirit of true, Diaspora Judaism); Jonah, the 'angry
chauvinist prophet'[279] plays the Zionist, a representative of those
who have duped the Jewish people into believing that Judaism
involves nationhood; and the Ninevites, after a quick costume
change, change out of their role as 'the gentiles' and into their role
as 'the Palestinians'. The dissymmetry of the text is both striking and
offensive, for though the Ruethers proclaim that their book is written
'out of concern for both wounded peoples',[280] they cast the Palestinians as 'wounded in body but not in spirit', having 'sustained over
many years of suffering an enormous sense of moral unity in the
rightness of the cause', whereas the Israelis are 'militarily strong' but
culpable, hence 'wounded in soul'.[281] (Indeed, there is no more
effective performance of the inadequacy and the offensiveness of the
old critical dichotomy between Jewish nationalists and gentile
universalists than the way in which it crumbles when clumsily
mapped onto the complex scene of contemporary Middle Eastern
politics.) Whereas the production of Jonah as satire has played to
full-houses and been run to several performances, this interpretation
has received far less enthusiastic reviews. The most caustic reviewer
is David Biale who attacks the production for reinscribing the myth
of the Jews, that 'stiff-necked people', for 'steal[ing] a Jewish book

---

[278] R. Radford Ruether and H. J. Ruether, *The Wrath of Jonah* (New York: Harper and Row,
1989). The book is a surprising one, coming from Rosemary Radford Ruether, the author
of *Faith and Fratricide*, an exposé of the Christian roots of anti-Semitism. The source for the
book is the *Database Project on Palestinian Human Rights*, and the baseline assumptions are that
Israel has no right to exist, that the bulk of the guilt for intolerance of Others lies with the
Israelis, that Israel's actions are 'indefensible' (p. xv) and even that the actions of the
Israelis are comparable with those of the Nazis (the conquest of Ranle and Lod is
described as a *Blitzkrieg*).

[279] Radford Ruether and Ruether, *The Wrath of Jonah*, p. xvii.

[280] *Ibid.*, p. xv.

[281] *Ibid.*, p. xv.

and tell us how to read it', and for 'turning the Hebrew Bible into a stick with which to beat the Jews'.[282]

The acerbic metaphors of Biale's review – the Ruethers have plundered a Jewish book, or turned the Jewish canon into a stick with which to beat the Jews – are an apposite comment on the violence of Christian appropriation. For once the Old Testament text is annexed to, and taken over by the New, Christian ideology is imported and naturalised, and the text brims over with a surfeit of Christian vocabulary. 'As so often', writes Allen (without irony), 'the effect of this Old Testament book is to lay a foundation upon which the New Testament can build';[283] Rudolph maintains that this *christlichen* Old Testament book encapsulates the very *Quintessenz des Evangeliums* and is full of the concept of 'grace';[284] and Trudinger tells how Jonah resisted the call to be a 'light to the nations'[285] and envisages the dove that alights on Jesus at his baptism flying across the intertestamental abyss, to carry New Testament messages into the Old Testament text. Indeed, it seems that, while Jonah wasn't looking, everyone in this most thoroughly Christian of texts converted: proto-Christian sailors and proto-Christian Ninevites people a proto-Christian book, conceived as written by a proto-Christian author, to stress the universalism of a proto-Christian God. Jonah the Jew is isolated in his Judaism, his anachronism, and the other characters, in league with the authoritative trinity of critic, author, and deity (whose identities all blur into one another) effectively militate against him, and try to convert him or pitch him overboard. New Testament intertexts multiply almost as prodigiously as with the Fathers: the template for the book is Romans 3.29, Rudolph invokes John 3.16, and Wolff's comment that 'the God of Jonah, the Hebrew, is able to find among completely strange people the obedience and trust which his own messenger denied him'[286] reverberates with the gospel's praise of the gentile centurion: 'Never before have I found faith like this in Israel' (Matthew 8.10; Luke 7.9). Allen develops 'extensive parallels' with the parable of the Prodigal Son and the Good Samaritan: in his reading, the book becomes a strange Old

---

[282] D. Biale, 'The Philo-Semitic Face of Christian Anti-Semitism', *Tikkun* 4.3 (1989), pp. 99–102 (101).

[283] L. C. Allen, *Joel, Obadiah, Jonah and Micah*, p. 194.

[284] W. Rudolph, *Joel, Amos, Obadja, Jona* (Gütersloh: Gerd Mohn, 1971), p. 371.

[285] Trudinger, 'Jonah: A Post-Exilic Verbal Cartoon?', p. 143.

[286] Wolff, *Obadiah and Jonah*, p. 123.

Testament proto-parable in which the Ninevites (alias the gentiles) get to play all the best parts: the Samaritan exposing the hypocrisy of the religious community; the young son who exposes all the 'narrow pretensions and uncharitable grudges' of Jonah/the elder brother. (Meanwhile Jonah and the group he represents become the scowling, muttering Pharisees, for whom the book is a 'trap', designed to trick a narrow-minded proto-Pharisaic audience into 'damning themselves as latter-day Jonahs'.)[287]

As the book becomes a gigantic echo chamber, swelling with a cacophony of New Testament voices, so it reverberates, somewhat farcically, to the tune of Christian hymns. As Bewer argues that the lesson of the book is 'to teach the narrow, blind, prejudiced, fanatic Jews, of which Jonah is but the type' that

> the love of God is wider than the measures of man's mind,
> And the heart of the Eternal is most wonderfully kind,
> But we make his love too narrow by false limits of our own . . .

the organ strikes up, the congregation stands, in an attempt to soothe the 'hot Jewish hearts' with the tranquil truths of Christian hymnody.[288] As the book of Jonah becomes a quasi-hymn, for use in Christian services, so it becomes an appropriate tract for Christian missionary societies. Payne uses Jonah as an example of the 'Reluctant Messenger and Intercessor';[289] Trudinger sees the book as a call to the Jews to stop 'feathering their own nest' and become a 'missional nation';[290] while Rowley, addressing the Baptist Missionary Society during the last years of the Second World War, produces a squirming, wriggling pamphlet on Jonah and the 'Missionary Message of the Old Testament'. Rowley claims that 'Judaism's rejection of its mission should not blind us for one moment to its greatness' and that we, 'who are heirs of its good things' should have 'no stones to throw at it', because 'Our Lord had only tenderness and yearning for it even in the hour of his rejection.' Though it is true that 'It was not ready for the fulfilment of the dreams it had cherished, and it regarded with horror, as traitors to its faith, those who were ready', and that 'It had our Lord crucified; it scattered His followers, it harried them to the places whither they had gone; it hated with an intense hatred the greatest of its sons who went over

[287] L. C. Allen, *Joel, Obadiah, Jonah and Micah*, p. 180.
[288] Bewer, *Critical and Exegetical Commentary on Jonah*, p. 64.
[289] Payne, 'The Prophet Jonah: Reluctant Messenger and Intercessor'.
[290] Trudinger, 'Jonah: A Post-Exilic Verbal Cartoon?', p. 143.

to the Crucified, persecuted Him wheresoever he went, and finally brought calamity on Him', yet this huge catalogue of crimes, infinitely expanded, is 'balanced' by the meagre assertion that 'this was not because Judaism was evil through and through'. Judaism is redeemed by the 'pity' of Christianity, and by the character reference given by its high-achieving 'daughter': 'Christianity was a growth out of Judaism, not a revolt against it, and if Judaism had been essentially evil it would not have had so much to pass on to the daughter faith'.[291] With the image of the Portia-like daughter, visiting and pitying the Jewish parent as he/she sits dribbling in the Home for Moribund Religion, the rhetoric of supersession writes itself garishly, and the 'growth' that comes from the body of Judaism begins to look increasingly like a cancer.

There is something highly provocative about the idea of Jonah as a proto-missionary text, that in turn preaches to and evangelises some of its retrogressive fellow-texts, that suggests associated metaphors about the colonisation (which is more than simply the Christianisation) of the Old Testament.[292] For while I have no objections to the reading of Jonah in the context of Christian theology – at least in works that consciously foreground themselves as such – there is something profoundly disturbing about a habitual and relentless assumption of a Eurocentric, Christian, critical standard, by which the primitive Hebrew text and the primitive Hebrew are judged. The Bible, of course, has always been intimately bound up with colonial power and missionising, and has functioned as a cipher of the values of the paternal guardian culture.[293] But (though

---

[291] All quotations are taken from Rowley, *The Missionary Message of the Old Testament*, p. 79.

[292] For a more detailed development of the metaphorical 'colonisation' of the Old Testament, see Y. M. Sherwood, '"Colonising the Old Testament" or "Representing Christian Interests Abroad"', in S. E. Porter and B. W. R. Pearson (eds.), *Christian–Jewish Relations Through the Centuries* (Sheffield: Sheffield Academic Press, 2000).

[293] At the same time as Pusey was writing his Darwinian dissection of the fish, Thomas Jones Barker was painting 'Queen Victoria Presenting a Bible in the Audience Chamber at Windsor' (1861): a picture of Victoria presenting the English Bible to a genuflecting African king and subtitled 'The Secret of England's Greatness', which now features in or on the cover of numerous colonialism and postcolonialism readers (see for example M. Ferro, *Colonization: A Global History* (London and New York: Routledge, 1997)). Everyone is familiar with the *general* position of the Bible in relation to colonialism: it is in the English Queen's hands and is being given to the African king; it is in the hands of the colonisers who come with a Bible in one hand and the conqueror's sword in the other; it is the emblem of the English Book, and the English language, 'an insignia of colonial desire and discipline' that displaces indigenous language, religion, and custom with the Christian ideolect of the West (H. K. Bhabha, 'Signs Taken for Wonders; Questions of Ambivalence and Authority under a Tree outside Delhi, May 1817', in *The Location of Culture* (London

the metaphor is bound to give way as soon as too much pressure is applied) I think it is vital to re-manoeuvre the alliance between Bible and imperialism, to look at imperialism *within* the canon, or what could be called the phenomenon of inner-biblical, or inter-testamental, colonisation. Such a move has already been suggested by Timothy Beal when he argues that 'supersession . . . plays out rather like colonialism: Jews have not managed their own scriptural territory rightly, and it is therefore the right of Christianity to take it over, renaming it "Old Testament"'.[294] Similarly, Harold Eilberg-Schwarz has provocatively described the Jew as the 'savage other'

and New York: Routledge, 1994), pp. 102–22). Though the general story is familiar, a more detailed story needs to be told, and this seems to be one of the crucial roles of Biblical Studies as it enters the twenty-first century. For not only has the Bible functioned wholesale as a legitimator and ally of imperialism, but it also offers all kinds of examples of violent displacements of the Other, of which colonising powers were only too ready to take hold. The Old Testament/Hebrew Bible supplies the ultimate ur-narrative of the gift of the land of nation A, by God, to nation B (in the narratives of Joshua and the Conquest); it offers models of the monstrous and faceless Other (the Canaanites are like 'giants' and are to be exterminated wholesale, lest they contaminate the Israelites); and it offers one of the earliest examples of the myth of the empty land (when God first gives the land to Abraham in Genesis 12, he says nothing of the minor detail that it has Canaanites in it – this particular revelation does not come until Genesis 15). A colonial history of the Bible would trace the way in which biblical texts echo colonising discourses back to the colonisers (the way in which the myth of the empty land, for example, rattles around in the ideas of an empty America (as opposed to a populated Europe) and with Hitler's invocation of *Lebensraum* in the East); it would expose the Bible to the same kind of ideological critique that has been inflicted on other cultural authorities, and would take in issues such as the influence of Bible translation on indigenous language and culture. There are also more subtle stories of the biblical history of colonialism that can be told, as hints and asides in Mainstream colonial/postcolonial studies suggest. Said, for example, suggests a clear relationship between the Bible and Orientalism (the mentally colonising abstraction of the East) when he observes that 'one of the important impulses toward the study of the Orient in the eighteenth century was the revolution in Biblical studies stimulated by such variously interesting pioneers as Bishop Lowth, Eichhorn, Herder and Michaelis' (some of whom have cropped up in this study) and that, since the first Orientalists were by and large biblical scholars, the Eastern lands associated with the Bible were the first to be 'academically conquered' (Said, *Orientalism*, pp. 17, 51). For some preliminary forays into the field of the colonial history of the Bible see: M. Prior, *The Bible and Colonialism: A Moral Critique* (Sheffield: Sheffield Academic Press, 1997); R. S. Sugirtharajah (ed.), *The Postcolonial Bible* (Sheffield: Sheffield Academic Press, 1998); and D. Gunn, 'Colonialism and the Vagaries of Scripture: Te Kooti in Canaan (A Story of Bible and Dispossession in Aotearoa/New Zealand)', in T. Linafelt and T. K. Beal (eds.), *God in the Fray: A Tribute to Walter Brueggemann* (Minneapolis: Fortress, 1998), pp. 127–42. For a discussion of the ideology of Bible translation, including missionary translations, see R. P. Carroll, 'Cultural Encroachment and Bible Translation; Observations on Elements of Violence, Race and Class in the Production of Bibles in Translation', *Semeia* 76 (1996), pp. 39–53, and 'He-Bibles and She-Bibles: Reflections on the Violence done to Texts by Productions of English Translations of the Bible', *Biblical Interpretation* 4.3 (1996), pp. 257–69.

[294] T. K. Beal, *The Book of Hiding: Gender, Ethnicity, Annihilation and Esther* (Biblical Limits; London and New York: Routledge, 1997), p. 5.

within European civilisation,[295] while Jonathan Boyarin has gone further, explicitly equating the violent Othering of the Jew to the violence of colonisation.[296] Though the nexus of ideas associated with 'the Jew' cannot be conflated with those associated with 'the Negro' or 'the Oriental', (for the European consciousness projects multitudinous others, to act as different foils for different projections of 'Self') all operate as vast repositories of typifying adjectives, scrutinised from the outside by the condescending imperial eye. The Jew, as we have seen, is jealous, vicious, and carnal; the Oriental is irrational, depraved, and childlike; and both are depicted as 'something one represents, something one judges (as in a court of law), something one studies or depicts (as in a curriculum), and something one disciplines (as in a school or prison)'.[297] In his laziness and his clownishness, Jonah in fact shows remarkable affinities to the Others of colonial discourse. For the native Other is typically comic in his attempts to ape civilised culture (one British educationalist compared the native learning English literature to a shamefaced 'clown' walking with 'hobnailed shoes through a lady's boudoir'[298] – a description that is strongly reminiscent of a shamed and comic Jonah, bunglingly trying to assimilate the higher points of Christian truth), and is also typically 'lazy',[299] unable to muster the energy to

---

[295] H. Eilberg-Schwartz, *The Savage in Judaism: An Anthropology of Israelite Religion and Ancient Judaism* (Bloomington: Indiana University Press, 1990).

[296] J. Boyarin, 'The Other Within and the Other Without'. Boyarin notes how Mainstream studies in colonialism and postcolonialism displace the Jew by equating the imperialist vision with a 'white Christian Europe', and yet neglecting the situation of those inside Europe who are not Christian. This tends to reinforce the othering of the Jew in European culture, whereby the Jew is seen as outside 'universal European history'. The paradoxical assumptions of postcolonial critics such as Edward Said and Gayatri Chakravorti Spivak are (a) that Jews are no longer a Diaspora people because they now have a homeland, and (b) that Jews can't be in a postcolonial situation because they are participating in a belated colonial venture (for a rare study of the Bible and colonialism, that concentrates all the force of the critique on the state of Israel, see Prior, *The Bible and Colonialism*). And yet the othering of the Jew within Europe is intimately related to the invention of Others outside Europe. As Said himself notes, 'hostility to Islam in the modern Christian West has . . . been nourished at the same stream as anti-Semitism', and therefore 'a critique of the orthodoxies, dogmas, and disciplinary procedures of Orientalism contribute to an enlargement of our understanding of the cultural mechanisms of anti-Semitism' – and vice versa (E. Said, 'Orientalism Reconsidered', *Cultural Critique* 1, pp. 89–107 (99)).

[297] Said, *Orientalism*, p. 40.

[298] The quotation is from one H. G. Robinson and is cited by C. Baldick, *The Social Mission of English Criticism* (Oxford: Clarendon Press, 1983), p. 66. The full quotation reads: 'As a clown will instinctively tread lightly and feel ashamed of his hob-nailed boots in a lady's boudoir, so a vulgar mind may, by converse with minds of high culture, be brought to see and deplore the contrast between itself and them.'

[299] Numerous examples are catalogued by Syed Hussein Alatas, *The Myth of the Lazy Native: A*

manage and distribute his vast God-given natural resources.[300]
Jonah's 'laziness' is a strange deduction from the biblical text, but
does link him with those other Others who have lacked the inclination or the capacity to distribute their vast natural wealth to the
rest of civilisation, and who are guilty of an intolerable (if unwitting)
selfishness. By an unconscious but telling logic, Jonah joins those
who have kept their resources to themselves, and so legitimated –
indeed cried out for – the intervention of a masterful, benign
colonial presence.

Now the violent appropriation of textual space is not the same as
the violent appropriation of geographical space, but the borders
between territorial and intellectual property are, as Edward Said has
shown, provocatively malleable and supple. And if fields of knowledge, or texts, like areas of land, can be 'academically conquered',
and colonial expansion involves 'epistemic violence',[301] then it is not
entirely inappropriate to construct a metanarrative about the New
Testament and Western Rationalism as Metropolis or imperial
centre, and the annexed, peripheral territories known as the 'Old
Testament'. A (potted) narrative of the book of Jonah's colonial
history would perhaps run as follows. Since the eighteenth century,
European Christian critics have been moving into and appropriating
the textual territory, speaking, with all the confident hubris of
Balfour on Egypt, of 'our author',[302] or *unser Buch*.[303] As the British/
German flag has been hoisted over the text, the text's indigenous
language and purpose (whatever that may mean) have been displaced by, or at the very least merged with, a new standard language
made up of New Testament vocabulary (grace, faith, conversion, the

Study of the Image of the Malays, Filipinos and Javanese from the Sixteenth to the Twentieth Century and Its Function in the Ideology of Colonial Capitalism (London: Frank Cass, 1977).

[300] According to colonial logic, by a perverse twist of fate, there appears to have been an error regarding the divine distribution of national resources. Albert Sarraut, Governor General of French Indochina from 1911 to 1914 and 1917 to 1919, later Minister of Colonies, comments on how Nature's 'double abundance' of intellectual and material resources have come adrift from one another: 'While in a narrow corner of the world nature has concentrated in white Europe the powers of invention, the means of progress, and the dynamic of scientific advancement, the greatest accumulation of natural wealth is locked up in territories occupied by backward races who, not knowing how to profit by it themselves, are even less capable of releasing it to the great circular current that nourishes the ever-growing needs of humanity' (A. Sarraut, *Grandeur et Servitude Coloniales* (Paris: Saggitaire, 1931), p. 109).

[301] Said, *Orientalism*, p. 51.

[302] Wolff, *Obadiah and Jonah*, p. 175.

[303] Friedrichsen, *Kritische Übersicht*, p. 39.

prodigal son, the Good Samaritan, Romans 3.29), and of the assured dichotomies of Western rationalism. In an imperial masterstroke, the annexed territory has been taught to echo back to the colonisers their own right to govern, speaking in its own voice the rightful mastery of Christianity over Judaism and condemning the kind of nationalism and hubris that would result in any claims to autonomy and home-rule.[304] The book has, as it were, internalised the image of the colonisers in the venerated figure of the Governor-Author, a symbol to recalcitrant primitive forces (i.e. figures like Jonah) of all that it means to be properly civilised and human. The Author, with his 'superior talents and unselfish conduct', stands at the heart of a primitive culture, hoping, through the example of his 'Code of Christian Morality' to win over the recalcitrant native population (here the blood-loving Ezra-Nehemites).[305] Over time, this figure of the Author (as projection of the Coloniser) has come to control the text and its potentially uncontrollable meanings, acting as what Foucault would term 'the principal of thrift in the proliferation of meaning'.[306] The centre has been consolidated, ex-centric meanings curtailed. The book has been packaged in what Edward Said calls that peculiar mixture of 'imperial vagueness and precise detail'.[307]

The colonial history of the book of Jonah is, of course, only part of a much wider narrative in which (under the influence of anti-Semitism and a huge neo-Marcionite hangover in biblical scholarship) the Old Testament becomes the 'dark continent' of the New, requiring missionising, amelioration, and containment by a higher, humanising power. And if colonialism, as Linda Hutcheon shows, classically results in a 'doubleness' in which the colonised becomes

---

[304] Compare the assertions of Lord Cromer Evelyn Baring (also known as 'Over-baring'), British governor over Egypt from 1882 to 1907. Baring rejected Egyptian demands for a self-sustaining national sovereignty on the grounds that 'the real future of Egypt lies not in the direction of a narrow nationalism which will only embrace native Egyptians . . . but rather in that of an enlarged cosmopolitanism' (cited in Said, *Orientalism*, p. 37). The kind of cosmopolitanism that Baring so reasonably argues for in fact justifies and legitimates a British stake in Egypt. Similarly the argument for universalism in the Old Testament justifies and legitimates a Christian stake therein.

[305] Compare Lord Cromer (again). The governing imperial forces, by operating a 'Code of Christian morality', aim to achieve allegiance 'grounded on the respect always afforded to superior talents and unselfish conduct' (Said, *Orientalism*, p. 37).

[306] M. Foucault, 'What is an Author?', in P. Rabinow (ed.), *The Foucault Reader* (Harmondsworth: Penguin, 1984), pp. 101–20 (118).

[307] Said, *Orientalism*, p. 50. Said describes Orientalism as vague and detailed, 'ignorant and complex' (*Orientalism*, p. 55). The same charges of gigantic skewed statements endlessly detailed would also suit the endlessly refined stereotypes of Jonah criticism, as well as other biased and detailed packagings of biblical texts.

both the *imitation* and the *antithesis* of, the coloniser,[308] this paradox is clearly inscribed across the map of Old Testament territories. Some elements of the colonised, such as Ruth, Jonah, Deutero-Isaiah, become mirrors of the colonial power reflecting, albeit in a glass darkly, the coloniser's face. But as these texts internalise imperial values, take up the cultural cringe,[309] other texts – Ezra-Nehemiah, Esther, Ezekiel, 'and the like' – are cast as the dark, uncivilisable antithesis, repelled to the primitive periphery. To return to the (irresistible) missionary metaphor, while some texts convert and learn to sing Christian hymns, albeit with the trace of a foreign accent, others remain stubbornly heathen, primitive (not 'Moham-medan' or 'Hindoostanee' in this case, of course, but Jewish). Beal fascinatingly shows how the book of Esther has habitually been sidelined in the canon as savagely 'Judaising', as the antithesis of the 'high and pure truths' (of Empire), an exotic country peopled by 'sensual despots', shallow beauty queens, and an author who 'gloats over the wealth and triumph of his heroes'.[310] The space between the noble book of Jonah (with its exemplary proto-Christian, proto-Western author) and the primitive book of Esther (with its base, sensuous and immoral author) maps the two extremes of the model-antithesis paradox: most books fall somewhere in-between and shift their identities in relation to the shifting self-identities of the Christian, rationalist centre.

If, as Gaston Bachélard has suggested, there is such a thing as a 'poetics of space',[311] an imaginative geography that we associate with various spheres of foreignness and pastness, then the 'Old Testament' is, among other things, a space devoted to colonising and missionary activity, where Jonah, Ruth, and other *Translations of the Gospel into the Hebrew Tongue* are handed out to a cringing, Caliban-

---

[308] Linda Hutcheon observes how 'Doubleness and difference are established by colonialism in its paradoxical move to enforce cultural sameness while, at the same time, producing differentiations and discriminations', and speaks of the 'doubleness of the colonized in relation to the colonizer, either as model or antithesis' (L. Hutcheon, 'Circling the Downspout of Empire', in B. Ashcroft, G. Griffiths, and H. Tiffin (eds.), *The Post-Colonial Studies Reader* (London: Routledge, 1995), pp. 130–5 (134)).

[309] For the way in which cultural domination produces 'cultural subservience', or what Arthur Phillips calls the 'cultural cringe', see B. Ashcroft, G. Griffiths, and H. Tiffin, *The Empire Writes Back: Theory and Practice in Post-Colonial Literatures* (London: Routledge, 1989), pp. 11–13; A. Phillips, 'The Cultural Cringe', in *The Australian Tradition: Studies in a Colonial Culture* (Melbourne: Cheshire, 1958).

[310] Beal, *The Book of Hiding*, pp. 7–8 (discussing L. B. Paton, *The Book of Esther* (International Critical Commentary; New York: Charles Scribner's Sons, 1908)).

[311] G. Bachélard, *The Poetics of Space* (trans. M. Jolas; New York: Orion Press, 1964).

like Esther and Ezra-Nehemiah. And for the moment I'm going to let the connection between missionary activity, colonialism, and the unenviable position of Jewish Jonah, isolated in his proto-Christian text, rest in the realm of analogy: a protected, imaginative, non-committal zone, where I do not have to cite dates and certifiable historical influences, although I have suspicions that such connections could be made, and can see them beginning to emerge. The beginning of colonialism 'proper', that is colonialism attached to monopoly capitalism, is dated from the late eighteenth century, and, as critics such as Sugirtharajah and Segovia have recently stressed, this new wave of imperialism originates in Protestant countries, is tied up with Protestant missionary activity, and coincides with the publication of William Carey's *Enquiry into the Obligation of Christians to Use Means for the Propagation of the Gospel among the Heathens* (1792) and the foundation of the Baptist Missionary Society.[312] In this context Jonah, with its command to 'Go and Preach in Nineveh' becomes a reactivated text, an Old Testament equivalent of Matthew's 'Go ye and preach' or the Acts appeal 'Come over and help us' (indeed, centuries later, Rowley could still instinctively use it as such in an address to the Baptist Missionary Society). And, strangely and tellingly, it is not the Ninevites who epitomise the savage needy Other, as one might expect, but the Jew. The Jew, it seems, is the proto-Savage, the archetypal Other, and readings of Jonah as a missionary text instinctively home in on Jonah, as at once the epitome of the recalcitrant convert and the convert that Christianity most desires.

Polonius-like, I have already cracked the wind of my poor colonial metaphor quite enough (for now) but need to call on it just once more before I let it collapse, exhausted, in a corner. For if the occupation of Jonah by (I would argue) alien words and themes is

---

[312] See R. S. Sugirtharajah, 'A Postcolonial Exploration of Collusion and Construction in Biblical Interpretation', in Sugirtharajah, *The Postcolonial Bible*, pp. 91–116, and F. F. Segovia, 'Biblical Criticism and Postcolonial Studies: Toward a Postcolonial Optic', in *The Postcolonial Bible*, pp. 49–65. Following other postcolonial critics Segovia divides the imperialism (and missionary activities) of the West into three distinct epochs: (i) the initial mercantile phase of European imperialism, accompanied by missions that are primarily Catholic in orientation and including the massive evangelisation of the Americas (1492–1792); (ii) high imperialism, tied to monopoly capitalism and European nation-states, accompanied by largely Protestant missionary activity in Africa, Asia and the remaining areas of the Americas (1792 to mid-twentieth century); and (iii) late imperialism, embracing both the end of formal colonialism and the continued impact of imperial culture in the world (mid-twentieth century to the present day).

tied in with a rationalist, Christian colonisation of the Old Testament, any critic who tries to write the book differently is caught up in the same theoretical complexities as the postcolonial writer.[313] Of course, I am arguing that readings that stigmatise the figure of the Jew and prioritise the civilisation and discipline of the primitive have over-lived in the critical tradition and are now well past their read-by date. Yet (before my metaphor calcifies into an absurdly rigid kind of counter-polemic) I need to make it clear that I am not simply arguing that imperial critical forces should pull out of the 'Old Testament', rename it the Hebrew Bible or Tanakh and so restore a genuinely Jewish book to its own people. Regarding the people of the Old Testament/Hebrew Bible as 'Jews', and failing to appreciate the differences between the Old Testament and post-biblical Judaism creates a minefield of ideological problems; moreover the history of Christian and Mainstream interpretation is part of the very fabric and actualisation of the book of Jonah, and the text is literally unthinkable without it. And no more than a territory or a people can be wiped clean of its colonialist history, the luxury of textual essentialism is no longer something that I can sink back into. I cannot claim (much as I would like to, because in certain quarters it might increase the impact of my reading quite considerably) that I am somehow stripping away a false reading to let the text speak in its own native, guttural, Hebrew accents – and indeed other attempts to do this have failed because the interpretative myths that cling to this text are too persuasive, too perennial, too strong.[314] But what I can do is to create another Author (who will be just as much a readerly construct) to replace 'Our Author' and to pluralise the voices competing for ownership of this text. If it is the critic's responsibility, as Alan Sinfield puts it, to 'help confirm or challenge the stories through which we tell ourselves who we are, to set the boundaries of the thinkable',[315] then I am more than keen to have a

---

[313] The prefix 'post', in the term 'postcolonial' is at least as fraught as the 'post' of 'postmodernism'. For a discussion of the complexities see, for example, A. Loomba, *Colonialism/Postcolonialism* (London and New York: Routledge, 1998), pp. 7–19.

[314] G. H. Cohn, for example, cogently argues that the Christian interpretation of the text is wholly without foundation in terms of both style and content. Yet, although his book was widely reviewed in Christian journals, none of them mentioned this rather key point, and the interpretative reflex remained unchanged (G. H. Cohn, *Das Buch Jona im Lichte der biblischen Erzählkunst* (Studia Semitica Neerlandica, 12; Assen: Van Gorcum, 1969), p. 99, n. 4).

[315] A. Sinfield, *Faultlines: Cultural Materialism and the Politics of Dissident Reading* (Oxford: Clarendon Press, 1992), p. 172.

go at the stories of a dissident Jonah who has his ego bashed out of him, and (particularly) the throwing overboard of Jonah the anachronistic Jew. But even as I read against the grain, enlisting alternative traditions, I know that there is no virgin territory, and that the space in which I read is set by my feelings about (in this case my absolute reaction against) these antiquated, venerated, canonised meanings.

So I am left holding a heavily encrusted, rusted, text, covered in barnacles and ideas that hold on, like limpets, coated by the 'language [that is] deposited on things by time'.[316] And while I can see that these layered language deposits testify to the reanimation of the text – in past times and other contexts – they seem merely to reinforce its alienation from my own. After Orwell and Foucault, the over-disciplined book of Jonah looks like an annex to a divine police state; after the Holocaust the anti-Semitic reflex is unbearable. And Victorian schoolrooms and skewed essay questions may be all very well, but how is one to read, and teach this text, at the turn of the millennium, in *Higher* Education?

[316] Foucault, *The Order of Things*, p. 130.

CHAPTER 2

Backwaters and underbellies

This book first arose out of a passage in Borges, out of the laughter that shattered, as I read the passage, all the familiar landmarks of my thought – our thought, the thought that bears the stamp of our age and our geography – breaking all the ordered surfaces and all the planes with which we are accustomed to tame the wild profusion of existing things, and continuing long afterwards to disturb and threaten with collapse the age-old distinction between the Same and the Other. This passage quotes a 'certain Chinese encyclopaedia' in which it is written that 'animals are divided into (a) belonging to the Emperor, (b) embalmed, (c) tame, (d) sucking pigs, (e) sirens, (f) fabulous, (g) stray dogs, (h) included in the present classification, (i) frenzied, (j) innumerable, (k) drawn with a fine camelhair brush, (l) et cetera, (m) having just broken the water pitcher, (n) that from a long way off look like flies'. In the wonderment of this taxonomy, the thing we apprehend in one great leap, the thing that, by means of the fable, is demonstrated as the exotic charm of another system of thought, is the limitation of our own, the stark impossibility of thinking *that*. (Michel Foucault, *The Order of Things*)[1]

It is no doubt a credit to the ingenuity of scholars that they have managed to squeeze something like a conventional prophetic lesson out of this most misfit and out-of-proportion 'prophetic' text. By a curious alchemy, the 'monstrous' has been converted into meaningful monsters – the Jew and the dangerous populace – and the fish has been demoted to a mere plot-transporter or red-herring. Under the pressure of a rather disembowelled rationalism, the *qiqayon*, the fish, and the city of Nineveh have been pruned, slimmed, and grafted onto a respectable scientific lexis of *ricinus communis*, the *cani*

[1] M. Foucault, *The Order of Things: An Archaeology of the Human Sciences* (New York: Vintage, 1994), p. xv.

cacharis, Ancient Near Eastern records, and mathematics. And the bodily/fleshy temptation of the text, the temptation to speculate on what kilos of blubbery flesh would have looked or felt like, has been repressed in favour of a meaningful fleshiness: Jewish carnality as opposed to Christian spirituality.

And so Jonah has become a textbook example of what Foucault terms a 'squared and spatialised knowledge': the desire to measure, define, tabulate, and contain. In other words, this shape-shifting little book, that has already become an exemplar of so many things, now obligingly proffers itself as an example of how:

Western knowledge . . . organises the universe into disciplines, each with its own teratology which refuses the eccentric, the abnormal and the monstrous in favour of those propositions that inscribe themselves within the theoretical horizons organised by the discipline.[2]

The lines that place the city of Nineveh within the circumference of the reasonable, and that connect the *qiqayon* and the big fish to tangible points in the 'real' world, are, as it were, extreme, cartoonish pointers to the disciplinary teratology that maps the field of biblical studies. Squeezed, squashed and rationalised and converted into a thesis, the book demonstrates how texts are forced into the contours of the *episteme*, the 'historical a priori' that 'in a given period, delimits the totality of experience in a field of knowledge, defines the modes of being of the objects that appear in that field, provides man's [*sic*] everyday perception with theoretical powers, and *defines the conditions in which he can sustain a discourse about things that is recognized to be true*'.[3] The logic of the *episteme* seems to have insisted that the book of Jonah be perceived as a *monologic* text in which a 'compact and unambiguous' central voice chomps all rival perspectives and in which 'every struggle of two voices for possession and dominance of the text . . . is decided in advance'[4] (when Jonah and God, Jew and gentile, particularism and universalism slog it out, the

---

[2] D. Spurr, summarising Foucault, in *The Rhetoric of Empire: Colonial Discourse in Journalism, Travel Writing and Imperial Administration* (Durham and London: Duke University Press, 1993), pp. 62–3.

[3] Foucault, *The Order of Things*, p. xxii (my italics).

[4] M. Bakhtin, *Problems of Dostoevsky's Poetics* (ed. and trans. C. Emerson, introduction by W. C. Booth; Minneapolis: University of Minnesota Press, 1984), p. 168. As Bakhtin writes, in the monologic text 'Every struggle of two voices for possession of and dominance in the word in which they appear is decided in advance – it is a sham struggle; all fully significant authorial interpretations are sooner or later gathered together in a single verbal centre and in a single consciousness, and all accents are gathered in a single voice.'

dialogue is only a rigged fight, a 'sham struggle', and the outcome is always a foregone conclusion). It has also insisted that the text be perceived as *realist*, coherent, governed by 'the principle of non-contradiction', stressing the '*compatible* nature of circumstances', and 'attaching narrated events together with a kind of logical paste'.[5] In the Mainstream there has been no place for the *fantastic*: a genre that 'plays the game of the impossible', that overtly violates 'what is generally accepted as a possibility', and that, by definition, disturbs and dislocates comfortably known worlds.[6] The intolerance for triffid-like plants and monstrous fish is but the most obvious symptom of a distaste for alterity or disruption, and the desire for a text that is smooth, easily digested, and purged of all that is potentially monstrous or abnormal. The Mainstream readings conform to a model of absolute solidarity – both the solidarity of the text with itself and the solidarity of the text with its readers; the official version of the book of Jonah reflects back to the reader an already pre-conceived notion of 'reality', and, in its order, simplicity, and predictability of form as well as content, it offers security and the 'power to console'.[7] The centralising slogans demonstrate the centripetal impulse of interpretation, the fact that, as Frank Kermode muses, 'We are all fulfilment men, [*sic*] *pleromatists*; we all seek the centre that will allow the senses to rest, at any rate for one interpreter, at any rate for one moment.'[8]

But scholars can also be found peering around the edges of paradigms, bumping up against the black-line boundaries of tables, to suggest that this book resists conventional strategies of containment, and that academic idioms run off it, like water off its (wax-proofed) back. Take Julius Bewer and Leslie Allen, for example – two scholars who featured prominently in the Mainstream. Even as

[5] R. Barthes, *S/Z* (trans. R. Miller; London: Blackwell, 1990; 1st edn 1973), p. 156.

[6] W. R. Irwin, *The Game of the Impossible: A Rhetoric of Fantasy* (Illinois, 1976), p. ix.

[7] Compare Wayne Booth's and Frank Kermode's comments on the 'kind of security' offered by the realist novel, and the 'power of form to console' (W. Booth, *The Rhetoric of Fiction* (Chicago: Chicago University Press, 1983), p. 352, and F. Kermode, *The Sense of an Ending: Studies in the Theory of Fiction* (Oxford: Oxford University Press, 1967), p. 151). Obviously the structures of expectation that we are discussing here extend far beyond the field of biblical studies: for example, literary studies have also long-prioritised values of unity, coherence, and realism, and demoted disjunction, incoherence, and the fantastic. For discussion of the disciplinary teratologies that have mapped English Literature, see L. Armitt, *Theorising the Fantastic* (London: Arnold, 1996), pp. 1–4, and especially A. Gibson, *Reading Narrative Discourse: Studies in the Novel from Cervantes to Beckett* (London: Macmillan, 1990), pp. 1–25.

[8] F. Kermode, *The Genesis of Secrecy: On the Interpretation of Narrative* (Cambridge, Mass.: Harvard University Press, 1980), p. 72.

they are busy doing emphatically Mainstream things, like converting the narrative into diatribe against the narrow-minded Jew, and lopping off the fantastic as surplus, they can be caught looking longingly at the colourful and strange-shaped offcuts that lie around their feet. Glancing wistfully at aspects of the book that it is beyond his remit to consider, Allen speaks of the 'accumulation of hair-raising and eye-popping phenomena': the 'violent sea-storm, the submarine-like fish in which Jonah survives and composes a song, the mass conversion of Nineveh, the magic plant'.[9] Bewer similarly indulges in the luxuriant excess of the fantastic – the 'exaggerated' size of Nineveh, the 'extraordinary speed of growth of the plant', and 'the psalm of thanksgiving in the fish's belly', all of which 'exceed the limit of credibility'.[10] What Allen and Bewer are free to acknowledge in their prefaces and asides, if not in their main text, is that reading Jonah is like drinking one of Alice's *Drink Me* potions: 'We are in Wonderland', exclaims Bewer, 'Where everything is so passing strange.'[11] Yes, but as both commentators know, it is not the critic's job to get punch-drunk on *Drink Me* potions, but rather to apply rationalising conversion mechanisms to (perhaps) precisely those elements that probably attracted them to this text (as opposed to, say, Obadiah or Deuteronomy) in the first place. To revel in the big fish, the big city, the big plant, would mean forfeiting the emphatically adult critical persona for a persona as wide-eyed as a child, or as Gulliver in Brobdingnag. If eyes pop, they must pop modestly, self-mockingly, or the critic runs the risk of creating a cartoonish version of the text – and himself.

This chapter is devoted to readings that do not flow as tributaries into the Mainstream: it is about the ex-centric, the marginalised, the ones that got away. It pursues Jonah with God-like obsession in his less conventional journeys through two fields that are generally considered peripheral to biblical scholarship – the Backwaters of Jewish Studies, and the underbellies of Cultural Studies – and so tours precisely the areas that the Mainstream has deemed surrogately and meaningfully monstrous: 'the Jewish' and 'the popular'. The collections are no respecter of persons: gathered with the

---

[9] L. C. Allen, *Joel, Obadiah, Jonah and Micah* (London: Hodder and Stoughton, 1976), p. 194.

[10] J. A. Bewer, *Critical and Exegetical Commentary on Jonah* (International Critical Commentary; Edinburgh: T. & T. Clark, 1912), p. 3.

[11] Bewer, *Jonah*, p. 4.

democratising impulse that has now become the trademark of Cultural Studies, they chase Jonah through the sacred and the secular as he surfaces in etchings and cartoons, scuttles through the Talmud and *Moby Dick*, washes up on the salt-stained pages of *The Ocean Almanac* and puts in a special guest appearance on TV. And they watch as both groups of 'texts' become irritants in the belly of the Mainstream, by refusing to act as subordinates to the official scholarly perception of the text (enriching it, feeding it fat on colourful anecdotes), and thinking the book of Jonah in ways that the Mainstream cannot and must not stomach.[12] Once again Jonah becomes a forum for larger disciplinary questions as this chapter questions the conventional partitioning of knowledge, the dam that keeps Christian readings in the Mainstream but leaves the Jewish sloshing up against the popular in the periphery.[13] As this book situates itself as part of an expansionist move to introduce the cultural afterlife of biblical texts into that sphere of enquiry known as Biblical Studies,[14] so it also argues, even more importantly, for Jewish Studies to become part of Biblical Studies, as Christian

[12] This is not the first time that Jonah readings of Jonah have been included in commentary: James Limburg, for example, looks at Jonah in Judaism in his appendices, alongside sections on Jonah in the apocryphal/deuterocanonical books, in literature of the first centuries CE, in Islam and in Reformation theology (see J. Limburg, *Jonah: A Commentary* (Old Testament Library; London: SCM, 1993), pp. 99–123). But although he is at pains to excise the anti-Semitic slant from Luther, Limburg does not yet allow the Jewish readings to make inroads into the traditional Christian frameworks through which the book is read. He provides a valuable service by making the reader aware of what goes on 'in Israel's classrooms', and yet the content of that teaching ultimately remains in those classrooms, hermetically sealed off at the back of the book.

[13] The distribution of knowledge about Jonah between Mainstream and Backwater is indicative of a general situation in which 'Christian Studies' is not named, but subsumed under New Testament *and* Old Testament Studies, and where to study the Bible without studying Christian theology is regarded by many as strange in the extreme, but where Jewish Studies is regarded as a separate specialist area (an extra string to one's academic bow?). The division of knowledge, which I attempted to explain on ideological grounds in chapter 1, has also been reinforced by related historical developments: since Theology departments were originally Christian and Protestant, Judaism has, like other religions, been regarded as something of an external add-on, as those departments have evolved into departments of Theology *and Religion*. The way in which the sheer familiarity of Christian exegesis has overtaken 'Old Testament' texts means that, though the field is now arguably more open, Jewish scholars tend to prefer to stay down the other end of the corridor in Religion departments in a nook marked 'Jewish Studies'. For a powerful expression of the alienation that many Jewish scholars feel when confronted with the professional study of the Bible, see J. D. Levenson, *The Hebrew Bible: The Old Testament Historical Criticism* (Louisville: Westminster/John Knox, 1993).

[14] For recent work in this area, see the list in the introduction, p. 3, n. 3. The diversity of that list is a fitting snapshot of the way in which this fledgling site of study is beginning to stretch its wings, try its limits, and experiment with what it may begin to do in the future.

Studies[15] always (implicitly) has been. It pushes for a clear re-distribution of disciplinary lines, in which Jewish and Christian interpretation both feature equally in the study of the texts' afterlife, and in which neither is anachronistically conflated with their origin. Jonah is not the only book that would be destabilised if Jewish biblical interpretation were brought into the equation, for centuries of primarily Christian exegesis of the 'Old Testament' have, inevitably, led to a conflation of the Christian understandings of a text with the legitimate 'historical' meaning, as if Old Testament texts were always somehow purposely engaged in the process of becoming Christian.

Entering the Backwaters is like browsing around a collection of curios, gathered from places foreign to the biblical critic, where critics tend to venture only when armed with hard hat and field glasses. The eclectic collection reminds me of the Pitt Rivers Museum of Ethnography in Oxford – a dimly lit showcase of exoticism, a museum of museums, crammed with weird and wonderful exhibits such as a 'sistrum called Junka', 'coolie cigarettes', a 'mask of Saaga, the Devil Doctor, the eyelids worked by a string', organised in cabinets labelled simply 'pipes', or 'snuff-boxes', or 'canoes'.[16] The exhibits in this chapter are not *intrinsically* stranger than nineteenth-century Jewish caricatures cloning themselves with Warhol-like regularity across a biblical text, but they *seem* stranger because they operate outside the limits and proportion of the Mainstream. They make Jonah precisely what the Mainstream decrees it cannot be: quirky, angular, anomalous, humorous, peculiar, and disproportioned. And, appropriately enough, since this is the 'main

---

15 The fact that no one calls it 'Christian Studies' shows to what extent Christian Studies are normalised and their presence taken as pervasive and assumed. An analogous situation is the way in which students take courses on Women and Religion, whereas courses on Men and Religion would sound rather ridiculous: the Jew, like the Woman is the Other, who needs, by definition, to be named.

16 The Pitt Rivers Museum is based on the collection of the Victorian anthropologist Pitt Rivers (1827–1900); the list of exhibits is taken from James Fenton's poem 'The Pitt Rivers'. In the spirit of the Great Exhibition of 1851 it is arranged to demonstrate the principle of inexorable and perfectly predictable progress. The organisation of the museum into generic cabinets – which looks, at first sight, as clumsy as my own ham-fisted organisation of material into the 'Jewish' and the 'Popular' – is designed to demonstrate the evolution of 'pipes' or 'firearms', from native artefact to Victorian showpiece. The poet James Fenton appropriately describes the museum as a hot-house of 'foreign logic' (as enticing as a trip abroad) and the 'land where myths/Go when they die' (thus evoking the sense in which myth is sucked up by, and becomes a foil for, rationalism).

course' of the book, the artefacts here seem to be inordinately concerned with meat (or flesh) and fish. Not only do they create their own genre of inner-space fiction – obsessed with the 'reeking ooze', 'mottled tripes', vast kidneys and 'yeastly liquors' of the whale's belly – but they imagine, with all the zest of a horror-movie, the impact of Jonah's three-day sojourn in the belly of the beast on his hair, his skin, his flesh. Freed from professional obligations, they ignore the disciplinary padlock on the gates to Wonderland, and travel down what Lucie Armitt calls 'the open gate [or mouth] leading down to the textual underworld',[17] often literally, into the zone of fantasy literature. And contra Bewer and Allen, they *propagate* the persona of the wide-eyed child, dosed up on *Drink Me* potions: Nineveh swells to forty parasangs (or light years) in diameter; the *qiqayon* becomes large enough to house a family of five; and the fish mutates into an underwater synagogue, an Imax Cinema, a New York subway. While the Mainstream is busy teaching the book of Jonah to articulate itself in adult idioms of the Enlightenment critic (and culture) come-of-age, the underbellies, as if hell-bent on regression, articulate the book in ways that will beg analogies with Jack's beanstalk, Superman, Pinocchio, Disney, the fairground ride, and the (second-rate) magic show. All this, of course, potentially reinforces a sense of this chapter being a kind of circus on the edge of scholarship, which in turn reinforces a sense of Jewish midrash as rather 'puerile', and Cultural Studies as the equivalent of a day off.

But it would be reductive to see these readings as nothing more than an assemblage of the charming, the a-critical, and the primitive, collected, Pitt Rivers like, as a foil for our own progress; and viewing the material with a charmed half-smile would only keep in place the distinction between Same and Other (since the Jewish as exotic, whimsical Other is only a nicer, milder form of the Other as negative foil for the self). A far more interesting and unsettling response to the material in this chapter is to consider how the '[seeming] exotic charm of another system of thought is the limitation of our own, the stark impossibility of thinking *that*', and to watch the contours of our own thought-geography, and the rules of disciplinary teratology, emerge, by way of contrast. Instinctive reactions against the lavishly described whale-belly and Jonah's bodily agonies tell us much about the cerebral disembodiment

---

[17] Armitt, *Theorising the Fantastic*, p. 81.

intrinsic to modern Western culture,[18] and reactions against gratuitous giganticism and the fantastic reveal much about our commitment to principles of realism and proportion as conditions for viable discourse. And the fact that some of the readings here may strike some readers as monstrously irreverent (and irrelevant) responses to the biblical, similarly intimates much about cultural and theological pre-conceptions of 'The Bible'. If we feel it a curious, transgressive alchemy when a biblical text is mixed with popular, mass literature and self-conscious storytelling, and if we feel that readings that empathise with a character who disobeys God cannot be legitimate readings of a biblical text, then those responses reveal the contours of our expectations and raise pertinent questions. Do biblical texts, by definition, then, automatically castigate disobedience and forbid interrogation of the deity?; are they always polemical (or even pious)?; and could a biblical text ever be conceived of as a story, if that story were not constrained and disciplined by a clear, polemical, monologic *intent*?

There is something very appropriate about taking voices on the edge of the interpretative tradition (the Jewish/the Popular) and using those voices to elucidate a text that has been classed as one of the strange books of the Bible, right on the edge of the canon.[19] Exploring these readings – and reading Jonah in the light of them – may enable us to short-circuit the natural reflex that Christianises the 'Old Testament' and that homogenises texts that come under the category of the 'biblical'. It may just be that these seemingly impotent and soft whimsies – these sucking pigs and sirens and 'fabulous' animals – have the power to break the ordered planes and surfaces within which the book of Jonah has been contained, and to articulate the book in ways that escape a disciplinary pedagogics and

---

[18] The way in which contemporary Western culture represses the body and its 'strange . . . and repugnant' biological underside is powerfully discussed in Z. Bauman, *Mortality, Immortality and Other Life Strategies* (Cambridge: Polity Press, 1992). As Bauman so memorably and persuasively puts it, contemporary culture 'slices the big carcass of mortality from head to tail into thin rashers of fearful (yet curable) afflictions' so that we tend to die of heart disease or cancer rather than unnamed vulgar mortality (p. 140). Presumably, Bauman would have something to say about the Polish poet Zbigniew Herbert's thoroughly modern Jonah, to be encountered later in this chapter, who dies banally, in hospital, of cancer.

[19] The classic statement of Jonah's strangeness comes in Elias Bickerman's *Four Strange Books of the Bible: Jonah, Daniel, Qoheleth, Esther* (New York: Schocken Books, 1967). But, as I intimated in the introduction, perhaps the strangest thing about Jonah is the way in which this gesture towards 'strangeness' has co-existed with a thoroughly normalising assimilation of the text in the scholarly Mainstream.

a sing-song Sunday School morality. For if, as Bewer and Allen intimate, modern disciplinary structures do not always map persuasively onto this pre-modern biblical text, peripheral interpretations may be the best way of beginning to articulate and explore the strangeness of Jonah, without feeling compelled to normalise this most maverick of 'prophets'.

Finally a note on the organisation of this chapter. Because they tend to operate independently of professional obligations and constraints, the alternative readings do not obligingly arrange themselves into neat chronological/conceptual blocks like the Mainstream. Instead, trying hopelessly to find a way of arranging the material that I scavenged, I have been forced, like the curator of the Pitt Rivers, into a rather crass form of organisation. I have set up two rather capacious cabinets, one labelled 'the Jewish' (any reading of Jewish authorship from the earliest midrash to the twentieth century), and the other called, even more flabbily, 'the Popular'. So as not to try the reader's patience too much, I have restricted myself to the most colourful, eye-catching artefacts,[20] and have attempted to tease out themes and trace trajectories rather than dealing with every artefact in depth. As with the Mainstream, the chapter concludes by teasing out conclusions and meditations from the material gathered in a way that hooks into wider issues of interpretation. Whereas the key tropes in the Mainstream were the survival and the over-living of readings past their read-by date, in the underbellies the key themes are survival and secularisation. In three sections:

On the strained relations between the Backwaters and the Mainstream; or how Jewish and popular readings are prone to bring on a bout of scholarly dyspepsia

Of survival, memes and life-after-death: on Jonah's infinite regurgitation and Endless Survival

Jonah on the oncology ward and the beached-up whale carcass, or the strange secular afterlives of biblical texts

---

[20] I have also tended to select texts that offer a variant on the readings of the Mainstream, which most literary/artistic interpretations in fact tend to do. One of the few exceptions is Robert Frost's 'A Masque of Mercy', which I have excluded partly because it is so much weaker than the 'A Masque of Reason', based on the book of Job, and partly because it regurgitates familiar Mainstream lessons: it ends with a figure named Paul suggesting that Jonah cure his penchant for justice by 'lying in self-forgetfulness/On the wet flags before a crucifix'. 'A Masque of Mercy' can be found in R. Frost, *The Complete Poems of Robert Frost* (London: Jonathan Cape, 1951), pp. 467–94.

I consider the chameleon-like survival of the book of Jonah, and explore how secular culture is still actively haunted by, and engaging with, biblical ghosts. For, in the strangest possible twist on the familiar religious trope of life-in-death, or life-after-death, it seems that the book of Jonah is living on, in perhaps its most *animated* contemporary form, in interpretations that foreground the death of religious credulity and question the relevance of the biblical text.

1. JEWISH INTERPRETATION

In the Mainstream, as we saw, 'the Jew' functions as proto-Christian and anti-Christian, foil and monster, virtual image and antithesis of the Christian self. 'Jonah the Jew' – clownish, lazy, savage, unable to manage his territory rightly – takes his place alongside the other extras in the 'colonial' charade: the lazy Oriental, the untruthful Hindu, the indolent African, the barbarous Turk. At the same time, in the hubris of the Christian/colonial enterprise, Jewish knowledge, like other pre- or sub-colonial knowledges, is sidelined or imperiously dismissed in sentence-long caricatures. Midrash is 'frivolous and puerile', writes Calvin;[21] while Pusey (lifting his head from his cetology textbooks for a moment) pronounces, with the absolutely incorrect pseudo-knowledge of the colonial observer, that 'Talmudic Jews identified Jonah with their Messiah ben Joseph, whom they expected to die and rise again'.[22]

The sheer assurance of these pronouncements is reminiscent of the views of English educationalists such as Thomas Babington Macaulay who was famously, bumptiously, of the opinion that 'a single shelf of a good European library is worth the whole native literature of India and Arabia'.[23] And they beg a long overdue counterblast in which the subjugated knowledge that is 'the Jewish' strides back into the interpretative arena, shakes off the constraints of 'the Other', and presents itself in its own complex terms. To explode the 'insularity and provincialism' of the Mainstream, or

---

[21] J. Calvin, *Commentaries on the Twelve Minor Prophets* (trans. J. Owen; Edinburgh: Calvin Translation Society, 1847), p. 26.

[22] E. D. Pusey, 'Jonah', in *The Minor Prophets with a Commentary, Explanatory and Practical* (London: Walter Smith and Innes, 1860), pp. 247–87 (248). Once again Judaism looks in the mirror and sees a fundamentally Christian self hankering after its own dying and rising messiah.

[23] T. Babington Macaulay, cited in B. Anderson, *Imagined Communities: Reflections on the Origin and Spread of Nationalism* (London and New York: Verso, 1991), p. 91.

Metropolis, argues Edward Said, we need to read 'not univocally, but *contrapuntally*', with a 'simultaneous awareness' of the history at the centre, and the other histories that jeopardise and potentially disassemble its 'incorporative, universalising and totalising codes'.[24] Diversification inevitably leads to destabilisation: if simply stretching out the 'Christian' across time leads to tensions between Church Fathers and Enlightenment critics, Chrysostom and Michaelis, then how much more will Jewish interpretation threaten the models of interpretation that are reliant on the 'Jew' as little more than the sidekick of the Christian imagination?

My aim here, then, is to subversively twist the motif of 'Jonah the Jew', to read Jonah from a place within Jewish culture and interpretation (though I need to say from the outset that this is not a tradition I inhabit, but one I visit from the outside as an occasional visitor or day-tripper).[25] I want to look at how Jewish tradition takes the flour and flax of this text and cooks it up/spins it out as part of a very distinctive cultural fabric. And I want to explore how the character who declares himself a 'Hebrew' (Jonah 1.9), becomes a 'Jew' in Jewish readings as well as Christian; or how, to be more (im)precise, he becomes a rabbi among the rabbis, a scholar poring over his books in a fish-belly *schul*,[26] a fellow-disputant with God, an apocalyptic super-hero, a character weighed down with suitcases and the freight of twentieth-century history, and a biblical Tevye the Dairyman,[27] shrugging his shoulders, and addressing wry Yiddish-isms at the inscrutable Holy One. Jonah, like God in Jewish tradition, has many faces,[28] faces that stymie any attempts to portray Jewish interpretation as something monolithic (in either an ideal or a derogatory sense). Together they produce a complex performance of 'Jewish interpretation' that sends a red-faced Jonah-as-Shylock caricature scuttling off the critical stage into obsolescence.

But inevitably there are problems and pitfalls in this utopian

---

[24] E. Said, *Culture and Imperialism* (London: Vintage, 1994), p. 59.

[25] This point is important. The view of Jonah presented here is emphatically a view-from-the outside: I am reading Jewish texts as I read Calvin, Luther, and Pusey, rather than from the point of view of someone who grew up within the Jewish tradition.

[26] *Schul* is the Yiddish word for 'synagogue', commonly used by Jews of Ashkenazi (German and East-European) origin.

[27] Tevye the Dairyman is the hero of Sholem Aleichem's *The Railroad Stories* (see S. Aleichem, *Tevye the Dairyman and The Railroad Stories* (trans. H. Halkin; New York: Schocken, 1987)) popularised (and sentimentalised) in the play and movie *Fiddler on the Roof* (N. Jewison, Mirisch, 1971).

[28] See for example *Pesikta Kahana* 109b–110a.

project; pitfalls that are (tentatively and precariously) analogous to those encountered in postcolonial situations. In the quest to rehabilitate themselves in regard to themselves and others, colonised peoples have often sought a collective one true self, stereotyped, idealised, and projected back onto pre-colonial time. Similarly, the sheer violence of anti-Judaism wearily catalogued in chapter 1 means that my first instinct is to stress and reify the absolute difference of Jewish interpretation, and then, flipping over the pantomime-like Manichean hierarchy, to clap at the Jewish and boo at the Christian. But, as with the relation between colonial and indigenous cultures, the relations between the two cultures are reciprocal, riddling, and complex, and the history of one is literally unthinkable without the other. Taking the hierarchy and simply reversing it, so that the Jewish trumps, teaches, and instructs the Christian, simply repeats the homogenising hierarchies of the critical master-discourse. There is a place, of course, for inverting the assumptions of the Mainstream (so, for example, in a twist on the universalist Christian versus the particularist Jew, I argue that a distinctive strength of Jewish interpretation is precisely its 'particularism', the way in which, to quote Emmanuel Levinas, it 'watches over the general from the basis of the particular').[29] And, since Christian commentators have for so long imagined Jonah the Jew in school, under their tutelage, learning about universalism and obedience, there is something fitting about the idea of 'the Jewish' giving an interpretative masterclass to the Christian (highlighting dimensions of the text that it had failed to notice hitherto, and pointing out, after a two-hour Christian lecture on the 'qualities of mercy in the book of Jonah', that it has already written a lengthy midrash on that very subject).[30] Thinking in terms of huge generalised abstracts 'the Christian' and 'the Jewish' will be necessary at some points. But I need to watch that they don't solidify into something lumpish and reductive – nothing more than the caricatures of the Mainstream, inverted.

[29] 'The great power of Talmudic casuistry is to be the special discipline which seeks in the particular the precise moment in which the general principle runs the risk of becoming its own opposite, which watches over the general from the basis of the particular. This preserves us from ideology. Ideology is the generosity and clarity of a principle which did not take into account the inversion stalking this generous principle when it is applied . . .' (E. Levinas, *L'Au-delà du verset* (Paris: Les Editions de Minuit, 1982), pp. 98–9; cited in and trans. A. Aronowicz (ed.), *Nine Talmudic Readings by Emmanuel Levinas* (Bloomington and Indianapolis: Indiana University Press, 1990), p. xxx).

[30] See *Midrash Jonah*, discussed below (pp. 104–5).

I say this at the outset because I plan both to resist, and participate in, a strand of post-modern culture that casts Jewish textuality – exemplified in Talmud[31] and Midrash[32] – as the idealised antithesis of Christian logocentricism. In what is, at least potentially, an inverted morality play, the Jewish (or Hebraic) has become iconic of the polyphonic, the dialogic, the open-ended, the open-minded, and the Christian (or Hellenistic) has come to represent the monologic, the closed, the dogmatic close-down of meaning. As they have 'taken the sacred elements of rabbinic thought and then inverted them against their sacred origins',[33] Jewish theorists such as Edmund Jabès, Jacques Derrida, and Emmanuel Levinas have popularised a sense of Jewish interpretation as haunting relentless questions, as inexhaustive textuality that resists transcendence, and as a type of enquiry that chases the general principle to the point where the general principle gives way.[34] And these readings have been sup-

---

[31] Just as in Christianity the Old Testament is only properly understood in the context of the thinner sequel, the New, so in Judaism the Hebrew Bible (known as *Tanakh* or *Miqra'*) is only properly understood in the context of midrash, rabbinic commentaries and, above all, Talmud. The Talmud contains the Oral Torah, or Mishnah, which according to tradition was given to Moses at Sinai alongside the written Torah. It also contains the Gemara, a vast body of rabbinic discussion of Mishnah, as well as additional commentaries. The arrangement of a page of Talmud (Mishnah in the centre, surrounded by Gemara, encased by commentaries) gives it a certain labyrinthine appearance. This, together with the fact that many different voices co-exist on a single page, has made it even more of a visual aid for the postmodern.

[32] Midrash (deriving from the Hebrew root 'to search out') is both a process of interpreting and a collection of texts which, together with the Talmud, make up the body of foundational Jewish learning. Midrash attempts to fill in the gaps – both within the biblical text and between the biblical text and contemporary culture – answering questions such as where Isaac went after his near-death experience under his father's knife, who God was talking to when he said 'Let us make man', and what exactly it means to love one's neighbour as oneself. As Daniel Boyarin explains, the interpreter 'slips' into the gaps left by the text 'interpreting and completing the text in accordance with the codes of his or her culture' (D. Boyarin, *Intertextuality and the Reading of Midrash* (Bloomington and Indianapolis: Indiana University Press, 1990), p. 14). There are two basic categories of midrash: *midrash halakah* (concerned with civil and religious law) and *midrash aggadah* (i.e. all the non-legal material, including narrative, parables and theological and ethical statements).

[33] S. Handelman, *The Slayers of Moses: The Emergence of Rabbinic Interpretation in Modern Literary Theory* (Albany: State University of New York Press, 1982), p. 211.

[34] The quintessential image of the postmodern is the infinite book, the book folded back on itself, question-crammed and infinitely self-reflective: the text that cannot escape to a truth behind or above itself, or that, to use the common jargon, cannot find refuge in a 'transcendental signified'. And Judaism, which in popular consciousness is the 'religion of the Book' (to coin the phrase of the emphatically *un*-post-structuralist George Steiner) becomes, by extension, the religion of this kind of book, this inescapable book, this text that scrutinises itself with meticulous exuberance and, in the process, breeds more text. Derrida sees the whole 'onto-theological' history of Western rationality as consigning both writing and the Jew to a position of fallen secondariness, as intruder, threat, and scapegoat; and,

ported by iconic prooftexts from the Talmud that spice up the sometimes clunky, sometimes colourless idioms of the postmodern (the sign *sous rature*, the interminable 'white spaces' and lacunae) and offer themselves as colourful illustrative doodles in the ghostly pale palimpsest of poststructuralism.[35] According to the metaphorising Talmudic logic by which postmodernism spawns Talmudic images of itself,[36] the inexhaustibility of meaning can be compared to Torah as a sea of ink,[37] *or again it can be compared to* God studying and interpreting his own Torah,[38] *or again it can be compared to* the

though he is keen to stress that he is not involved in something as simple as reversing the Pauline promotion of Spirit over Law, his writing 'reinstates' both writing and Judaism defined as 'the birth and passion of writing . . . the love and endurance of the letter itself' (in J. Derrida, *Writing and Difference* (trans. A. Bass; London: Routledge, 1990), p. 64). In a similar vein, Levinas proclaims 'the volume of the book as living space', and Edmund Jabès, who occupies 'the book' as 'universe, country, roof and enigma', observes that 'the difficulty of being a Jew coincides with the difficulty of writing', and that 'Judaism and writing are but the same waiting, the same hope, the same depletion' (Levinas, *L'Au-delà du verset*, p. 159; E. Jabès, *Livre des questions* (Paris: Gallimard, 1963), pp. 32, 132). So Derrida, Levinas, Jabès, *et al.*, bring a sense of Jewish interpretation into popular consciousness, and trounce anti-Semitic stereotypes of an insularly bookish Judaism, rigidly sticking to the letter, with an image of the Jew wandering through a different kind of book, and skidding on, sliding off, and ricocheting through the letter(s). But, in the process, Judaism risks becoming an exotic transgressive Other to the edifice of a 'Greek' western rationalism, the enticing and seductive '*heretic* hermeneutic', as Handelman puts it (Handelman, *The Slayers of Moses*, pp. 179ff.).

[35] Why is midrash so appealing to the postmodern *Zeitgeist*? On one level, I think it has something to do with the physical, almost cartoonish images of interpretation that midrash provides (for all its talk of privileging body over soul, and of 'semiotic stripteases', postmodern writing can be surprisingly abstract and disembodied). It may also be that midrash somehow 'roots' postmodernism, and gives it a colourful, historicised image of itself. Daniel Boyarin speculates that the appeal of midrash perhaps has something to do with the way it 'preserves contact with the tradition while it is liberating' and so replicates postmodernism's own troubled and creative relationships with modernism and 'the past' (*Intertextuality and the Reading of Midrash*, p. 20).

[36] Since Talmud and midrash constantly stack up new and ingenious textual analogies using the phrase 'again it can be compared to' or 'again it is like', there is a certain poetic justice in the way in which they have themselves become the subject of large-scale comparison between the midrashic and the postmodern.

[37] Levinas's *Difficile Liberté* and Derrida's *Of Grammatology* both cite Rabbi Eliezer, who muses on the infinitude of Torah: 'If all the seas were ink, and all ponds planted with reeds, if the sky and earth were parchments, and if all human beings practised the art of writing – they would not exhaust the Torah I have just learned, just as the Torah itself would not be diminished any more than is the sea by the water removed by a paint-brush in it' (cited in E. Levinas, *Difficile Liberté: Essai sur le Judaïsme* (Paris: Albin Michel, 1963), p. 44; J. Derrida, *Of Grammatology* (trans. G. Chakravorty Spivak; Baltimore and London: Johns Hopkins University Press, 1976), p. 16; no reference given).

[38] B. Berachot 6a and 7a. As Michael Fishbane comments, 'The well-known Talmudic image of God studying and interpreting his Torah is nothing if not tradition's realisation that there is no authoritative teaching which is not also the source of its renewal' (M. Fishbane, *The Garments of Torah: Essays in Biblical Hermeneutics* (Bloomington: Indiana University Press, 1992), p. 3). (Compare God's 'hands-off' commandment in *Yer. Hag.* 1.7; *Eikah Rabbah*, intro.

exposition of the verse 'Man is born into trouble' (Job 5.7) to mean 'man is born into study'.[39] And the God of *Baba Mezia* 59b, who declares himself outwitted by the interpretation of the rabbis and chuckles, good-humouredly, 'My children have defeated me',[40] becomes both a sign of the dying author (who generously abdicates the interpretative rights to the book he has authored)[41] and a modestly shrunken, human God for an increasingly secular age. Like the God of *The Satanic Verses*, who is balding, with salt-and-pepper beard, dandruff, and glasses,[42] or the God of a recent pop song who rides public transport,[43] God-in-the-text or God-at the-mercy-of-the text becomes a markedly un-authoritarian God for the late twentieth century.[44] And as Judaism becomes the indelible sign of exile, and exile the universal figure for the postmodern condition,[45] God

ch. 2: 'So it should be that you would forsake me, but would keep my Torah', and Levinas's gloss, 'To love the Torah more than God (is) protection against the madness of direct contact with the sacred' (Levinas, *Difficile Liberté*, p. 218).)

[39] *B. Sanhedrin*, 99b.

[40] In this amazing narrative (often taken as a prooftext for the Talmud's postmodern sensibilities), Rabbi Eliezer and a group of other rabbis are debating the purity of an oven. Rabbi Eliezer supports his argument with amazing acts (a carob tree uproots itself and travels one hundred feet, a water pipe flows backwards, the walls of the study-house incline) and finally the Holy One himself supports him with a booming voice from heaven. But as the rabbis argue, Heavenly voices cannot authenticate Eliezer's position, since God himself located interpretative authority firmly on earth when he wrote 'Incline after the majority.' The prophet Elijah later reports that, on hearing the ingenuity of their arguments, the Holy One could be heard laughing 'My children have defeated me', so by implication admitting the capacity of the text he authored, and its interpreters, to outwit and outmanoeuvre him.

[41] Derrida describes the absent God of Judaism/postmodernism as a God 'who, in a more or less defined way, is said to have given us the use of his pen' (*Writing and Difference*, p. 10).

[42] S. Rushdie, *The Satanic Verses* (Dover, Del.: The Consortium, 1988), p. 318.

[43] Joan Osborne's 'One of Us' asks 'What if God were one of us? Just a stranger on a bus, trying to make his way home', and imagines a lonely God who has no one calling his mobile, except perhaps the Pope (Joan Osborne, 'One of Us', on *Relish*, Polygram Records, 1995). The lyrics are hardly astounding but the popularity of the song suggests that it somehow struck a chord with a contemporary sense of a little God, a lonely God worthy of pity, since he is losing followers and is stranded in anachronism. Compare the journalist Jack Miles's recent biography of God, where the author makes much of the idea of a schizophrenic God and God as 'cosmic orphan' (J. Miles, *God: A Biography* (London: Simon and Schuster, 1995), p. 231).

[44] As well as laughing, God also weeps (*B. Berakhot* 3a, 59a), puts on *tefillin* (phylacteries), studies Torah in the heavenly academy (*B. Berakhot* 6a, 7a), regrets his actions, and laments his old age (*Eikah Rabbah*, twenty-fourth poem). See D. Stern, '*Imitatio Hominis*: Anthropomorphism and the Character(s) of God in Rabbinic Literature', in *Prooftexts* 12 (1992), pp. 151–74 (157–61).

[45] The way in which Judaism has become synonymous with exile and alienation is writ large across twentieth-century literature, for example in James Joyce, who imitated Jewish strategies of writing and identified himself as a 'Jew' in exile (see I. B. Nadel, *Joyce and the Jews* (London: Macmillan, 1989)). Postmodern discourse similarly underlines the figure of

(generously) joins the people in anomie, wading through seas of ink and working in a dense, inexhaustible labyrinth of words.

But it is the very palatability of this presentation of 'the Jewish' that should make us suspicious. Derrida, Levinas, *et al.* work from a select portion of Jewish material (midrash aggadah, and very selective mystical texts) and tend to studiously avoid halachic material, Hasidic legend, and mysticism in its most esoteric, transcendent, and 'Christian' manifestations. And while the characterisation of the Jewish as expansive and polyphonic is certainly a neat, and necessary, refutation/inversion of the expansive Christian/ narrow Jew hierarchy, it can also congeal into an equally stereotyped projection of the Jewish in (narcissistic?) relation to the self. Personally, I suspect myself of the desire to make Judaism into an idealised Other: a repository for the playful, the open-minded and modestly text-bound, and the humble meaning that is always under renegotiation. And I worry that a secular appropriation of 'the Jewish' may, to different, more Calvinesque minds, continue to cede the higher religious/moral ground to the Christian by reinforcing the perception of Jewish interpretation as frivolous and non-serious.

Yet, despite this caveat, Jewish readings of Jonah tend to support the contemporary characterisations of Jewish textuality, *generally* speaking. Insofar as Jewish interpretation is characterised as emphatically textual, physical, quizzical, prone to bringing everything (even the deity) into the realm of questions, and prone to multiply contradictions and empathies so that texts ricochet in all directions, *most* of the readings gathered here seem to conform to the general photofit. But, taking the advice of Levinas and the Talmudists, and watching over the abstractions and generalisations that emerge from the basis of each *particular* Jewish reading of this *particular* biblical text, I need to confess that there are also readings that – doggedly doing precisely what the typically 'Jewish' does not do – close down meaning and reduce the text to a single moralising principle. The temptation is to compress these texts down below (in ten-point footnotes) or to put them at the end (as an afterthought) where they cannot disturb the general pattern that emerges. But, since the work of midrash is typically to expose precisely those points that may embarrass the main claims of the text, the most appropriately

the wandering Jew, with sand on his/her shoes, and reifies the figure of exile as a universal warning against the homogeneity.

'midrashic' thing to do seems to be to put these misfits at the beginning, up front, where they can do most damage to any cliché that may congeal.

My two leftover texts are the fourteenth-century mystical text *Sefer-ha-Ẓohar*, or the 'Book of Splendour',[46] and *Midrash Jonah*, a tenth-century midrash that is typically midrashic in its detail[47] but not in its general argument. Both could easily set up residence in the Mainstream, since both roundly condemn the sinner-prophet and exalt in his punishment with seemingly 'Calvinist' relish.[48] *Midrash Jonah* compares Jonah, who coldly refuses to take up the role of prophet-as-nurturer, to a wet-nurse who runs away rather than suckle the King's own son.[49] It lavishes empathy on God and the Ninevites and heaps tortures on Jonah, putting him in a pit of snakes

[46] The Zohar is the magnum opus of Jewish mysticism, or Kabbalah. Written in obscure and often contrived Aramaic, it was circulated by a Spanish mystic, Moses de Léon, in the late thirteenth and early fourteenth centuries. De Léon claimed to be transcribing ancient midrashim from the circle of a second-century Palestinian Rabbi, Simeon bar Yohai, but in fact was using bar Yohai, and Aramaic, as a talmudic alter-ego. The Zohar is the most esoteric document in Judaism: it conceives of Torah as a beautiful veiled woman, who reveals her face to her lover for fleeting moments, and speaks in cryptic symbolic language about celestial bridegrooms and brides, lights and sparks, flowing streams and rivers, and God as Ein-Sof (the Without End). Because it works on the assumption that the real meanings of Torah are hidden, like kernels within a nut, its readings, or crackings, of Jonah are unlike any other readings elsewhere in Judaism. For general discussions of the Zohar see G. Scholem, *Major Trends in Jewish Mysticism* (New York: Schocken Books, 1974; 1st edn 1941), pp. 156–243, and M. Idel, *Kabbalah: New Perspectives* (New Haven and London: Yale University Press, 1988). The Zohar's discussion of Jonah can be found in *The Zohar* (trans. M. Simon and P. P. Levertoff; London: Soncino Press, 1934), iv.172–6, and in easy and accessible form in G. Scholem (ed.), *Zohar, the Book of Splendour: Basic Readings from the Kabbalah* (New York: Schocken Books, 1977; 1st edn 1949), pp. 103–6.

[47] *Midrash Jonah* is also discussed below as a typical example of midrashic stories that grow from a slight discrepancy in grammar or the subtle tweak of a letter. The original text of *Midrash Jonah* can be found in J. D. Eisenstein (ed.), אוצר מדרשים: *A Library of Two Hundred Minor Midrashim* II (New York: 1915), pp. 218–22; a German translation can be found in A. Wünsche, *Aus Israels Lehrhallen* II (Hildesheim: Georg Olms, 1967), pp. 39–56. James Limburg translates selections of the text into English in *Jonah*, pp. 109–12.

[48] Although as we saw in chapter 1 Calvin is not always 'Calvinist' – or at least not in the sense we might expect. And if Judaism is assumed to have the monopoly on quizzicality, then Luther seems positively 'Jewish' when he comments on how God plays with life and death as if they were 'trivial playthings' and 'toys with Jonah' in the plant–worm scenario (M. Luther, 'Lectures on Jonah', in H. C. Oswald (ed.), *Minor Prophets* II: *Jonah, Habakkuk* (Luther's Works 19; Saint Louis: Concordia, 1974), pp. 82, 94). Clearly the Jewish–Christian dichotomy is already starting to leak.

[49] In contrast to Christian theologians, and indeed to Jewish medieval philosophers, rabbinic exegesis tends to amplify the embarrassing divine anthropomorphisms that can be found in the Hebrew Bible. The most common figure in the midrashim is the Holy One as a 'king of flesh and blood', modelled directly upon the known figure of the contemporary Roman emperor or one of his representatives. As David Stern points out, the image is not just a bland representation of God's sovereignty, but a way of allowing him to act with all kinds of

and scorpions, and giving him not one, but two prison-belly sentences, in the belly of a male and then a female fish.[50] The Zohar reads Jonah allegorically as a story of Everyman's journey through life, and is caught between a view of man as oppressed/maltreated (which is how it interprets Jonah's name),[51] and as a 'rank droplet' deserving thorough punishment. It sees the fish-belly as a sign of the grave, which is also a torture chamber, where man is punished in 'each organ, and in his eyes and hands and feet', and it reads the 'three days and three nights' as the time it takes for a corpse to 'burst apart' and 'cast forth . . . putrescence on his face', as the body castigates the soul with the words:

Receive back that which you put into me; all day long you ate and drank, nor ever gave a thing to the poor; like feasts and holidays were all your days, but the needy did not share your food and were left hungry.

In the Zohar, Jonah (or man) is so sinful that even his belly throws up a sermon on him; in *Midrash Jonah*, Jonah falls off the end of the biblical text onto his knees, pleading with God to 'Direct your word according to the principle of Mercy.' The Zohar allegorises and *Midrash Jonah does* read the text through generalised abstractions (justice versus mercy) and *does* condemn Jonah according to those general principles; and both subversively illustrate the way in which the Jewish and the Christian nestle up against one another. The Zohar, which reads Jonah as a sign of the soul/body in purgatory, clearly imbibes large doses of the medieval Christianity with which it co-exists. *Midrash Jonah* clearly demonstrates, if demonstration is needed, that Jewish tradition also sees the Ninevites as 'God's children' – in this case literally, since they need the tender suckling of prophet-as-wetnurse.[52] Lines between 'the Christian' and 'the

---

'shockingly undivine' emotions – as in this text, where he seems rather emotionally volatile, and prone to torture and despotism. (For a full discussion, see Stern, '*Imitatio Hominis*'.)

50 The basis of this curious double punishment is discussed on pp. 116–17.

51 The Zohar reads the prophet's name as a participle of יונה (*ynh*), to oppress/maltreat, and sees Jonah as the 'aggrieved one'. And the explanation of why Jonah is aggrieved underscores the fragility and pain of human life: 'Why is Jonah aggrieved? Because as soon as (the soul) becomes partner with the body in this world she finds herself full of vexation. Man, then, is in this world as in a ship that is traversing the great ocean and is like to be broken, as it says "so that the ship was like to be broken" [Jonah 1.4].'

52 It would obviously traumatise the Mainstream to realise that numerous Jewish commentators stress that the Ninevites, as well as the Israelites, are God's handiwork, and that this taps into a whole vein of Jewish tradition stressing compassion for one's enemies. Like many of their Christian counterparts, Jewish readers are troubled by the more bloodthirsty and vindictive passages in the Hebrew Bible/Old Testament and detach themselves from them. Even God gets uncomfortable: as the Israelites/the angels revel in the death of the

Jewish' are clearly vulnerable on conceptual, historical, and stylistic grounds: for example, the distinctively 'Jewish' empathy with Jonah that emerges later in this chapter overlaps with the Church Fathers' sympathy with the prophet (their 'silly deference' to him, in the view of the Reformers). And crucially, the central liturgical use of the book of Jonah on the holiest day of the Jewish calendar, Yom Kippur, the Day of Atonement, the 'Sabbath of Sabbaths', establishes a thoroughly Mainstream reading of Jonah based on sin, repentance, and the oceanic mercy of God, right at the heart of Jewish tradition.[53]

Clearly 'the Christian' and 'the Jewish' are porous to one another: they seep into one another, breathe the same cultural air. Yet, just as surely, their readings are shaped by the urge to resist the Other, to shape themselves in such a way that they emphatically *do not touch*. The agenda of the scholarly Mainstream is clearly set by the presence of Judaism-as-Father: Jonah takes the grotesque shape that he does in order to intimidate into oblivion the ever-present spectre of 'the Jew'. Jewish readings, similarly, find that their agenda is pre-set by the Other: that they are re-deflected by the pressures of living in close proximity with Christianity. There are, in fact, two different versions of the Talmud, one written in Babylon (*Bavli*) and one written in Palestine (*Yerushalmi*),[54] and so two readings of Jonah and two readings of the repentance of the Ninevites. In *Bavli* the Ninevites repent superlatively, excessively: even if someone had used a stolen joist to build a palace, he would raze the entire palace to

---

Egyptians in the Reed/Red Sea (Exodus 15) the God of the Talmud chides: '*My handiwork* is drowning in the sea and you presume to sing praise' (*B. Megillah* 10b; my italics).

[53] The reading of Jonah as the *haftarah* reading (that is, the reading from the Prophets) at the *minhah* (or afternoon) service on Yom Kippur seems to have been established very early in Jewish tradition: it can be traced back at least as far as the Babylonian Talmud (*B. Megillah* 31a) and some scholars argue that it was in place by the second century CE. Though the liturgy for Yom Kippur is complex and diverse, as are the resonances of Jonah within it, the overt lesson of the text is clearly that 'sincere repentance can reverse even the harshest Heavenly decree' and that the Ninevites are an exemplary case of repentance (N. Schwerman, H. Goldwurm, and A. Gold, *Yom Kippur: Its Significance, Laws and Prayers* (New York: Mesorah, 1989), p. 85). To reiterate the point, the reading flows into an addendum from Micah 7.18–20, which turns the sea in the book of Jonah into an image of the God who throws sins into the sea.

[54] *Bavli* (completed around 500 CE) and *Yerushalmi* (written down around 380 CE) contain basically the same Mishnah chapters (though there are several significant differences), and different *gemarot* (for a definition of Mishnah and Gemara, see n. 31). *Bavli* is the more complete and is generally considered the more skilful and elegant of the two, and it is to *Bavli* that people refer when they speak of 'the Talmud'.

return the beam to its owner.[55] But in *Yerushalmi* the same excessive repentance of the Ninevites becomes a pantomime farce, a 'repentance of deception', a cynical exercise in divine blackmail (instant repentance: just add sackcloth).[56] The difference between *Yerushalmi* and *Bavli* is clearly rooted in their respective geographical and political contexts, for whereas the Babylonian interpreters are responding to the text in a free, relatively uncluttered interpretative space, the Palestinian interpreters live in close contact with Christian readings that habitually identify the Ninevites with the gentiles and the Church.[57] The Palestinian readings of Jonah are clearly dented and restricted by the pressure of the Christian reading; they need strategically to vacate certain interpretative trajectories to avoid playing into Christian polemicists' hands.[58] It may well be the supreme irony of Christian and Jewish interpretation of the book of

---

[55] *B. Taanit* 16a. Fascinatingly, the repentant Ninevites are seen as being 'clever at asking'. As part of their repentance, they separate mother animals from their offspring, and tell God that they will only reunite them when God has mercy on them (this image, incidentally comes from reading בחזקה (*beḥazeqah*) in Jonah 3.8 as 'hardheartedly') and they direct clever rhetorical questions at God such as 'if one is long-suffering and the other is quick-tempered, if one is righteous and the other is wicked, who yields before whom?' Far from being a negative trait, this rhetorical skill only reinforces a sense that the Ninevites are like David and the Israelites, who, according to *Lev. R. Wayikra* v. 8, 'know how to appease and win the favour of the Creator'. In a fascinating exegesis of David's psalms, *Leviticus Rabbah* shows how David knows how to butter God up with Ninevite-like ingenuity, and how God, in his more chuckling manifestations, responds affectionately and knowingly to his strategies: '[David] first sang God's praises and said "The heavens declare the glory of God" [Psalm 19.1]. God said "Perhaps you want something?" . . . [David said] "Thou art a great God and my trespasses are great; it befits a great God to pardon the great trespasses, as it is written 'For the sake of they name [which is great], pardon my iniquity, for it is great'" [Psalm 25.11]' (*Lev. R. Wayikra*, v. 8, cited in C. G. Montefiore and H. Loewe, *A Rabbinic Anthology* (New York: Schocken Books, 1974), pp. 235–6).

[56] The difference between *Yerushalmi* and *Bavli* is only the most obvious example of the impact of Christian polemic on Jewish readings. The Aramaic Targum to Jonah, a translation/interpretation also written in Palestine, is also forced into some fancy footwork to avoid replicating and reinforcing anti-Jewish readings. In the Targum, the repentance of the Ninevites is short-lived, as in *Yerushalmi*, and they soon relapse into bloodshed and violence. More subtly, Jonah proclaims emphatically 'I am a Jew' (rather than 'I am a Hebrew'), so as to disentangle himself from typological association with Christ. For similar reasons, he complains 'It is better that I die than I live' in Jonah 4.8 rather than 'My death is better than my life', to stymie analogies with Luke 23.46. (For text, translations and commentaries see E. Levine, *The Aramaic Version of Jonah* (New York: Sepher Hermon Press, 1981); K. J. Cathcart and R. P. Gordon, *The Targum of the Minor Prophets* (The Aramaic Bible 14; Edinburgh: T. & T. Clark, 1989).)

[57] St Bede, for example, declared that Nineveh signifies 'the Church ornate with the glory of all virtue' (cited in R. H. Bowers, *The Legend of Jonah* (The Hague: Martinus Nijhoff, 1971), p. 40).

[58] In another Talmudic passage (*Av Zar* 4a) a Palestinian Rabbi tells an unidentified opponent that 'We [of Palestine] who frequently meet with you set ourselves the task of thoroughly studying it [the Bible], but they of Babylonia do not study it carefully.' This may just be

Jonah that, for several centuries, a pro-Ninevite, universalist Jewish reading was eliminated because *Jews feared the power of Christian supersessionist logic, that would gobble up such readings into vindication of the Church.*

As it curls up in order to protect itself, *Yerushalmi*'s reading of Jonah shows how the difference between Christian and Jewish interpretation can sometimes be an emphatic difference, a result of interpretative self-defence. But this is the only example that I have come across where the difference between Jewish and Christian readings of Jonah is cut deeply and emphatically like a siege trench. For the most part, the difference is not manned by border guards or fenced around with barbed wire, it results from a different kind of relation with the sacred word. The remainder of this tour is given over to Jewish readings that deflect the book of Jonah in ways that are radically different to the Mainstream, and to looking, through these examples, at the distinctive traits of midrash that result in these 'deflections'.[59]

We begin with the ninth-century midrash, the *Pirke de Rabbi Eliezer,*[60] and the story of 'Jonah Superprophet': a refreshing (if unintentional) antidote to the Mainstream story of 'Jonah the Eminently Vomitable Nationalist'. It follows the biblical storyline (with insertions) until Jonah 1.17, where it departs from the biblical surface text altogether, and dives into an underwater subplot, a sensational adventure from which it never re-surfaces. The point of transition is the fish's mouth, which, rather like Lewis Carroll's rabbit hole or C. S. Lewis's wardrobe, functions as gateway to a magical other- (or in this case under-) world. The fish has been

---

simple rivalry or bumptiousness, or it may be an allusion to the fact that, in Palestine, Jews are *forced* to read carefully.

[59] An apologetic footnote for Jewish specialists. In this study, focused as it is around the book of Jonah, I will inevitably be losing some of the finer distinctions that can be made in more lengthy and specialised tours of midrash for its own sake. I will not be referring to the many distinctions between the *aggadot* of the *tannaim* and the *amoraim*, and will be using 'the rabbis' in the very loosest sense to refer to the authors of the *Mekilta de Rabbi Ishmael* and the *Pirke de Rabbi Eliezer*. In an interdisciplinary study such as this, it is sometimes necessary to paint in broad strokes, lest the main text get completely swamped in footnotes.

[60] Like the Zohar, the *Pirke de Rabbi Eliezer* (or 'The Chapters of Rabbi Eliezer') takes its authority from an early rabbi, the first century Rabbi Eliezer ben Hyrcanos. The excursus on Jonah can be found in *Pirke de Rabbi Eliezer: The Chapters of R. Eliezer the Great* (trans. G. Friedlander; New York: Sepher Hermon Press, 1981), ch. 10, pp. 65–73. The midrash is less explicitly homiletic and exegetical than many midrashim, and sits more loosely with the biblical text (the reading of Jonah, for example, only stays with the biblical text until 2.10, and loses all trace of chs. 3 and 4 and the Ninevites).

appointed from the first six days of creation to swallow Jonah, and its belly is not filled with guts and ooze and intestines (unlike other less salubrious bellies to be visited later in this chapter), but opens into a great synagogue (perhaps an allusion to the famous synagogue at Alexandria)[61] illuminated by glass eye-windows and by a pearl that hangs from the stomach-roof.[62] Just as the prophet is settling down into his top-of-the-range, tastefully lit, *schul*-submarine, his fishy host tells him, trembling, that his day has arrived 'to be devoured in the midst of Leviathan's mouth'. And realising that it is for this purpose (rather than for punishment) that he has been swallowed, Jonah steers the fish alongside Leviathan, scares him into retreat by showing him the 'seal of our father Abraham' (that is, the sign of circumcision),[63] and vows to return, tow him off, and cut him up in juicy chunks for the great messianic feast of the righteous.[64] As

---

[61] So Friedlander, *Pirke de Rabbi Eliezer*, p. 69.

[62] 'He entered its mouth just as a man enters the great synagogue, and he stood therein. The two eye-windows were like windows of glass giving light to Jonah. Rabbi Meir said: "One pearl was suspended in the belly of the fish and it gave illumination to Jonah, like the sun which shines with its might at noon; and it showed to Jonah all that was in the sea and in the depths, as is said, 'Light is sown for the righteous'" [Psalm 97.11]'. (In *B. Baba Bathra* 74b, the sea-monsters of the deep also have luminous eyes.)

[63] Reading in the late twentieth century it is tempting to see the James-Bond-like figure of Jonah as a virtual cartoon illustrating Masculinity for Beginners. If, at least according to J. Doyle, to be a man is to be successful, to be aggressive, and to be sexual (see J. Doyle, *The Male Experience* (Dubuque, Indiana: William C. Brown, 1989)), Jonah Superprophet is manly on all counts: he not only floors the beast but does so by using his penis as a weapon. Officially of course, the sign of circumcision is a sign of obedience to the covenant, and a sign of God's fidelity to Israel inscribed on the flesh. But is it so very inappropriate to think that there is at least an element of this showdown that is enjoying the spectacle of Jonah as male hero, with a not inconsiderable bulge in his tights?

[64] Clearly a rather large footnote is required to chart the dimensions of the beast, Leviathan, and the chomping of his body at the apocalyptic feast of the righteous. In the Bible, the Leviathan denotes various real marine animals (the sea-serpent, the crocodile) *and* the supernatural chaos monster who, according to the ancient mythology which the Hebrew Bible imbibes, as well as resists, struggled with God in the primordial battle between the creator and the sea. Leviathan has his natural habitat in biblical texts such as Isaiah 27.1; Psalms 50.10; 89.10–12; 104.26; Job 26.12; 40–1. A monster- and myth-shy Christian tradition tends to leave these particular stones unturned, but the Talmud develops both the physical and supernatural dimensions of the beast. In typically midrashic fashion, *Baba Bathra* 74b–75a puts together a whole physical anatomy from snippets of biblical texts (Job 41.20 shows how fire from Leviathan's mouth makes the deep boil like a cauldron; creative philological exegesis on Job 41.21 demonstrates that he had such bad breath that it constantly had to be deodorised by putting his head into the perfumes of Eden) but at the same time it tells an apocalyptic narrative stretching from the beginning to the end of time. It tells how there were originally two Leviathans, a male and a female who, had they mated with one another, would have destroyed the whole world, and how in response to the threat the Holy One castrated the male and killed and salted the female. It tells how 'in the future', Gabriel will lead the hunt for Leviathan, and draw him out with a fish-hook (Job 40.24); and it tells how the Holy One will 'make' something for the 'righteous' out of the

a reward, Jonah demands from the fish an underwater tour in which he visits the 'foundations of the world'. At this point superprophet turns supertourist (I imagine him with his face pressed up against the glass of the fish's eye-windows). The subplot briefly resurfaces within the text which now seems shamefacedly pedestrian in contrast, as the lines of Jonah's psalm are transformed, effectively, into a series of postcards home.[65] Jonah's proclamation 'The reeds were wrapped around my head' (Jonah 2.5) is a report from the Reed Sea, the site of the Exodus; his exclamation 'Out of the belly of Sheol I cried' (Jonah 2.2) is written at a stop-off in Sheol or Gehinnom;[66] and the line 'I went down to the bottom of the mountains' (Jonah 2.6) is penned from the foundation stone beneath the Temple Mount in Jerusalem, where he also bumps into the Sons of Korah, who authored some of the psalms.

I choose the *Pirke de Rabbi Eliezer* as the first stop-off in our tour of the distinctiveness of Jewish tradition because it's an appropriately 'foreign', and typically midrashic, place to start. Clearly it goes in a radically different direction to Christian homily and exegesis: it steers clear of the showdown between justice and mercy, universalism and particularism; it counters Jonah the anti-prophet with Jonah the superprophet; and it audaciously and graphically departs

body of Leviathan: either tabernacles (*sukkot*) from his skin, or more commonly a banquet from the monster's flesh. (The idea of an eschatological banquet has its origin in texts like Isaiah 25.6, where the menu consists of *shemanim* (fat things, oozing with goodness) and *shemarim* (plentiful fortified wine made from the lees), but in later apocalypses it comes to include the body of Leviathan who is also to be slaughtered at the end of time (see Isaiah 27.1).) Though it would be wrong to try and systematise Talmudic stories of Leviathan, which often grow from folk culture and then are read back into the Bible, it presents an intriguing view of a present in which God tolerates the chaos monster (and even plays with him according to Psalm 104.26), but restrains him, and ultimately promises that evil will be literally consumed and chaos subdued in the apocalyptic climax of the Leviathan banquet. For an illuminating dissection of the body of Leviathan in *Baba Bathra* 74b–75a, see M. Fishbane, 'The Great Dragon Battle and Talmudic Redaction', in *The Exegetical Imagination: On Jewish Thought and Theology* (Cambridge, Mass.: Harvard University Press, 1998), pp. 41–55. References to the popular image of the Leviathan banquet can also be found in *Song of Songs Rabbah* 1.4; Ethiopian Enoch 40.7–9; 4 Ezra 6.49–52; and *The Apocalypse of Baruch* 29.4 – see A. Jellinek (trans.), *Bet ha Midrash* VI (Jerusalem: Wahrman Books, 1967), p. 150, 'Leviathan Banquet'.

65 The tradition of Jonah's fabulous journey probably comes from the Targum's translation of סוף (*suf*, 'reeds') as an abbreviation of the 'Sea of Reeds' or the Red Sea (cf. Aquila's *eruthra* (*thalassa*)). For discussion, see E. Levine, *The Aramaic Version of Jonah*, pp. 75–6.

66 In the Hebrew Bible, the dead all go, without distinction between good and evil, to Sheol, the place of shades, or shadowy non-existence. But in later Judaism, as in Christianity, Sheol becomes less shadowy and more defined and merges with the more recognisably hellish site of Gehinnom (for an outline of the dimensions of Gehinnom, see *b. Shab.* 152–53a).

from the expected storyline, without apology – in fact advertising its departure – by diving down into a kind of Judaised *Twenty Thousand Leagues under the Sea*. Like the readings of the Fathers, the *Pirke de Rabbi Eliezer* is clearly on a collision course with post-Enlightenment rationality: it seems to exemplify the absurdity that Calvin would have deemed 'frivolous' and 'puerile', and I have done nothing but exacerbate this with my Itzik Manger-ish[67] images of Jonah with tights and leotard and a giant 'S' on his chest, postcards home, and *schul*-submarines. And the strange cultural waters in which it fishes only compounds the sense of foreignness: though they are no more alien to the book of Jonah than Christ's tomb, the Good Samaritan, Romans 3.29, and European anti-Semitism, when motifs like the *Even Shethiyah*, the fish with eye-windows, Leviathan, and the messianic feast of the righteous are washed up on the shores of contemporary 'scholarly' consciousness, they seem like interpretative flotsam, primitive exotica, something to bring a fascinated smile to the face of the colonial anthropologist.

But although it seems like a fabulous foreign ocean teeming with exotic cultural life, the *Pirke de Rabbi Eliezer* is a profoundly religious text that links the book of Jonah to the apocalyptic defeat of chaos by Go(o)d. Jonah (like the readers of the midrash) lives in a time when a hook has not yet been put through the body of chaos that disturbs the world, but where everything – biblical characters, ritual, memory – is working to that (assured) end. With an ebullience that is reminiscent of the Mainstream, it celebrates the power of God that brings the sailors to their knees,[68] and proclaims God's future victory. In the meantime it offers the reassurance that chaos is

---

67 Itzik Manger (1901–69) was a Romanian-born Yiddish poet who lived in Poland, France, Great Britain, and later the United States. His novel *The Book of Paradise: The Wonderful Adventures of Shmuel-Aba Abervo* (New York: Hill and Wang, 1965; 1st edn 1939) is an irreverent and affectionate fantasy in which angels get drunk and have double chins, Elijah rants about 'shoshialists', the prostitute Rahab keeps a manicure shop, and the patriarchs live in an elitist suburb on Three Patriarch's Allée. In Manger's vision, paradise is like the shtetl crossed with the secular modern world.

68 'The sailors saw all the signs, the miracles, and the great wonders which the Holy One, blessed be He, did unto Jonah, and they stood and cast away every one his god, as it is said, "They that regard lying vanities forsake their own shame" [Jonah 2.8]. They returned to Joppa and went up to Jerusalem and circumcised the flesh of their foreskins, as it is said, "And the men feared the Lord exceedingly; and they offered a sacrifice to the Lord" [Jonah 1.16].' According to the *Pirke de Rabbi Eliezer* and *Midrash Jonah* the repentance of the sailors is linked to the thirteenth benediction of the Amidah (the core prayer in the daily service) that asks God to have mercy on 'the righteous, on the pious, on Israel's elders, on its remaining sages, on sincere converts, and on us'.

intimidated by obedience and the seal of the covenant with Abraham, and it anchors the reader, like Jonah on his underwater tour, in the security of the recitation (or re-visiting) of tradition.

But the main value of this midrash, at least for my purposes, is the way it proffers itself as a graphic midrashic demo- or teaching-text – a midrash on midrash in a sense. In *Bavli* (*Menahot* 29a), Moses turns up at the Academy of Rabbi Akiva (though he doesn't understand a word of what is going on), as if to demonstrate the intimate relationship between biblical text and house of study which is intrinsic to midrash.[69] Similarly, the way in which the fish's belly becomes a *schul* and Jonah by implication becomes a rabbi/scholar who needs nothing so much as a good light (to study by?) graphically demonstrates how midrash opens the biblical text up into a place for study. Just as the fish's belly becomes a synagogue, or *bet-midrash*, so the narrative in the *Pirke de Rabbi Eliezer* conveniently 'houses' the distinct features of midrashic writing. With its monsters, its fish-hooks-through-lips, and its flashed (circumcised) penises, it demonstrates the midrashic tendency to seize on and embellish the physical, as opposed to the Christian tendency to veer towards abstraction.[70] And by diving beneath the surface meaning in such a sensational way, it illustrates the exuberant hermeneutic opportunism by which stories spawn more stories, and any grammatical quirk, inconsistency, or lacuna, becomes the excuse for another narrative. Spying a small (half a centimetre?) space between Jonah 1.13, where the

[69] As Philip Alexander points out, the anecdote about Moses not understanding the teaching of the school of Rabbi Akiva is a quintessential rabbinic anecdote in that it can be turned and turned in all directions. It may be a joke by members of another school on the complicated nature of Akiva's teaching (so complex that even Moses can't understand it) and/or – and perhaps this is more likely – it may be a statement that Torah has evolved, and legitimately evolved, so much since Sinai that if Moses were to come back he would hardly recognise it. To compound the puzzle, Moses's mind is set at rest when Akiva tells him that his teaching is all Oral Torah (or literally *Halakhah le-Mosheh mi-Sinai*): it is justified as a tradition which Moses himself has passed on. This raises, then, a third possibility, that the anecdote is an attack (or a joke) on the idea of Oral Torah – the traditions of Moses which Moses himself is unfamiliar with – a typical rabbinic joke in that it exploits the tensions between biblical ur-text, and the interpretations that come 'from' it. (For a description of Oral Torah, see n. 31; for a discussion of rabbinic joking, see n. 83. I am grateful to Philip Alexander for turning over the ambivalence of this passage in private correspondence.)

[70] Two excellent recent studies that turn Augustine's accusation that the Jews are 'indisputably carnal' back on itself, and explore the physicality of Talmudic tradition, are D. Boyarin, *Carnal Israel: Reading Sex in Talmudic Culture* (Berkeley: University of California Press, 1993), and D. Biale, *Eros and the Jews: From Biblical Israel to Contemporary America* (New York: Basic Books, 1992).

sailors try to row back to shore, and 1.15, where they throw Jonah overboard, the *Pirke de Rabbi Eliezer* crams in the following dunking drama:

> [The sailors] took [Jonah] and [cast him into the sea] up to his knee joints, and the storm abated. They took him up again to themselves and the sea became agitated again against them. They cast him in up to his navel, and the sea-storm abated. Again they took him up among themselves and the sea again was agitated against them. They cast him in up to his neck and the sea-storm abated. Once more they lifted him up in their midst and the sea was again agitated against them, until they cast him in entirely and forthwith the sea-storm abated, as it is said 'So they took Jonah and cast him forth into the sea and the sea ceased from her raging.' (Jonah 1.15)

The expansion, which goes through the process limb by limb, body part by body part, demonstrates the elasticity of midrash, its exuberant 'prolongation of scriptural speech through the exegetical imagination'.[71] It also graphically externalises the fear of the sailors, as they find themselves not only caught up in a game of cat and mouse between Jonah and God, but also trapped in a Catch-22 situation between Jonah's death and their own.[72] The virtually vaudeville scene where the sailors try to negotiate and get Yhwh to settle for a piece of the prophet, and give up only when he refuses to settle even for Jonah from the head down, dramatically illustrates the delicateness of their position. The sailors are, quite literally, testing the waters of Yhwh's mercy, and, finding them to be turbulent and unrelenting, reluctantly drop Jonah into the sea.

But what is the sea in the *Pirke de Rabbi Eliezer*? Not just a place where, as Herman Melville puts it, 'one can have one's hands among the unspeakable foundations, ribs and very pelvis of the world',[73] but a place where one can visit and probe the ribs and landmarks of Jewish/biblical tradition. In other words, like the fish-schul, it is an image of midrash, a place where past meets present, where Jonah the Hebrew becomes a 'Jew' – just as in other midrashim Abraham bakes matzot for Passover and Moses goes to the yeshiva – and where, in one fabulous synchrony, symbols from a biblical past (Jerusalem, Exodus, the Sons of Korah) lap up against symbols of a

---

[71] Fishbane, *The Exegetical Imagination*, p. 2.

[72] In the biblical text the sailors cry to God, 'We beseech you, O Lord, let us not perish for this man's life, and lay not on us innocent blood, for you, O Lord, have done as it pleased you' (Jonah 1.14). They are concerned not to be found guilty of murder, and the *Pirke de Rabbi Eliezer* simply 'performs' this concern.

[73] H. Melville, *Moby Dick* (Ware, Hertfordshire: Wordsworth, 1992), p. 135.

Jewish present (circumcision, the synagogue, the messianic feast of the righteous). If the role of interpretation, as the Jewish mystics said, is to create a huge glossed living space, a new heaven and earth for human habitation,[74] here we seem to have a whole ocean. And Jonah's grand tour – where each line from his psalm is anchored in a different biblical scene, and elements of tradition are connected in a fabulous itinerary – vividly literalises the midrashic tendency to conduct fabulous intertextual tours, and to explore new routes 'from the Torah to the Prophets and the Prophet to the Writings'.[75] Midrash is a generative space where words and passages are strung together like beads or pearls on a string and where words as raw material are combined in new, often seemingly infeasible ways. The *Pirke de Rabbi Eliezer* is typically midrashic because, in the process of weaving in and out of fragments of the book of Jonah, it strings them together with extracts from Job, 2 Kings, Psalms, Micah, Exodus, and Isaiah.

One thing Jonah is compared to, at least by implication, is a scholar or interpreter or rabbi. Not only does his chief need in the belly of the fish appear to be an angle-poise lamp, but his marvellous exploits within the text seem to mirror the interpreters' triumphant exploits in, through, and over the text-as-text. At the beginning of the *Pirke de Rabbi Eliezer* we find Jonah, as midrashist within the midrash, surveying the biblical corpus and trying to find an (inter-pretative) space to move into. Resolved to flee from Yhwh, he decides that he cannot go anywhere on earth because 'the whole earth is full of his glory' (Isaiah 6.3) and that he cannot go to the heavens because 'Above the heavens is his glory' (Psalm 113.4), and so he flees to the only place where opposing prooftexts do not

---

[74] Fishbane, *The Exegetical Imagination*, p. 2.

[75] Strictly speaking, all texts are intertextual, but midrash is emphatically so, referring to itself as 'stringing (like beads or pearls) the words of Torah together . . . from the Torah to the Prophets and the Prophets to the Writings' (*Song of Songs Rabbah*, cited in D. Boyarin, *Intertextuality and the Reading of Midrash*, p. 109). As Daniel Boyarin puts it, the words of Torah are literally raw material in that 'The verses of the Bible function for the rabbis much as do words in ordinary speech. They are the repertoire of semiotic elements that can be recombined in new discourse, just as words are recombined constantly into new discourse' (*Intertextuality and the Reading of Midrash*, p. 28). Not only does midrash operate on the general principle that 'the words of Torah are rich in their own context [lit. in their place] and rich in another context' (*Yer. Rosh Hashanah* 58d), but it also sets itself the task of stringing the most unlikely texts together. It is common for a midrash on a particular biblical passage to open with a totally different (and seemingly unconnected) text as if stranding itself in the forest of Torah, and then setting itself the task of finding its way home, through analogy and wit, like a homing pigeon.

harangue him, the sea.[76] Admittedly, like all (desperate) interpreters he finds that you have to exclude some texts to get the meaning you want, or need, and he strategically averts his eyes from texts like Psalm 139 and Zechariah 4.10. Thus he becomes an image of the rabbis, strategically trying to negotiate their way around a dense space of words and quotations which both restrict room for man-oeuvre and offer up endless new possibilities.

In the self-consciously textual world of midrash, words become virtually physical objects: pearls on a string, shuttlecocks, objects that can be 'turned and turned' because everything, potentially, is contained within them and every word contains 'at least three score and ten topsytypical readings'.[77] They must be felt, 'kneaded', tested, 'tried in all possible positions, in the most varied locutions, turned round to show all their facets in the hope that a gleam will break forth' or a 'meaning twinkle'.[78] Words can be obstacles in your path that need to be strategically negotiated, or parcels so densely packed with meaning that you need to go at them with tweezers. No vowel, consonant, or suffix is superfluous: if you pick at the word שכרה (*sekarah*) in the phrase 'and Jonah paid her [i.e. the ship's] fare' (Jonah 1.3) for example, you can find a whole story packed in miniature, in the ה (the letter *heh*). And if you look closely and follow the directions of the Talmud and the medieval interpreter Rashi, you will see that the suffix clearly means that Jonah not only paid in advance, but that he paid the ship's whole fare.[79] Similarly if you get the midrashic eye-glass out to the phrase 'the ship' in Jonah 1.4 and train it on the definite article (again coincidentally a *heh*), you

---

[76] This is very different to the Mainstream, where Jonah is smugly castigated for not knowing that God is everywhere.

[77] One rabbi says of Torah, 'Turn it and turn it for everything is in it' (*Pirke Avot* 5.27); the word for turn here is הפך, the same word on which the book of Jonah turns (see the following discussion of Jonah 3.4). Words are described as shuttlecocks in *Pesikta Rabbati* (*Piska* 3): 'Like a shuttlecock flying back and forth, or like a ball that children play catch with – one tosses it here and another tosses it there – so words fly back and forth when the wise come into a house of study and discuss Torah, one stating his view, and another stating his view, still another stating his view, and another stating a different view.' They are described as pearls on a string in *Song of Songs Rabbah* (see n. 75 above). The allusion to 'topsytypical readings' comes from James Joyce, self-styled Jew-in-training, in *Finnegan's Wake* (New York: Viking, 1966), p. 20.

[78] V. Jankélevitch, *Quelque part dans l'inachevé* (Paris: Gallimard, 1978), pp. 18–19.

[79] *B. Nedarim* 38a, followed by Rashi (cf. L. Ginzburg, *The Legends of the Jews* I (Philadelphia: Jewish Publication Society, 1909–38), p. 247). (Rashi is an acronym for Rabbi Solomon ben Isaac (1040–1105), the most influential of the medieval Jewish commentators. He wrote two commentaries, one on the Talmud and the other on the Bible, and wrote in such a concise manner that legend has it that 'in Rashi's time every drop of ink was a precious stone'.)

will see a whole fabulous storm scene being played out. To the trained eye, the article is meaning-ful, in fact meaning-crammed – according to the *Pirke de Rabbi Eliezer* it means that Yhwh sent a storm that was concentrated on *the* ship, the *one* ship, and that this ship was tossed and buffeted while others sailed blithely past.[80] Both *heh*s are condensed clues, and both, when unravelled, result in stories that compliment, and inflate, hints in the biblical text. In the biblical text Jonah is anxious to flee; in the midrash he pays the ship's whole fare to escape; in the biblical text God relentlessly pursues and targets Jonah; in the midrash, he sends a storm cloud that doggedly attaches itself to just one vessel. The midrashic tendency, as with the anxious dunking of Jonah, is to inflate textual elements that are already there. (In a similar vein, *Midrash Jonah* opens up the bigness of Nineveh to phenomenal – and labyrinthine – proportions: 'Nineveh was forty parasangs square.[81] In it were twelve streets, in every street were 12,000 people and every street had two market-places, and every marketplace had twelve corridors, and every corridor had twelve courts, and every court had twelve houses, and in every house were twelve strong men, and every strong man had twelve sons.')

But the prize for the most fabulous expansion from a single letter (yet again a *heh*) goes to another expansion. In Jonah 1.17 the fish is masculine הדג (*ha-dag*) and in 2.1 it is feminine הדגה (*ha-dagah*), although this is probably not so much an early attempt at inclusive language in the Hebrew Bible as a scribal error. But in *Midrash Jonah* the extra ה (*heh*, the feminine suffix) is unravelled into a fabulous tale of *two* fishes. Jonah is first swallowed by a male fish, but after three days, when he still has not shown any signs of remorse, the Holy One concludes that the belly must be 'too roomy' and that the prophet is not 'anxious' enough to pray. This most Calvinesque and right-wing of midrashim begins to suspect that fish-belly prisons are too comfortable, that they have too many televisions and snooker tables, and that the regime must be made harsher and more punitive. So Yhwh has Jonah moved to a smaller cell, in a block with no day

---

[80] 'They had travelled one day's journey, and a mighty tempest on the sea arose against them on their right hand and on their left hand; but the movement of all the ships passing to and fro was peaceful in a quiet sea.' The scene is reminiscent of the suffering of Job, where every conceivable disaster – Chaldeans, Sabeans, lightning, whirlwind, skin disease – all converge on the single man.

[81] A parasang is a phenomenal unit of measurement: a modern equivalent would be a light year.

visitors and restricted privileges – or in the midrash's terms, he has him swallowed by 'a pregnant fish, with 365,000 small fish in it' so that he will 'become afraid and pray to me'. A female fish swims up alongside the male fish and tells him that she has been appointed to 'swallow the man, the prophet, that is in [his] body' and (perhaps hormonally agitated from her pregnancy) snaps that if he does not spit him out forthwith, she will simply swallow both the fish and the prophet wholesale. The male fish promptly spits Jonah out, the pregnant fish swallows him, and, cramped among the 365,000 baby fish and 'very much afraid because of the dirt and refuse', Jonah yields up to God the 'prayers of the righteous' which God 'desires'. As the contemporary Jewish writer Norma Rosen puts it: 'There he felt the squeeze. There he felt what narrowness is'[82] – though there is evidently something joking as well as punitive about all this.[83]

Because they are so aware of the punning potential of words – the way in which they can be held between thumb and forefinger and lovingly rotated, the way in which they can be unhinged from their obvious sense, or unravelled through various loopholes – the rabbis are also sensitive to similar rotations/unravellings in biblical texts. Jewish interpreters tend to zone in on Jonah 3.4, where Jonah pronounces God's verdict on Nineveh: נינוה נהפכת or 'Nineveh will be overthrown/overturned'. The irony is that the Hebrew verb הפך (*hfk*), 'to overturn', can also be turned over to mean the very opposite – i.e. that Nineveh will be 'turned around'. Thus the word that Jonah is given is a hinged word, a curse-blessing, a word that declines to fulfil its obvious referential responsibilities, a word that booms 'Nineveh will be destroyed', then, when no one is listening any longer, whispers the parenthesis '(or restored)'. The writers of the Talmud appreciate that this would have been rather disorientating for Jonah: 'Jonah was originally told that Nineveh would be turned, but did not know whether for good or for evil.'[84] Rashi notes that if the real meaning of the oracle is present but craftily hidden

---

[82] N. Rosen, 'Jonah: Justice for Jonah, or a Bible Bartleby', in D. Rosenburg (ed.), *Congregation: Contemporary Jewish Writers Read the Jewish Bible* (New York and London: Harcourt Brace Jovanovich, 1987), pp. 222–31 (226).

[83] As James Kugel has argued, there is 'often something a bit joking about midrash', and the ultimate subject of that joke is the 'dissonance between the religion of the rabbis and the Book from which it is supposed to be derived' (J. L. Kugel, 'Two Introductions to Midrash', in G. Hartman and S. Budick (eds.), *Midrash and Literature* (New York: Yale University Press, 1986), pp. 77–103 (80)).

[84] *B. Sanhedrin* 89b.

from Jonah, then Yhwh is only fulfilling his contract with the prophets not to do anything without telling them first (Amos 3.7), in the most cursory and playful sense. Like the Delphic oracle that seems to encourage Croesus to attack the Persians by telling him that if he does 'he will destroy a great empire' (but omits to mention that that 'great empire' will be his own),[85] Yhwh speaks a cryptic word that means destruction-salvation. In certain mystical texts, this becomes a prooftext for the way in which the real meanings of Tanakh whisper, flirt with, and tantalise the mystic, and lie concealed within the surface text like the kernel within the shell.[86]

The image of Jonah caught up in a divine word, like someone trapped in revolving doors, elicits a certain sympathy for the prophet. And this vein of empathy with Jonah, *as human being, prophet, and as member of a people,* is an integral part of Jewish interpretation. The Mainstream tends either to repress Jonah's suffering and repeated death-wishes, or to play up his torture for purely disciplinary purposes (though Luther does let slip the idea that God seems to toy cruelly with Jonah as a plaything, before he hastily clears his throat, apologises, and gets on with the sermon). But Jewish interpretation, in contrast, describes at great length the suffering of Jonah's sun-and-fish-tormented flesh, often by way of a gloss on Jonah 4.3 and 4.8, and by way of an explanation of *why* he feels that it is 'better to die than to live'. *Midrash Jonah* speculates that 'because of the great heat in the belly of the fish', Jonah's 'clothing, jacket and hair must have been all burned up, and flies, mosquitoes and ants would have settled on him and irritated his raw flesh'. Maharai Kara and Abraham Ibn Ezra imagine Jonah's skin, raw from the effect of fishy gastric juices, salt water, and belly heat, being fried under the heat of the sun applied in chapter 4, and Radak imagines that Jonah's sufferings were so intense that he almost died.[87] Whereas Christian interpretation seems interested in pur-

---

[85] Herodotus, *The Histories* (trans. A. de Selincourt, intro. A. R. Burn; Harmondsworth: Penguin, 1972), p. 60. I am grateful to Loveday Alexander for drawing my attention to this analogy.

[86] Drawing an implicit analogy between the prophet and contemporary readers of the Torah, the kabbalist R. Moshe Chaim Luzatto (1707–46), uses this text to explain 'how it is possible for a prophet to comprehend the truth of his prophecy . . . yet not to perceive all of the (hidden, later to be understood) truths which may be included in it' (*Derek Hashem* III 4.7; cited in N. Scherman and M. Zlotowitz, *Jonah: A New Translation with a Commentary Anthologised from Talmudic, Midrashic and Rabbinic Sources* (Artscroll Tanakh Series; New York: Mesorah Publications, 1988), p. 121).

[87] Mahari Kara (Rav Yosef Kara, *c.* 1060–1130), Abraham Ibn Ezra (1089–1164) and Radak

suing the literalism of the text in one (Puseyish) sense only, and wants to know whether there is a 'big fish' capable of swallowing a man, and whether the world of the Bible and the world of hard-core fact can comfortably co-exist, Jewish interpretation chases the literal implications down far more disturbing avenues.[88] The exquisite awfulness of Jonah's skin complaint takes him to the very dermatological depths of suffering in the Hebrew Bible – alongside Job (scraping his loathsome sores with a potsherd), and the sufferers of Lamentations with their skin hot, dry, shrivelled, and blackened by famine. As the adversary in Job knows, to really get at a human being, you must get under their skin (Job 2.4–5). And the spectacle of Jonah-Job makes the all-too-human, skin-cased reader want to rush in with bottles of aloe vera, or soothing, cooling calamine lotion.

Thus the midrashic superstructure erected around the text begins to provide solid textual justification for Jonah's dissidence and Jonah's cries. And while the Mainstream is busy stacking up accusing adjectives and cramming Jonah's psyche with poisonous xenophobic thoughts, Jewish interpretation is entering the textual maze from Jonah's (as well as Yhwh's) side. From the very first, it is less concerned to spin off into homiletic riffs on the perils of disobedience, and more concerned to analyse *why* Jonah ran away. One answer lies in the riddles of prophecy and the way in which prophecy, by definition, is a self-defeating career. According to the

---

(Rabbi David Kimhi, 1160–1235?) are all medieval Jewish commentators. Compare the comments of Eliezer of Beaugency who glosses Jonah's protest in 4.2–3 as '*I struggled and broke my body and had my strength exhausted along the way for nothing*, for I realized that you would renounce evil without repentance' (*Kommentar zu Ezechiel und den XII kleinen Propheten* (ed. S. Poznanski; Warsaw: Mekize Nirdamim, 1909), p. 159, cited by and trans. A. Cooper, 'In Praise of Divine Caprice: The Significance of the Book of Jonah', in P. R. Davies and D. J. A. Clines (eds.), *Among the Prophets: Language, Image and Structure in the Prophetic Writings* (Sheffield: Sheffield Academic Press, 1993), pp. 145–63 (154); my italics).

[88] Although there is no discussion, to my knowledge, of the impact of the fish-trauma on Jonah's flesh in Christian tradition, it is striking that in early to medieval Christian iconography Jonah is always bald. The *Dictionary of Biblical Tradition in English Literature* catalogues several instances in art and literature from the early Christian period to the twelfth century (H. Sumerfield, L. Ryken, and L. Eldredge, 'Jonah', in D. L. Jeffrey (ed.), *A Dictionary of Biblical Tradition in English Literature* (Grand Rapids, Mich.: Eerdmans, 1992), pp. 409–11), and David Clines remarks on the curious baldness of Jonah, adding that 'there is a PhD thesis topic here, one feels' (D. J. A. Clines, *The Bible in the Modern World* (Sheffield: Sheffield Academic Press, 1997), p. 38). Although it may not be enough to spin a PhD out of, it seems to me that Jonah's hair-loss is due to the imagined impact of fishy fluids on his flesh, and that there is some cultural leakage between the Christian and the Jewish on this point.

neat binary logic of Deuteronomy 18.21–2, a true prophet's prophecies come true, and a false prophet's prophecies do not, but the
prophet with his wits about him realises that he is caught in a
revolving aporia, whereby negative predictions ideally have the
performative function of annulling themselves. In other words, the
riddling word הפך (*hfk*), which twists from curse to blessing, is not an
aberration so much as a visual demonstration, in microcosm, of
what should *ideally* happen with negative prophetic words. The irony
is cleverly illustrated in a cartoon from *Judaism for Beginners*, with its
punchline 'a good prophet is one who is wrong' (fig. 6). The post-
Enlightenment Mainstream deems Jonah the worst or most reluctant
of the prophets, who is totally upstaged by the real 'prophetic'
persona, the proto-Christian author. But in fact, according to
prophecy's own self-subverting internal logic, Jonah is actually the
best of the prophets because he has a success rate in annulling his
own prophecies that is second to none. Many Jewish interpreters
find it hard not to empathise with a character who does not want to
enter a plot where the words may turn on him, trip him up, and
(mis)represent him as a liar. Jonah is frequently depicted as someone
who has already had a long and unpredictable prophetic career and
is somewhat weary with the inherent instability of his profession.[89]

Another take on prophecy, or *dabar aher* ('something else') as the
midrashists would say: according to a second-century midrash, the
Mekilta de Rabbi Ishmael,[90] representing the interests of God is only
one half of the prophetic job-description. The ideal prophet should
speak for both God and nation (or in the *Mekilta*'s terms for 'father'
and 'son'): he must be prepared to take issue with the son on behalf
of the father *and vice versa*. The ideal prophet, in other words, is a
mediator, a riven figure representing in a single person the site of
arbitration between God and nation. For the *Mekilta*, the exemplary
prophet is 'Jeremiah' (here considered the author of Lamentations)[91]

---

[89] According to the *Pirke de Rabbi Eliezer*, Jonah's mission to the Ninevites is his third prophetic
mission. On the first occasion God sent him to restore the borders of Israel and his words
were fulfilled (cf. 2 Kings 14.25). But on the second occasion he was sent to prophesy the
destruction of Jerusalem, but God in his mercy did not destroy it and the people called him
a lying prophet. Jonah resists his mission because he is already known as a lying prophet in
Israel, and he does not want to have a similar reputation internationally.

[90] The *Mekilta de Rabbi Ishmael* is the earliest midrashic commentary and is based on the book
of Exodus. The relevant passage can be found in Lauterbach (trans.), *Mekilta de Rabbi
Ishmael* (Philadelphia: Jewish Publication Society of America, 1933), tractate *Pisha*, pp. 7–10.

[91] Though early tradition ascribes Lamentations to Jeremiah, the book is in fact a collection of
anonymous laments.

who in Lamentations 3.42 declares to God '*We* have transgressed and rebelled; *you* have not pardoned.' Jeremiah is voted rabbinic Prophet of the Year because he presents the people's protest to God ('you have not pardoned') and God's protest to the people ('you have transgressed and rebelled') in a single hinged sentence that implies that the covenant is being violated *from both sides*. Jonah and Elijah, in contrast, are paraded as examples of prophets whose sentiments are lop-sided. Elijah – the classic blood-and-thunder prophet – is concerned only with justice for the father, ardently proclaiming that 'I am moved [only] by zeal for the Lord, the God of hosts' (1 Kings 19.10); Jonah, in contrast, is exclusively concerned with the son, and flees from God's command because he reasons that 'since the gentiles are more inclined to repent, I might be causing Israel to be condemned'. Logically, Elijah and Jonah should share joint second place, but in fact the distribution of sympathy is not this neat or logical. Whereas the *Mekilta* seems to celebrate the come-uppance of the over-brittle, over-zealous Elijah, it empathetically develops Jonah's story, emphasising his despair and his dark death-wishes, and reporting how *he went to sea to drown himself because he would rather commit suicide than co-operate in Israel's potential destruction.*[92] Whereas Elijah's replacement by Elisha is read, effectively, as Elijah's sacking, Jonah's story is read as the story of a prophet caught in the impossible impasse between disobedience to God and the condemnation (and even the annihilation) of his own nation. In his passion for his people, Jonah is ranked highly in the *Who's Who* of Ancient Israel, alongside Moses (who pleads with the deity: 'If Israel cannot be forgiven erase me from your book' (Exodus 32.32)), David (who takes responsibility upon himself when a plague strikes the nation (2 Samuel 24.17)) and other 'patriarchs and prophets [who] offered their lives on behalf of Israel'.[93]

Like the *Pirke de Rabbi Eliezer*, the *Mekilta* is both foreign and, at the same time, exemplarily midrashic. It seems to empathise with, and

---

[92] To muddy the waters between the Mainstream and the Backwaters, it should be stressed that this defence of Jonah is echoed in certain strands of the Fathers. Rewinding right back to the beginning of the first chapter, we find Jerome, for example, proclaiming that 'Jonah acts thus as a patriot, not so much that he hates the Ninevites, as that he does not want to destroy his own people.' Just as *Midrash Jonah* and the Zohar show Mainstream tendencies, so the Christian Mainstream mimics the Backwater tendency to empathise with Jonah.

[93] This interpretation is adopted by Radak and Ibn Ezra, and also echoed by modern commentators (see Scherman and Zlotowitz, *Jonah*, p. 135).

in fact actively encourage, protest against the deity and to work on the basis that, as Elie Wiesel puts it, 'The Jew may oppose God as long as it is in defence of God's creation.'[94] And it seems to promote rather than to resolve friction, and to embody that friction in the riven persona and speech of the prophet. The statement of 'Jeremiah' in Lamentations 3.42 is ideal precisely because it is aporistic: because the two halves confront one another across the same sentence, the same speaker, and refuse to settle out into a hierarchy or an arbitrated median position. The schizoid persona of Jeremiah becomes the image of the ideal rabbi or student, though in a different sense to the scholar-hero of the *Pirke de Rabbi Eliezer*. Jeremiah-as-rabbi is exemplary because he 'walks' or 'hops'[95] between the opinion of different masters, in this case the father and son, and because he acts as prosecuting attorney for both, pursuing both cases to their disjunctive conclusions. In other words, Jeremiah's sentence is extracted and highlighted by the rabbis as an exemplary image of the *dialogism* or polyphony of midrash,[96] and is read as a (narcissistic?) mirror for students – a meta-textual image of study/interpretation. The implication is that it is like a page of Talmud where voices 'mingle and jostle in the splendour of a wild disorder',[97] and where, in the round-table discussions between the rabbis, an argument that resolves a controversy is called a difficulty (*kushia*), while one that restores a controversy is called a solution (*terutz*). Or again, *it can be compared to* the cacophony of the yeshiva, where students study in pairs and where 'the words of the wise fly back and forth like shuttlecocks, one stating his view, and another stating his view, and still another stating his view and another stating

---

[94] E. Wiesel, *A Jew Today* (New York: Vintage, 1978), p. 135. For a fascinating discussion that traces the motif of arguing with God through the Bible and Talmud, medieval poetry, liturgy, and Hasidic folk-tales and Holocaust poetry, see A. Laytner, *Arguing with God: A Jewish Tradition* (Northvale, N.J.: Jason Aronson, 1990).

[95] Nahman of Bratslav taught that the ideal student should 'make his ears like a hopper' and jump between the opinions of different masters (*Likkutei Moharan* 1.64). That is, he must operate like God, who decrees that the differing opinions of the schools of Hillel and Shammai are both 'words of the living God' (*B. Eruvin* 13b).

[96] In Midrash and Talmud, strangely, dialogue itself is authoritative: one cannot say 'the Talmud says X' or the 'Midrash says Y' so much as 'Rabbi X says, but Rabbi Y says'. Through Franz Rosenzweig's *Philosophie als Dialogik: Philosophie auf dem Boden Neuzeit* and Martin Buber, *Ich und Du*, the term 'dialogism' entered the common philosophical vocabulary of the twentieth century, but the concept is fundamentally Jewish in origin.

[97] Arsène Darmesteter, cited in M. Ouaknin, *The Burnt Book: Reading the Talmud* (trans. L. Brown; Princeton: Princeton University Press, 1995), p. 30.

a different view'.[98] Fascinatingly, this view of Jonah as a text strung out between dissonant inner voices, was revived by the Jewish scholar Etan Levine in the 1980s,[99] though his article was soon swallowed by the voracious, overwhelming Mainstream. Taking issue with the way in which the book has been reduced to 'moralistic tripe of . . . love versus hate, universalism versus tribalism etc.', he argued that the book is an exercise in *situational ethics*.[100] The author, he argues, avoids weighing the dialogue in either Jonah's or God's favour, and deliberately makes God's final point weak, and represses Jonah's answer, in order to keep the tension alive. Thus the reader has no alternative but to hop, and to keep hopping, between the dissonant inner trilogy of Jonah's view (that evil must be punished), God's position (that repentance warrants forgiveness), and the view of the author (aka the 'Thinker') who is 'more disturbed by the philosophical problem than he was convinced of the concrete answer'.[101]

Postmodernism and midrash do not always see eye to eye; after all, two parties are involved, and it seems to be absolutely intrinsic to both that, as Levinas puts it, 'as soon as two are involved everything is in danger'.[102] But where they map onto one another most effectively is in their joint tendency to fight shy of the universal, which runs the risk of 'evaporating' if not embodied in a particular instance,[103] and to refuse to yield themselves to disembodied truths and an abstract, transcendent 'metalanguage of meaning'.[104] According to Levinas, rabbinic discourse actively pursues 'the precise moment in which the general principle runs the risk of its opposite' – a principle that we have already seen demonstrated in the discussion of Jonah-as-prophet. For while it would seem that it is the general duty of the prophet to obey without question and deliver God's message, Jonah's particular story seems to deconstruct this central premise, and virtually vindicate him in his act of

---

[98] *Pesikta Rabbati, Piska* 3.

[99] E. Levine, 'Jonah as a Philosophical Book', *Zeitschrift für die alttestamentliche Wissenschaft* 96 (1984), pp. 235–45.

[100] *Ibid.*, p. 244.

[101] *Ibid.*, p. 243.

[102] Levinas, 'Toward the Other', in Aronowicz, *Nine Talmudic Readings*, pp. 12–29 (16).

[103] A. Aronowicz, 'Introduction' to *Nine Talmudic Readings*, p. xxix.

[104] J. Genot-Bismuth observes that 'Talmudic rabbinical thinking loathes the metalanguage of meaning. In vain will one seek to find the expounding of a principle, even less of a theory' ('De l'idée juive du sens', in *Hommage à G. Vajda* (Louvain: 1980), pp. 105, 116, cited in Ouaknin, *The Burnt Book*, p. 66).

resistance. The injunction 'Jonah should have delivered God's message' is besieged and interrogated by the counter-injunction 'Jonah should not have delivered God's message', and the conflict between them is rotated, in condensed form, in all the complexities of the turning word הפך (*hfk*). Jonah is not read as Anyprophet or Everyprophet, but is habitually read as *this* prophet, in *this* plot and *this* situation. Similarly, the Ninevites *tend* not to be read as a huge globalised abstraction – the Nations, or the Gentiles – but, at least from the medieval period onwards, are located specifically as the 'Assyrians'.

This is a crucial twist, because Assyria plays a key role in the (his)story of the Hebrew Bible: it is the Empire responsible for the exile and dispersal of the northern kingdoms of Israel and Samaria in the eighth century BCE and the unsuccessful siege of Jerusalem in the southern kingdom of Judah. But it not just a political player whose role can be exhaustively rendered by historiography or by the archaeological exhibits in the Louvre or the British Museum; it also has a rich metaphorical life in the densely allusive story that the Hebrew Bible tells about itself. Within the Bible's own narrative web, Assyria features, as (among other things) the swarm of (killer) bees that Yhwh whistles for from across the river (Isaiah 7.18); the razor that God uses to shave the nation's genitalia and expose its shame to the world (Isaiah 7.20); the rod of God's anger and the staff of his fury (Isaiah 10.5, cf. 13.5) and the force that devours the surrounding countryside, leaving Jerusalem tottering like a pathetic allotment hut (Isaiah 1.8). And Assyrians can typically be found striding through the biblical corpus, hands on hips, plaguing Judaean Kings with taunts like: 'I will give you two thousand horses, if you are able to set riders on them' (Isaiah 36.8) and proclaiming to the inhabitants of Jerusalem, in the Judaean tongue, with loud-speaker, that they are destined to 'eat their own dung and drink their own urine' (Isaiah 36.12). In early (seventh century BCE) biblical literature Nineveh is the 'bloody city, full of lies and booty' (Nahum 3.1) and the lion that tears its prey, brings back enough torn flesh for its whelps (Nahum 2.11–12); in later apocryphal literature (post 200 BCE) it becomes detached from its specific historic referent, and floats free as a cipher for Every-enemy (including the Babylonians and the Persians): thus the book of Tobit foregrounds the Assyrian threat to the national body, and depicts the righteous Tobit relishing and anticipating the bloody judgement of Nineveh predicted by

Nahum;[105] the book of Judith conflates the Assyrians with the ultimate aggressor against Judah, the Babylonians, as the generic 'enemy';[106] and 2 Esdras sees the Assyrians as the quintessential 'wicked nation' (2 Esdras 2.8). Assyria functions essentially as an icon of the 'threat to Israel's existence',[107] and in the wish-fulfilment world of the Hebrew Bible both Jerusalem's survival of the siege and the destruction of Nineveh in 612 BCE are heightened and revelled in through extension-by-metaphor and miracle. An angel of the Lord slays eighty-five thousand Assyrians in an evening, thus putting a rather decisive stop to the siege (Isaiah 37.36–8); and Nineveh is raided by Yhwh the divine 'shatterer' and his troops, with their cracking whips, rumbling wheels, and chariots like fire, or lightning or flame. In the gloating book of Nahum, recording the destruction of Nineveh in 612 BCE, Nineveh-as-water dissipates and disappears; Nineveh-as-woman is raped, her skirts lifted up, and filth thrown upon her (in punishment for her previous shaving activities); and 'all who hear of the news of her destruction 'clap their hands over [her]/ for upon whom has not come [her] unceasing evil?' (Nahum 3.19).

Clearly 'Assyria'/Nineveh is no neutral signifier, like Jericho or Megiddo, and contemporary commentators are perhaps not too far off the mark when they suggest that its meaning is not dissimilar to the Berlin of the Third Reich.[108] In the emphatically intertextual

---

[105] See Tobit 14.3–4. The book of Tobit depicts Nineveh as the iconically evil city: imagining the consequences of Isaiah 37.36–8 it describes how the Assyrian king, thwarted in his attempts to capture Jerusalem, returns to Nineveh and (like a typical Assyrian) slays many of the exiled Israelites and throws the corpses over the city walls (see Tobit 1.17–18). For a fascinating discussion of the way in which the book of Tobit foregrounds anxieties over the vulnerability of the national body in exile, see A.-J. Levine, 'Diaspora as Metaphor: Bodies and Boundaries in the Book of Tobit', in J. A. Overman and R. S. MacLennan (eds.), *Diaspora Jews and Judaism: Essays in Honour of, and in Dialogue with, A. Thomas Kraabel* (Diaspora Jews and Judaism 41; Atlanta: Scholar's Press, 1992), pp. 105–17.

[106] The central catastrophe that shapes much of the literature of the Hebrew Bible is the Babylonian Exile (580s BCE): the destruction of Jerusalem and the temple by the Babylonians under Nebuchadnezzar and a series of deportations of the upper classes of Judah to Babylon. Fascinatingly, the apocryphal book of Judith (written around the middle of the second century BCE) conflates the two exiles: it begins 'In the twelfth year of the reign of Nebuchadnezzar, who ruled over the Assyrians in the great city of Nineveh . . .' (Judith 1.1).

[107] J. S. Ackerman, 'Jonah', in R. Alter and F. Kermode (eds.), *The Literary Guide to the Bible* (London: Fontana, 1989), pp. 234–43 (244).

[108] Though I have certain reservations about this analogy, which tends to be somewhat overplayed, Lacocque and Lacocque have no such reservations: for them Nineveh is 'as *gemütlich* as a Gestapo torture chamber', 'the concentration camp for God's people', inhabited by the 'barbarian killers of Israel's children'; Jonah is like 'the Auschwitz survivor' who understandably would not want to 'go to Berchtesgaden or Berlin carrying God's salvation'; and 'Jonah's theology cannot reconcile a God who stands in covenant

world of Jewish interpretation, the larger biblical narrative about
Assyria spills into, and informs, the book of Jonah: Rashi identifies
the anonymous 'King of Nineveh' as Sennacherib, the ruler of
Assyria during the time of the destruction of the northern kingdom
and the siege of the south;[109] and the medieval commentator
Mahari Kara reads the 'wickedness of Nineveh' in Jonah 1.2 as the
wickedness that the Assyrians are *about* to commit against the
northern kingdom of Israel. Clearly the book situates itself in a time
before the destruction of Nineveh: before the 'bloody city' disintegrated into a pool of water or blood. But if this book belongs to a
time when the Assyrians were, or were about to be, killer-bees and
staves of Yhwh's aggression, then this makes Jonah's commission the
more perverse. Jonah is called to help Yhwh to spare the Assyrians,
who will then go on to bring destruction, humiliation, on his own
people. That is, he is called to participate in a plot designed to defeat
himself – self as nation as well as self as prophet. Just as the plot
seems to intensify and highlight all the self-defeating ambiguities of
prophecy, so, on a much larger and more momentous scale, it places
Jonah/Israel in a profoundly self-defeating, self-imploding storyline.
Christian interpretation has always acknowledged the strange twist
that makes the protagonist the victim of the plot, but has banalised
and politicised this curious phenomenon as the story of the-Jew-
who-gets-egg-on-his-face. But reading Nineveh not as the exemplary
'gentiles' (so precariously close to repentance that the slightest whiff
of an oracle will tip them over), but as 'the Assyrians' (so precariously
close to destroying the northern kingdom of Israel) entirely alters the
distribution of the text and brings the implied masochism of the plot
into stark relief. The book can no longer be resolved into a simple
morality play based around a triangulation of Jew, God, and gentile,
but becomes a tortuous labyrinth of argument and counterargument.
And the case for the prophet resisting the father on behalf of the son
becomes not only feasible but compelling. Many Jewish interpreters

with the SS' (A. Lacocque and P.-E. Lacocque, *The Jonah Complex* (Atlanta: John Knox,
1981), pp. 19, 56, 68, 80).
[109] Another tradition has it that the Pharaoh of the Exodus was the King of Nineveh. Though
the *Pirke de Rabbi Eliezer* cuts off its excursus on Jonah before Jonah gets to Nineveh, the
Ninevites are discussed in chapter 43 under the theme of repentance. And the reason that
they repent so quickly is that Pharaoh knows of God's power and – stunned by memories
of frogs, boils, locusts, and rivers of blood – understandably wants to avoid a second,
perhaps fatal, round with Yhwh. Identifying the king as Pharaoh is a way of explaining the
speed and scale of repentance. But it also (inadvertently?) reinforces the sense that
Nineveh is the locus of evil, the home of Israel's oppressors.

find themselves empathising with and reinforcing the 'protests in Jonah's heart'.[110] Even in one of the more orthodox of contemporary Jewish commentary series, you can find the statement that 'Jonah's objections have validity, because the continued existence of Nineveh would result in harm to Israel', as well as the disturbing speculation that had Jonah not preached to Nineveh, the Assyrians would have been too wicked to have been used as the 'whip' with which Israel would be punished.[111]

This contrast between Jewish commentaries that empathise with a prophet who (having pre-read his Bible) is justifiably traumatised by his mission to the Assyrians, and Christian commentaries that regularly discipline and dismiss Jonah as errant pupil, points to a fundamental distinction between 'the Jewish' and 'the Christian'. Jews *can* oppose God as long as it is in defence of God's creation, and Jewish interpreters continue to take up this prerogative, though with increasing discomfort, right up to the text's strange vegetable-parable finale. When God uses a *qal va homer* (literally a 'little' and a 'large')[112] to compare his feelings for Nineveh to Jonah's feelings for the *qiqayon* plant (Jonah 4.10–11) he is less likely to be saying that Jonah is emotionally attached to plant-life, just as he is emotionally attached to Nineveh, than that he finds Nineveh useful, just as Jonah finds the *qiqayon* useful.[113] The utility of Nineveh to God can be

---

[110] The phrase is from Isaac ben Judah Abravanel (1437–1508), whose reading is discussed in more detail below. Abravanel was one of the first Jewish scholars to be influenced by humanism and the ideas of the Renaissance; his commentary on the minor prophets was published in 1505.

[111] Scherman and Zlotowitz, *Jonah*, pp. 143–4. (The Art-Scroll Tanakh Series advertises itself as 'a traditional commentary on the Books of the Bible' and is aimed at a largely Orthodox readership.)

[112] The practice of using a minor case to illustrate a major one (often on the basis of 'how much more' or 'how much less') can be found in the New Testament parables, in rabbinic literature, and in the Hebrew Bible (see for example Ezekiel 15.1–6; 2 Kings 5.13; Luke 12.24).

[113] The problem arises from the fact that the verb חוס (*hus*, which can mean anything from regret at losing something you need to selfless mercy/compassion) is applied both to Jonah's feelings for the *qiqayon* plant and to Yhwh's feelings for Nineveh. Critics try and get around this problem either by translating the two verbs differently (Jack Sasson has Jonah 'fretting' over the plant, whereas God has 'compassion over' Nineveh (see Sasson, *Jonah*, p. 300)) or by arguing that Jonah was such a fanatical lover of the eco-system that he loved the plant as God loved Nineveh: Danna Nolan Fewell and David Gunn argue that the death of the plant elicits Jonah's 'pity' for its 'vulnerability'; Elie Wiesel, even more strangely, argues that 'Jonah came to love that plant more than anything in the world' because it 'offered him protection and asked nothing in return' and ultimately 'died for him' (D. Gunn and D. N. Fewell, *Narrative in the Hebrew Bible* (Oxford: Oxford University Press, 1993), p. 143; E. Wiesel, 'Jonah', in *Five Biblical Portraits* (Notre Dame: University of Notre Dame Press, 1981)), p. 137. The one solution that cannot be tolerated is that Yhwh

interpreted in many ways: it may mean that God basks in the shade of the Ninevites' acknowledgement and glorification (just as Jonah basks in the shade of the *qiqayon*);[114] or it may mean (and this reading is rather more sinister) that Nineveh is an investment, something prepared for a purpose, and that God has specific functions in mind for this particular nation. A small group of interpreters begin to link this utility with Assyria's role as rod of God's anger or weapon of his wrath, and the most explicit of them, Abravanel, says that God saved Nineveh 'so that he might take vengeance against Israel by means of them'.[115] Many interpreters do not get this far, and those that do soon trail off into silence. But Abravanel sits there, virtually alone, turning and turning the difficult questions.

According to Vladimir Jankélevitch, Jewish study is a dizzying, disorientating process that:

> consists of thinking everything that is possible in a question, thoroughly, at all costs. You must entangle the inextricable and only ever stop when it becomes impossible to go any further . . . This rigour must sometimes be achieved at the cost of an illegible discourse: you sometimes come very close to contradicting yourself; you just have to follow along the same line, slide down the same slope, and leave your starting point further and further behind, and the starting point ends up by refuting the finishing point.[116]

needs Nineveh as Jonah needs the plant – that as Abravanel suggests he basks in its shade, or has specific plans for the city. But it is precisely this pragmatic reading that seems to be enforced by God's declaration not of abstract commitment to mercy, but of concern for the one hundred and twenty thousand Ninevites and their 'many cattle' (4.11).

[114] Abravanel glosses God's speech to Jonah in Jonah 4.10–11 thus: 'You cannot argue that you did not care about the plant for its own sake, but rather, for the benefit that it provided you with, namely the shade, because Nineveh provides me with acknowledgement and glorification that are like the shade' (Abravanel, cited in A. Cooper, 'In Praise of Divine Caprice', p. 157).

[115] Commenting on Jonah 4.1, Abravanel writes: 'Why, then, did God renounce the punishment that he had planned to bring upon [the Ninevites]? . . . So that they might become the "rod of his anger" [Isaiah 10.5] and the "weapons of his wrath" [Isaiah 13.5], in order that he might take vengeance against Israel by means of them. The prophet protested against God in his heart: Why should it be his intention to destroy Israel for idolatry, while pardoning Nineveh for the same offence?' (Abravanel, cited in Cooper, 'In Praise of Divine Caprice', p. 149). Malbim (Meir Leibush ben Yechiel Michel, 1809–1909) follows Abravanel and argues that God saved Nineveh specifically to use it as a rod of his anger against Israel. In his opinion, at the time of Jonah Nineveh was too wicked to be used as God's tool, and so God sent Jonah to bring the Ninevites to repentance, precisely so that they could be used to harm Israel (Malbim, *Gei Chizayon*, cited in Scherman and Zlotowitz, *Jonah*, pp. 81–2).

[116] Jankélevitch, *Quelque part dans l'inachevé*, pp. 18–19.

Jewish interpretation of Jonah 'rigorously slides' as oxymoronically as Jankélevitch suggests: it rotates and diffracts words, and, in flagrant defiance of the principle of non-contradiction, it pursues the prosecution and defence for both 'father' and 'son'. But at the same time it seems that there are moments where it stops before the logical end is reached, and the aporistic moment where God forgives the aggressor, precisely to perpetrate aggression against Israel, is one such point. Arguments and words can be endlessly rotated, but the point where God, Israel, and the aggressors against Israel so radically change places is a place that is rarely and briefly visited. And it seems that this is not so much to preserve the integrity and justice of God (and so resist the point where conventional theodicy closes down) but to avoid dwelling on the moment when the counter-intuitive turns masochistic in the motif of God-against-Israel. For all its pursuit of tension, and multiplication of complications, midrash also shows a general counter-tendency to *elide* tensions between God and Israel, to convert words of judgement/divine aggression into palliative words of comfort, as it teaches the blood-and-thunder biblical deity to learn to soften his voice in the reality of the Diaspora.[117] Interpretation of Jonah, similarly, may be prepared to open up Jonah's 'wounds' and to explore the possibility of the over-mighty hand of God, but ultimately it stops short of the nihilistic conclusion that (adapting the words of Herman Melville) the 'favourites of heaven' are inherently 'hapless', and the 'embrace of the deity' may be somehow 'fatal' or 'cruel'.[118]

But in the twentieth century, cracks within the text – and between

---

[117] In the Bible, Yhwh is frequently depicted as enraged husband ranting against his adulterous nation-wife, but in the midrashim the emphasis is often on the faithful wife who waits for her husband to return, holding onto her Torah as *ketubah* (marriage contract). Midrash devotes a considerable proportion of its energies to converting devastating prophetic oracles into sustained words of comfort: in *b. Ber* 4b, Amos's awful prediction 'She has fallen and will no more rise, the virgin of Israel' (Amos 5.2) is tweaked to 'She has fallen and will no more; rise, O virgin of Israel!' (For a discussion of this passage see Kugel, 'Two Introductions', pp. 77–80.) Similarly, the daily liturgy tweaks Isaiah 45.7 to a statement of praise to God who 'forms lights and creates darkness, Who makes peace and creates *all things*' (rather than who makes peace and creates *evil*). In the context of the catastrophes of first centuries of the Common Era, when much of the prayerbook came together, the concept of a God responsible for evil needed to be muted and euphemised.

[118] Melville, *Moby Dick*, p. 172. This raises the question to what extent a text must be shaped to gratify the reader. Mainstream Christian interpretation clearly reads Jonah in such a way as to provide comfort for the interpreter, bolstering the Christian ego in opposition to 'the Jew'. Jewish interpretation may not be so negatively self-affirming, but it nevertheless stops short of the extreme discomfort of a self-annihilating reading. The question resists absolute complicity with the text's logic of self-defeat.

the text and the contemporary – are prised open further, and the
resulting dissonance becomes both comic and poignantly absurd.
And a whole host of contemporary resonances tumble into the ever-
open mouth of the book, mixing with elements of the biblical text
and the midrashic tradition on the way down. The final part of this
book is devoted to the way that Jonah goes in contemporary Jewish
art and literature in a short meditation on Jonah by the writer
Stephen Mitchell; in Wolf Mankowitz's play *It Should Happen to a Dog*;
in Eugene Abeshaus's painting *Jonah in Haifa Port*; and in Norma
Rosen's haunting update of the *Pirke de Rabbi Eliezer* and *Midrash
Jonah*. The strange metamorphoses that begin here – as Jonah
becomes a client on a psychoanalyst's couch, a European Jew
making *aliyah*[119] to Israel, a travelling salesman, and a traumatised
spectator of the Holocaust – lead naturally into the 'popular' section.

In Stephen Mitchell's brief meditation 'Jonah',[120] a relatively well-
adjusted Jonah, now used to his story, inhabits it comfortably and
meditates on its resonances. He finds himself 'a dry, mildly fluorescent corner near one of the ribs, and settles down on some huge
organ (as springy as a waterbed)'; then 'with nothing to do now until
the next instalment, he leans back against the rib and lets his mind
rock back and forth'. The huge organ/waterbed seems to mutate
into a therapist's couch, as he thinks how 'everything – the warmth,
the darkness, the odour of the sea – stirs in him memories of earlier
comfort'. 'His mother's womb' perhaps, or maybe something before
that 'at the beginning of the circle which death would, perhaps soon
complete'. Jonah, who is evidently something of a Jungian, knows
that the fish is simply a mythical archetype, one of the 'strange,
gurgling, long-breathed out, beautiful songs' of the universe. And, as
a regular reader of Robert Alter, Harold Bloom, and the *New York*

---

[119] *Aliyah* ('ascent') describes the act of going to Israel/Jerusalem.
[120] S. Mitchell, 'Jonah', in 'Five Parables', *Tikkun* 4.3 (May/June 1989), p. 31. Since the
meditation is very short, it can be quoted in full: 'After the first few hours he came to feel
quite at ease inside the belly of the whale. He found himself a dry, mildly fluorescent
corner near one of the ribs, and settled down there on some huge organ (it was springy as
a waterbed). Everything – the warmth, the darkness, the odor of the sea – stirred in him
memories of an earlier comfort. His mother's womb? Or was it even before that, at the
beginning of the circle which death would, perhaps soon, complete? He had known of
God's mercy, but he had never suspected God's sense of humour. With nothing to do now
until the next installment, he leaned back against a rib and let his mind rock back and
forth. And often, for hours on end, during which he would lose track of Nineveh and
Tarshish, his mission, his plight, himself, resonating through the vault: the strange,
gurgling, long-breathed-out, beautiful song.'

Literary Review, he knows how to analyse his story, as it were, from within. Jonah is a Jungian within the archetype, literary critic within the text, a modern for whom the spiritualised, ironised narrative has lost all capacity to terrify. For him the fish is like a yoga-class, a water-tank, a 'vault' in which 'for hours on end, he loses track of Nineveh and Tarshish, his mission, his plight, himself', and his book is a good read, well constructed and well reviewed, that makes him smile appreciatively at the unexpected 'humour' of the divine author.

The Jonah figure in Wolf Mankowitz's one-act play *It Should Happen to a Dog* (1956)[121] is decidedly less appreciative of the plot he inhabits. His God is more like a 'twittering bird' or an incessantly nagging Jewish harpy than a deep, resonant comforting darkness, and the fish is not so much a relaxation tank as a place that 'smells like Billingsgate' (the East London fish market). Unlike Mitchell's Jonah who seems relatively content with his lot, and on good (if distant/aesthetic) terms with God-as-author, Mankowitz's Jonah has about him the weariness of the poor and sorely put upon.[122] He works as a tobacco salesman (presumably because there is not much call for prophecy these days), he goes by the name of J. B. Amittai, and his story is presented not as a pleasingly crafted whole but as a tetchy, vaudeville slapstick piece, in which J.B. highlights, and clownishly grates against, the absolutely self-defeating biblical story-line. Finding himself hooked up to an impenetrable, perhaps certifiable deity, and an impenetrable and perverse plot, this Jonah does the one thing that it remains in his power to do: he distances himself from, and wryly comments on, the life that he is scripted to occupy with the kind of ironising, self-deflating comments that have come to be seen as the trademarks of 'Jewish humour'. Tevye-like, J.B. captions each scene of his perverse life with muttering, shoulder-shrugging Yiddishisms: when he is plagued by God's voice, or when he is thrown overboard, he mutters 'it should happen to a dog, what happens to me'; when he decides to drop in on friends in Tarshish '*en route*' to Nineveh he reasons 'it's a crime?' (in contrast to Main-stream commentary's adamant 'it *is* a crime'); and in response to the

---

[121] W. Mankowitz, *It Should Happen to a Dog* (1956), in M. Halverson (ed.), *Religious Drama* III (New York: Meridian Books, 1957), pp. 123–35. I am grateful to Robert Carroll for sending me a copy of the play.

[122] Compare the authorial persona in the medieval poem *Patience*, discussed in the 'Popular interpretation' section below.

King of Nineveh's faithfully recited biblical lines: 'Who can tell if
God will turn and repent, and turn away from his fierce anger, that
we perish not?', he simply shrugs: 'Who can tell? But if you ask my
opinion, I don't think so. Otherwise he doesn't go to all this trouble.'
As the plot/his life uncoils in such perverse and unpredictable ways,
he offers a running commentary of protest and questions: 'If God
knew he wasn't going to destroy Nineveh what did he want with my
life?'; and 'What's the point of all this expensive business with whales
and palm trees and so on?'; and 'This is a terrible way to treat
someone who goes through all the trouble I go through. For what –
only he knows.' And when he finds that God has flipped his oracle
over, leaving him looking like the 'biggest bloody fool in the Middle
East', he tells the inscrutable, exasperating deity: 'You can do what
you like with Ninever, Minever, Shminever – I'm finished.'

Jonah, in other words, embodies that quintessentially Yiddish
sense of life as 'an overbearingly scented rubber-ice pick, a
chocolate pacemaker, or an open tub of chicken giblets cast out to a
man besieged by tetchy sharks'.[123] His story becomes something
like the story of *Leon the Pigfarmer*, the North London Jew who finds
that he was conceived by artificial insemination, that his father is in
fact a Yorkshire pig farmer, and that the whole story of his life to
date is, through no fault of his own, un-kosher, hence un-tenable.[124]
In a twist on the Mainstream image of Jonah the clownish dupe,
Mankowitz's Jonah turns stand-up comic, playing his text for laughs
in the manner of Jackie Mason or Woody Allen. 'The lion and the
calf shall lie down together but the calf won't get much sleep',
smirks Allen,[125] while J.B. inside the whale quips, 'Who'd have
thought that being dead was a black-out in a fish and chip
shop?'[126] In this alienated, secularised world even the angels mock
their lines and the archangel-commentator explains the plant-worm
mashal in the style of David Attenborough (the naturalist and BBC

---

[123] I'm cheating. The quotation is actually from a collection of short stories by a Scottish
writer (A. L. Kennedy, *Now That You're Back* (London: Vintage, 1995), p. 115), but it seems
such an irresistibly appropriate quote.
[124] *Leon the Pigfarmer* (Gary Sinyor/Vadim Jean 1992, GB).
[125] W. Allen, *Without Feathers* (London: Sphere Books, 1980), p. 25.
[126] In a similar comic vein the captain of the ship boasts: 'We got all the passengers making
sacrifices to all the different gods. That way we must hit the right God sooner or later . . .',
and a wide-eyed Jonah draws attention to the absurd cattle footnote in Jonah 4.11: 'You got
a point there, there never was any harm in those cattle.' In the storm scene, relations
between God and Jonah degenerate into slapstick as Jonah nonchalantly throws a half-
eaten meat pie overboard as sacrifice, and an unseen hand throws it right back.

broadcaster).[127] The play ends with J.B. and angel heading off-stage right, Tarshish-wards, into comic alienation, muttering 'What can you do?' and 'It should happen to a dog.'

Mankowitz's Jonah – unfolding the *Tarshish Gazette* and gleefully reporting that 'Mrs Zinkin has been presented with her third daughter' and that 'Young Fyvel is opening a café expresso bar in the High Street' – is a gently self-mocking and affectionate descendant of the Yiddish-speaking shtetl Jew, and so an (unconscious) antidote to the more sinister caricature that haunts the Mainstream.[128] Equally unintentionally, but even more powerfully, the artist Eugene Abeshaus offers an antidote to that nasty recent mutation, Jonah the hard-hearted Zionist. In *Jonah in Haifa Port* (1978, fig. 7) Jonah looks like a fugitive from a Chagall painting or *Fiddler on the Roof*: his expression is world-weary, as if he's played this part many times before. Images of twentieth-century Jewish history – wandering, suitcases, Shoah, socialism – are imported or smuggled into the biblical frame; indeed the picture seems to be as much about the migration of contemporary resonances into the biblical text as about Jonah's migration to Eretz Israel. The fish that previously only inadvertently looked like a car-ferry, now deliberately evokes famous twentieth-century Jew-carrying ships, like the *Exodus*, or the *St Louis*. (I wonder how this picture would look snuggling up

---

[127] 'A small worm crawls through the arterial system of the tree and cuts off the life from the heart.' His explanation of the *mashal* is similarly tongue-in-cheek (though remarkably faithful to the biblical original): 'If you feel sorry for the tree, which after all didn't cost you anything, why shouldn't (God) feel sorry for Nineveh, that great city, in which there are one hundred and twenty thousand human beings with whom after all He has taken a great deal of trouble, even if they still don't know what time it is, or their left hand from their right. Also much cattle.'

[128] Of course, Mankowitz is simply replacing one Jewish caricature with another – but the crucial difference is that this caricature comes from inside the Jewish community. Freud's comments are still helpful in this respect: 'the jokes made about Jews by foreigners are for the most part brutal comic stories in which a joke is made unnecessary by the fact that Jews are regarded by foreigners as comic figures. The Jewish jokes which originate from Jews admit this too; but they know their real faults as well as the connection between them and their good qualities, and the share which the subject has in the person found fault with creates the subjective determinant . . . of the joke-work' (S. Freud, *Jokes and Their Relation to the Unconscious* (transl. J. Strachey, Harmondsworth: Penguin, 1994), pp. 156–7). Homi Bhabha, exegeting Freud, suggests that the Jewish joke be seen as a 'destablising encounter with alterity', a 'way for minority communities to confront and regulate the abuse that comes from "outside"' (H. Bhabha, 'Joking Aside: The Idea of a Self-Critical Community', in B. Cheyette and L. Marcus (eds.), *Modernity, Culture and 'the Jew'* (Cambridge: Polity Press, 1998), pp. xv–xx (xviii)). In contrast to 'the death-dealing mummifying gaze of racist discourse and its fixated images of "otherness"', joking allows a 'play with one's words and thoughts' – it is a subversion of solid and static structures that allows the community to generate its own playful versions of self (p. xviii).

against von Rad's condemnation of Jonah as 'monstrous', or Bewer's invective against 'narrow, blind, prejudiced and fanatic Jews'; I wonder how the scholarly image of Jonah would be irreparably distorted if this picture were used as a commentary illustration.)

But the crucial element in Abeshaus's painting is the gangplank – the gangplank that connects the aquamarine (dissolving?) biblical world to the solid realistic terra firma of Haifa port, and that acts as a cipher for the thin connection between the biblical and the twentieth century. It is possible to read the painting as an allegory of the relations between 'the Bible' and 'Culture': Jonah's suitcases are full of contemporary material carried into the fish and biblical resonances carried back out, and the thin gangplank is an image of the increasingly precarious, and mutually destabilising, relationship between the two worlds. Reading the biblical text in the present is not just a case of dropping contemporary allusions (the *Tarshish Gazette*, or fish-markets, or Haifa) into the mouth of the biblical text, it is a case of exploring how the two work in tandem, or how one acts as a spanner in the cogs of the other. In *It Should Happen to a Dog* there is a strong sense that Jonah and his fellow characters are lost moderns, stranded in a perverse little plot from the past that they can neither believe nor comprehend ('You could live a thousand years', says a sailor, 'you wouldn't see a man swallowed by a whale. But who would believe such a thing?'). In Abeshaus's painting there is an even greater sense of disjunction as Jonah carries the knowledge of pogroms, and Dreyfus, and Herzl, and perhaps Hitler, into and out of the fish, and so brings to the text a sense of chronological and epistemological trauma that it may, or may not, be able to bear.

But it is in Norma Rosen's haunting twentieth-century midrash[129] that the tension between these days and those days becomes most acute: for Rosen's aim is to show how the Shoah has 'broken the back of the continuum between the past and present'[130] and intervened decisively in our relations with biblical texts. Rosen's reading, like Abeshaus's, subjects the biblical text to a disorientating prolepsis, in which the text is performed (stutteringly, and with ever decreasing conviction) in the full, bleak knowledge of the twentieth century. In a sombre twist on the *Pirke de Rabbi Eliezer*, the fish is still a creature from the dark mythical substructures of the world, created

---

[129] Rosen, 'Justice for Jonah or a Bible Bartleby?'
[130] *Ibid.*, p. 223.

during the first six days of creation, and appointed to swallow Jonah from the beginning of time. But, as it has lain at the bottom of the ocean in a mythical time out-of- and below-time, it has 'soaked up the events of the millennia'[131] and taken history into its skin. This fish does not take Jonah on a tour of the fabulous landmarks of biblical history; it takes him on a journey through the dark underside of the biblical canon:

First there is the Babylonian exile: how the tongue of the sucking child cleaved to the roof of his mouth for thirst; how the young children asked for bread, and no one gave it to them; how skin was blackened like an oven, because of the terrible famine. 'He hath broken my bones . . . He hath bent his bow, and set me as a mark for the arrow.'[132]

Then the biblical references break off and the fish's cavernous interior mutates into an Imax (horror) Cinema filled with scenes from inquisitions and expulsions and ghettos and pogroms and death camps and crematoria. As the most disturbing documentaries of the modern world spool round, Jonah sees 'Times for which new names will be learned: "eclipse of God", a "turning away of God's face"',[133] times when the familiar judgement–mercy dichotomy falls in splinters at his feet. Rosen imagines Jonah reacting with all the terror of Milton's Adam, hearing for the first time that his biblical paradise is not to last.

Because she is familiar with his story through the liturgy of Yom Kippur, Rosen sees Jonah as the blithe believer in God's infinite mercy, the happy antithesis of 'twentieth-century man'.[134] And she wants to startle him out of his naïvety, to make him inhabit the same back-broken discontinuum between biblical past and present that she is forced to inhabit; she wants him to experience the disorientation from this story, and the tradition that she experiences.

Show me a text that speaks of God's unbounded mercy and images of the holocaust appear before my eyes. It's not anything I can help. Theology doesn't help. This is visceral. I don't imagine I'm alone in this. Perhaps my generation will have to die out in the desert before God can appear again on an untarnished mercy seat . . . Before the Holocaust it was possible for piety to say, as we read in Lamentations 'We are punished for our sins'. After the Holocaust, none but a twisted piety dares say it . . . Every Yom

---

[131] *Ibid.*, p. 228.   [132] *Ibid.*, p. 228.   [133] *Ibid.*, p. 228.

[134] 'Happily for Jonah', she writes, 'his glimpse into later centuries has not made of him a twentieth-century man. He is alive in an age of faith, and could not conceive of replying in a nihilistic vein' (Rosen, 'Justice for Jonah', p. 229).

Kippur I ask myself how Jonah would speak if he could somehow learn what happened to us. Mercy, pity, judgement, punishment; in what proportions might Jonah ascribe these attributes to God if he knew our condition? Might Jonah study us with the same astonishment as we study him?[135]

And yet is Jonah (as book and character) such an ingénu? Indeed, could he be after assimilating all the interrogations and speculations contained in Jewish tradition, let alone the ambiguities of the biblical text? Yom Kippur is perhaps the one occasion on which the text speaks unequivocally of mercy: paradoxically, it is precisely Rosen's sense of disjunction from the biblical text that makes her so much a part of (at least one trajectory of) Jewish tradition.

So, as the lights go out in the belly of the fish and the magical mystery tour turns nightmarish history tour, our own tour of Jonah's Jewish afterlife has come full circle. Jonah is no longer wide-eyed Superprophet/Supertourist, full of apocalyptic hope, looking forward to the moment when he'll put a hook through the mouth of Leviathan; his eyes hang heavy (Abeshaus), he is traumatised and disillusioned (Rosen), able only to enter into his story as a literary-critic or Jungian analyst (Mitchell) or a secular Jewish humourist who turns every element of the plot into sardonic one-liners (Mankowitz). On one level, these disillusioned Feuerbach- and Rubenstein-reading[136] Jonahs are profoundly at odds with the voices of the interpretative past, but on another they live, consciously or unconsciously, among the quotations. Mitchell's Jonah, scrutinising his story from within, is perhaps only a modern extension of the *Pirke de Rabbi Eliezer*'s Jonah-rabbi; Mankowitz's shoulder-shrugging Jonah was probably always implicit in the musings on the perversities of

---

[135] *Ibid.*, pp. 222–3. Elsewhere Rosen puts the problem even more starkly: 'The story of Jonah, in which God chides Jonah into remembering mercy, on Yom Kippur, is the very one we cast at the feet of God to stay the death-dealing hand, to stir up the memory of mercy. Nineveh had only 120,000 souls; on Yom Kippur we think of Europe's eleven million who perished in the Holocaust, six million of them Jews, one-third of their number in the world, cut off from the pity of Nineveh' (*ibid.*, p. 231).

[136] Ludwig Feuerbach (1804–72) famously argued that 'religion is the dream of the human mind' and 'theology is anthropology': in his view religion is a compensatory device and 'The more empty life is, the fuller, the more concrete is God' (L. Feuerbach, *The Essence of Christianity* (trans. G. Eliot; New York: Harper and Row, 1957), pp. xxxix, 73, 270). Richard Rubenstein expounds a 'death of God' theology: now that all illusions about God have been so dramatically snatched away, Jews are called to face up to their existential situation, and to find meaning in the meaninglessness of existence through the existence of the Jewish people and forms of Jewish religion (R. Rubenstein, *After Auschwitz: Radical Theology and Contemporary Judaism* (Indianapolis: Bobbs-Merrill, 1966)).

prophecy; and the immense empathy with Jonah expressed by Mankowitz, Abeshaus, and Rosen is perhaps only the logical culmination of the human orientation of the midrashim, their empathy for the 'son' that leads them to challenge (and in the case of the secular critics, eventually dissociate themselves from) the 'father'.

In the reverberating echo-chamber of Jewish interpretation, all the textual notes of these contemporary writers, all their accumulating whys and hows and wherefores, have all been noted before. When the angel in *It Should Happen to a Dog* makes it clear that God wants to keep the Ninevites because they took him 'so much trouble' to make, he is only making comic capital from a rather pragmatic vein in the text that other Jewish readers mined several centuries earlier. When J.B. asks, 'If God knew he wasn't going to destroy Nineveh what did he want with my life?', and Rosen asks, 'Why should mercy be expressed so cruelly?', they merely condense related questions and debates in *Bavli*, Rashi, and Abravanel. And that is where I'll leave them – J.B. disputing with the rabbis, Rosen mulling the text over with Abravanel – in strangely productive *zuggot*, or study-pairs, between the past and the present. 'Why should it be God's intention to destroy Israel for idolatry, while pardoning Nineveh for the same offence?' asks Abravanel, and Rosen nods, pauses, then replies slowly, deliberately, with a counter-question:

Can it be right to say that after the fish Jonah wanted only judgement, not mercy? Perhaps he wanted more than that. Consistency. Judgement you could count on. A mercy that was meet. Wanted there never to be a time when there would be no judge and no judgement for if they are lacking, how can there be mercy?[137]

2. POPULAR INTERPRETATION

The great floodgates of the wonderworld spring open.[138]

Judaism, the religion of the Book, clearly lives what Thomas Mann called a *zitahaftes Leben*, a textualised existence, inhabiting the dense and infinitely extrapolatable space among the quotations.[139] But there is a sense in which Western culture similarly lives in and among the words of the Bible, albeit far less densely and more

---

[137] Rosen, 'Justice for Jonah', p. 228.
[138] Melville, *Moby Dick*, p. 16.
[139] So Fishbane, *The Exegetical Imagination*, p. 1.

selectively arranged. Milan Kundera may well be overstating when he observes that 'All of us – believers and nonbelievers, blasphemers and worshippers – belong to the same culture, rooted in the Christian past, without which we would be mere shadows without substance, debaters without a vocabulary, spiritually stateless',[140] as may Northrop Frye when he describes the Bible as a stubborn, inscrutable, sprawling book that sits in the very midst of our cultural heritage, 'frustrating all attempts to walk around it'.[141] But it is at least true to say that, adapting a metaphor that Valentine Cunningham applies to Roland Barthes, we all live in the 'crackle, the static of the Judaeo-Christian past' (though the 'Judaeo-Christian' as I defined it in chapter 1 – strong on the Christian, rather lighter on the Judaeo-) and that 'the Bible' and 'Culture' are constantly jamming one another's frequency.[142] Jonah is a book that people somehow seem to 'know', even if they have never consciously read a Bible: they think of it as a double act – 'Jonah and the Whale', like 'Laurel and Hardy' or 'Gilbert and Sullivan'. And this seems to confirm Patricia Hampl's suspicion that Jonah, 'unlike its slender prophetic neighbours in the canon, is the story known in the bones, the story you can't remember not knowing, a memory so old it's like an ounce of yourself',[143] the story that, to put it another way, and to pick up a theme that I'll be returning to later, is one of the most successfully replicating memes in Western culture.[144]

Now 'Culture' may be a less assiduous reader than the 'Jew' – it may not live in such concatenated chains of association and such dense word-labyrinths – but it goes on reading the book of Jonah and, in its own fashion, turning it and turning it, and finding everything refracted in it. Just as Jewish tradition mixes and stirs the text with the synagogue, Leviathan, Yiddish humour, the Shoah, memories of the shtetl and hints of psychoanalysis, so culture appropriates Jonah, and (narcissistically?) mixes it with itself. In George Orwell's famous essay 'Inside the Whale', fragments of the book of Jonah appear like a few loose beads shaken up among 'a whole

---

[140] M. Kundera, *Testaments Betrayed: An Essay in Nine Parts* (New York: Harper Collins, 1993), p. 11.

[141] N. Frye, *The Great Code* (London: Routledge and Kegan Paul, 1982), cover notes.

[142] V. Cunningham, *In the Reading Gaol: Postmodernity, Texts and History* (Oxford: Blackwell, 1994), p. 365.

[143] P. Hampl, 'In the Belly of the Whale', in C. Büchmann and C. Spiegel (eds.), *Out of the Garden: Women Writers on the Bible* (New York: Ballantine, 1995), pp. 289–301 (291).

[144] For more on memes, see pp. 196–201.

world of stuff', including Aldous Huxley, Ezra Pound, John de Passos, Henry Miller's *Tropic of Cancer*, Housman, Swinburne, Walpole, the Georgian poets, *Ulysses*, Dostoevsky, and the Second World War.[145] Jonah hovers behind the title but doesn't put in an appearance until page forty-two (though Balaam's ass does pop up rather unexpectedly on page nineteen as a sign of the 'average sensual man' given the power of speech). The first specific allusion to Jonah comes in a paragraph on Henry Miller's *Max and the White Phagocytes*, which contains a chapter on the 'introverted' writing of Anaïs Nin, whom Miller compares to the cloistered figure of Jonah in the whale. And then Orwell refers *in passing* to a comment that Miller makes on Aldous Huxley *in passing* about El Greco's picture *The Dream of Philip the Second*. Apparently Huxley thought that 'the people in El Greco's pictures always look as though they were in the bellies of whales' and he found the idea of a 'visceral prison' repulsive, but Miller seemed to find the idea rather attractive.[146] And Orwell writing on Miller writing on Huxley/Nin thinks that Miller finds the idea of 'being inside a whale is a very cosy, homelike thought' because the whale is simply a 'dark cushioned space that exactly fits you', that cossets you in an adult-womb, and that puts 'a yard of blubber between yourself and reality'.[147] True, Orwell concedes, the original Jonah was 'glad to escape', but in the dense space of quotation that develops between Huxley, Orwell, and Miller (with Nin in the background) Jonah is squeezed into the meaning of absolute passivity. The essential 'Jonah act' is 'allowing oneself to be swallowed, remaining passive, accepting', and Jonah's typifying attitude is *je m'en fous* or 'Though He slay me, yet will I trust him.'[148]

In the fabulously showy, densely allusive 'in' conversation that Orwell constructs between himself and a century of cultural literati, Jonah becomes a sign of the amorality of Miller's writing: Miller, according to Orwell, is 'an unconstructive, amoral writer, a mere Jonah, a passive acceptor of evil, a sort of Whitman among the corpses',[149] although (and here the metaphor begins to run away with all the audacity of the *Pirke de Rabbi Eliezer*) the walls of the whale in which Miller cossets himself are at least 'transparent' (double-glazed?).[150] But Jonah-ism, being inside the whale, becomes

---

[145] G. Orwell, 'Inside the Whale', in *Inside the Whale and Other Essays* (Harmondsworth: Penguin, 1979; 1st edn 1940), pp. 9–50 (11).
[146] *Ibid.*, p. 42.   [147] *Ibid.*, pp. 42–3.   [148] *Ibid.*, p. 43.
[149] *Ibid.*, p. 50.   [150] *Ibid.*, p. 43.

something much broader and all-encompassing: nothing less than a dangerous a-political quietism that is tantamount to acceptance of (and the list is a strange one) 'concentration camps, rubber truncheons, Hitler, Stalin, bombs, aeroplanes, tinned food, machine guns, putsches, purges, slogans, Bedaux belts, gas masks, submarines, spies, provocateurs, press censorship, secret prisons, aspirins, Hollywood films, and political murders'.[151] Orwell's point is clearly that the intellectual in society should take up his/her post outside the whale; forty-four years later, appropriately enough in 1984, Salman Rushdie picks up Orwell's metaphor to make the point that modern reality is 'whaleless', 'without quiet corners in which there can be easy escapes from history, from hullabaloo, from terrible unquiet fuss'.[152] Thus Jonah – passed from Miller on Nin and Huxley on El Greco, to Orwell on Miller then to Rushdie on Orwell – becomes a symbol of a-political introversion, and his whale becomes, variously, a cosseting womb for the hard-of-living, and a glass-walled vessel where the most courageous of life's refugees can at least look out.

I mention this extended conversation to show how convoluted Jonah's cultural journeys are: how he becomes an ism, Jonah-ism, and how he somehow gets mixed up with the Second World War and tinned food and barbed wire and politics. Curiously, as he is buffeted along this particular trajectory, he ends up precisely where the Mainstream deposits him – as a slur, the epitome of all that is bad – but not because he is a Jew, but because he refuses the kind of political engagement that is required of anyone living in Europe during the Second World War. Orwell's Jonah has some features in common with Rosen's Jonah who, inhabiting the insulating blubber of the biblical tradition, is also naïvely unaware of the Second World War, though of course the two have never met. And what, if anything, would Orwell's and Rosen's Jonahs with their bland beliefs in God's mercy have to say to the *Mekilta*'s Jonah, who bravely counters the 'father' on behalf of the 'son', as they perplexedly confront one another across the centuries?

Though Jonah's cultural journeys clearly take him to places as conceptually far-flung as Nineveh and Tarshish, my aim here is at least to try and trace the ways that Jonah goes. And a clear theme that starts to emerge is that popular readings of Jonah are concerned

[151] *Ibid.*, p. 17.
[152] S. Rushdie, 'Outside the Whale', in *Imaginary Homelands: Essays and Criticism 1981–1991* (London: Viking/Granta, 1991), pp. 92, 101.

with precisely this: tracing literally, viscerally, viscously, the way in which Jonah goes. Biblical critics may deem the fish to be an interpretative minnow, but for most readers it is the veritable centre (or navel) of the text, the vortex into which our attention is sucked. For centuries artists have speculated on the nature of Jonah's monster and produced a fabulous menagerie of potential hosts. Jonah's monster has eyes the size of saucers and a huge trampoline-like tongue (fig. 8); he shifts species and becomes a hybrid serpent-dog (fig. 9); his eyes are fierce, his skin armour-plated, his incisors the length of Jonah's index finger (fig. 10) or the size of Jonah's head (fig. 11). In the most fabulous mutations of all the beast grows flamboyant gill-feathers (plain or spotted), a pugnacious snout, and eyes that are glassily fish-like or tiny, peering from heavily armoured eye-sockets (figs. 12 and 13). Like the fabulous creatures that skulk and snarl on the borders of medieval maps beyond the boundaries of the known world, or like the mutant and subversive creatures that clamber around the margins of sacred manuscripts or fill Hieronymus Bosch's visions of hell,[153] Jonah's fish becomes a site of fabulous mutation, the perfect place for playing out fantasy and fear. And the way in which art rewinds and replays, with stuttering compulsion, the moment where Jonah goes into and out of the fish suggests an obsession with the carnival theme of the eater eaten, the consumer consumed, the man-in-the-fish as opposed to the fish-in-the-man, that is played out in works such as Bosch's *Vision of Tondalys*, *St Christopher*, and the *Temptation of Anthony* triptych.[154]

---

[153] For an intriguing discussion of the subversive functions of medieval manuscript marginalia and the displacement of monstrosity at the edges of the world, see M. Camille, *Images on the Edge: The Margins of Medieval Art* (London: Reaktion Books, 1995). For a tantalisingly illustrated discussion of Bosch, see W. Gibson, *Hieronymus Bosch* (London: Thames and Hudson, 1995).

[154] In the visions of hell in the *Vision of Tondalys* humans are force-fed at a table inside the mouth of a monster; in *St Christopher*, monks inhabit a building composed from the body of a fish; and in the lower foreground of the central panel of the *St Anthony* triptych a man imprisoned in a fish struggles to escape, peering out from the bars that are cut away in the fish's back, and thrusting his hands through the fish's body. The fascination with swallowing fishes and bodies consumed by other bodies that is so evident in the work of Bosch can also be seen in slightly later Netherlandish art – for example in Pieter Brueghel (the elder's) etchings based on the proverb 'The Big Fish Swallow the Little Fish'. As art historians explain, monstrous mutations of fish breed so prodigiously on Last Judgement scenes because swallowing by a fish is seen as an appropriately hellish punishment for greed – but it seems to me that the fascination with the swallower swallowed is not confined to this symbolic function. Unfortunately, there is no study that I know of that looks at the resonances of fish (beyond the symbolism of greed) nor that explores the relationship between fish and hellish monsters and the book of Jonah.

Meanwhile literature ventures into areas where artists cannot or dare not tread, penetrating deep into the inner organs and belly of the beast. According to the contemporary novelist Julian Barnes, what sucks the reader into this book is fear – 'fear of being devoured by a large creature, fear of being chomped, slurped, gargled, washed down with a draught of salt water and a school of anchovies as a chaser; fear of being blinded, darkened, suffocated, drowned, hooded with blubber etc. etc. etc.'[155] (and in literature this 'etc. etc. etc.' is stretched out to something like a high-velocity fairground ride). From antiquity to the present there seems to be a feeling that the text cannot be properly digested without ruminating on what it would be like to be a digested prophet, and threading an investigative optic fibre down the fish's gullet. Even Luther can barely resist the temptation: 'How often lung and limb must have pained [Jonah]!', he speculates, 'How strange his abode must have been among the intestines and the huge ribs.'[156] (But for Luther speculations about Jonah's discomfort must be subordinated to the serious sermonic business of exposing how the 'real wild plant' of Judaism is nibbled and consumed by the advent of the Christ-worm.)

The literary obsession with the fish (internal view) erupts early: the early Latin poem *Carmen de Jona de Ninive* tells how the fish 'sucked with slimy jaws a living feast' and speculates how Jonah must have lived among 'half-eaten fleets' and 'digested corpses, dissolved and putrid'.[157] The late fourteenth-century Middle English poem *Patience* imagines the prophet 'malskred in dread', and flung in 'like a mote in at a minster door' – miraculously 'without a touch from any tooth' because the fish's jaws are so '*mickle* [huge]'.[158] In an image

---

[155] J. Barnes, *A History of the World in Ten and a Half Chapters* (London: Picador, 1989), p. 178.

[156] Luther, 'Lectures', p. 68.

[157] The poem, which was once ascribed to Tertullian, can be found in R. Peiper (ed.), *Corpus Scriptorum Ecclesiasticorum Latinorum* XXIII (Vienna: Akademie der Wissenschaften, 1891), pp. 221–6 (see also *PL* II, 1166–72). A translation and discussion of authorship can be found in A. Roberts and J. Donaldson (eds.), *Tertullian* (Ante-Nicene Christian Library 18; Edinburgh: T. & T. Clark, 1870), pp. xviii–xix, 279–83.

[158] *Patience*, a poem of 531 lines written in unrhymed alliterative verse, is the work of a north-western contemporary of Chaucer known as the *Pearl*-Poet or the *Gawain*-Poet after his two more famous works, *Pearl* and *Sir Gawain and the Green Knight*. *Pearl*, *Patience*, *Sir Gawain* and a fourth poem *Cleanness* (or 'purity'), are preserved on a single manuscript (British Library Cotton Nero A. x.) which was almost destroyed by fire in 1753, and gathered dust, unread, until the works first appeared in print in the nineteenth century. The complete original text with translation can be found in P. Vantuone (ed.), *The Pearl Poems* II: *Patience and Sir Gawain and the Green Knight* (New York and London: Garland, 1984) and this is the translation that I am mostly using here, though sometimes with alternatives from B. Stone (ed. and trans.), *Medieval English Verse* (Harmondsworth: Penguin, 1981), pp. 118–35. A

reminiscent of the *Pirke de Rabbi Eliezer's* fish-synagogue, the fish-cathedral's lips swing back on their hinges to receive the high-velocity prophet, who this time does not step in, glasses on, books in hand, but is ignominiously hurled into the *wild waterande whal* (the 'wild, wallowing whale'). And, as his entrance is less decorous, so his accommodation is far less luxurious: unfortunately, the place-of-worship metaphor does not stick in *Patience* as in the *Pirke de Rabbi Eliezer*, and Jonah finds no pearl eye-window, study booths, or well-equipped learning resource centre, but rather a huge body, full of endless intestines and 'murky slime'. Jonah's thoroughly disgusting journey through the tubes and folds of the cetacean digestive system – the way he glides in through mucus, somersaults head over heels until he is deposited in a huge cavernous gut, and then looks through every 'nook of his navel' for a dry place to sit – begs to be savoured in full:

> [Jonah] glides in near the gills through slimy mucus,
> Rolling in by a gut which seemed to him a rood's length,
> Always heel over head, whirling about,
> Until he stopped in a cavern as broad as a hall.

> And there he fixes his feet and gropes about,
> And stood up in that stomach, which stank like the devil,
> Where in fat and in filth, that savoured as hell,
> There was built the abode of one who will suffer no pain.

> And then he lurks and looks for a sheltered place
> In every nook of his navel, but nowhere does he find
> Either relief or safety – nothing but muck and mire [or 'reeking ooze']
> Whichever gut he explores: but God is sweet.

Curiously, at a time when the book of Jonah is saturated in allegory, when the belly is 'hell', and Jonah is 'Christ', Jonah ends up in a place that is emphatically not hell – but a place that smells 'like hell', and a stomach that stinks 'like the very devil' (a place reminiscent of Mankowitz's Billingsgate belly). Although the poet is quite capable of creating graphic pictures of hell (in the companion poem *Cleanness*, the devil and his angels tumble thick as snow, like fine meal through a sieve, into the pit of hell that is forty-days-falling deep), here hell and the devil are present only in metaphor, dispersed in colloquialisms (as Jonah sleeps, 'slobbering and

useful edition with original text and glossary can be found in A. C. Spearing and J. E. Spearing (eds.), *Poetry in the Age of Chaucer* (London: Edward Arnold, 1974), pp. 113–35, although unfortunately this only gives selected extracts from the poem.

snoring',[159] the sailor kicks him, curses him in the name of the 'fettered fiend' and asks *wot the devel* he has done, while Jonah beneath the gourd is so content that he does not care 'a devil of a bit'). Jonah may be in *warlowe's guttes* (hell's guts) or *hellen wombe* (hell's womb) but hell is the vehicle, and guts/womb are the tenor, and the stomach acids and fishy fats that flow around Jonah's feet never turn into those typically hellish liquids – pitch, or sulphur, rivers of fire, lakes of blood, or molten lead. And Jonah's emergence, similarly, is a messy purgation of the fish's belly that is a long way from resurrection.[160] In an emphatically biological reading, the human 'mote' is an irritant in the fish's guts, that causes him to thrash about in distemper so that Jonah is eventually 'sput spakly' (quickly spat) upon the land. Jonah is 'spat' and 'spewed' out and his clothes are 'sluched' (or soiled): 'I leave it to you to decide', adds this mercilessly realistic poet, grinning, 'whether Jonah's mantle needed a wash . . .' (*Hit may well that mester were his mantile to washe!*)[161]

---

[159] These passages give a good sense of the grotesque realism and vivid language of the poem: the Middle English comically conveys a sense of Jonah's brutal awakening: '(the sailor) *freke him frunt with his foot and beded him ferk up*'. Since the poet is working from the Vulgate, he is probably unaware of the Septuagint translation in which Jonah also snores, but this physicality is typical of poetry of this period (cf. Langland's *Piers Ploughman*, where Sloth begins his confession with a belch and the inebriated Gluttony sways to and fro like a *glewannes bich* ('an entertainer's dog')).

[160] It does have something in common with popular descriptions of the harrowing of hell, however. As Ad Putter points out, in medieval sermons Christ is often depicted entering the 'bowels' of hell, and hell is forced to vomit up the 'indigestible bread' of Christ (see A. Putter, 'Patience', in *An Introduction to the Gawain-Poet* (Harlow: Longman, 1996), p. 131).

[161] Although it is impossible to do justice to a work like *Patience* in a whistle-stop tour like this, I at least want to give an impression of the extraordinary use of language in this poem. The prophet's psalm gushes with every possible variety of water – sea, floods, whirlpools, waters, streams, currents – all flowing, swelling, folding, dashing, rippling and bubbling, and Jonah gives the impression of drowning in labials as he burbles his liquid (and perfectly alliterative) lines:

> The gret flem of thy flod folded me umbe
> All the gotes of they guferes and groundeless pooles
> And thy strivande stremes of strindes so many
> In on daschande dam dryueth me ouer.

> (The strong flow of your sea folded around me.
> And the swells from your whirlpools and bottomless waters,
> And your struggling streams from so many currents
> Drive over me in one dashing flood).

The way in which the poet unravels Jonah 2.1 into a coil of intestines is only one example of how he unravels the biblical text into a three-dimensional poem space: in the storm scene, red-tinged storm clouds loom darkly, winds wrestle, frightened fishes huddle to the bottom of the sea, masts split, sails rip in a crash of onomatopoeia, and the sailors hurl out

Six centuries later, Aldous Huxley's Jonah finds himself in a similarly viscous environment, where even the dim 'phosphorescent light' is described as 'creamy', but where he does at least find a place to sit 'on the convex mounds/of one vast kidney'.[162] Like the author of *Patience* (the so-called *Gawain*-Poet), Huxley uses dripping, sensuous onomatopoeic language, luring the readers, against all their better instincts, to positively revel in the fluid spectacle of:

> Many a pendulous stalactite
> Of naked mucus, whorls and wreaths
> And huge festoons of mottled tripes
> And smaller palpitating pipes
> Through which a yeastly liquor seethes.

The belly is metaphorically a machine (where pipes ooze yeastly liquor); a function room (adorned with Rabelaisian tripes rather than more conventional carnival ribbons); and a cavern where we, Huxley, and Jonah are, absurdly, pot-holers through the fish's intestines. More absurdly still, Jonah's presence seems to anthropomorphise his host: as he sings hymns and make the 'hollow vault resound' with 'God's goodness and his mysterious ways' it seems as if the 'fish spouts music as he swims'.

Huxley and the *Gawain*-Poet are of course only imagining what it would feel like to be in the belly of the beast. But it seems that this kind of deeply metaphorical, soft, fluid experience is a perfectly *factual* rendition of what it is actually like to be in the belly of a whale, at least if survivors' testimonies are to be believed. The most sensational and sumptuously written of these strange liminal documents is the testimony of one James Bartley, British harpooner, swallowed and regurgitated in 1891. (The testimony can be consulted in *The Ocean Almanac*, in a chapter called 'Survival at Sea: Of Those Who Were Saved and How to Save Yourself', squeezed between stories of a modern-day Crusoe, and a south Korean who escaped

---

bags, feather beds, bright clothes, and prayers to Diana, Neptune, and Mohammed. Motifs spill over from one scene to another: the hold of the boat is compared to the bowels of the beast, while Jonah (obviously collecting metaphors from his own experience) warns the Ninevites that they will be 'swallowed swiftly by the swart earth' and 'rages against God like a roaring gale'. Similarly words do double duty on a spiritual/metaphorical and all-too-concrete level. Jonah, soaked by the 'reeking ooze' of the fish, confesses himself the *gaule of prophetes* ('the scum of the prophets'), and, when he is almost overcome by the devilish stench, he begins to think of (or smell) the sweetness or purity of God.

[162] A. Huxley, 'Jonah', in G. Grigson (ed.), *The Cherry Tree* (London: Phoenix House, 1959).

drowning by travelling one hundred miles on a sea-turtle).[163] Bartley reports how a whale with 'piglike eyes' surrounded by 'seaweed and barnacles' catapulted him into his mouth with its tail, and how he 'slipped' into a 'big ribbed canopy of light pink and white', and found himself hemmed in by a 'wall of flesh on either side' that 'gave way like soft India rubber before [his] slightest movement'. He tells how he was 'drawn downward, feet first' into a 'strange darkness', a 'sack much larger than his body' full of a 'yielding, slimy substance' where living fish still squirmed, and where the heat was so oppressive that it seemed to 'open the pores of his skin'. Only the next day, when his shipmates caught the whale and the flensers began to remove the blubber from its stomach, did Bartley and his story, together with 'thousands of shrimp', emerge. (Bartley's appearance, incidentally, testifies to the accuracy of Ibn Ezra's and Maharai Kara's speculations: he was covered in whale blood, so traumatised that he had to be tied, thrashing and screaming, to a bunk in the captain's cabin, and for the rest of his life the skin on his hands, neck and face remained bleached white by acids and gastric juices.)

Bartley's sumptuously metaphorised whale's stomach (as pink canopy, dark sack and soft India rubber) clearly represents a kind of Bermuda Triangle of the imagination where 'fact' collapses into something deeper, darker, and more metaphorical/liminal and reality springs a leak. And his gravestone in Massachusetts with the inscription 'James Bartley, 1870–1909: a modern day Jonah' represents one of those strangely tangible points where the mythical sub-world of the 'Bible' emerges, or literally thrusts itself up from, the solid ground of reality, briefly entwining itself with it, mutually affirming it, asserting that in this place at this time the book of Jonah could have, might have, 'happened'.

A similar but more complex collapse of the contemporary into the biblical takes place in a sur- (or sub-) real Jonah sequence on the Canadian TV series *Northern Exposure*. The series is set in Alaska, already an alternative, liminal world on the borders of the 'real', like E. Annie Proulx's Newfoundland or the lives of the New England whalers. And in this particular episode the New York doctor, Joel Fleischman, is out rowing on the lake and contemplating whether to allow his non-Jewish girlfriend, Maggie O'Connell, to cook him

---

[163] R. Hendrickson, *The Ocean Almanac* (London: Hutchinson), pp. 322–4. I am grateful to Anne Datta, zoology librarian at the Natural History Museum, for digging *The Ocean Almanac* out for me.

Passover dinner, when his childhood rabbi materialises in the boat beside him, the boat tips up, and the two find themselves within the whale. Beneath a tent-like heaving canopy on which ribs and spine are clearly discernible, and against a backing track of long languorous breathing and lapping water (rather like New Age relaxation tapes), the following conversation ensues:

JOEL: Rabbi?

RABBI: Right here.

JOEL: Where are we?

RABBI: [*Lighting a match.*] Wait a second, I'll make this brighter.

JOEL: You smoke?

RABBI: Just the occasional one, Joel. I don't inhale . . .

JOEL: Gee, this stinks.

RABBI: Hey, what's this? [*Finds a light already wired up and plugged in. Takes the lead and hooks it on the spine above.*]

JOEL: [*Picking something up from the ground.*] Hey, my baseball bat. Hey Rabbi, this is mine . . .

RABBI: [*Also picking something up from the ground.*] My father's Mishnah . . . I haven't seen one like this in fifty years.

JOEL: Oh, look at this. Spiderman. I *knew* I didn't throw this away. What's going on here?

RABBI: We're inside, Joel.

JOEL: Inside what?

RABBI: The fish, the belly of the beast.

JOEL: O my God, O God. [*Pause, looks*]. Hey Rabbi, that looks very much like alveoli. Let me tell you something, if that is, we stand a very good chance of being slimed to death by digestive enzymes and I think we better get out of here, like, fast.

RABBI: We could make a fire. I took my son Neil to see a movie just like this.

JOEL: What? You're talking about *Pinocchio*?

RABBI: That's right. The whale just coughed them right out.

JOEL: That's Walt Disney. It's a *movie* . . . All right, look, I mean stomachs and coughing anatomically have no correlation but . . . I can't believe I'm having this conversation . . . but if we attempt an oesophageal exit we have a small matter of teeth to consider. I think it would be best if we went colo-rectal.

RABBI: You mean – ?

JOEL: I mean every living creature has to excrete and I think this is safest – come on.

[*They make their way to the back of the fish, which mutates into a turnstile for the New York subway. They leap over the turnstile and from this point on the belly becomes a train*]

Clearly the contemporary and the biblical are nesting in each other here in all kinds of complex and cunning ways, and the scriptwriters are playing with the Chinese-box relationships between reality and fiction. Joel and the rabbi on TV, descend into the biblical subworld, which is hardly real; but it's more real, apparently, than Walt Disney, because when the rabbi suggests using Gepeto's and Pinocchio's tactics for getting out of Monstro, Joel replies scathingly that *that's* just a movie. The whole sequence is packaged in the corny film cliché of the dream sequence: later Joel wakes up, sans rabbi, on the shore of the lake, murmuring something strange about a fish bringing him to shore. But the relationship between the unreal and the real is actually far more devious than this – the contemporary fills the myth-fish with 'junk' culture including Spiderman, baseball bats, the New York subway, even Clinton's famous statement about 'not inhaling' marijuana – rather as if it were forcing the biblical to swallow great drafts of the present. And the effect is comic: it makes the reality of the biblical world hiccup and choke when you bring an anatomical specialist (with *Gray's Anatomy* in his head) down into the belly of the whale. 'Going colo-rectal' (a solution that echoes the Catholic martyr John Fisher's speculations about Jonah being 'voyded' from the fish 'in the manner of dung'), as opposed to being 'slimed by digestive enzymes', is a perfect way of playing off the incongruity of the harsh world of post-Enlightenment fact against biblical credulity ('I can't believe I'm having this conversation', mutters Joel, in parenthesis). It points to the huge abyss between the contemporary and the book of Jonah, between a world where God is God, and a world where God is just a saying that has lost all edge of worship or even blasphemy ('Oh God, Oh God', murmurs Joel, when he realises that he's in the belly of the beast). The misty, credulous biblical world, or whale's belly, seems to be the world of childhood (of Spiderman and baseball bats) or of the past (my father's Mishnah) and yet it still lurks somewhere down below, beneath the 1990s, or adult life, somewhere deep *within*. But for the scriptwriters, the biblical and the contemporary can only be linked by means of the tongue-in-cheek surreal, and for the characters within the whale, who share the scriptwriters' alienation, biblical messages are opaque and notoriously difficult to discern. Puzzling over what the Jonah story could possibly 'mean' in Joel's situation, the Rabbi hazards something about Maggie being Joel's 'Nineveh', and something about 'the evasion of responsibility'; but both meanings have to be

Figure 1a. Hell mouth, Winchester(?) Psalter, twelfth century

Figure 1b. *The Mouth of Hell*, the Book of Hours of the Master of Catherine of Cleves, fifteenth century

Figure 2. *Jonah en de walvis*, 1564, by Dirk Crabeth, in St Janskerk, Gouda

Figures 3a & b. Jonah is spat out from the whale/the resurrection, two
details from the Jüngeres Bibelfenster, *c.* 1280, in Cologne cathedral

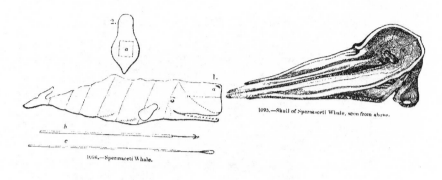

1095.—Skull of Spermaceti Whale, seen from above.

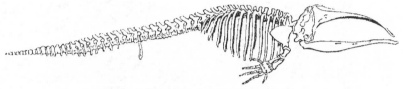

1096.—Spermaceti Whale.

1104.—Skeleton of Greenland Whale.

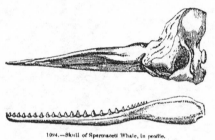

1094.—Skull of Spermaceti Whale, in profile.

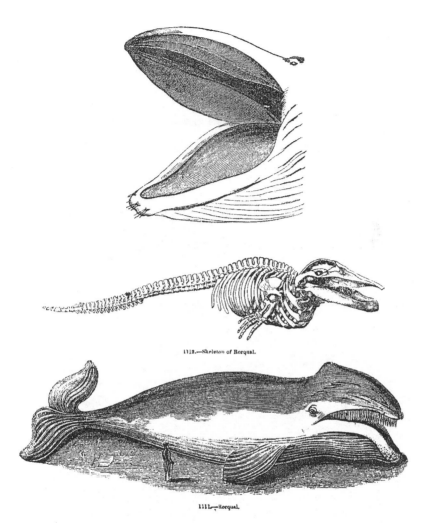

1112.—Skeleton of Rorqual.

1111.—Rorqual.

Figure 4. Skeletons, diagrams and dissections of fish/whales/porpoises, as found on the pages of nineteenth-century cetology/ichthology textbooks (the kind of books that I imagine sprawled out alongside the Bible on the Reverend Pusey's desk). Pictures taken from Charles Knight's *Popular Natural History and Pictorial Museum of Animated Nature* and Jim Harter, *Animals: 1419 Copyright-Free Illustrations of Mammals, Birds, Fish, Insects*

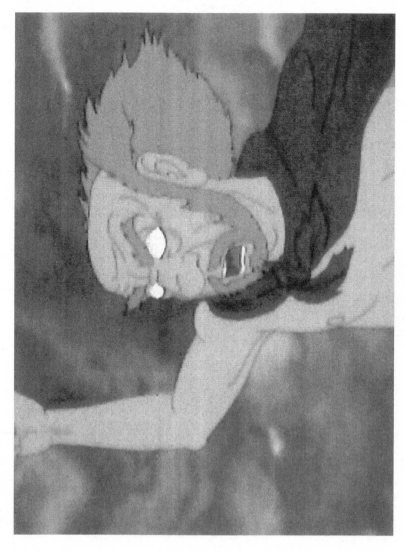

Figure 5. Jonah anticipating the destruction of Nineveh, *Testament: The Animated Bible*

Figure 6. The dilemmas of prophecy, from *Judaism for Beginners*

Figure 7. *Jonah in Haifa Port*, 1978–1979, by Eugene Abeshaus

Figure 8. *Jonah Being Thrown to the Whale*, by Daniel Lindtmager the Younger
(1552–1606)

Figure 9. Engraving by Luca Ciamberlano, after a drawing by Augustino Caracci (1560–1606)

Figure 10. *Jonah is Cast Ashore by the Fish*, by Maarten van Heemskerk (1498–1574)

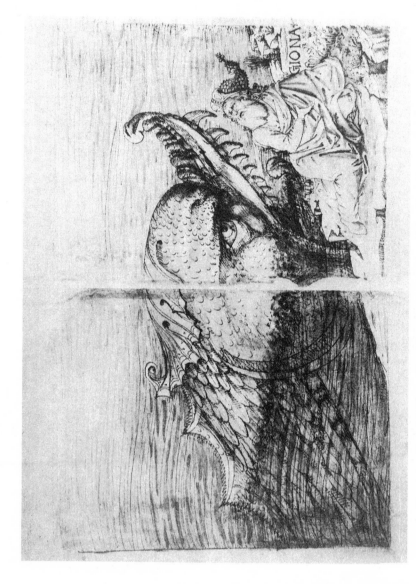

Figure 11. *Florentine Picture Chronicle* II, plates 72 and 73 (this edition London, 1898)

Figure 12. 'Jonah Cycle', by H. Wierix (1549–1615)

Figure 13. *Jonah and the Whale*, by Pieter Lastman (1583–1633)

Figure 14. *Jonah Preaching to Nineveh: the City Repenting,* 1566, by Maarten van Heemskerk (1498–1574)

Figure 15. *Jonah Preaching to the Ninevites*, by Philip Galle (1537–1612), after Maarten de Vos (1532–1603)

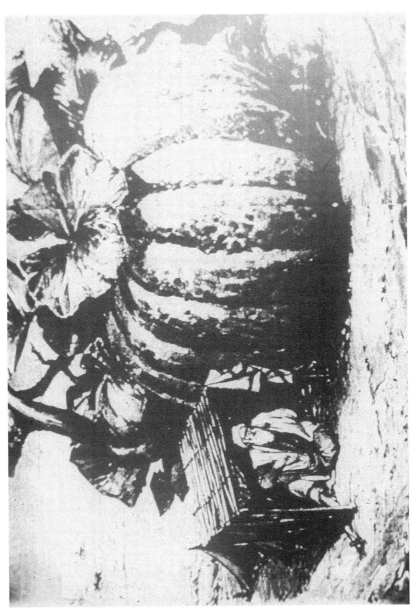

Figure 16. Jonah, from *The Hamlyn Children's Bible in Colour*

extracted by such allegorical twists and sweaty interpretative work that he finds them ultimately unconvincing. Indeed the very difficulty of extracting a lesson points to the more convincing (counter-) lesson that the biblical and the contemporary are simply on a different wavelength and losing any tangible sense of the other's frequency. As the Rabbi muses, from the midst of the fish-subway:

We live in a very confusing age, Joel. Here we are, as close to the Almighty as we're likely to get in this life, and still there's no clarity, I mean do you hear any voices? The Lord spoke to Moses directly – there was no allegory involved. And what was Moses' problem? You don't like slavery? Get out of Egypt. What's to ponder?

These days, it's not so much that when Moses visits the yeshiva, the rabbis are so ingenious that he doesn't know what's going on. Rather the rabbis look back, wistfully, at his simplicity, as they try to milk some contemporary sense from these texts.

The absurdist comedy of *Northern Exposure* comes from lowering a medical expert into the belly of myth, then leaving him to tick off the body parts and find a way out. For as even Bartley seems to know instinctively, the experience of being in a whale is terrifying/ awesome when described in metaphorical terms of heaving pink and white canopies and dark sacks, and absurd when defined in terms of oesophagus, digestive enzymes, colons, rectums, and kidneys. The Mainstream is definitely onto something in its constant tendency to translate the text into language other than its own: to convert it into an abstraction, or iconography, to make it about Jews and gentiles and universalism, or the resurrection of Jesus. For as soon as this text is taken literally and its physical detail midrashically expanded, comic incongruity inevitably results. The iconographic stained-glass presentation of Jonah – cleanly stepping out of the car-ferry fish, and stepping forward as a sign of Christ – is not one that disturbs the sanctity of the church or cathedral. But imagine instead Maarten van Heemskerk's Jonah or Pieter Lastman's Jonah hanging in the sancti-fied and reverent space of the church. These Jonahs are assiduous literalists: they follow the Hebrew text, rather than the hygienically modified Septuagint, which states that Jonah was not 'cast' but 'vomited/spewed' out.[164] Heemskerk's Jonah (fig. 10) does not step out of the fish but is propelled out of it on what looks like a propulsive tide of fish-phlegm, and Pieter Lastman's Jonah (fig. 13) runs from the

---

[164] The Hebrew verb is קיא (to vomit).

fish, clearly pursued by traces of fish-sputum. These Jonahs –
ignominiously belched and sneezed out, clothes tattered, or in
Lastman's case practically removed altogether (apart from a strategically draped piece of cloth) – suggest that the artists are applying the
same kind of speculative literalism as the medieval Jewish interpreters: presumably Jonah's clothes have corroded because of the
same acids and enzymes that would have burnt his skin raw, the same
enzymes presumably that Joel Fleischman spots oozing from the
fish's alveoli. And a similar assiduous literalism is applied to the
repentance scenes at Nineveh: Heemskerk, reading that the King of
Nineveh proclaimed: 'let man and beast be covered with sackcloth,
and let them cry mightily to God' (Jonah 3.8), and seeing that God
repents on account of the 'twenty thousand people' *and* the 'many
cattle' (4.11), faithfully depicts the (very Athenian-looking) city as a
veritable zoo of repentance (fig. 14). Two cows and goats lead the
fasting, and (in an imaginatively midrashic touch) seem to be making
so much noise in their anguish that a person behind them is telling
them to hush. Similarly in Galle's Nineveh (fig. 15) sheep form the
front row of the prophet's attentive congregation, and a cow kneels
behind Jonah in a pseudo-human posture of repentance.

    To modern eyes, like mine, such fantastically literal interpretations
of the text look like intentionally cartooning, lampooning, secularising pastiches of the biblical. They are reminiscent of the kind of
twentieth-century interpretations that pursue the literal, precisely
because that way the absurd lies: 'Where would Jonah have sat?'
asks Huxley – presumably on one vast kidney; 'What would it have
looked like, from the outside, if a prophet on the inside of the fish
were singing psalms?' – it would have looked as if the 'great fish were
spurting music' and praises to God, rather like the ticking crocodile
in *Peter Pan*. But according to art historians, these grotesque depictions of Jonah are thrown up by a distinct moment in the history of
European art, and the effect of absurdity is the product of anachronism, not design. According to John Knipping, sixteenth-
century Netherlandish art, in the wake of the Counter-Reformation,
moves away from iconography to materialistic literalism and tends
to interpret all biblical texts in an 'earthy, tangible, somatically
approachable' way.[165] And this leads to all kinds of interpretations of

---

[165] J. B. Knipping, *Iconography of the Counter-Reformation in the Netherlands: Heaven and Earth* 1
(Nieuwkoop: B. de Graaf, 1974), p. 14.

the sacred that appear dissonant/shocking/comic to contemporary eyes: for example, Jerome Cock's illustration of Luke 6.41 as two men arguing with a huge beam and a not inconsiderable speck projecting out of their eyes; Theodor Galle's depiction of Romans 12.20 as an enemy with a real pile of coals on his head; and Maarten van Heemskerk's etching of Christ on the cross, with a clearly visible penis beneath his loincloth, at least half-way to erection. Historically, these seeming-lampoons of Jonah need to be contextualised as part of a world where Maarten van Heemskerk seriously, literally, imagines what Christ would have looked and felt like on the cross, and where proverbial logs and specks and fish-vomit and repentant goats are all graphically, faithfully illustrated (with a faithfulness that is emphatically not the mock-faithfulness of a parodying secularity). But at the same time – just as Maarten van Heemskerk's Christ has recently become a hot topic in Christian theological circles, precisely because his image is incompatible with the de-sexualised Christ of tradition – so these Jonah pictures point to a sense of revelry in the physicality of the text that has been all but drowned out in the Mainstream. I inhabit an age where the idea of the sicked-up prophet or cows in sackcloth cannot readily be paired with the disembodied sacred, but the fact that Heemskerk, Lastman, Galle, *et al.* do not, means that they provide a fascinating and seemingly sur-real (or heightened-real) counter-current where all the embarrassing, and long-repressed details of the biblical book of Jonah are vividly and graphically made flesh. And, Knipping's warnings apart, I personally suspect that we tend to over-stress the piety and seriousness of past generations – as if such reverence for the biblical were impervious to smiles about repentant cattle, and goats in sackcloth.[166]

A similar kind of unintentional comic literalism can be found in a rather less lofty source: the *Hamlyn Children's Bible in Colour* (fig. 16). In this Bible (the one I grew up with; the one that taught me how to picture biblical texts), Jonah and his huge, outsize *qiqayon*/gourd/pumpkin blurs with Jack and the Beanstalk, James and the Giant Peach, Cinderella-and-the-pumpkin-that-is-magically-transformed-into-a-coach, and other childhood tales of outsize, fabulously en-

---

[166] Compare the comments about *Patience* below. The reductive (modern?) sense that a writer/artist will interpret a biblical text with either straight-faced piety *or* a desire to satirically debunk it, is too simplistic, and excludes all kinds of ironic, mixed modes of relations between text and reader.

hanced fruit and vegetables. The big-ness of the pumpkin is taken absolutely literally: Jonah's giant pumpkin is big enough for him to live in. But Heemskerk-like, the illustrator also pays scrupulous attention to the minutiae of the text, and the disjunction between Jonah 4.5, where Jonah builds himself a booth and sits under it in the shade, and Jonah 4.6, where God causes a *qiqayon* to be a shade over Jonah's head and saves him from his discomfort. The curious thing about this picture is that the pumpkin is not only huge, it is hugely superfluous, for Jonah has already built himself a small, quite serviceable hut. (The problem has troubled Mainstream and Jewish critics for centuries and forced them to try and find solutions:[167] redaction critics remove the hut verse as a flimsy and unnecessary addition;[168] Rashi, somewhat similarly, suggests that the hut was only a temporary structure, a badly built flat-pack that soon fell down.)[169]

If the Dutch painters of the sixteenth century and the *Hamlyn Children's Bible in Colour* unconsciously ruffle the calm surface of the Mainstream reading of Jonah, Herman Melville consciously and deliberately sends a gale through the book. The gargantuan novel *Moby Dick* is obsessed with, and modelled on, the body of the whale; it begins, appropriately enough, with a collection of clippings on the whale collected by a 'sub-sub-librarian' from sources as diverse as

---

[167] For example, J. P. Lettinga goes out on an obfuscating grammatical limb to claim that the phrase 'Jonah made a booth for himself there' (4.5) is in fact an example of the conversive imperfect bearing 'connotative-voluntative' nuances so that the meaning is *really* 'There, [Jonah] wished to build for himself a hut [but presumably did not]' (J. P. Lettinga, *Grammaire de l'Hebreu Biblique* (Leiden: E. J. Brill, 1980), p. 169). Lacocque and Lacocque take a rather idiosyncratic Jungian tack and argue that, since the booth is purely symbolic, it is of no practical use in giving shade (Lacocque and Lacocque, *The Jonah Complex*, pp. 87–8).

[168] Redaction criticism is a branch of so-called historical biblical criticism that focuses on the composite nature of the text and often posits successive layers of editing (or redaction). The most common solution to the double-shade problem is to propose that Jonah 4.5 originally belonged after 3.4, but was moved either in response to God's query in 4.4 or because of a so-called 'scribal error'. For this kind of relatively minor textual surgery at work see, for example, H. Winckler, 'Zum Buche Jona', *Altorientalische Forschungen* 2 (1900), pp. 260–5, and more recently, P. Trible, 'Studies in the Book of Jonah' (PhD diss., Columbia University; Ann Arbor, Mich.: University Microfilms International, 1963; order no. 65–7479), pp. 101–2. Major textual surgery is not usually applied to Jonah on the grounds that it appears to be a narrative unity, but for a dramatic exception, see E. Nielsen, 'Le message primitif du livre de Jonas', *Revue d'histoire et de philosophie religieuses* 59 (1979), pp. 499–507.

[169] Rashi, a proponent of *peshat* (or straight) interpretation, as opposed to midrashic detours, shows how Jewish interpretation can sometimes look very like Christian exegesis. In this case he is clearly trying to eradicate the textual difficulty, just like the Mainstream exegetes.

Pliny, Plutarch, *Paley's Theology, Cook's Voyages* and the book of Genesis.[170] As Captain Ahab hunts it down, the narrator dissects its body, inch by inch, in whole chapters entitled 'The Sperm Whale's Head'; 'The Right Whale's Head – Contrasted View'; 'The Spirit Spout'; and 'The Great Heidelburgh Tun'. He gets inside the whale with 'cisterns and buckets', contemplates the whale as a dish, as a breakfast of whale balls, and a meat pie 100 feet long; he crawls inside the whale's gullet, exclaiming 'Is this the way the prophet Jonah went?',[171] and he ruminates how you might cure a sperm whale's indigestion by 'administering three or four boat loads of Brandreth pills, and then running out of harm's way, as labourers do when blasting rocks'.[172] He surveys with (mock) contempt romantic 'monstrous pictures of whales' (which are so exaggerated and out of proportion that they might just as well have shown Jonah peeping out of the eye-socket),[173] and investigates, in copious detail, 'Less Erroneous Pictures of Whales and the True Pictures of Whaling Scenes' and 'Whales in paint; in teeth; in Wood; in Sheet Iron; in Stone; in Mountains; in Stars'. In 583 word-crammed pages he amply demonstrates how the whale's mighty bulk 'affords a most congenial theme whereon to enlarge, amplify and generally ex-patiate'; and as befits his subject matter he uses the 'weightiest words of the dictionary' and the 'dictionary compiled by the corpulent Samuel Johnson at that'.[174]

Within this gargantuan novel and these huge folds of whale's flesh are woven distorted images from the book of Jonah – what Father Mapple terms 'one of the smallest strands in the mighty cable of Scripture'.[175] Motifs from the biblical text float overtly on the surface, as in Mapple's sonorous sermon or a chapter entitled 'Jonah Historically Regarded', but also materialise in a more submerged, carnivalised form, like images distorted under water. Among these incidental transpositions of the biblical text are the little withered old Jonah who officiates at the bar of the Spouter Inn, serving

---

[170] The extracts can be found in Melville, *Moby Dick* (Norton Critical Edition; ed. H. Hayford and H. Parker, New York: W. W. Norton & Co., 1967), pp. 2–11; elsewhere all quotations are taken from *Moby Dick* (Ware, Hertfordshire: Wordsworth, 1992) unless otherwise stated.

[171] Melville, *Moby Dick*, p. 343. Melville constantly makes allusions to Jonah as he tours the insides of the whale. In the midst of yet another detailed inventory of the whale's innards, he cautions himself for 'seizing the privilege of Jonah alone; the privilege of discoursing upon the joists and beams; the rafters, ridge-pole, sleepers and underpinnings, making up the framework of leviathan; and belike of the tallow-vats, dairy-rooms, butteries and cheeseries in his bowels' (*ibid.*, p. 458).

[172] *Ibid.*, p. 420.   [173] *Ibid.*, p. 272.   [174] *Ibid.*, p. 465.   [175] *Ibid.*, p. 42.

'deliriums and death' from a bar shaped from an old whale jaw, and
stacked with 'shabby shelves, ranged round with old decanters,
bottles and flasks'.[176] Elements of the biblical text are also wrinkled
and resorted: as a Dickensian Jonah (old, unrescued, unperturbed)
shuffles round dispensing drafts of delirium rather than oracles of
doom, sailors actively seek to swallow (and vomit?) at this whale bar
(so stealing the fish's prerogative), and look for the fuggy delirium of
alcohol – a death-by-swallowing of a far more palatable kind. Later
in the novel, another incidental Jonah, the harpooner Tashtego
explores first hand (accompanied by 'horrible oily gurgling' sound-
effects) the 'way that Jonah went'. In a bowdlerised performance of
the biblical original he tumbles into the head of a decapitated
sperm-whale but is saved by an act of 'midwifery': comically the
weight of his body seems to animate the whale's head making it bob
knowingly beneath the surface of the water, 'as if just seized by an
idea'.[177]

Had Tashtego perished in that head, Melville/Ishmael ruminates,
while his 'Jonah' lies unconscious in the oily afterbirth, 'it would
have been a very precious perishing; smothered in the very whitest
and daintiest of fragrant spermaceti; coffined, hearsed, and tombed
in the secret inner chamber and sanctum sanctorum of the
whale'.[178] Yet, he muses, tipping over into heads is not an uncommon phenomenon, for how many have fallen into Plato's honey
head and sweetly perished there?[179] In a viscous, and comically
specialist, rhetoric cobbled together from whaling laws and whale
heads and whale oil, Melville enforces the absolute imperative of
keeping one's own head. He compares the picture of the Pequod
caught in an intricate balancing act between a right whale's head
hoisted up on one side, and a parmacetti's on the other, to the

---

[176] *Ibid.*, p. 12. Compare the way in which Stubb, speaking to his shipmate Flask, offers a
parodic exegesis of the book of Job: 'I don't know Flask, but the devil is a curious chap,
and a wicked one, I tell ye. Why, they say as how he went a sauntering into the old flag-
ship once, switching his tail about as devilish easy and gentleman-like, and inquiring if the
old governor was home. Well, he was at home, and asked the devil what he wanted. The
devil, switching up his hoofs, ups and says, "I want John." "What for?" says the old
governor. "What business is that of yours?" says the devil, getting mad – "I want to use
him". "Take him" says the governor – and by the Lord, Flask, if the devil didn't give John
the Asiatic cholera before he gots through with him, I'll eat this whale in one mouthful'
(*ibid.*, p. 334).

[177] *Ibid.*, p. 351. The bobbing, comically anthropomorphised head is reminiscent of Huxley's
hymn-singing fish.

[178] *Ibid.*, p. 353.   [179] *Ibid.*, p. 353.

individual trying to balance between Kant's and Locke's outsize heads: 'So, when on one side you hoist in Locke's head, you go over that way; but now on the other side, hoist in Kant's and you come back again; but in a very poor plight.'[180] And he appropriates the Dutch whaling laws of 1695 to encourage the reader not to be 'loose fish', that is fish that are 'fair game for anybody who can soonest catch them' (just as, say, America in 1492 was a loose fish to John Bull the harpooner).[181] All too aware of how prone readers are to slip into the nearest available sweet-sounding honey head, Melville makes his own narrative voice bob up and down, and lurch between register and styles in a way that is prone to bring on sea-sickness.[182] At one point (for a whole chapter in fact) 'Ishmael' engages in a lengthy metaphysical speculation on 'whiteness' in the manner of a French literary theorist; and then, snapping out of his proto-Derridean reverie on the abyss, he takes his own temperature, apologises that he must be sickening for a fever, and shifts to a more earthy kind of contemplation – of whale balls for breakfast.[183] The lurching of styles, registers, and concepts – which led one reviewer to describe the novel, rather disparagingly, as an 'intellectual chowder'[184] – expresses a sense that 'any human thing supposed to be complete must for that reason be faulty'.[185] Or to put it another way, that 'all of us, Presbyterians and pagans alike, are dreadfully cracked about the head'[186] and that no head – or novel – should present itself as smooth, finished and reliable.

Throughout *Moby Dick*, Melville gives the reader plenty of opportunity to practise responding with appropriate scepticism to the pronouncements of other people's heads. And 'Jonah Historically

---

[180] *Ibid.*, p. 336.

[181] *Ibid.*, p. 409.

[182] Sophia Hawthorne, Nathaniel Hawthorne's wife, primly misread this strange lurching quality in Melville, pronouncing that 'he is a boy in opinion – having settled nothing yet' (quoted in W. Berthoff, *The Example of Melville* (Princeton: Princeton University Press, 1962)). More to the point, I think, is an early and astute description of what we now might call Melville's dialogism by Lawrence Thompson. Thompson observes that 'Melville is inclined to see at least two possible values for all images, all concepts', and that 'as soon as he was able to turn away from one value and call it illusion he was victimised by the realisation that the new value which he had embraced might also contain elements of illusion' (L. Thompson, *Melville's Quarrel with God* (Princeton: Princeton University Press, 1952), p. 149).

[183] Melville, *Moby Dick*, p. 307.

[184] Evert Duyckinck, cited in Melville, *Moby Dick* (Norton Critical Edition), p. 613.

[185] Melville, *Moby Dick*, p. 135.

[186] *Ibid.*, p. 25.

Regarded' is one of its most elementary exercises. Here we meet various 'learned exegetists' and theological authorities who suggest:

(a) that Jonah was 'not ensconced in the whale's belly, but was temporarily lodged in some part of his mouth';

(b) that Jonah was ensconced in the mouth of a 'Right Whale' which could 'easily accommodate a couple of whist tables, and comfortably seat all the players';

(c) that maybe Jonah lodged in a 'hollow tooth' (until he remembers 'on second thoughts' that 'the Right Whale is toothless');

(d) that Jonah took refuge in the floating body of a dead whale 'even as the French soldiers in the Russian campaign turned their dead horses into tents and crawled into them';

(e) that a whale is merely a convenient metaphor for a 'life-preserver' or 'an inflated bag of wind' (a kind of ancient life jacket?);

(f) that Jonah was taken on board by 'some vessel with a whale for its figurehead' and named *The Whale*, just as craft are nowadays christened *The Shark*, *The Gull* and *The Eagle*.[187]

Clearly the theologians are, like the whale-life-jacket they describe, no more than 'inflated bags of wind' whose less-than-honey-heads are easily resisted (but whose arguments are not so far-fetched to those familiar with the Mainstream). However, negotiating one's way between different heads in regard to Jonah is not always this easy – as the more advanced exercise, Father Mapple's Jonah sermon, clearly demonstrates. Mapple's flowing rhetoric, so brilliantly performed by Orson Welles in John Huston's film version of the book, is pure rhetorical honey. The 'billow-like and boisterously grand'[188] current of the sermon sweeps over us, taking us with Jonah to the 'kelpy bottom of the waters', boxes, bales, and jaws clatter overboard, the open maw of the whale 'cleaves' through the waves. As his own labour-intensive rhetoric engorges his own body, and he enters into the effort of the 'howling, shrieking, slanting, storm', Mapple's chest heaves with a 'ground swell' and 'thunders roll off his swarthy brow'. Rarely has the biblical text had an expositor this mesmerising, this *animating*: Jonah is a burglar with 'slouched hat and guilty eye', 'skulking' from his policeman God; the ship is the 'first recorded smuggler' carrying the prophet as 'contraband'; the white

---

[187] All of these fabulous suggestions are catalogued by Melville, *Moby Dick*, pp. 374–5.

[188] Melville, *Moby Dick*, p. 42. (All of the following extracts from Mapple's sermon can be found in Melville, *Moby Dick*, pp. 43–50.)

moon is 'affronted', the gale is 'indignant', and the 'queasy sea rebels' and 'refuses to bear the wicked burden'. As Jonah is catapulted onto shore, his ears like two sea-shells 'still multitudinously murmuring of the ocean', everything propels the reader to situate herself as an open-mouthed member of the adoring congregation, and to see the sermon, as many literary critics have done, as the moral high ground and axiomatic centre of the novel.[189]

Except for the contexts. First there is the context of Melville's own meta-description of his novel as a 'wicked book', 'written while feeling as innocent as a lamb',[190] or as a novel that requires the health-warning:

Moby Dick is not a piece of fine feminine Spitalfields silk – but is of the horrible texture of a fabric that should be woven of ships' cables and hawsers. A Polar wind blows through it, and birds of prey hover over it.[191]

And then there is the context of the novel's own cetology-theology, and its highly selective use of the biblical canon. *Moby Dick* draws on Job and Jonah and chooses as its central characters not David and Isaac, but Ishmael and Ahab, the outcasts and the unchosen, the victims of divine deselection, who wander into *Moby Dick* still smarting from their biblical experiences (by the time the novel begins, Ishmael is already an agnostic, and Ahab is aflame with fury against the inscrutability of the beast).[192] And as the outline of the

---

[189] The famous Melville biographer Newton Arvin argues that the sermon is 'intended to make us understand that Ahab, like Jonah, has . . . sinned in his proud refusal to obey God's will' (N. Arvin, *Herman Melville: A Critical Biography* (New York: Carbondale, 1964; 1st edn 1950), pp. 179–80). Howard Vincent maintains that 'if Ahab had been one of the worshippers at the Seamen's Bethel he would have fared much better' (H. P. Vincent, *The Trying-Out of Moby Dick* (New York: Carbondale; 1st edn 1949), p. 121). The few biblical scholars who refer to *Moby Dick* in their analyses of Jonah or Job typically take the sermon as the moral high-point of the novel. Jack Sasson, for example, uses an extract from Mapple's sermon as an introduction for his commentary.

[190] Quoted from correspondence with Nathaniel Hawthorne. See J. Leyda, *The Melville Log: A Documentary of Herman Melville* (2 vols.; New York: Cordian Press, 1969), I, p. 415.

[191] Quoted by S. Cameron, *The Corporeal Self: Allegories of the Body in Melville and Hawthorne* (Baltimore and London: Johns Hopkins University Press, 1981), p. 15 (no further reference given).

[192] Ishmael is the first son of Abraham and his concubine Hagar, who, under persecution by Abraham's wife, Sarah, is expelled into the wilderness in favour of Isaac, the true son and heir; Ahab is one of the superlatively bad kings of the book of Kings and is deliberately deceived by God through a lying spirit so that he is seduced to his death in battle (see 1 Kings 22). Although Melville draws chiefly on Job and Jonah, the book is saturated with a number of incidental biblical images, from virtual throwaways such as Mrs Hosea Hussey (a comic allusion to the prophet Hosea's adulterous wife) to the more resonant image of the ship *The Rachel*, looking for the drowned lost child. For a discussion of biblical images in Moby Dick see N. Wright, *Melville's Use of the Bible* (Durham, N.C.: Duke University

Judaeo-Christian deity blurs into Egyptian, Hindu, and Greek mythology,[193] 'God' becomes, variously, an 'unseen and unaccountable old joker',[194] 'the unseen, ambiguous, synod in the air, the vindictive princes and potentates of fire',[195] the 'universal thump'[196] that is passed around, and a 'heartless void' into which the narrative (as well as Ahab and his crew) is sucked.[197] Ultimately Godness and whaleness blur: 'Dissect [Moby Dick] how I may', laments the narrator-turned-cetologist/theologian, conjuring the elusive, encrypted I AM of Exodus 34.23, 'I but go skin deep . . . Thou shalt see my back parts, my tail, he seems to say, but my face shall not be seen.'[198] As God fades into the whiteness of the whale, he becomes a 'dumb blankness full of meaning', a self-imploding, signification-crammed space of 'colourless all-colour' that evokes, alternately, soft fur, purity, absence, innocence, terror, and a metallic coldness and arctic chill.[199]

If the polar chill that Melville speaks of can be found, at least in part, in the arctic freeze of God, something reminiscent of the birds of prey lurks in the whaleman's chapel, where a blood-sucking 'faith,

---

Press, 1949), and more recently, L. J. Kreitzer's excellent study, '*Moby Dick*: Encountering the Leviathan of God', in *The Old Testament in Fiction and Film* (The Biblical Seminar 24; Sheffield: Sheffield Academic Press, 1994), pp. 49–93.

[193] For a discussion of the unorthodox mythologies that Melville incorporates in Moby Dick, see H. B. Franklin, *The Wake of the Gods: Melville's Mythology* (Stanford: Stanford University Press, 1963).

[194] Melville, *Moby Dick*, p. 232.

[195] *Ibid.*, p. 475.

[196] *Ibid.*, p. 4: 'Everyone is a slave . . . either in a physical or a metaphysical view . . . and so the universal thump is passed around.'

[197] Or as Queequeg puts it, in another of Moby Dick's counter-intuitive theologies: 'Queequeg no care what God made him shark, wedder Fejee god or Nantucket God; but de god what made de Shark must be one dam Injin' (*ibid.*, p. 311).

[198] *Ibid.*, p. 388.

[199] The quotations are taken from the famous chapter 'The Whiteness of the Whale' (*ibid.*, pp. 191–200) in which whiteness, hence Godness, is associated with the 'innocence of brides' *and* 'gauntleted ghosts', with polar sharks and bears *and* the 'benignity of age', with 'the majesty of justice and the ermine of the judge', *and* the terrifying strangeness of an albino face. In the mass of meanings that stockpile in this chapter, whiteness simultaneously enfolds the purity of Christ, the alb of Christian priests, *and* the 'king of terrors personified by the evangelist, who rides on his pallid horse'; it is the purity of orthodoxy, the comfort of purity and the horror of nothingness, the 'colourless all-colour of atheism from which we shrink'. Melville takes the theological truism of the indescribability of God and twists it in a meditation on the ambiguity of the colour that transcends the spectrum. The sense of groundlessness (sea-ness?) that results is typical of the whole novel – as Leslie Fielder comments: 'Multiple ambiguities undercut the simple polarities between good and evil, Ishmael and Ahab, contradictions and their reconciliation which the book superficially suggest' (L. Fielder, *Love and Death in the American Novel* (New York: Stein and Day, 1975), p. 387).

like a jackal, feeds among the tombs'.[200] In the more immediate context of Mapple's sermon – urging us to take his words with more than a pinch of sea-salt – is a sense that faith feeds on corpses, that the chapel is soaked in death and melancholia, and the congregation 'refuse to be comforted for those who they nevertheless maintain are dwelling in unspeakable bliss'.[201] Parody, like the jackal, also sneaks into the chapel: the hymn 'The Ribs and Terrors of the Whale' (that Huston brilliantly sets to a minor key, with yearning unresolved cadences) is, as D. Battenfeld has shown, a slightly tweaked parody on a Dutch Reformed hymn.[202] The real congregants sing the 'death and terrors of the grave'; Melville's sing of 'the ribs and terrors of the whale'; the real congregants sing of a noble deity flying to the rescue 'as on a cherub's wings'; Melville's of a rather absurd aquatic deity riding to the rescue 'as on a radiant dolphin borne'. Mapple himself is besieged by irony; he thinks himself 'impregnable' in the 'self-contained stronghold' of his pulpit, which he bumptiously conceives of as the prow of the world, [203] he apostrophises a deity 'chiefly known to [him] by [his] rod', and he cuts off the biblical text that he is preaching on at the end of chapter 2 – to curb what can be seen as Jonah's continuing protest.[204] To compound the sense of alienation from the sermon, we exit the chapel with Ishmael who spends the night with Queequeg, the 'soothing savage', and concludes that he'll 'try a pagan friend . . . since Christian kindness has proved a hollow courtesy'.[205]

---

[200] Melville, *Moby Dick*, p. 37.

[201] *Ibid.*, p. 37. In a comment that reminds me of the Talmud's rather knowing observation that 'all sailors are pious' (*b. Kiddushin* 82a), Ishmael observes that 'Few are the moody fishermen shortly bound for the Indian ocean or the Pacific who fail to make a Sunday visit to the (chapel)' – and so implies that faith is not just a jackal, but an insurance policy (Melville, *Moby Dick*, p. 35).

[202] D. Battenfield, 'The Source for the Hymn in Moby-Dick', *American Literature* 27 (1995), pp. 393–6. (Melville was brought up in the Dutch Reformed Church and reared on evangelical Calvinist piety.)

[203] Melville, *Moby Dick*, pp. 40–1. In Huston's film, Mapple's/Welles's extreme elevation is conveyed by awkward camera angles, implying craning necks. The pulpit is literally a ship-prow and a huge cross juts from it, symbolically casting a shadow over the congregation.

[204] The meaning of the telling adumbration of Mapple's text is discussed by J. Holstein, 'Melville's Inversion of Jonah in Moby-Dick', *The Iliff Review* 35 (1978), pp. 13–19 (17). Holstein argues, somewhat sensationally, that Melville 'broiled Mapple's sermon in hell-fire and baptised it in pagan blood' (p. 13). My own opinion is somewhat less sensational: Melville is certainly playing with Jonah but his playing amounts to something less than a black mass.

[205] Melville, *Moby Dick*, pp. 52–3. The scene is profoundly homoerotic: 'In our heart's honeymoon', writes Ishmael, 'lay I and Queequeg – a cosy, loving pair'.

If the reader misses a fang-toothed Christianity and a dolphin-riding deity, then the 'barbed sentences'[206] of Mapple's sermon may still yet warn her not to swallow, hook, line and sinker, Mapple's truth, and so become entangled in the springs of 'Mapple's sermon trap'.[207] For Mapple, who has clearly not only read his Calvin but Calvin's sermons on Jonah,[208] transforms the biblical book into a veritable torture chamber. Mapple's rhetoric takes specific images from Calvin's sermons on Jonah and pushes them to the point where they are overstretched and collapse – just like the body/conscience of the flailing Calvinist subject. Calvin's Jonah 'languishes' in 'continual torments' in the fish-belly hospital; Mapple's Jonah undergoes stifling confinement in the smallest 'wards' of the whale's bowels. Calvin's Jonah learns that God 'sharply pricks us . . . so as to constrain us to tremble';[209] in Mapple's sermon, words 'prick' the 'wrestling' prophet, 'plunge' into his flesh like spurs, drag him underwater and (virtually) drown him, as he undergoes even more brutal soul-surgery. In the belly of the ship, Jonah is:

Like one who after a night of drunken revelry hies to his bed, still reeling, but with conscience yet pricking him, as the plungings of the Roman race horse but so much the more strike his steel tags into him; as one who in the miserable plight still turns and turns in giddy anguish, praying God for annihilation until the fit be passed; and at last amid the whirl of woe he flees, a deep stupor steals over him, as over the man who bleeds to death, for conscience is the wound, and there's naught to staunch it: so after sore wrestlings in his berth, Jonah's prodigy of ponderous misery drags him drowning down to sleep.[210]

As terror digs into him like spurs (and not just any spurs, the spurs of a Roman race horse) and blood gushes from the conscience-wound,

---

[206] L. Thompson, *Melville's Quarrel with God*, p. 164.

[207] *Ibid.*, pp. 10, 428.

[208] T. Walter Herbert has undertaken a detailed survey of Calvin's theology in Mapple's sermon, showing, for example, how the fish, whose teeth close 'like so many white bolts, upon [Jonah's] prison', is very reminiscent of a seventeenth-century Calvinist commentary on Job which speaks of how God 'can destroy us, sooner than Leviathan can crush us, were we beneath his teeth' (T. W. Herbert, 'Calvinist Earthquake: Moby Dick and Religious Tradition', in R. H. Brodhead (ed.), *New Essays on Moby Dick* (Cambridge: Cambridge University Press, 1986), pp. 109–40 (125)). But as far as I am aware, no one has pointed out the specific correspondences between Calvin's Jonah sermon and Mapple's – though surely the reference to the hospital/ward seems to point in that direction. (Given his subtle and sophisticated play on the Dutch Reformed hymn, such a joke would be typical of Melville, even if the joke has remained largely private until now.)

[209] Calvin, *Commentaries*, p. 36.

[210] Melville, *Moby Dick*, pp. 45–6.

Calvin's capacity to turn words into lexical instruments of torture is pushed to hyperbolic extremes. The point is pushed until Jonah's body, and Calvinist rhetoric, stop struggling and acknowledge defeat, falling satisfyingly submissive and limp, 'bruised and beaten'.

Mapple's sermon is not so much about the orthodox punishment of Jonah-as-rebel, but about the satisfying punishment of punishing (Calvinist) rhetoric. And so Jonah-as-dissident is conscripted into a larger narrative campaign which has been described as anti-Calvinist, or even gnostic.[211] As Melville pushes the reader away from land (aka security, comfort, and 'all that's kind to our mortalities') towards the 'howling infinite' where the solid turns watery and the 'stateliest stiffest frigate' – and the stateliest stiffest truths – are in danger of being pulverised,[212] the lines between the deity and the demonic crash inwards. In a pursuit that climaxes in a chapter called 'The Devil's Chase' (but in which the distinction between hunter and hunted, subject and object is magnificently blurred) the 'grand-ungodly god-like man' Ahab, who metaphorically hosts a black mass and yet is also crucified, meets the colourless all-colour of the God-Whale who simultaneously provokes to faith and atheism.[213] In this context, Jonah functions not as a corrective to Ahab, but as a proleptic story of a nascent mini-Ahab, just as Ahab's story is explicitly Jonah-like (when Moby Dick first attacked him, he 'lay like dead for three days and three nights').[214] Mapple's sermon unwittingly brings into the novel the story of a 'headstrong, recalcitrant God-challenging prophet, whose one supreme moment of surrender to God's will only occurred after God had scared poor Jonah

---

[211] The now well-established argument for Melville's anti-Calvinism is set out by T. Walter Herbert, who argues that 'Melville sets forth a Calvinistic analysis of Ahab's moral strife in order to form a drama in which Calvin's God appears morally dubious on liberal principles, yet in which liberal principles lose their validity as a description of religious truth' (T. W. Herbert, *Moby Dick and Calvinism: A World Dismantled* (New Brunswick, N.J.: Rutgers University Press, 1977)). The argument for narrative gnosticism in Moby Dick is set out by T. Vargosh, 'Gnostic Myths in Moby Dick', *Proceedings of the Modern Language Association* 81 (1966), pp. 272–7. (See also T. Y. Booth, 'Moby Dick: Standing Up to God', in *Nineteenth Century Fiction* 17 (1962–3), pp. 33–43.)

[212] Melville, *Moby Dick*, pp. 109, 283.

[213] The tangled dialectic between good and evil, Ahab and God/Moby Dick is powerfully discussed by Kreitzer, 'Moby Dick: Encountering the Leviathan of God', (see especially pp. 80–90). John Huston's film climaxes in a scene in which Ahab and Moby Dick are literally tangled up together, 'bound together forever through eternity' as the screenwriter Ray Bradbury put it, as Ahab is lashed by coiled ropes to Moby Dick's side, spread-eagled in a kind of crucifixion (*Moby Dick*, Warner Brothers, 1956; see L. Grobel, *The Hustons* (London: Bloomsbury, 1990), pp. 416–23).

[214] Melville, *Moby Dick*, p. 96.

witless',[215] and so introduces us to one of those distressing, excessively suffering characters who refuse to acknowledge God's kingly
rights without (to use Ahab's phrase) asserting their 'queenly' rights
of protest.

For what Ahab (and by implication Jonah) poignantly express is
the terror of human impotence: the littleness of 'baby man', buffeted
by the realisation that 'however baby man may brag of his science
and his skill, and however much, in a flattering future, that science
and skill may augment, yet, forever and ever, to the crack of doom,
the sea will insult and murder him'.[216] They represent the fragility of
human flesh in a novel that focuses obsessively on human as on
whale bodies – on the skin that wraps the body up and offers a
'brace' against the world,[217] on milk and sperm, on unscrewable legs
and navels, leaky bodies and unpluggable holes,[218] on brains and
vertebrae and bone dust.[219] The Ahab who cries 'Rat-tat. So man's
seconds tick',[220] who rails against his creator with all the poignancy
of Frankenstein's monster, who feels himself 'turned round and
round in this world, like yonder windlass, with Fate as the hand-
spike',[221] and who is maddened by 'truth with malice in it' and 'all
that cracks the sinews and cakes the brain',[222] is only an outsize
Everyman, or gnostic/modern 'Adam', 'deadly faint, bowed and
humped . . . staggering beneath the piled centuries since Paradise'.[223] Lear-like, he represents the terror of man as 'poor naked
wretch', and the defiance of man as he probes the boundaries
between sinned against or sinning, and asks (reworking the words of
Job): 'Who's to blame when the Judge himself is dragged to the bar?'

The spectre of baby man, mewling, puking, and subjected to
perverse whims of fate pops up with remarkable frequency in
readings of Jonah outside the Mainstream – sometimes in the most
unexpected places. The medieval homily *Patience* constantly reiter-
ates Jonah's littleness (he is a mote in the fish's mouth, a minor
irritation in the fish's stomach, and his God, who sits on a throne so

---

[215] L. Thompson, *Melville's Quarrel with God*, p. 164.
[216] Melville, *Moby Dick*, p. 283.
[217] *Ibid.*, p. 115.   [218] *Ibid.*, p. 484.
[219] All of these examples are discussed in Cameron, *The Corporeal Self*, pp. 15–75.
[220] Melville, *Moby Dick*, p. 535.
[221] *Ibid.*, p. 551.   [222] *Ibid.*, p. 187.
[223] *Ibid.*, pp. 549–50. Compare the earlier description of Ahab as one who 'piles upon the
      whale's white hump all the general rage and hate felt from his whole race from Adam
      down' and then 'bursts his hot heart's shell upon it' (*ibid.*, p. 187).

high, thinks his expressions of misery are 'paltry') – as well as his quest for survival, shelter, and 'sweet' security. An all-too-human Jonah 'huddles' in the 'hurrock' (or keel) of the ship, he seeks out a corner that is 'safe from harm' in the fish's belly, and he shelters in the 'greenness of the glimmering leaves' that provide him with a 'haven', a 'leafy bower of bliss'.[224] And given that God tells him to accept his commission 'without another word', he is curiously eloquent about his terrors, despairs, and fears.[225] Trembling, he confides in the reader his fear that the Ninevites will 'confine him in a fetterlock, wrest out [his] eyes', and that God, from the security of his heavenly throne, will:

> frown very little,
> Though I be seized in Nineveh and stripped naked,
> [And] piteously torn apart on a cross by many knaves

(clearly he has read the stories of Samson and Jesus and knows what can happen to biblical heroes). When God overturns his oracle he protests:

> It would be more agreeable to perish at once, so it seems to me (*as me thynk*)
> Than to teach longer your doctrine which thus makes me false.

And when God takes away his 'leafy bower of excellence' 'at a wap' (all at once) and the heat 'burns hotly', a 'gryndel' (angry) Jonah cries 'hotly', with an 'anguych' and temperature that is totally justified:

> Ah, you Maker of man, why does [it] seem a victory to you
> Thus to destroy your prophet, more than all the others,
> With all [the] misfortune that you can [send]? Will you never spare me?
> I obtained for myself one consolation that is now taken from me . . .

Though the ostensible purpose of at least one of these speeches is to show how far Jonah falls short of his allegorical association with Christ,[226] his soliloquised whimperings are surprisingly poignant. This empathetically human perspective is only consolidated by the

---

[224] For a discussion of the way in which the *Gawain*-poet emphasises Jonah's desire for protection and shelter, see S. Stanbury, 'Space and Visual Hermeneutics in the *Gawain*-Poet', *Chaucer Review* 21 (1987), pp. 476–89.

[225] It is interesting that Jonah also once addresses God as *renk* – or man – an intimate mode of address that is extremely uncommon in medieval poetry and implies that Jonah is speaking with 'midrashic' frankness.

[226] So Spearing and Spearing: 'The figural allusion to the crucifixion is present only as part of Jonah's realistic forebodings, and its presence serves only to make us aware of Jonah's inadequacy to play the part he foreshadows' (*Poetry in the Age of Chaucer*, p. 119).

prologue, which by implication associates the fate of Jonah with the lot of the feudal peasant. As if to give us a clue that this is no conventional exercise in medieval homiletics, the poet situates himself in the pew, rather than the pulpit, and reports how he heard a sermon on the Beatitudes at Mass. He is no medieval Mapple, no poet-preacher or morality play narrator: rather, like Gower or Chaucer, he takes up a position as a 'layman of good-will . . . an "I" that is like "you"'.[227] Medieval poems often begin with complaints of poverty addressed by the poets to their patrons – either to advertise their own religious vows of poverty or, quite simply, to elicit more cash – but the *Gawain*-poet gives the convention a 'new twist'.[228] He sits in the congregation and identifies himself as poor, and his poverty affects his readings of both Jonah and the Beatitudes. Whereas medieval sermons habitually stress that the needy must wait to reap the rewards of their misery in future bliss (rather than try and rebel against the current social order), the *Gawain*-poet reads the 'happiness of the poor' in the context of now, in a wryly Chaucerian and utterly pragmatic fashion. His conclusions are fourfold:

(a) 'Poverty and patience' are inevitably 'playmates': Dame Poverty and Dame Patience always hang out together.

(b) Though they may not be the most attractive of female companions (in fact they are depicted as ugly pantomime dames) those forced to associate with them will get on better if they flatter them and learn to get on with them, rather than insult them and just make things worse.

(c) It's best to refrain from raging and ripping your clothes – if only because you must sit with the torn stuff and sew it back together.

(d) Lessons learnt by obeying earthly Sires or liege Lords can be applied, *mutatis mutandis*, to divine Sires. Feudal Lords may choose to keep you waiting, or send you on an errand, and may give you scant reward for your pains, but you know that grumbling gets you in trouble, whereas submission brings you profit.

Given that the poet's task is to sell 'patience', the most 'displeasing' of the virtues,[229] his choice of Jonah (rather than the more obvious

---

[227] A. Middleton, 'The Idea of Public Poetry in the Reign of Richard II', *Speculum* 53 (1979), pp. 94–114 (99).

[228] Spearing and Spearing, *Poetry in the Age of Chaucer*, p. 113.

[229] It is indicative of the whole tone of the poem that it begins 'Patience is a virtue, though it displease often.'

example of Job) is a curious one – and one that seems to work on two levels. On the first (official) level the poem extols the Patience of God (who is patient with both Jonah and with Nineveh)[230] and it adopts the 'foolish wretch' Jonah, the self-confessed 'gaule [or scum] of prophetes' as the counter-example of Patience. So far, so Mainstream, apart from the messy physicality of the poem, which we waded through above. But on another level the poem clearly implies that the book of Jonah is a supremely trying narrative and that Jonah is the ultimate biblical exemplar of those who are buffeted by forces beyond their control, and who are therefore *obliged* to practise patience. As the official voice of the poem extols the Boethian ideal of 'steering [or governing] one's heart', and warns against trying to resist 'Goddes windes' or the motions of Wyrde (Fate), a wryer, more subliminal countervoice suggests that to the poor (and to Jonah) Boethian philosophy can appear comically luxurious.[231] Those who are only too aware that life blows you about with or without your consent know only too well that, as a stoic and pragmatic deity tells Jonah, 'he that is to rakel to renden his clothez/Mot efte sitte with more unsounde to sewe he to-geder'.

Rather than being a conventional sermon on the Beatitudes or Jonah, the poem gives the impression of itself being a wry, and perhaps ultimately unconvinced, palliative to ugly Dame Patience.[232] And although the *Gawain*-poet is perfectly capable of treating biblical characters to strong doses of discipline, Jonah escapes remarkably unscathed. In the companion poem *Cleanness*,

---

[230] The God of Patience seems to be making an overt point when he tells Jonah: 'Were I as harsh as you sir, misfortune would have befallen.'

[231] The biblical text stresses how the plot falls out exactly according to God's design: how he 'appoints' the fish the worm and the storm to do exactly as he bids. In fact so strong is the plot's current that the sailors are depicted as futilely 'digging' against it (Jonah 1.13). Appropriately enough for a poem that advocates submission to 'Goddes Windes', *Patience* emphasises the inexorable flow of fate/the divine plot. The fish, 'arranged' by Wyrde, swings round alongside the ship right on cue and opens his *swolwe* (gullet); and the sailors, futilely trying to row against the current, find that the 'seething of the dark flood shatters [*bursten*] their oars'.

[232] The original draft of this chapter included a few lines on the fact that this reading could not be found in any work by medieval specialists, who, on the whole tended to read the poem as 'straight' homiletic. I suggested that this was maybe due to a too flat sense of medieval piety, and a sense that mockery/wryness and piety cannot be 'bedfellows' like Poverty and Patience. This is no longer true, as Putter's reading explores the subversive qualities of the poem and shows how it clashes with contemporary sermons and commentary. But at the same time he shows how this profoundly (and unconventionally) religious poem paints a very anthropomorphised picture of a deity who must also exercise patience (see Putter, 'Patience', pp. 103–46).

the poet tells how Lot's wife puts too much salt in the soup of her husband and his guests, though they have repeatedly told her not to, and so God turns her, quite happily and appositely, into a pillar of salt. *Patience*, in contrast, is a very 'humanly attractive'[233] poem in which the 'poet rides our consciences lightly'[234] and castigates Jonah openly only twice.[235] Jonah becomes a character like Gawain, who feels his own powerlessness acutely as he realises himself to be but a pawn in a masterplot against which resistance is useless.[236] And God, like Bertilac/the Green Knight, is a cunning and tricky plot-wielder: as he relates how God 'arranges' the fish and summons the winds, the poet comments: 'For the wielder of wit, who knows all things, who always wakes and watches, has tricks up his sleeve.'

But, though God in *Patience* is a wit-wielder, master-trickster, and quasi-feudal authority, this is no secular protest poem, and, for all his empathy with Jonah, the poet in no way dissents from the principle that divine lords must be obeyed. Six centuries later, the novelist Julian Barnes engages in a full-frontal attack on the absolute power of God in this text, describing him as a fascist dictator or Western Superpower attacking a third-world nation. For Orwell, Jonaism is blindness to 'concentration camps, rubber truncheons, Hitler, Stalin, bombs'; for Barnes the book of Jonah gets entangled with different pages of the twentieth-century history book. God becomes, by

---

[233] D. C. Fowler, *The Bible in Middle English Literature* (Seattle and London: University of Washington Press, 1984), p. 187.

[234] Stone, *Medieval English Verse*, p. 120.

[235] The two incidences have already been noted: Jonah is called a 'foolish wretch' by the narrator, and calls himself the 'scum of the prophets'. He is also referred to as 'Jonah the Jue', but, interestingly, this never becomes a negative appellation and a way of playing him off against the 'gentiles'.

[236] A potted summary of *Sir Gawain* may be helpful here. During the revelry at King Arthur's court one new year, the Green Knight enters, carrying an axe, and challenges anyone to strike him with it, provided he can give a return blow the following year. Gawain, the king's nephew, takes up the challenge and cuts off his head and the knight, still living (and now carrying his head), tells Gawain to come to meet him in the Green Chapel next new year. The next Christmas, on his way to the Green Chapel, Gawain comes across a castle, and the Lord of the castle, Bertilac, offers him rest. He says that he shall go out hunting every day, leaving Gawain alone with his wife, and at the end of the day they shall exchange whatever they have gained. Every day the wife visits Gawain's bedroom, but gets no more than kisses, and the noble knight gives the kisses to Bertilac in exchange for his hunting trophies at the end of every day. But when Bertilac's wife gives Gawain her girdle, Gawain keeps the present a secret from Bertilac, and goes to keep his meeting with the Green Knight. Gawain goes to the chapel, where the Green Knight gives him two feigned blows and a slight nick in the neck, and then reveals that he is Bertilac, and that the slight neck-wound is for the failure to reveal the gift of the girdle. Gawain laments his fault, and then goes back to court, where his fellow-knights judge that he has brought honour to the Round Table.

implication, like Stalin, Mussolini, Hitler, or Western Imperial forces; Jonah becomes an Afghanistan or Vietnam, and the text that the Mainstream reads as glorifying universality is critiqued from the moral high-ground of democracy (of which the supremacy of God itself falls foul). God features as an infuriated judge who places Jonah in a 'floating prison' for 'contempt of court'; a crazed war-game-admiral who gleefully fingerflips the blubbery jail hither and thither across his sea-map; a commander of air- and sea-space who has, 'complete operative control over the winds and water of the Eastern Mediterranean'; a 'paranoid schizophrenic', pushing his servant over the edge; and a 'moral bully' enforcing a 'routine and fairly repellent morality'.[237] Protesting against an overload of divine authorial control, Barnes complains that the plot is not interesting because 'God holds all the cards and wins all the tricks'; so much so that the only suspense is 'how the Lord is going to play it this time: start with the two of trumps and lead up to the ace, start with the ace and run down to the two, or mix them all around?'.[238]

The *Gawain*-poet introduces the idea of (quite literally) 'poor Jonah', Melville critiques the Calvinistically sharpened spurs that dig into poor Jonah's conscience, and, extrapolating a modern deflation of the text that really begins with *Moby Dick*, Barnes totally inverts the morality of the text and lays into divine fascism and torture. Jonah's position is totally vindicated: both his fear of 'being stoned to death by partying Ninevites', and his irritation when, having been 'put to a lot of trouble to bring a message of destruction', he finds that the Lord has decided to annul his decree are both sardonically pronounced to be healthy and 'normal'. In fact it is the schizophrenic God's inversion of his decree that seems perverse, since, contra Christian protestations of divine mercy, the biblical God has a 'well-known, indeed historic taste for wrecking cities'. In another reading that shows that it is hard for Jonah to pass through the twentieth century without picking up resonances from the Second World War, Barnes compares the fate of Jonah, pushed hither and thither by Superpower(s), to the *St Louis*, fingerflipped between nations in its ill-fated flight from Nazi Germany.

For Barnes, Jonah is a grim, oppressive text: indeed the only point in which he seems to take pleasure is the 'fancy [plant-worm] parable' which, as a 'little piece of street theatre' achieved with the

[237] Barnes, *A History of the World*, p. 177.   [238] *Ibid.*, p. 176.

'wave of a silk handkerchief',[239] seems to suggest that the once magnificent 'wielder of wit' with endless 'tricks up his sleeve' has now shrunk to the dimensions of a children's party magician. The Marxist literary critic Terry Eagleton seizes on the same narrative moment and relates it to God's diminished role in contemporary society: no longer top of the bill, he is more a 'magician on a ropy night at the Hammersmith Palais' (his bow-tie badly tied, with traces of soup down his shirt), 'pulling worms and winds from his sleeve like so many rabbits'.[240] For both Barnes and Eagleton the plant-worm trick not only fits with a post-Enlightenment sense that the divine emperor is no longer wearing any clothes, but it reinforces the 'surreal, absurd, 'Dadaist' quality of the narrative, since 'anyone can see there's a world of difference between a castor-oil plant and a city of 120,000 people'.[241] Applying liberal doses of J. L. Austin's theory of performativity to the biblical text, Eagleton argues that plants and worms are only the tip of the iceberg of this narrative's intrinsic dysfunctionality, since Jonah is caught in the paradox in which 'the only successful prophet is an ineffectual one, one whose warnings fail to materialise'.[242] Prophetic words belong to that special class of words known as 'performatives', words that get things done, but they belong to a perverse sub-group of that class in which 'what they get done is to produce a state of affairs in which the state of affairs won't be the case'.[243] To compound Jonah's anomie, God not only reverses

---

[239] *Ibid.*, p. 176. Clearly it is not just modern readers such as Barnes and Eagleton who feel there is something bizarre about the plant-worm *mashal*. Augustine reports a 'loud laughter' and 'scorn' that erupted among Pagans as they goaded him with the question 'Then what is the purpose of the gourd which sprang forth above the disgorged Jonas? What was the reason for its appearance?' (Augustine, *Epistulae* 102, 30, cited in A. Cooper, 'In Praise of Divine Caprice', p. 156).

[240] T. Eagleton, 'J. L. Austin and the Book of Jonah', in R. M. Schwarz (ed.), *The Book and the Text* (Oxford: Blackwell, 1990), pp. 231–6 (236).

[241] Barnes, *A History of the World*, p. 177.

[242] Compare Paul Auster's meditation on Jonah's predicament as a true prophet who 'knows', as opposed to a false prophet who only guesses. 'This was Jonah's greatest problem. If he spoke God's message, telling the Ninevites they would be destroyed in forty days for their wickedness, he was certain they would repent and thus be spared. For he knew that God was "merciful, slow to anger, and of great kindness". "*So the people of Nineveh believed God, and proclaimed a fast, and put on sackcloth, from the greatest of them even to the least of them.*" And if the Ninevites were spared, would this not make Jonah's prophecy false? Would he not, then, be a false prophet? Hence the paradox at the heart of the book: the prophecy would remain true only if he did not speak it. But then, of course, there would be no prophecy, and Jonah would no longer be a prophet. "Therefore now, O Lord, take, I beseech thee, my life from me; for it is better for me to die than to live"' (P. Auster, *The Invention of Solitude* (London: Faber and Faber, 1982), p. 126).

[243] Eagleton, 'J. L. Austin and the Book of Jonah', p. 233.

his decree in a predictably liberal fashion (leaving Jonah doubting whether he has done anything with words or not) but he then goes on to treat Jonah to a rather 'bizarre sadistic taunting', and so 'rubs Jonah's nose' in the 'sheer unfounded gratuitousness of meaning'.[244]

As it mixes with 'concentration camps, rubber truncheons, Hitler, Stalin, bombs', Austin's theories of language, and post-Imperialist politics, the book of Jonah is inevitably traumatised by the experience. In twentieth-century literature and culture the book becomes both a shadow of its former self *and* the subject of virtually compulsive repetition. Sometimes the book is diluted to a mere *reductio ad absurdam* of the biblical original: in the 1960s school musical *Jonah Man Jazz*,[245] wickedness is deflated to 'jazzin' and 'jivin'' (like playing your guitar in your bedroom too loudly, '*wickedly*'), punishment is reduced to a mocking threat to the Ninevites to 'smite 'em/Ad infinitum', the whale survives only as a pun as, in a banalised scene of redemption, the Ninevites learn to play Gospel and everyone has a 'whale of a time'. Sometimes the biblical and the contemporary are put together so lightly that they barely touch. In Paul Auster's *The Invention of Solitude*, a shifting meditation on chance, the Holocaust, memory, isolation, (in)security, and the 'Chinese-box nature of reality',[246] set in motion by the death of his father, Jonah surfaces as a fragment in the 'Book of Memory' (in the strangely assorted company of Pinocchio, Pascal, Mallarmé, Goldilocks and Freud) as part of a fragile fabric of 'stories of life and death'.[247] The story is read, hauntingly, as 'more dramatically a story of solitude than anything else in the Bible':[248] Jonah curled up and sleeping, Jonah-in-the-belly-of-the-ship, Jonah-in-the-belly-of-the-whale becomes both an image of sought-for security/retreat, and the spectre of a 'solitude so crushing, so inconsolable that one stops breathing for hundreds of years'.[249] As the book of Jonah becomes one of the many 'rhymes' that Auster finds between his own and his father's life and the deep pool of memory, Jonah merges with meditations on the individual struggling to understand his future, to 'prophesy', to cope in a world where individual stories do not have plotlines and 'the world is too big and one's life is too small'.[250] Jonah-in-the-belly resonates with the home, with the

---

[244] *Ibid.*, p. 236.
[245] M. Hurd, *Jonah Man Jazz* (London: Novello, 1967).
[246] Auster, *The Invention of Solitude*, p. 117.
[247] *Ibid.*, p. 149.   [248] *Ibid.*, p. 124.   [249] *Ibid.*, p. 83.   [250] *Ibid.*, p. 161.

heimlich and *unheimlich*, with rooms and tombs, and images of Auster, and Auster's father, walled-up and seeking protection and stability in their rooms. In Albert Camus's *Jonas, Or the Artist at Work* the belly is also transformed into a modern-day room. The biblical narrative survives, but only just, in the 'drowning face' of the artist's wife, and in an apartment like 'un aquarium vertical . . . où les êtres, perdus dans la lumière blanch et violente, semblaient flotter comme des ludions' ('A vertical fishtank, in which humans, engulfed in the white, violent light, seem to float like bottle imps').[251] As Peter Dunwoodie observes, the traces of biblical text in the narrative are so slight that critics who try to find overt linkages become like the sycophantic art critics who find in the protagonist's work 'une foule de choses qu'il n'y avait pas mises' ('heaps of things that he had never put there').[252] And yet the sense of compression and constraint around Jonas suggests that what he may have in common with his biblical namesake is the experience of being trapped in a plotline that is directed by others (agents and fans on the one hand, and the Big Other on the other) and that is therefore Absurd, in the technical sense. Camus's Jonas is squeezed by a whole succession of objects – paintings, dogs, cups, papers, people, children, admirers, hangers-on, conversations, lunches, calls, appeals – just as graphically as *Midrash Jonah*'s Jonah is squeezed in the pregnant fish's belly: he is '*swallowed up* by demands which obliterate the meaning of his life'.[253] Though he wants nothing more than to make a space for himself in the present, he is forced into an endless *fuite en avant*. As Auster's Jonah taps into a sense of alienation, detachment, and loneliness, Camus's Jonas suggests something of the 'divorce' or confrontation between human beings and their world. A thoroughly twentieth-century Jonah becomes an image of the quest for meaning and connection, and a symbol of the man who experiences life as Absurd.[254]

---

[251] A. Camus, 'Jonas, ou l'artist au travail', in *L'exil et le royaume* (Paris: Gallimard, 1957), pp. 101–39 (111). The English translation is taken from 'The Artist at Work', *Exile and the Kingdom* (trans. Justin O'Brien; Harmondsworth: Penguin, 1962), pp. 83–115 (90).

[252] P. Dunwoodie, *Camus: L'Envers et l'endroit et L'Exil and le royaume* (London: Grant and Cutler, 1985), pp. 59–60.

[253] *Ibid.*, p. 57.

[254] In his clearest statement of his understanding of the Absurd in *The Myth of Sisyphus*, Camus writes: 'The Absurd is not in man (if such a metaphor could have a meaning) nor in the world, but in their presence together', and 'The Absurd is essentially a divorce. It lies in neither of the elements compared; it is born of their confrontation' (A. Camus, *The Myth of Sisyphus* (trans. J. O'Brien; Hamish Hamilton: London, 1971; 1st edn 1942), p. 30).

If twentieth-century fiction bristles with a sense of abrasion between individuals and their world, it also grates with the disjunction between the 'real' and the 'biblical'. This tour grinds to a halt with five contemporary poems in which the book of Jonah misfires, winds down and dysfunctions in locations as far-flung as Chile, Israel, Poland, and the United States. In the four poems that deal with Jonah – by Enrique Lihn, Gabriel Priel, Zbigniew Herbert, and Hart Crane – Jonah reaches his apotheosis as the type of alienated humanity, caught in the paradoxes of agnosticism/atheism. Elucidating a reading that seems to have been struggling for articulation at least since the *Gawain*-poet, the Chilean poet Enrique Lihn (1929–88) invokes Jonah as a kind of patron saint of all those who feel the need to curse, who are so tossed on the 'ups and downs of good and evil' and the 'fickle circumstances of history' that their lives are 'grotesque and unfinished'.[255] Jonah is squeezed into an absurd plot in which he is forced to play the 'clown of heaven' and to march off to Nineveh with an 'explosive briefcase/tucked under a sweaty armpit' (presumably packed with pounds of prophetic rhetorical explosive). Jonah, divine secret agent, is tossed up and down by:

> Jehovah's doubts about him, wavering between mercy and
>   anger, grabbing him and tossing him, that old instrument
>   whose use is doubtful
> no longer used at all any more.

The poet and Jonah blur into one another and the poem ends with a strange plea to a riddlingly self-deconstructing, self-absenting, violent-sensitive deity, 'clenching his delicate fingers awkwardly':

> Blindly, I see the hand of a lord whose name I don't remember,
> his delicate fingers clenched awkwardly. And also something else
>   that has nothing to do with it. I remember something like . . .
> no, it's only that. Just a thought, it doesn't matter. I just don't
>   know where I am going again.
> 'Help me Lord in thy abandonment'

The American poet Gabriel Preil (1911–93) similarly entwines his own life with Jonah's, identifying with him in his bewilderment and his flight:

> The prophet Jonah ran from his angry master
> and I to my ship empty of God and man

---

[255] E. Lihn, 'Jonah' (trans. J. Cohen), in D. Curzon (ed.), *Modern Poems on the Bible: An Anthology* (Philadelphia and Jerusalem: Jewish Publication Society, 1994), p. 267.

> From a certain nightness which strikes root,
> From a net spread to maim,
> from a shadow that swallows me,
> like Jonah in the belly of the fish.[256]

To compound the sense of disorientation, the familiar elements of
the narrative are missing or twisted: God and the sailors have
vacated the ship; the fish and the sea are diluted, metaphorised, as
nets spread to maim, 'shadows that swallow', fears that engulf '*like*
Jonah in the belly of the fish' (as if to suggest that the closest alliance
that we can form with the text these days is a distant, metaphorical
strained relation). The biblical text is presided over not by the moral
abstract – disobedience – but by the emotional abstract – fear – and
after the fantastic plants, fish, and worms have drained from the
text, all that endures is darkness, nightness, the desire to run away
and hide. Blessing and mercy disappear; curse remains:

> All the black things envisioned by the prophets
> tangible, as in a returning mirror, penetrate to me;
> all words of consolation are white petals
> that flutter, fragile, on over-calm waters.

Like Lihn, Preil ends with a tangled, riddling anti-prayer in which
he speaks of fleeing from his Master to a refuge of faith, and finding
peace in eluding God, 'God willing':

> I, God willing, while escaping my Master, hope to find
> a minute of refuge in a season of faith and ripeness.

The American poet Hart Crane (1899–1932) in 'After Jonah'
invokes the absurd familiarity of the biblical Jonah, and recounts
how:

> We have his travels in the snare so widely
> ruminated – of how he stuck there, was reformed,
> forgiven, also –
> and belched back like a word to grace us all.[257]

The implication is that Jonah the text like Jonah the man is a
strange, soiled, and comically burped up little book, for which we
are supposed, ironically, to be grateful. Rewriting holiness as queasi-

---

[256] G. Preil, 'Jonah' (trans. Preil and D. Curzon), in Curzon (ed.), *Modern Poems on the Bible*,
p. 259. Preil, living at the intersection of different cultures, was born in Estonia, emigrated
to the USA, but writes in Hebrew.

[257] H. Crane, 'After Jonah', in Curzon (ed.), *Modern Poems on the Bible*, p. 260. The poem was
not published by Crane, but was published posthumously in M. Simon (ed.), *The Poems of
Hart Crane* (New York: Liveright, 1986), based on one extant typescript.

ness, Crane describes how the God-whale has a sensitive stomach, and reacts to sinners like a bad case of salmonella:

> There is no settling tank in God. It must be borne
> that even His bowels are too delicate to board
> a sniping thief that has a pious beard.

The poem ends in an apostrophe to God as a white whale/cloud in the sky, imploring him to cater for the poet with hellish hospitality:

> O sweet deep whale as ever reamed the sky
> with high white gulfs of vapour, castigate
> our sins, but be hospitable as Hell.
> And keep me to the death like ambergris,
> sealed up and unforgiven in my cell.

These days Jonah does not fall down on his knees, but asks to be preserved, sinful, rebellious; just as God, his role confused, becomes hellish, angry, and anxious about his receding role in the modern world, his outline fading, his fingers clenched nervously.

'After Jonah' – a title that suggests both 'after' in the sense of 'departing from' and 'after' in the sense of 'in the manner of'[258] – evokes the intense paradox of fleeing from the Bible through lines crammed with biblical allusions. As Lihn asks the God who abandons him to help him, Preil hopes to escape from God (God willing), and Crane asks a hellish God to seal him unforgiven, all three distance themselves from the Bible and its God and yet relentlessly reinscribe and transpose it/him. In these three poems the elements of the biblical are metaphorically diluted and re-arranged: in the maiming nets, shadows that swallow, the doubts that toss, the God who is at once a dissipating cloud, a whale, and a settling tank. The book is still discernible in the shadows, but is radically re-sorted almost beyond recognition. Although it survives only by ingesting twentieth-century idioms to produce strange biblical-contemporary amalgams like the God-whale hospitable as hell, or a Jonah who gets to stay in his cell unforgiven, there is at least a sense in each poem that the biblical text is still functioning, albeit in some (radically re-sorted) sense. But for the Polish poet Zbigniew Herbert (1924–),[259] the ancient text, deprived of the nourishing air of credulity, simply breaks down. Herbert begins, rather like Crane, by recounting the

---

[258] These ambiguities of writing 'after' someone/something are brilliantly foregrounded by Nicholas Royle in *After Derrida* (Manchester: Manchester University Press, 1995).

[259] Z. Herbert, 'Jonah' (trans. C. Milosz), in Curzon (ed.), *Modern Poems on the Bible*, pp. 257–8.

burped up story with childhood automaticity (how Jonah son of Ammitai ran away from a dangerous mission, how the 'well-known things happened', how the 'foreseen fish' swallowed and vomited the prophet, and so on) but then suddenly lifts Jonah out of his biblical context (where the story happily spools round and around endlessly) and strands him in the modern world. And once Jonah is out of the insulating world of monsters and miracles, his story plays itself out very differently. With no 'big fish' to cushion his fall, Jonah sinks and drowns:

> the modern Jonah
> goes down like a stone
> if he comes across a whale
> he hasn't even time to gasp

And if, by some freak of chance, he were saved, Herbert speculates, he would 'behave more cleverly/than his biblical colleague':

> the second time he does not take on
> a dangerous mission
> he grows a beard
> and far from the sea
> far from Nineveh
> under an assumed name
> deals in cattle and antiques

Today's Jonah is at once more 'real' than his biblical namesake – and a mere shadow of his former (fantastically surviving) self. Taking advantage of the fact that these days God is less omnipresent than he used to be (and less omniscient than Interpol), the modern-day Jonah puts on a false moustache, opens an antique shop, keeps his head down, lives a quiet life. Once outside the cushioning, insulating world of the biblical, Jonah does not die a spectacular mock-death in the Calvinistic hospital-belly, but he dies in a 'neat hospital'

> . . . of cancer
> himself not knowing very well
> who he really was

His body and the body of the text that bears his name collapses:

> the parable
> applied to his head
> expires
> and the balm of the legend
> does not take to his flesh.

The balm does not soothe, the story has passed its read-by date, the legend does not take to his (or our) flesh. In a world governed by blind chance, rather than providence,[260] the plot malfunctions, and our magical mystery tour ends, appropriately, with us gathered around 'Jonah' in the morgue or the hospital bed.

The fish, appropriately enough, is also dying: in 'Tidings', the Israeli poet Dan Pagis (1930–86) invites us to stand around the great beached corpse of the hollowed out fish:

> The great fish that vomited out Jonah
> swallowed nothing more.
> Without any prophecy in his guts he pined away.
>
> The great fish died and the sea vomited him out onto dry land,
> three hundred cubits of disappointed and forsaken flesh
> in the light of the end of day.
>
> Then they were merciful to him, an omen of things to come in a moment
> gangs of crabs
> surrounded him, delighted in him, picked him clean
>
> After all the tidings, there remained on the deserted beach
> the skeleton; caverns, columns, gates, secret entranceways –
> a city of refuge for an escaped wind. Everything had been fulfilled.[261]

Pagis is known for his perverse midrashic distortions of biblical texts, for reading the flood from the perspective of the fish who 'lived off/ the mishap like smooth speculators', but who are now 'drowning in air'; or, most famously, for chillingly applying Ezekiel's vision of the dry bones to post-war reparation for Holocaust victims, as he sardonically reassures the corpses that gold teeth will be returned to the gums, the scream back to the throat, and the smoke to the chimneys, as everything returns to its place.[262] In 'Tidings' he reads the book of Jonah from the perspective of the fish, who is no longer comically animated by Jonah's hymns from its belly, but is now

---

[260] Stanislaw Baranczak comments that 'Any attempt to sum up what this poem presents as the nature of the incompatibility between the biblical and the "modern" Jonahs must certainly begin with the opposition of "fate" and "chance". The past's heritage seems to have been determined by a providential order of things, while the modern disinheritance is the dominion of blind chance . . . Today's Jonah . . . cannot become a hero of myth, which would give significance to his experience by sanctifying it or at least preserving it in posterity's collective memory' (S. Baranczak, *A Fugitive from Utopia: The Poetry of Zbigniew Herbert* (Cambridge, Mass.: Harvard University Press, 1987), pp. 19–20, cited in Curzon, *Modern Poems on the Bible*, p. 336).

[261] D. Pagis, 'Tidings' (trans. S. Mitchell), in Curzon (ed.), *Modern Poems on the Bible*, p. 257.

[262] The fish-eye view of the flood can be found in 'Ararat'; the twisted resurrection of Ezekiel's dry bones is from 'Draft of a Reparations Agreement'.

stranded, disappointed, forsaken, pining for the spirit of prophecy that once filled its guts. The biblical original is jumbled, reassembled: the fish is vomited, mercy is (sardonically) being picked clean by crabs, and the 'city of refuge' (the biblical image of security)[263] is reduced to a hollowed-out skeleton, refuge only for 'an escaped wind'. In the late twentieth century, 'Scripture' is still 'fulfilling' and reinscribing itself, but in far bleaker senses than we could ever have envisioned.

If we started this tour with the body of the monster (externally recorded, internally explored), we end with 'three hundred cubits of disappointed and forsaken flesh' and the washed-up skeleton of a text. When all the humour, all the credulity, and the lessons that have clung to the text like limpets have been stripped away, all that remains is the hollowed-out body of the biblical, lying beached up on the shores of the contemporary, the skeleton of a text that has been picked clean by scavenger critics until there is literally nothing left. Everything has gone, it seems, everything has been fulfilled in the bleakest of senses: all that remains is only a haunting sense of nostalgia for the spirit of biblical credulity and innocence that once filled our guts. And yet the paradox that I want to explore further in a moment is that the book of Jonah goes on living, sur-viving, overliving its die-by date, sustaining itself even through poems about its death.

We shall be returning to visit Jonah on the oncology ward and to wander round the beached-up whale carcass when we come to consider the question of the curious secular afterlives of the book of Jonah. But first I want to look back over the material in this chapter, with an occasional glance even further back to the Mainstream, in an attempt to draw some common threads from this monstrous, whale-sized collection together.

3. ON THE STRAINED RELATIONS BETWEEN THE BACKWATERS AND THE MAINSTREAM; OR HOW JEWISH AND POPULAR READINGS ARE PRONE TO BRING ON A BOUT OF SCHOLARLY DYSPEPSIA

I started my voyage into the Backwaters by borrowing a term from the Russian literary theorist Mikhail Bakhtin and suggesting that

---

[263] See Exodus 21.13; Numbers 35.9–15; Joshua 20.7–9.

Mainstream productions tend to package Jonah as *monologic*. And since Bakhtin's distinctions between the monologic/satirical and the dialogic/parodic help to define the dam that separates the Mainstream from the Backwaters, it might be helpful for these terms to be developed. According to Bakhtin, monologic texts reduce all seeming dialogue to 'sham struggles', and when they laugh they can only laugh satirically, using humour as an educative device, a whip or scourge.[264] Monologic readings tend to 'surgically remove' ideological theses and to 'juxtapose them in absolute and irreducible antinomies',[265] and they tend to regard the text as something 'sacred and sacrosanct, evaluated in the same way by all and demanding a pious attitude towards itself'.[266] Dialogic texts, in contrast, allow unorthodox voices to exist in intimate contact with the orthodox voice without the tradition 'fusing with it', 'swallowing it up', or 'dissolving into itself the other's power to mean'.[267] They give characters (or 'idea-heroes') *specific* concerns and set them loose in *specific* circumstances, instructing them to fight their corner with conviction, to develop their positions to '[their] maximal force and depth', so that the book is always 'warm from the struggle within it'.[268] Even as they encourage rival perspectives to develop (so that

[264] Bakhtin's depiction of satire as a 'laughter that has forgotten how to laugh' is echoed and developed by other writers. Vladimir Nabakov observes that 'Satire is a lesson' whereas 'parody is a game'; Linda Hutcheon describes satire as a form of humour that mocks potentially anarchic points of view in order to 'bring deviation into line'; and Northrop Frye classes satire as the conservative end of comedy which enforces didacticism and supports the status quo (see V. Nabakov, *Strong Opinions* (New York: McGraw-Hill, 1973), p. 75; L. Hutcheon, *A Theory of Parody: The Teachings of Twentieth Century Art Forms* (London: Methuen, 1985), p. 79; N. Frye, *Anatomy of Criticism* (Princeton: Princeton University Press, 1967), p. 224).

[265] Bakhtin, *Problems of Dostoevsky's Poetics*, p. 9.

[266] This comes from Bakhtin's definition of 'epic', which can be seen as a version of the monologic, in M. Holquist (ed.), *The Dialogic Imagination: Four Essays by Mikhail Bakhtin* (trans. C. Emerson and M. Holquist; Austin: University of Texas Press, 1994), pp. 3–40 (16). An epic text is 'closed as a circle; inside it everything is finished, already over'; it 'admits no loopholes' and 'it is impossible to change, to re-think, to evaluate anything in it'.

[267] From Bakhtin's definition of the 'monologic' and the 'dialogic', in P. Morris, *The Bakhtin Reader: Selected Writings of Bakhtin, Medvedev and Voloshinov* (London: Edward Arnold, 1994), p. 93. The autocratic spectre of monologism manifests itself in philosophical idealism that assumes a 'single consciousness or truth', and recognises 'only one principle of cognitive individualisation: error' (pp. 80–1).

[268] Bakhtin, *Problems of Dostoevsky's Poetics*, pp. 30, 69. In the dialogic, or polyphonic novel, of which Dostoevsky is the master, 'the most diverse and contradictory material' is laid out 'extensively side by side', and 'every point of view is allowed to extend to its maximal force and depth, to the outside limits of plausibility' (pp. 30, 69). Meanings are inextricably, inoperably bound up with characters and contexts, so that there are 'no ideas, no thoughts,

the reader cannot tip over into any tempting honey-heads) so they allow dialogue to 'penetrate inside the word, provoking it into battle', so that 'two contending voices can be heard within the word, and cracks appear in every expression'.[269] Dialogic readings bring the text into a 'zone of crude contact where one can finger it familiarly on all sides, turn it upside down, peer at it . . . experiment with it'.[270] And when the dialogic text laughs, it laughs parodically, with the kind of laughter that 'does not place itself above a single object of mockery',[271] but that exalts in the 'contradictory and double-faced fullness of life'[272] and toys with every perspective, every character, without exception.

Although these rather simplistic dualisms (implying their own 'sham struggle' or morality-play showdown between the forces of good and evil) by no means do justice to the complexity of Bakhtin's thought,[273] or indeed the material in this chapter, they are at least a suggestive place to start. The Mainstream does, on the whole,

---

no positions, which belong to no one, which exist in themselves' and which do not live a 'tense life on the borders of someone else's thought' (p. 32).

[269] Bakhtin, *Problems of Dostoevsky's Poetics*, p. 30. This point is crucial: dialogism is not simply a tendency to produce dialogue (monologic works include dialogue), but a tendency towards bifurcation, that enters the text even at the level of the word, provoking it into what Bakhtin calls 'microdialogue'. The dialogic spirit is perfectly expressed in Bakhtin's panegyric to his dialogic hero, Dostoevsky: 'Where others saw a single thought, he was able to find and feel out two thoughts . . . But none of these contradictions and bifurcations ever became dialectical, they were never set in motion along a temporal path or evolving sequence: they were, rather, spread out in one place, as standing alongside or opposite one another, as consonant but not merging or as hopelessly contradictory, as an eternal harmony of unmerged voices or as their unceasing and irreconcilable quarrel' (*Problems of Dostoevsky's Poetics*, p. 30). Dostoevsky's dialogism can be demonstrated, fortuitously enough, by a multiply embedded and highly ambiguous allusion to Jonah, the 'chap who skulked in the whale's belly for three days and three nights' (F. Dostoevsky, *The Brothers Karamazov* (trans. D. Margarshack; Harmondsworth: Penguin, 1964), p. 354). The allusion would seem simple enough to interpret (surely Jonah's recalcitrance is being condemned), were it not that it comes in the context of the speech of the Devil to an atheist (Ivan) trying to tempt him to faith – a context in which all tangible frameworks of good and evil, belief and unbelief, turn to dust.

[270] Holquist, *The Dialogic Imagination*, p. 23.

[271] M. Bakhtin, *Rabelais and His World* (cited in Morris, *The Bakhtin Reader*, p. 201).

[272] M. Bakhtin, *Rabelais and His World* (trans. H. Iswolsky; Bloomington: Indiana University Press, 1984), p. 62.

[273] It is one of the drawbacks of a plundering work of this nature that I am simply borrowing a set of basic conceptual tools, and so painting a rather reductive and cartoonish picture of 'Bakhtin'. Luckily one of the good side-effects of what Caryl Emerson calls the *bakhtinskii boom* of the 1980s and the 1990s is that there are many more nuanced works on the market. I particularly recommend M. Gardiner, *The Dialogics of Critique: M. M. Bakhtin and the Theory of Ideology* (London: Routledge, 1992), a discussion of Bakhtin as a contributor to social and political theory, and C. Emerson's brilliant *The First Hundred Years of Mikhail Bakhtin* (Princeton: Princeton University Press, 1997), which sets Bakhtin firmly in a Russian

surgically extract ideological dualisms from the text (reducing it to a sham struggle between universalism and particularism) and in its latest laughing manifestations it laughs sardonically with Jonah as its target. The distinctiveness of the Backwaters clearly begins with a tendency to give weight to Jonah's voice: even as Jewish interpreters imagine Jonah engaging with the 'father' on behalf of the 'son', as if God and Jonah were a study-pair in a yeshiva, the popular readings are busy scripting Jonah with lines such as: 'If God knew he wasn't going to destroy Nineveh what did he want with my life?', and 'Why it seems a victory to You/Thus to destroy your prophet more than all the others?' The 'Jewish' and 'Popular' readings are prone to fatten Jonah as a character: they tend to maintain Jonah's and God's positions and maximise the friction between them; and they refuse to remove the problems of the text to the laboratory of abstract, generalised analysis where they can be so easily dissected and resolved. They tend to apply the kind of humour that does not merely hover over Jonah, like the Talmud's ship-hugging storm cloud, but that falls on Jonah and God without distinction. They bring the book into a 'zone of crude contact', finger it, turn it, experiment with it[274] (I'm thinking particularly of the word-turning rabbinic commentaries here); and they relish the battles within words, pointing out the friction in the two-edged הפך (*hfk*, 'to (over)turn').

'Why do you try and enlarge your mind?', asks Herman Melville, 'subtilise it'. On a general, morality-play scale, this book tells the story of how, as it passes through the Backwaters, the same small book of Jonah becomes more fraught, more seething, more subtle, more *written*. The limpet-like polemical readings (which clung to the book at the end of the last chapter) fall away; the smooth homiletic coating starts to bristle with puzzles and question marks; the book comes out of its neat filing cabinets (Jew versus gentile, Universalism versus Xenophobia) and begins to disintegrate into a thick pile of miscellany (menageries of monsters, prophets on oncology wards). But watching over the general from the basis of the particular, the waters muddy at all kinds of points, both stylistic and conceptual. The Church Fathers empathise with Jonah like the rabbis; *Midrash Jonah* and the Zohar read the book in a very Mainstream fashion;

context, and defies any attempts to make Bakhtin into a 'guru', or to conscript him unproblematically into French or Anglo-American 'postmodernism'.

[274] Holquist, *The Dialogic Imagination*, p. 23.

and Luther is quizzically 'rabbinic' in his query about whether God toys with Jonah as a plaything. And lest we are in danger of setting up the Backwaters as a dialogic utopia, a refuge from the narrow-minded polemic of the Mainstream, it needs to be stressed that there comes a point where – as authors like Eagleton and Barnes ally themselves with Jonah against God – the Backwater production of the book reverts to monologism and satire, albeit in an inverted fashion. As if to reverse the one-hundred-and-eighty degree twist where the Jonah-ideal (Jonah-Christ) twists to Jonah the anti-ideal (Jonah the Jew), Jonah becomes, once again, the site of empathy, the projection of the self: not this time because he is Christ-like, but because he represents a means of defying and debunking religious tradition. In a demonstration of the story's fundamental flexibility, the story of the expulsion of a few select Old Testament texts becomes the story of the expulsion of the Bible from within the Bible, and the book that functioned as the story of the expulsion of a Jewish Jonah to make way for Christianity twists into a rather different narrative about throwing God/Christianity overboard.

In fact, wading through this chapter after wading through chapter 1, one cannot fail to be impressed by the book of Jonah's capacity to spread its influence, octopus-like, and to spawn alternative versions of itself. As it has reached out its tentacles to the Christian tradition – as it has sucked in New Testament idioms and has fed itself fat on the anxiety attached to the spectral figure of the Jew – so it has saturated itself in the language and collective traditions of Judaism. While it is not surprising to see the book surface in the two major biblical religions,[275] it is more surprising to watch it insinuate and multiply itself in, for want of two better words, 'popular' and 'secular' culture. ('You're working on Jonah?', a friend of mine asked when this project was incubating, 'is that in the *Bible*?')

The obvious points need to be made – if only to tie up loose ends left at the end of chapter 1. Jonah's career in the Backwaters is as plastic as his career in the Mainstream: he features as a passive

---

[275] This is not to deny the third major religion based on the Book – Islam. Islam's reading of Jonah, which spills beyond the boundaries of this study, can be found in the Qur'an, Sura 10 (Yunus or Jonah). A midrashic retelling of Jonah's story (including his encounters with a wolf as well as a fish, his trip to the Mediterranean and the Coral Castle, and the way in which Gabriel restored his skin when he emerged from the fish's belly like a 'featherless chick') can be found in the medieval collection, *The Tales of the Prophets of al-Kisa'i* (trans. W. M. Thackston; Boston: Twayne Publishers, 1978).

martyr-figure (Orwell) and as noble dissident (the *Mekilta*, Abravanel); as naïve ingénu (Rosen) and as a character more subtle and knowing than God (Eagleton); and, trapped in the pincers of a rather unconducive plot, he performs his predicament in comic and tragic mode, as stand-up comic in the style of Jackie Mason, Tevye the Dairyman, or Woody Allen (Mankowitz), and as poignant hero contemplating suicide (the *Mekilta*). And if we focus on the Jewish readings and take away the barriers that separate the Backwaters from the Mainstream (just as earlier we took away the arbitrary lines that separated readings within the Mainstream from one another), it is almost superfluous to point out how the binary distinction between Jewish legalism/xenophobia and Christian mercy disintegrates.[276] The mercy of God who throws all sins into the sea and the efficacy of true repentance are such strong themes in Jewish interpretation (underlined in *Midrash Jonah*, proclaimed annually on Yom Kippur) that it becomes clear that a Jewish book of Jonah is also dripping with mercy. Indeed, the supreme irony is that, historically, a Jewish reading foregrounding mercy and repentance was eliminated precisely to avoid playing into the hands of Christian polemicists.

But 'the Jewish' does far more than justify itself (and consolidate its virtual role) by demonstrating its ability to reflect Christian values back to the Christian community: it fundamentally stymies any attempt to situate the Jew within the economy of the Same and the Other. As Luce Irigaray observes, in a different context, as soon as the 'object' speaks, the fundamental 'disaggregation' of the subject

---

[276] This needs to be stressed, since certain cartoonish impressions of 'postmodernism' or 'interdisciplinarity' suggest that this kind of analysis tends to avoid commitment by getting away from an 'essentialist' view of the text. On the contrary, expanding our view of the text by diffracting it through different interpretative traditions frequently leads not to an amorphous relativist mass, but to a situation in which readings fight with and consume one another. The realm of the battle might not be staged in and across the text, it may take place in an ethical/political domain outside the text, but the Mainstream reading of Jonah the Jew is nevertheless clearly proved 'wrong, that's right, wrong, not right' (to use Derrida's phrase). Further, this particular case questions the assumption that proper biblical studies can only take place between an individual specialist and a text, or within the context of Christian theology. The case of 'Jonah the Jew' suggests that it is precisely by de-specialising, or rather by specialising plurally, that the danger of mutual confirmation between text and myopia is avoided. Rather than preserving an established reading, with minor variations, because it is established, perhaps we should be looking for doses of healthy defamiliarisation (only by seeing how Jonah is spun out as part of very different cultural fabrics, can we stand back and defamiliarise the naturalness with which we read Jonah 'in the light of' Romans 3.29).

results.[277] The Mainstream constructs a spectral image of 'the Jew', split between the positive Author and the negative Jonah, as if these two images could work bifocally to make a Christian self who is the precise image of what we need to be. But the Backwaters present a 'Jew' who walks through the looking glass, escapes 'his' virtual role, and who sends back images of the Self in distorted, disaggregated form. The Christian reading about 'Jews under threat in the book of Jonah' is refracted back, virtually unrecognisable: the threat is from the Assyrians, not the Christians, and triumphalism shifts to anguish and uncertainty as the Jewish storyteller poignantly contemplates the threat to his own people. Ruether's and Radford Ruether's projection of 'Jonah the Zionist' is refracted, splintered and inverted in *Jonah in Haifa Port*; and 'Jonah the butt of satire' is fractured in Mankowitz's wry, self-mocking Jonah as caricature combats caricature, and the image of the Jewish 'monster' is confronted with other spectral self-generated clichés. Most traumatic of all, from the perspective of the Mainstream Subject, is Rosen's midrash, not only because it raises theological questions that Mainstream biblical scholars have barely begun to consider ('How can biblical affirmations of divine mercy possibly survive in the wake of the Holocaust, the "eclipse of God", and the "turning of God's face"?'), but because it draws attention to the complicity of Christian theology and biblical interpretation in generating the imaginative marginalisation/annihilation of the Jew. When Rosen speaks of the 'antisemitic garnish' scattered through Jonah interpretation and invokes 'ghettos and pogroms and death camps and crematoria', the tensions for a discipline that has, as late as the 1970s and 1980s, perpetuated images of Jonah as 'religious monster' or 'nest-feathering' Jew, become virtually unbearable; for the persistence of these images on the pages of commentary uncomfortably confirms, as Bauman suggests, that the 'allo-semitism [or othering of the Jew] endemic to Western Civilisation is to a decisive extent the legacy of Chris-

---

[277] L. Irigaray, *Speculum of the Other Woman* (trans. G. G. Gill; Ithaca: Cornell University Press, 1985), p. 135. Of course the other context is feminism, and the 'Object' of which she speaks is the woman as object of patriarchal discourse. The feminist image of the woman as the 'virtual other side of the mirror', or the pure ungraspable reflection of the masculine Self, resonates provocatively with the projection of the Jew as the reverse of the Christian mirror. For a brilliant study that explores and disrupts the specular image of the Other Woman and the Other Jew, and that draws feminist theory and theories of allo-semitism together, see T. K. Beal, *The Book of Hiding: Gender, Ethnicity, Annihilation and Esther* (London and New York: Routledge, 1997).

tendom' and the 'Christian Church's struggle with the inassimilable, yet indispensable, modality of the Jews'.[278]

The Jewish readings gathered here not only have the capacity to make the Mainstream more than slightly queasy by refashioning Jonah-Shylock in the mode of Arnold Wesker's Shylock,[279] they suggest alternative reading strategies and stances towards the text. In a nicely ironic twist on the particularist Jew versus the universalistic Christian dichotomy, Jewish readings are emphatically particularist in the sense that they watch over the general from the basis of the particular (in a way that threatens the parabolic readings of the Mainstream) and they graft onto the book synagogues, circumcision, the 'messianic feast of the righteous', and the *even shethiyah* in a way that forces the Christian reader to appreciate how the 'Old Testament' is differently distributed and interpreted in Jewish tradition, even to gain a point of entry into these strange-seeming texts. As if to compound the sense of foreignness, midrashim like the *Pirke de Rabbi Eliezer* seem to indulge in the fantastic in a way that seems almost strategically designed to alienate the largely Protestant scholarly Mainstream, and to provoke disdainful dismissals of the material as 'puerile'. Although Judaism encompasses its own Enlightenment, or *Haskalah*, and its own rationalist mutinies against the fantastic, Jewish tradition is full of stories which move freely, without any sense of clear division, between the real world and the world that in Yiddish is called *Yenne Velt* (the other world).[280] Here, looking from the other side of the Enlightenment, we can probably only understand those stories as a separate genre of 'fantastic' or 'fairytale', divided from the real or the rational in a way that they would not

[278] Z. Bauman, 'Allosemitism: Premodern, Modern, Postmodern', in B. Cheyette and L. Marcus (eds.), *Modernity, Culture and 'the Jew'* (Cambridge: Polity Press, 1998), pp. 143–56 (148).

[279] Arnold Wesker's *The Merchant* (1976) is a retort to Shakespeare's *The Merchant of Venice*. It presents Shylock as impetuous, kind, and above all scholarly (the play opens with him cataloguing his copies of Kimhi's *Hebrew Dictionary* and Maimonides' *Guide to the Perplexed*) and it exposes, by contrast, the anti-Semitism of the Venetians (see A. Wesker, *The Journalists/The Merchant/The Wedding Feast* (Harmondsworth: Penguin, 1980), pp. 191–266).

[280] For a discussion of the deep vein of the fantastic that runs from aggadah through to contemporary Jewish literature, see H. Schwarz, *Reimagining the Bible: The Storytelling of the Rabbis* (Oxford: Oxford University Press, 1998). For a collection of works of Jewish fantasy, including Hasidic legends, and stories from the Eastern European collection of Jewish folktales known as the *Maaseh Book*, see J. Neugroschel (ed.), *Yenne Velt: Great Works of Jewish Fantasy* (London: Picador, 1976). As Neugroschel observes: 'It is the legacy of the West European Enlightenment that makes us talk of fantasies and fairy-tales. The polarity of the rational and the irrational in regard to such literature does not historically exist' (p. 9).

have been for the compilers of the *Pirke de Rabbi Eliezer*; or, perhaps more accurately, we can see them as the equivalent of a Jewish magic-realism[281] – a kind of Jewish Derek Walcott, Salman Rushdie, or Gabriel Garcia Marquez. For stories about fish that mutate into synagogues and prophets that scare Leviathan with the sign of the circumcision are, like magical realist narratives, not so much an escape from reality as heightened reality. In Rushdie's *The Satanic Verses*, Saladin Chamcha mutates into a beast with horns as the truism of racist prejudice ('They have the powers of description, and we succumb to the pictures they construct') takes to his flesh;[282] in Gabriel Garcia Marquez's *One Hundred Years of Solitude*, the blood of a murdered son trickles out of a house and turns corners to find his mother (to demonstrate the proverbial thickness of blood, the strength of family ties); and in the *Pirke de Rabbi Eliezer*, the tour of deep mythology seems to indicate a way-of-seeing that is so funda-mental and so powerful that these myths have the power to bring on metamorphosis. Admittedly, the rabbis may not be using the fantas-tic as a way of deliberately goading realism and challenging the genre and content of 'colonial' truth, but the effect is the same: the violation of proportion and normality that Christian readers may feel in reading the *Pirke de Rabbi Eliezer* comes from the double alienation – seeing the familiar made strange from the perspective of the Other, and seeing it rendered in a way that violates the centre's own constructions of rationality and reasonableness.

Jewish readings not only destabilise Mainstream constructions of knowledge, but they show a strange tendency to read towards insecurity. If we compare the Jewish readings to the Christian readings in the Mainstream, it seems that they are staging a fundamentally different relationship between the reader/religious community and the book. The Mainstream gratifies the reader, comforts and reassures her, places her above the vacillations of the text. The role of the book is not to teach, to surprise, or even less to dislocate us; the view of life is sanguine: God is on our side, the plot flows in our interests, it vindicates our position, and God,

---

[281] 'Magic realism' is a brand of post-colonial or counter-colonial fiction that deliberately shakes itself free from the mimetic constraints of nineteenth- and twentieth-century realism (and its more sardonic offshoots), and that uses magic and ontological disruption as a form of political and cultural disruption. (For a discussion of magic realism, see L. Parkinson Zamora and W. B. Faris (eds.), *Magic Realism: Theory, History, Community* (Durham, N.C. and London: Duke University Press, 1995).)

[282] Rushdie, *The Satanic Verses*, p. 168.

throughout, is demonstrating his love for us, his Ninevites. With the potential exception of Calvin's and Hooper's threats of a disciplinary God (who can throw us overboard or cause us to tremble), the interpretations invite us to read from a secure position where we already know the lessons that Jonah has to learn, where we can smile at his lack of understanding, and where our identity is shored up by 'the Jew' as antithesis to us. They offer the comfort that comes from the recitation of the familiar and the recapitulation of the already-learnt lesson. The story does not surprise, it does not take unexpected twists; but it does something more foundational, more essential. By telling a story that ends conclusively with God's assertion of love for the gentiles (and that in turn is subsumed into the greater teleological thrust of the New Testament), it circumscribes us in the familiar, and it makes us feel safe in a way that resonates with salvation as security, safety, being safe and sound.[283] Such readings seem to support contemporary definitions of the 'religious' as that which satisfies the profoundly human, deep-rooted psychological/social desire for stability, legitimacy, worth, power, and order.[284] And while it may be that the particular form that this desire takes in Mainstream interpretation is ethically and politically problematic, it is a bold critic who can detach him/herself from and critique, as if from above, the all-too-human desire for bulwarks

---

[283] Compare Jacques Derrida's provocative meditation on 'salvation' in connection with security, health, the unscathed, the *heilig*, and the immune, in J . Derrida, 'Faith and Knowledge: The Two Sources of "Religion" at the Limits of Reason Alone', in J. Derrida and G. Vattimo (eds.), *Religion* (Cambridge: Polity Press, 1998), pp. 1–78 (esp. p. 49).

[284] Putting aside the question of whether or not such definitions are adequate, and whether any definition of religion can be adequate, contemporary definitions of the sociology/ psychology of religion are clearly full of words like power, serenity, meaning, stability, and so on. For example, J. M. Yinger: Religion is 'an attempt to explain what cannot otherwise be explained; to achieve power . . .; to establish poise and serenity in the face of evil and suffering . . .' (*The Scientific Study of Religion* (London: Routledge, 1970), p. 7); Max Weber: religion provides a theodicy of good and ill fortune and behind the social psychology of world religions lie the implicit demand that 'the world order in its totality is, could and should somehow be a meaningful "cosmos"' ('The Social Psychology of the World Religions', in H. H. Gerth and C. W. Mills (eds.), *From Max Weber: Essays in Sociology* (London: Routledge, 1991), pp. 267–301 (281)); Clifford Geertz: religion is a 'system of symbols which acts to establish powerful, persuasive and long-lasting moods and motivations in men [*sic*] by formulating conceptions of a general order of existence' ('Religion as a Cultural System', in M. Banton (ed.), *Anthropological Approaches to the Study of Religion* (ASA Monographs 3; London, Tavistock, 1966), p. 4); Peter Berger: 'Men [*sic*] are congenitally compelled to impose a meaningful order [or *nomos*] upon reality . . . Religion has been one of the most effective bulwarks against anomie throughout human history' (*The Social Reality of Religion* (Harmondsworth: Penguin, 1973), pp. 31, 94).

against anomie, and for self-affirming, as opposed to self-destabi-
lising, meanings.

But, as if to question a definition of the 'religious' that tends
towards self-enforcing meaning or security, Jewish interpretation is
less prone to gratify the reader, or, rather, it gratifies the reader in
different ways. The closest analogy to the Mainstream is the *Pirke de
Rabbi Eliezer*, in that it presents a Jewish hero who is comfortably and
uncomplicatedly allied with God. Effacing the tension between God
and Jonah in the ur-text, it fulfils the desire for reassurance by
showing how Jewish tradition and heroism triumph over the forces
of evil and chaos. It presents Judaism as adventure, Judaism as
positive quest, and it locates the reader in a present dripping with a
fabulous past and on a trajectory towards a glorious future when we,
the righteous, will be vindicated.

But in doing so, it only highlights how many of the Jewish texts do
not do this. Indeed, rather than reading in a way that gratifies and
comforts, it seems that many are set on unnerving us. The *Mekilta*
emphasises the friction between God and Jonah, and presents the
potentially terrifying possibility of a father who cannot always be
guaranteed to act primarily in the interests of the son. Abravanel
et al. go one step further and speak of an all-powerful, unaccountable
God, who may decide, should he so desire, to save the Assyrians to
be a 'rod' against Israel. Whereas the Christian readings, albeit
under the guise of universalism, nurture the comforting idea of a
deity who does protect his special-interest group, the Jewish tradition
offers a far less comforting perception. The book of Jonah is
uncomfortably underwritten by a sense that God's protection is not
guaranteed; that the plot may not work towards a fulfilment of our
desires; and that, rather, the ending may well be tragic and self-
defeating for Israel.

If the meanings that popular stories generate 'are themselves
magical shape-shifters, dancing to the needs of their audience',[285] if
they survive by 'sensing the aspirations and prejudices, the fears and
hungers of [their] audience',[286] then Jewish readings of Jonah seem
to have developed in surprisingly vulnerable ways. It seems that
rather than reading the book in ways that answer, and so adumbrate,
social 'anxieties and desires', they use the text as a forum for fears

---

[285] M. Warner, *From the Beast to the Blonde: On Fairy Tales and Their Tellers* (London: Chatto and
Windus, 1994), pp. xix–xxi.
[286] *Ibid.*, p. 408.

and troubling questions, to be played out without resolution. Questions such as 'What if God sided with our enemies, against us?' and 'What if God were acting against our interests' are all explored, without flinching, without foreclosing questions because of their implications for us. It is this aspect of Jewish interpretation that gives an impression of Jewish study as of 'entangling the inextricable', asking the unaskable, and 'thinking everything that is possible in a question, thoroughly, at all costs'.[287]

But asking everything that is possible in a question does not deny so much as displace desire. Jewish interpretation may not offer the comfort of a familiar self-affirming story, but it does offer the gratification of an intellectual/philosophical quest. These two variations of desire – seeking the comfort of familiar stories and the thrill of turning and turning questions – so often tug in different directions that it seems impossible to satisfy one without forfeiting the other. The Mainstream absorbs social anxieties (about social discipline, a retrogressive Old Testament, a troubling Jewish Father, a Bible superseded by science) then processes and answers them and gives back to society a coherent solution: all dissidents purged, a rational Bible, the inferior and demoted Jew, a scientifically plausible, naturalised text. The Jewish underbellies, in contrast, take anxieties about the protection of God and the waywardness of life and its plots, and stage those anxieties, multiplying question marks. Instead of the reassurance that God is on our side, we get the philosophical dilemma of whether, and under what circumstances, one should take the case of the 'son' up over and above the case of the 'father'; instead of the bolstering affirmation of Self over and against the Other, we get the spine-tingling exhilaration of mulling over what exactly God can mean when he says that Nineveh is 'useful' to him. Jonah, in Jewish interpretation, might not become a comforting, cotton-wool text (the Yom Kippur interpretation is actually anomalous in this respect),[288] but it does become the equivalent of a Mensa puzzle or a Rubik's cube. It might not satisfy an essential yearning for comfort, but you can turn it and turn it and take delight in the way it intrigues and discomforts you.

The 'popular' interpreters of Jonah often read the book in ways

---

[287] Jankélevitch, *Quelque part dans l'inachevé*, pp. 18–19.

[288] Arnold Band has recently argued that the use of Jonah on Yom Kippur 'swallows' the original subversive/parodic nature of the book. See A. J. Band, 'Swallowing Jonah: The Eclipse of Parody', *Prooftexts* 10 (1990), pp. 177–95.

that the Mainstream may well perceive as monstrous but that also resonate with their Jewish companions on the periphery. Whereas Mainstream interpretation tends to be centripetal – shaping Jonah into a book that upholds social and religious order, that punishes dissidents, and that booms lessons of discipline and obedience ('Submit to God', 'Don't Rock the Boat') – Backwater interpretations tend to be more centrifugal in orientation.[289] They resist the restrictions of a typically restrained rational idiom, stretching the range of permissible expression to include the bowdlerising 'going colo-rectal', being 'sput [or spat] out' and the 'belched up word of grace' (which gives the Backwaters, at least to those used to operating in the smooth rational idiom of the Mainstream, something of the air of an 'intellectual chowder'). And rather than repressing the fantastic because it distorts familiar secure worlds and implies that there is something a-rational about the Bible, they revel in the possibility of fantasy as 'an overt violation of what is generally accepted as possibility',[290] and foreground the strange features that may make Jonah, and by implication the Bible, not so much a rationalist tract as 'our culture's most seminal fantasy work'.[291] They use Jonah as a site for interrogating/lampooning the bastions of religion and scholarship (Melville's cartoonish Calvin and his 'learned exegetes' pull faces at the sacred text of theology/scholarship from the margins), and they actively jeopardise the coherence and self-satisfaction of the book by injecting it with the most difficult

---

[289] Even a text like *Patience*, which anchors itself firmly within a Christian worldview, allies itself with Jonah as the man-in-the-pew, for whom the lesson of the book of Jonah is essentially 'Though you often cannot see the rationale for obeying Divine or Feudal Sires, obey them nevertheless, because, as you know too well, disobedience will just prolong your agonies.' Even as it affirms social order and promotes obedience, it offers a sense of wry identification with the poor, the put-upon, the Jonahs who languish under the machinations of the Wit-Wielder and the plot of Wyrde, and it embellishes Jonah's script and encourages him to ask questions such as: 'Ah, you Maker of man, why does (it) seem a victory to you/Thus to destroy your prophet, more than all the others?'

[290] Irwin, *The Game of the Impossible*, p. ix.

[291] So D. Palumbo, 'Sexuality and the Allure of the Fantastic in Literature', in D. Palumbo (ed.), *Erotic Universe: Sexuality and Fantastic Literature* (New York: Greenwood Press, 1986), cited in T. Pippin and G. Aichele, 'Introduction', in Aichele and Pippin (eds.), *The Monstrous and the Unspeakable: The Bible and Fantastic Literature* (Sheffield: Sheffield Academic Press, 1997), pp. 11–18 (11). Not surprisingly, there have been few studies prior to Pippin and Aichele's collection exploring the fantastic as a biblical genre. But for an intriguing exception (that nevertheless feels compelled to demote such stories as primitive hangovers) see H. Gunkel, *Das Märchen* (i.e. fairy-tale/folk-tale) *im Alten Testament*, translated as *The Folktale in the Old Testament* (trans. M. D. Rutter; Sheffield: Sheffield Academic Press, 1987; 1st edn 1911).

questions. (Why is Jonah treated more cruelly than the others? If this book is about mercy, why is God not merciful? Who's to judge when the judge himself is dragged to the bar?). And flaunting the Mainstream desire for security, for feeling safe-and-sound and at home in the text, they deliberately aim to make the book of Jonah *unheimlich* (uncanny) to itself or to the religious tradition by introducing a power-abusing deity, a Jonah who sinks like a stone, or a fish picked clean until it is nothing more than a skeleton. If texts quote other texts using what Bakhtin calls 'intonational quotation marks' that span the whole spectrum from the 'pious and inert' to the most 'ambiguous, disrespectful, parodic-travestying use of a quotation';[292] if a text's use of an ur-text can involve 'acceptance and rejection, recognition and denial . . . [and be] supporting and undermining',[293] then these texts tend to quote the biblical ur-text in every possible register and link it to every possible genre. Not only do they cross the line between the Bible and pulp fiction, but they begin to suggest analogies with the pulpiest of pulp fiction, fiction that plays on the fear of becoming pulp – horror. With their frequent allusions to 'being chomped, slurped and gargled' or descending into horrible oily gurglings, to being 'stripped naked' and having one's eyes 'wrested out', to descending into a belly full of human corpses 'dissolved and putrid', to being drawn downwards into 'darkness' and 'oppressive heat' and emerging so traumatised and freakish that you have to be tied up screaming in the captain's cabin, they suggest that the allure of Jonah may be something like that of Stephen Spielberg's *Jaws*. As the fascination of *Jaws*, as Kingsley Amis put it, lay in the fear of 'being eaten by a great big bloody shark',[294] so Jonah, with its great big bloody fish, has the potential to become that latent B-movie within the canon.

To pick up another (rather over-used) term found lying on the desk of Mikhail Bakhtin, the Backwater readings show something of a tendency towards carnival – the mock-inversion of the sacred on the sacred's own territory. As Bakhtin's development of the concept is based on pre-Renaissance carnival ritual, it is not surprising that the carnival tendency (as most strictly defined) is most manifest in

---

292 Holquist, *The Dialogic Imagination*, p. 69.

293 P. D. Miscall, 'Isaiah: New Heavens, New Earth, New Book', in D. Nolan Fewell (ed.), *Reading Between Texts: Intertextuality and the Hebrew Bible* (Louisville: Westminster/John Knox, 1992), pp. 41–56 (44).

294 Cited in Barnes, *A History of the World*, p. 178.

Patience and in the fifteenth- and sixteenth-century artwork of Heemskerk, Lastman, and Galle. With its fish-belly as broad as a hall, and the image of Jonah hunting for a nook in the navel amidst slime and guts and reeking ooze, *Patience* has more than a little in common with medieval rituals such as the *festa stoltorum* (feasts of fools) *parodiae sacrae*, and mock liturgies like the 'liturgy of drunkards', where 'yeast' is added to 'reality', where 'life comes out of its usual legalised and consecrated furrows', and where the 'icy petrified seriousness' of 'official truth' is subjected to a momentary, but satisfying thaw.[295] And as it shifts winkingly between the iconographical association of the fish with Hell and the metaphorical dissipation of the hellish in 'fat and filth that *savours as* hell' and '*stinks like* the very devil', it imitates the tendency of carnival rituals to bring icons of finality (such as death, hell, and the Eschaton) down to the un-cerebral 'lower bodily stratum', and to convert the jaws of death and hell into bodily orifices and gaping human and animal mouths.[296] Just as carnival typically conducts strange conversions between the symbolic/metaphorical and the fleshy, just as Rabelais takes the image of 'chewing over a problem' and turns it into a giant mouth stretching to the skies, so fifteenth- and sixteenth-century artists' impressions of Jonah's monster reverse the alchemy first successfully completed by the Church Fathers and turn the fish emphatically, gloriously, back into flesh. The endless rewinding and replaying of the moment where Jonah is swallowed and regurgitated by the fish suggests a fascination with the inversion of order intrinsic to carnival, the spectacle of the human eater becoming a 'living feast' or tasty morsel, in a fabulous distortion of the food-chain.[297] Heemskerk's and Lastman's prophet, clearly being messily sneezed or belched out of the fish's mouth, and Heemskerk's and Galle's Ninevehs with their foregrounded kneeling cows, or fasting goats, seem to exploit the physicality of the text for carnival purposes, and to use Jonah 3.8 as an excuse for taking down the barrier that

---

[295] Bakhtin, *Rabelais and His World*, pp. 89, 73. For Bakhtin's survey of medieval carnival ritual, see pp. 1–58.

[296] *Ibid.*, pp. 329, 334. Bakhtin discusses 'The Grotesque Image of the Body' and 'Images of the Material Bodily Stratum' in chs. 5 and 6 of *Rabelais and His World* (pp. 303–436).

[297] In carnival there is 'no longer the movement of finished forms, vegetable and animal, in a finished and stable world; instead the inner movement of being itself is expressed in the passing of one form into the other'. Human beings turned into meat/animals are brought down to earth with a bump, and rituals of absorbing and ejecting, swallowing, excreting and giving birth stress the openings of the body, its lack of secure definition, and its link with other bodies (see Bakhtin, *Rabelais and His World*, pp. 20, 29, 32).

cordons off the human from the animal world. Not only do the popular 'underbellies' typically obsess, in true carnival fashion, on the 'inner features of the body: blood, bowels, heart and other organs',[298] they also betray a Rabelaisian fascination with the material status of bodies, the slime of bodies, the way in which humans cross over with animals, and with specimens in butcher's shops.

A circular letter defending carnival ritual, issued by the Paris School of Theology in 1444, describes men as 'barrels poorly put together, which would burst from the wine of wisdom, if this wine remains in a state of constant fermentation of piousness and fear of God'.[299] The Backwaters seem to be of a similar opinion: the biblical canon must breathe, and it breathes through the outlet of Jonah, or, to be more accurate, Jonah carnivalised in images of Jonah sitting on a giant kidney, Jonah and his rabbi going colo-rectal, or Jonah 'belched' back as a word to grace us all. Just as the biblical is subjected to carnivalisation through this vent in the Minor Prophets,[300] so the inversion by which Jonah becomes heroic and God is reduced to a 'twittering bird' or a 'second-class magician' is reminiscent of the defrocking of the clergy in carnival ritual, the elevation of the congregation, and the devolution of the spiritual authority to the fool. But, as we move beyond the fifteenth and sixteenth centuries through the Enlightenment to the nineteenth- and twentieth-century readings of Jonah, we move beyond the disruption of the sacred from within the boundaries of the sacred, and exit the zone of the strictly carnivalesque. The Enlightenment has just as profound an influence on the Backwaters as it has on the Mainstream (though the consequences are very different): *Moby Dick*, like *Patience*, may 'hear' the book of Jonah from the perspective of the-man-(Ishmael)-in-the-pew, but it's a sign of the times, and of the abyss between the thirteenth century and the 1850s, that the man-in-

---

[298] *Ibid.*, p. 162. Just as Dostoevsky is the icon of the dialogic, so Rabelais is Bakhtin's prime example of the carnival spirit. If Dostoevsky seems to let characters develop autonomously, independently of a circumscribing authorial consciousness, Rabelais is more likely to turn them into animals/meat (he dwells relentlessly on 'tripe (the consumable intestine), stomach, bowels . . ., the very life of man', and describes sex, memorably, as 'playing the two-backed beast' or 'rubbing the *bacon* together' (my italics).

[299] Cited in Bakhtin, *Rabelais and His World*, p. 75.

[300] The Minor Prophets, otherwise known as the Book of the Twelve, are Hosea, Joel, Amos, Obadiah, Jonah, Micah, Nahum, Habakkuk, Zephaniah, Haggai, Zechariah, and Malachi. They are minor in the sense that the books are shorter, as opposed to the books of the Major Prophets, Ezekiel, Jeremiah, and Isaiah.

the-pew is now an (a)gnostic, prone to subversive readings of biblical literature. In *Moby Dick* the God of Jonah mixes, as he could never have done before, with Egyptian and Hindu deities and the gods of Greek mythology to become the 'universal thump', the 'unaccountable old joker', and a member of the 'unseen, ambiguous synod in the air'. For Barnes and Eagleton the book becomes an opportunity for exposing God as crazed Superpower and for permanently defrocking God-as-conjurer. For Enrique Lihn it becomes a forum for enacting the very modern uncertainty of a deity experiencing his own erosion, 'waver[ing] between mercy and anger' and clenching his 'delicate fingers' awkwardly.[301] The book that has acted as a defence of Christianity and religious faith now lends itself to exposing the nakedness of the Divine Emperor, and the ideological and moral plot that tended towards conservatism in the Mainstream now bends towards anarchism and dissent. The book that so comfortably grafts itself onto the wider cultural canons of Judaism and Christianity now becomes accommodatingly porous to existentialism and humanism, and the sympathies of the Mainstream double back on themselves as Jonah becomes the focus of empathy, and God becomes remoter and remoter, curiouser and curiouser, finally dissipating into the whiteness of the whale.

This empathy with Jonah takes distinctive and symptomatic forms. In a reading that has its roots in *Patience*, but that really begins to flourish in the nineteenth and particularly the twentieth centuries, Jonah becomes a sign of 'baby man' rattling around in a disproportionate plot and world.[302] A range of authors from the *Gawain*-poet to Melville to Auster and Barnes extrapolate from Jonah's physical littleness (as a mote in the whale's belly, the mere pawn of a divine superpower) to Jonah's powerlessness and his inability to control his own life. 'When I consider the short duration of my life', wrote Pascal, 'swallowed up in an eternity past and to come, the little space that I fill . . . engulfed in the infinite immensity of spaces of which I

---

[301] Lihn, 'Jonah', in Curzon (ed.), *Modern Poems on the Bible*, p. 267.

[302] The theme of baby man, and the exploration of insecurity and alienation, brushes up against the rabbinic 'what ifs' that ask 'What if being a prophet is about invalidating one's own words?' and 'What if God were to save Assyria to be a rod against Israel?'. The exploration of the lack of human control, and insecurity, also resonates with the treatments of Jonah that nudge towards the territory of the horror genre: for horror is based on the awareness of the vulnerability of the flesh, and is, in effect, the exploration of the lack of control taken to its ultimate extreme. (For a discussion of the 'loss of control' inherent in the horror genre, see S. McCracken, *Pulp: Reading Popular Fiction* (Manchester: Manchester University Press, 1998), p. 129.)

am ignorant and which know me not, I am terrified'.[303] And Jonah –
who wanders through a narrative world where everything is big (the
city is big, the fish is big, the *qiqayon* is big) – comes to exemplify a
profound and disturbing sense that, to quote Auster, 'The world is
too big and one's life is too small.'[304] In a development that parallels
the *Mekilta* and the Talmud's sense of a Jonah caught in a plot that
goes against the grain of his own interests, the *Gawain*-poet, Mankowitz, Preil, Auster, Lihn, Camus, Herbert, Eagleton, and Barnes –
albeit in different registers and idioms – all see in Jonah a man who
is in some way netted by, or at odds with, his plot. Whereas the
Mainstream is at pains to normalise Jonah's story, the Backwaters
exacerbate and exploit that strangeness; and whereas the Mainstream is at pains to assimilate the book of Jonah into the Prophets,
the Backwaters, where they allude to biblical intertexts at all (which
is quite rarely), move Jonah closer to the strangest zone of the
Hebrew canon, where the human is at his/her littlest and God is at
his most 'omnipotent, inscrutable, capricious and dark'.[305] The
Backwaters suggest a link between Jonah and the so-called Wisdom
tradition,[306] particularly Job: Melville explicitly weaves Jonah and
Job together as the warp and weft of his anti-canon; *Patience* implies
an analogy between Jonah and Job by seeing Jonah as iconic of
'Patience', and scripts his Jonah with all the passion and boldness of
a Job.[307] Jonah, for these authors, fits more easily with a book where

[303] Pascal, *Pensée* 205, cited in Nathan A. Scott Jr, *The Modern Vision of Death* (Richmond, Va.:
John Knox Press, 1967), p. 12.
[304] Auster, *The Invention of Solitude*, p. 161.
[305] R. E. Murphy, *The Tree of Life: An Exploration of Biblical Wisdom* (New York: Doubleday,
1990), p. 36.
[306] The 'Wisdom' books in the Old Testament/Hebrew Bible are Proverbs, Job, and
Ecclesiastes (also known as Qoheleth), and in the Apocrypha Ben Sira and the Wisdom of
Solomon. They share a common style, vocabulary, and understanding of life that is
powerfully influenced by Egyptian and Mesopotamian Wisdom traditions and that differs
from what could be termed the theological Mainstream of the Old Testament. Proverbs,
Job, and Qoheleth have nothing to say about the covenant and God's intervention in
history and they present a God who is hidden in the processes of daily life. And what
makes this 'Wisdom trilogy' additionally strange is the way in which Job and Qoheleth
turn in on, and question, fundamental Wisdom premises. Orthodox Wisdom thinking, as
presented in the book of Proverbs, is concerned with the order of life (both moral and
aesthetic) and it upholds the principle that the wise will prosper whereas the foolish, or
evil, will perish. Job (the story of the righteous sufferer) and even more extremely Qoheleth
(the musings of a teacher who finds life crooked, and fundamentally disordered) radically
disorientate this neat moral aesthetic.
[307] As I look at the Backwaters, both the Jewish and the popular, analogies with Job seem to
multiply (though I concede that this is at least partly due to my own imagination). For
example, the Jonah depicted here seems to share with Job a skin complaint and a verbal

suffering is not explained, where the disparity between experience and paradigms for understanding that experience leads to frustration and to protest, and where God is so remote and so inscrutable that we can know but a 'whisper' of him and perceive the 'outskirts' or the edges of his ways (Job 26.14).

The inscrutability and hugeness of God – a topic for praise – can so easily shift to a site of blame, as it does in Qoheleth (Ecclesiastes), the most radical of the Wisdom trilogy, where God is described (indirectly, in the third person) as the one who makes life crooked so that none can make it straight (Ecclesiastes 7.13). And insofar as Qoheleth becomes a kind of 'theistic Camus',[308] it parallels Jonah's latest, twentieth-century mutations. The theme of 'baby man' develops in distinctly twentieth-century idioms, and the book becomes a book about alienation, summed up in the slogan 'Absurd'. Jonah becomes the man who is so 'tossed by the vacillations of history' that his life feels 'grotesque and unfinished'; the man who feels alienated and looks desperately for connection; the man who feels that his actions may well be self-negating; and the man who, to quote Camus again, is caught in an absurd encounter between 'human need [for rationality] and the unreasonable silence of the world'.[309]

Such readings, touching as they do on themes that could loosely be called 'existentialist',[310] are likely to prove anathema to the

complaint. Like Job, he demonstrates all too clearly the fact that humans are not made of 'stones' or 'bronze' but of vulnerable soft fleshy stuff (compare Job 2.7–8; 6.12; 7.5 with the Jewish descriptions of Jonah's raw skin). And Jonah's death-wishes and his protests against the deity only reinforce the connections with a character who (in a sardonic riff on Psalm 8.4) accuses God of being a Big Brother figure, and who aims a rhetorical arsenal at annihilating the day of his birth (Job 3.1–26; 7.17–20).

308 M. V. Fox, *Qoheleth and His Contradictions* (Sheffield: Sheffield Academic Press, 1989). Fox explores the resonances between Albert Camus and Qoheleth ('the teacher') throughout his book, but see especially pp. 13–15. To emphasise the connection, he translates the word הבל (*hbl*) which is usually translated 'vanity' (as in the famous translation 'Vanity of vanities, all is vanity') as 'Absurd'.

309 Camus, *The Myth of Sisyphus*, p. 22.

310 Since existentialism has received rather a bad press, I need to be clear what I mean by it here. Existentialism is not a self-indulgent, bourgeois indifference to life, as exemplified by Camus's hero Meursault in *L'Etranger* (The Outsider) as he sits smoking on his mother's coffin, kills an Arab without remorse, and finds no value in life. (Not only is this a huge reduction of Camus's novel but Camus is, as David Cooper points out, perhaps the least typical of existentialist thinkers in that he seems, at time, to revel in the perception of life as Absurd.) Existentialism is the perception of, and the attempt to overcome alienation from one's world, from one's fellow human beings and from oneself; it is the attempt to live life with energy and commitment, as if the ground beneath the individual were solid, while at the same time aware of the exigency with which life is lived. For a discussion of

Mainstream. But, as it would be too easy to consign them to a drawer of 'mere play', it needs to be stressed that the Backwaters are not always simply toying with Jonah, they are also concerned with the ultimate questions belonging to the realm of religion/philosophy. Though they might not be immediately recognisable to readers accustomed to seeing the 'religious' packaged in terms of grace, salvation, and distinctly Christian idioms, the Backwaters are also engaging with 'religious' themes, with the perennial questions of the human condition, and with issues of 'frustration and suffering and death'.[311] The fact that they do not necessarily overcome alienation so much as see the book of Jonah as a performance of that alienation merely demonstrates the infinite plasticity of this little text.

At this point it is probably appropriate to pause for a moment, to stand back and admire the book of Jonah's capacity to reinvent itself. Jonah has absorbed religious and secular metanarratives, it has told stories of acquiescence and subversion, it has learnt to comfort and to disturb and to imitate the ideology/(a)theology of figures as diverse as Martin Luther and Albert Camus. It has somehow managed to conscript atheists/agnostics like Terry Eagleton and Julian Barnes into its dissemination, and it has achieved such a permanent hold in popular consciousness that, although approximately a third of my students on an 'Introduction to the Bible' module have never consciously opened a Bible (or so they say), I have never yet met one who has not heard of Jonah and the whale. Like Rosen's myth-fish, this book has lain at the bottom of the ocean taking the history of millennia into its skin: it has responded to the Enlightenment and Darwin, has processed anxieties about the Jew and about Science, and most recently has imbibed (and sometimes choked on) the Second World War, the Holocaust, the state of Israel, and the loss of religious faith.

If the last chapter ended with a quasi-scientific meditation on the survival of the fittest readings, and the way in which the readings of

existentialism that challenges all the conventional clichés, see D. E. Cooper, *Existentialism: A Reconstruction* (Oxford: Blackwell, 1999).

[311] These descriptions of religion are taken from B. Clack and B. R. Clack, *The Philosophy of Religion: A Critical Introduction* (Cambridge: Polity 1998), pp. 4–5. Moving away from what they call the Parson Thwackum Fallacy, after Thwackum's remark in Fielding's *Tom Jones* ('when I mention religion I mean the Christian religion; and not only the Christian religion, but the Protestant religion; and not only the Protestant religion, but the Church of England'), Clack and Clack move towards a functionalist definition of religion as a means of dealing with ultimate questions. For a further discussion of Clack and Clack's definition of 'religion', and a comparison with the field of Biblical Studies, see p. 208.

the dead live on, or over-live, this chapter ends with two rather different meditations on the theme of survival. The first (Of survival, memes and life-after-death) is a pseudo-scientific meditation on the amazing living-on of the book of Jonah. The second (Jonah on the oncology ward and the beached-up whale carcass) considers the Chinese-box relations between the Bible and 'reality', and looks at the way in which the secular and the biblical (contrary to popular report) are currently finding all kinds of ways of nesting in one another and commenting on one another – rather than simply fighting to the death.

4. OF SURVIVAL, MEMES AND LIFE-AFTER-DEATH: ON JONAH'S INFINITE REGURGITATION AND ENDLESS SURVIVAL

I'm intrigued by (the book of) Jonah's survival in secular culture: a survival that, like the survival of Jonah after three days in the fish, tries the very limits of credulity. And I'm fascinated by descriptions of Jonah as, for example, a 'book that has always been there' in the 'blood' and in the 'bones', the 'story that you are born into', to quote Patricia Hampl.[312] Hampl's description of a book that inhabits the human body/consciousness echoes Frank McConnell's provocative statement that 'The Bible is less a book and more a living entity in the evolving consciousness of Western man [*sic*].'[313] As it positions Jonah, and indeed the Bible, as living in and off the human mind, it edges curiously close to the idea of the biblical text as 'meme' – the cultural equivalent of the gene, popularised by Richard Dawkins[314]

---

[312] Hampl, 'In the Belly of the Whale', p. 291. The full quotation (with my italics) reads: 'How many people recall the first time they heard of the cowardly man swallowed by a big fish? *He's always been there.* Like all abiding tales that carry heavy psychological freight, *Jonah is not a story you merely read or hear, but one into which you are born, as into a family, recognising the blood relation* . . . Jonah, unlike its slender neighbours, is *the story known in the bones, the story you can't remember ever not knowing,* like a memory so old, it isn't a memory but *an ounce of yourself.*'

[313] F. McConnell (ed.), *The Bible and the Narrative Tradition* (New York: Oxford University Press, 1986), cited in Clines, *The Bible and the Modern World*, p. 40 (no page reference given).

[314] The popular scientist Richard Dawkins famously argued that cultural evolution can be compared to evolutionary biology, on the basis that 'just as genes propagate themselves in the gene pool by leaping from body to body via sperm or eggs, so memes [small replicating elements of culture, such as tunes, fashions, or even biblical texts] propagate themselves in the meme pool by leaping from brain to brain' (R. Dawkins, *The Selfish Gene* (Oxford: Oxford University Press, 1976), p. 206). The idea 'caught' on (to use an appropriately memetic idiom): as if to testify to the memetic success of the word 'meme' the *OED* now contains a definition, and Dawkins recently found no less than 5,042 references to meme on the internet (as reported in Dawkins, 'Foreword', in S. Blackmore, *The Meme Machine* (Oxford: Oxford University Press, 1999), pp. vii–xvii (viii)). For one of the many popular

– the cultural unit that ensures its own survival by grafting itself onto, and incubating itself in, human culture and the human mind.

The question of the survival of biblical texts, the way they continue to replicate themselves in a secularised, contemporary meme-pool was recently raised by Hugh Pyper, biologist turned Hebrew Bible scholar, in one of the most interesting meditations on the Bible in Culture to date.[315] In 'The Selfish Text: The Bible and Memetics', Pyper provocatively, and emphatically metaphorically, takes a Bible's-eye view of the world, and shows how the Bible – as a memeplex, or association of memes – has ensured its faithful propagation by hooking up its own interests with the interests of the host community.[316] Like all successful replicators, the Bible, he argues, has ensured its faithful copying, but has also demonstrated an extraordinary capacity to produce variation when variation is required. In 'The Triumph of the Lamb: Psalm 23, Darwin and Textual Fitness', he homes in on a specific text and asks what it is about Psalm 23 (surely one of the most successful of biblical memes) that has made this text so fit to survive? The answer seems to lie in ambiguity: because it hovers between want and fulfilment, anxiety and promise, because it promises a glorious future involving cups that runneth over, but speaks with fraught and poignant ambiguity of the present, Psalm 23 is used, strangely, both at weddings and funerals, these 'two major loci of . . . the anxiety of survival'.[317] The psalm's non-committal ambiguity in terms of language and sentiment means that it can 'jump ship between communities of readers': with its allusions to sheep (and by implication (good) shepherds) it so

---

disseminations of the idea of meme, including reflections on the human brain as 'meme-nest', see D. Dennett, *Darwin's Dangerous Idea* (London: Allen Lane, 1995).

315 H. S. Pyper, 'The Selfish Text: The Bible and Memetics', in J. C. Exum and S. D. Moore (eds.), *Biblical Studies/Cultural Studies: The Third Sheffield Colloquium* (Sheffield: Sheffield Academic Press, 1998), pp. 70–90; and 'The Triumph of the Lamb: Psalm 23, Darwin and Textual Fitness' (unpublished paper presented at the *Reading, Theory and the Bible* section of the *Society of Biblical Literature* Annual Meeting, Orlando, 21–24 November 1998). I am grateful to Hugh Pyper for letting me see a copy of this paper.

316 To be specific, Pyper proposes that Bibles ensure their faithful propagation by containing their own message of evangelisation; by promising the benefits of immortality to their hosts; by offering a whole plethora of strategies for survival; by linking their own survival to the survival of the host community; and by warning the host of the disasters that will ensue by abandoning them or allowing foreign ideas to infiltrate them (see 'The Selfish Text', pp. 78–9).

317 Pyper, 'The Triumph of the Lamb', p. 4. As Pyper elaborates, Psalm 23 works, and works so disparately, because the ambiguous phrase 'I shall not want' can mean 'I have nothing now, but will be satisfied in the future', or 'I am satisfied and will continue to be in the future.'

easily grafts itself onto the 'Christianity of convention', and yet it can
also 'slip back into a more open unitarian universalism without
effort'.[318]

What happens if, like Pyper, we enter this strange metaphorical
zone where the Bible becomes 'alive' in anything but a conventional
sloganeering sense, and examine the book of Jonah's strategy, and
capacity, for survival? In times when the Bible lives on by an
increasingly slim metonymic margin – when texts like Psalm 23,
Jonah, the Nativity, the Ten Commandments, Armageddon, and
fragments like 'holier than thou' or 'wheels within wheels' carry the
texts like Obadiah or the book of Jude[319] – Jonah is clearly one of
the dominant texts, one of the books that the Bible leads with in its
quest for cultural presence. It survives by hooking itself up with the
survival of communities (with Christian anxiety about the Jew, and
Jewish questions of survival) and it shows an extraordinary capacity
for variation and mutation (in the effort to re-contemporise itself it
has regenerated itself by *grafting*: by attaching itself to contemporary
landmarks and idioms – Haifa Port, the New York subway, Yiddish
humour, espionage, J. L. Austin – that stop it sinking into irrelevance
in a biblical 'past'). Like Psalm 23, it survives because it carries what
Patricia Hampl terms 'heavy psychological freight',[320] because it
taps into the anxiety of survival and lends itself to stories of 'life and
death'. The swallowing and emergence of Jonah suggest the triumph
of humanity, survival against the odds, even as it resonates with the
fear of being consumed. And, rather as the Mainstream extracts
iconic moments from the text – like pins with magnets – so popular
culture extracts its own resonant images. Jonah becomes a book
about seeking security: 'huddling in the hurrock' and seeking shade
in the 'green bower' of the *qiqayon* are profoundly human gestures
foregrounding human vulnerability, and the belly of the whale can
be stretched to a sign of returning to the insulating security of the
womb (so Mitchell), or, more negatively, of escaping from life and
huddling in whale blubber (so Orwell). Going to Nineveh or running
away to Tarshish become attenuated metaphors for accepting or

---

[318] Pyper, 'The Triumph of the Lamb', pp. 6–7.

[319] This is not only true of the Bible, but also of other weighty cultural tomes. 'Shakespeare',
for example, tends to be disseminated through *Macbeth*, *Romeo and Juliet*, the 'To be or not
to be' speech, and 'Alas poor Yorick . . .', rather than, say, *The Two Gentlemen of Verona* or
Timon of Athens.

[320] Hampl, 'In the Belly of the Whale', p. 291.

fleeing from risk and responsibility – 'What is your Nineveh?', the Rabbi asks Joel Fleischman in *Northern Exposure*.

But the key to Jonah's survival, like the key to Psalm 23's survival, lies in the 'hinged' quality that mimics the hinged oracle at the book's centre. Jonah can be read as comedy or tragedy, self-bolstering or self-annihilating, the stuff of 'marriages' or 'funerals': you can read it in a way that makes theological/pedagogic capital out of the forgiveness of Nineveh and the disobedience of Jonah, or you can read it in a way that makes comic capital out of potentially absurd features like cattle in sackcloth, the *qiqayon* and worm, or hymns sung from the fish's belly. For those who seek lessons, the book offers reduction to a parable; but for those who like their texts to come as Rubik's Cubes or Mensa puzzles (like Barnes, Eagleton, and the rabbis), it also offers mind-bending hooks such as the oracle that tips over, or Yhwh's puzzlingly inadequate *qal ve homer*. But the most fundamental hinge of all – and the key to Jonah's capacity to 'jump ship' – is the fact that you can enter the text from the perspective of God and/or Jonah. The capacity of the book to be read dialogically or to lend itself to two equal and opposite monologic readings means that, even as a God-centred reading lends itself to the 'Christianity of convention', the book can also slip into the idioms of existentialism and humanism without effort. And as Jonah becomes the patron saint of the lost, and the confused, those who experience their lives as (comically and/or tragically) disjunctive and bizarre, the book throws out an anchor to more secular shores, and guarantees its survival outside the sea of religious affiliation.

Jonah's strategies for survival are ultimately more extreme (and desperate?) than those of Psalm 23. For two of the major ways in which the book survives in a secular environment is by making itself Absurd – and absurd. The book of Jonah survives by offering itself as an outlet for the spirit of carnival (or secular debunking) within the Bible, and by allowing scope for turning this rather inert and straightfaced icon of piety and culture into a vent for the bizarre and the baroque. The book that has already added large helpings of yeast to reality offers the opportunity to trump hyperbole with hyperbole, and to satisfy an appetite for strange novelties that, in this 'postmodern' age, has become increasingly acute. Jonah squatting on one vast kidney, Jonah with false beard and glasses running from God-as-MI5, Jonah in the fish belly/New York subway and so on and so on remind me of nothing so much as the array of the bizarre and the quirky wheeled on stage in the postmodern show in Donald Barthelme's short story 'The Flight of the Pigeons from the Palace'.[321] In an attempt to satisfy a public who want 'wonders piled on new wonders' and who know, in this jaded age, that 'things that seem wonderful in the beginning are not wonderful at all when you are familiar with them', the showmakers audition earthquakes, volcanoes, and a 'seventy-five-foot highly paid cacodemon', in a desperate attempt to 'raise even the tiniest frisson'.[322] But what ultimately seems to engage the showmakers, their public, and indeed Barthelme, albeit briefly, is the regurgitation and re-sorting of images from the past in comic, nostalgic and mocking modes: the line-up of oddities includes a black and white reproduction of Jael and Sisera captioned 'Scenes of Domestic Life'; 'theological novelties'; cut-and-pasted images from old-fashioned medical textbooks; and 'sad themes' played by a band 'bereft of its mind by the death of tradition'.[323] It is in this time, under these circumstances, that the book of Jonah, with its attendant menagerie of monsters and its capacity for throwing up theological novelties, seizes its opportunity and exerts its appeal on the (post)modern imagination.[324]

Thus Jonah becomes, in a sense, a kind of biblical Judas, surviving precisely by betraying the Bible as a lofty cultural icon. Curiouser and curiouser still in its most extreme survival tactic to date, it seems to make a living, like Barthelme's band, by playing on the 'death of tradition'. Not only does it live by subverting the Bible, by twisting biblical images, and by carnivalising the sacred, but in the strangest twist of all it survives by becoming a place for probing strange secular attachments to, *in detachment from*, the biblical text. In a culture where the death-of-God and the related ill-health of the Bible are something of a well-established truism,[325] the book of

---

[321] D. Barthelme, 'The Flight of the Pigeons from the Palace', in *Forty Stories* (London: Minerva, 1988), pp. 130–40.

[322] *Ibid.*, p. 140.

[323] *Ibid.*, pp. 133, 135.

[324] Of course, this book is itself a testimony to the allure of the Jonah-meme, as well as to the book's capacity to satisfy a (contemporary?) taste for the whimsical and the baroque. Although this study began purely as an attempt to unpick the motif of Jonah the Jew, it soon grew as I discovered motifs like the man-in-the-belly-of-the-pregnant fish, the repentant goats, and Jonah hunting for a navel-nook, and could not resist erecting a book-length show-hall to display them.

[325] The death of God is not a one-off event in Western Culture, but something that has been regularly announced (with associated media sensation) since the Enlightenment. The most famous obituaries for God have included Nietzsche's prophetic shriekings over the death of the (Christian) 'God of the sick, God as spider, God as the will to nothingness sanctified';

Jonah lives on, parasitically, feeding from the shrinking of biblical authority and a sense of the loss of religious faith. In the interpretations of Rosen, Preil, Crane Pagis, and Herbert (to name only the most obvious examples), Jonah reproduces itself precisely by becoming a site for exploring the decay of tradition, the death of God; it lives off the grating between the credulity of the past, and the doubt of the present. But in doing so, it suggests that the 'secular' and the 'biblical' are not as alienated from one another as popular wisdom would have us believe, and that they are finding all kinds of mutually provocative ways of changing, interrogating, and indeed goading one another.

5. JONAH ON THE ONCOLOGY WARD AND THE BEACHED-UP WHALE CARCASS: OR THE STRANGE SECULAR AFTERLIVES OF BIBLICAL TEXTS

> The secularization of the European spirit of the modern age does not consist solely in the exposure and demystification of the errors of religion, but also in the survival of these 'errors' in different, and in some sense degraded, forms. A secularized culture is not one that has simply left the religious elements of its tradition behind, but one that continues to live them as traces, as hidden and distorted models that are nonetheless profoundly present.[326]

> The postmodern 'overcoming' of myth . . . proposes to salvage myth in the transposed form of an ironically distanced or diluted reinterpretation. By not taking itself seriously (that is, literally), myth can be taken seriously once again.[327]

Thomas Hardy's account of 'God's Funeral' (1910), in which he reports how he sang the requiem of God as 'man-projected figure' and followed behind God's coffin; and Thomas Altizer's 'death of God' theology in the 1960s, leading to *Time* Magazine's announcement that 'God, Creator of the Universe, principal deity of the world's Jews, Ultimate reality of Christians, and most eminent of all divinities, died late yesterday during major surgery undertaken to correct a massive diminishing influence' (*Time* 82, 1966). To check out the obituaries see T. Hardy, *The Complete Poems* (London: Macmillan, 1974); F. Nietzsche, *The Anti-Christ* (trans. R. J. Hollingdale; Harmondsworth: Penguin, 1990), p. 138; T. J. J. Altizer and W. Hamilton, *Radical Theology and the Death of God* (Harmondsworth: Penguin, 1968). Recent accounts of God's dotage and demise can be found in D. Jasper, 'The Death of God: A Live Issue?', *Biblicon 3* (May 1998), pp. 19–26, and A. N. Wilson, *God's Funeral* (London: John Murray, 1999) – a suitably weighty, black tome charting the God's demise (and the emotional loss that accompanied it) from the late eighteenth century to the present.

[326] G. Vattimo, *The Transparent Society* (Cambridge: Polity Press, 1992), p. 40.

[327] R. Kearney, *Poetics of Imagining: From Husserl to Lyotard* (London: Harper Collins, 1991), p. 183.

There is a popular cultural myth that packages and manages
relations between the Bible on the one hand, and contemporary
Secular Reality (as arbitrated and defined by Science) on the other.
According to this rather simple dualism, the two are at loggerheads,
and ultimately we are on a one-track Hegelian trajectory in which
the primitive (the religious, the biblical) is inexorably being eroded
by the corrosive cumulation of facts.[328] 'It is certain that religions
are mistaken in the real nature of things: science has proved it',[329]
proclaimed Emile Durkheim in 1915, while a recent article in *The
Guardian* strangely 'expose[s]' the fact that the Bible got the value of
pi 'rather wrong' in 2 Kings, and then, unable to resist the pun,
implies that the superiority of science suggests religion is all 'pi in the
sky'.[330] Meanwhile Creation and Evolution (fighting for 'the Bible'
and 'Science' teams respectively) still wearily slog it out in the sham
struggles or rigged fights staged regularly on Christian bookshop
shelves, as well as on the pages of popular science. It was inevitable,
of course, that Jonah – the story of a man gobbled and regurgitated
by a big fish – would get caught up in these struggles (that is, when
anyone bothered to make it past Genesis 1–3) and it was equally
inevitable that, as the book became another prooftext for the biblical
tried in the scales of facts and found wanting, the assault on biblical
faith would send Keil and Delitzsch and Pusey and their pseudo-
scientific descendants scurrying off to re-package the book in
plausible scientific language. The sense of showdown and victory
spilt over into popular culture in the well-known song where the
biblical claim that 'Jonah lived in a whale' proves, rather conclusively, that 'things that you're liable/to read in the Bible/ain't
necessarily so'.[331]

But while scholars, journalists, and George Gershwin have been
distracted by the idea of a mythological showdown between Reality
(as Science) and Religion, 'Culture' and 'the Bible' have been
playing a more sophisticated – and infinitely more interesting –

---

[328] The Hegelian trajectory of secularisation, and the influence of Hegel on Feuerbach, Marx, and Comte is discussed by G. Graham, 'Religion, Secularization and Modernity', *Philosophy* 67 (1992), pp. 183–97.

[329] E. Durkheim, *The Elementary Forms of the Religious Life* (London: Allen and Unwin, 1915), p. 83.

[330] T. Radford, 'Babylon belittled by brothers' pi in the sky', *The Guardian*, 29 August 1992, p. 6. The example is discussed by Clines, *The Bible in the Modern World*, p. 75.

[331] Gershwin's famous song from *Porgy and Bess* (Goldwyn, 1959) is itself a happily replicating meme: it was covered by *The Communards* in the 1980s.

game. In this game the secular does not trump the biblical, then crumple it up and throw it in the cultural wastebasket, but rather the secular plays out its concerns and its disaffections *within the forum of the biblical text*. Ever since *Patience*, contemporary reality and the biblical have been meeting one another in all kinds of mutually destabilising, ironic modes, where both are present and (inter)active, and neither can be said to win. To take that most obvious grating point between the Bible and reality, the sojourn in the fish, as an example, it seems that this has been a site of ironic distantiation long before the dawn of Modernism and scientific empiricism. When the *Gawain*-poet, an indisputably religious writer, says: 'What became of that man after he was plunged into that water?/It would be a marvel to believe if Holy Scripture were not in existence', he is clearly drawing attention to – and exploiting the comedy of – the dissonance between the real world of 'natural laws' and the biblical world of miracles, and using a kind of humour that antitheses between the secular and the religious inevitably miss. At the other end of the scale Joel Fleischman, an almost totally secular creation, mutters 'I can't believe I'm having this conversation' as he contemplates going colo-rectal through the bowels of the fish. The sheer complexity of the *Northern Exposure* sequence – the way in which medical textbooks are levered into the stomach of myth, and a whole series of Chinese-box relations are set up between various sub- or virtual- or heightened-realities (including Disney, TV, and the Bible) – suggests that the idea that reality and the Bible either confirm one another or have no truck with one another is crassly over-reductive and over-restrictive. Similarly, Abeshaus's spectacle of the myth-fish docking in Haifa suggests that tenuous gangplank-like connections can be set up between the Bible and the present, and that the dissonance created by traffic between them is a fundamental part of the experiment. This chapter is crammed full of examples of the modern and the biblical querying one another, jamming one another's frequency – from Stephen Mitchell's playful exploration of his distance from the biblical text within the framework of the biblical original, to Rosen's bitterly nostalgic and alienated reflections. Instead of simply conforming to a modernist Hegelian trajectory or a mythical dualistic show-down, these readings edge close to a postmodern mode of being in which incompatible modes of reality provocatively – and gratingly – co-exist. They come close to a postmodern reappropriation of myth in which myth is retained as a 'secular interplay of multifaceted meanings' and preserved in 'the transposed form of an ironically distanced or diluted reinterpretation', and is taken seriously precisely by not taking itself too seriously.[332] But, at the same time, they never entirely shake a sense of looking back on myth from a demythologised present; indeed, they often work by exploiting the contrast between a knowing 'now' and an innocent/credulous 'then', and they tend to read from the playful/mocking/yearning vantage point of a surplus of knowledge.

If midrash is, as Daniel Boyarin argues, a tradition that regenerates through disruption, that preserves contact with the tradition while it is liberating, and that treats the words of Torah as a 'repertoire of semiotic elements' that can be recombined in new discourse,[333] there is evidently something very 'midrashic' about contemporary culture's relation with the biblical. And, if we concentrate on the twentieth-century readings, it seems that relations with the biblical text are most commonly violent or nostalgic and are often, incongruously, a combination of both. As if to demonstrate Harold Bloom's thesis that creativity is an Oedipal struggle in which sons imitate and displace fathers,[334] these readings sometimes deal with the father-text as violently, and anxiously, as Christianity deals with its precursor Judaism in the Mainstream. Many readers, such as Rosen and Barnes, are clearly forcing the biblical text to swallow twentieth-century models of thought or events that it simply cannot digest without poisoning (or deconstructing) itself. As this book of mercy chokes on knowledge of the Shoah, Rosen points up its inadequacy, and as Barnes condemns a fascist deity through models of democracy, he makes it all too clear that we no longer live in days (as Hooper did) where the State and the Bible automatically collude with one another, like wearers of the same school tie. The privatisation of religious belief (and unbelief) – the fact that we are able to dissent from biblical and Church/synagogue authority – means that readers are more prone to sympathise with the biblical dissenters and outcasts – with the Ahabs, the Ishmaels, and indeed the Jonahs. Not only is the book of Jonah read dialogically, but the dialogue is sometimes skewed in

---

[332] Kearney, *Poetics of Imagining*, p. 183.

[333] D. Boyarin, *Intertextuality and the Reading of Midrash*, p. 28.

[334] Bloom's famous argument that strong poets are always, necessarily, 'perverse' in relation to the precursor, and the processes of rewriting the past are never 'polite', is mapped out in H. Bloom, *The Anxiety of Influence* (New York: Oxford University Press, 1973).

Jonah's favour, and the words of the text are re-sorted and realigned so that the text becomes the gnostic inversion of its Mainstream self. In the Backwaters and underbellies, Jonah is victimised by the nets spread to maim, tossed hither and thither by an uncertain deity (who has become a barely tangible presence, like a cloud), and begs to be sealed up, unforgiven, in ambergris, in the whale's belly.[335] As if to express his disaffection from the text he finds himself in, and to adapt to the contemporary world, he gives up prophecy, starts selling tobacco or antiques, and puts on a false beard and dark glasses to evade God-as-MI5. God, meanwhile, finds that a sceptical (post)modernity is beginning to corrode his sovereignty: his rather feudal *modus operandi* criticised, he becomes increasingly unsure of himself and his place in the world. For readers like Barnes and Eagleton, there is clearly a considerable amount of pleasure involved in shrinking the booming brittle deity of a Protestant Christian heritage down to a two-bit magician, and to do so via the text, thus hoisting the biblical by its own petard.

The secular, then, is not always *kind* to the biblical,[336] and sometimes seeks to expose it, and the God behind it, as an old, moribund, and dribbling parent. It aims to make the text stammer and stutter; to use the present as a spanner in the mechanisms of its logic: to show how Jonah sinks like a stone, unsaved, in the less conducive climate of the (post)modern world. And yet an intrinsic part of this traumatic unhinging of the text is simply to make it as puzzled and alienated by us as we are by it, to register within the Bible the sense of disjunction between the naïve past and the knowing present. Many of the secular reinscriptions of Jonah are profoundly nostalgic, as if pining, like Pagis's fish, for the prophecy and the belief that once filled our bellies. The flipside of the Hegelian march from primitive childhood to rational adulthood is that the adult longs to be a child again. Jonah – with its big fish and big plants – becomes a perfect site for staging the longing for the lost world of baseball bats and 'my father's Mishnah', and for exploring the sense of loss that

---

[335] See Preil, 'Jonah', Lihn, 'Jonah', and Crane, 'After Jonah', in Curzon (ed.), *Modern Poems on the Bible*, pp. 259, 257, 260.

[336] Bloom would argue, of course, that interpretation is never kind, and that reading is always an 'act of defensive warfare'. The curious thing (as I argued in *The Prostitute and the Prophet: Hosea's Marriage in Literary-Theoretical Perspective* (Sheffield: Sheffield Academic Press, 1996), pp. 35–6) is that sometimes the most faithful and pious readings are caught up in a strange paradox of being cruel-to-be-kind to the parent-text.

attends the coming of a knowledge that can be (certainly in Rosen's case) almost too terrible to be borne.[337]

Once again, it seems that the ever-obliging book of Jonah is merely the tip of the iceberg, a convenient microcosm of the mutations of 'the Bible' in the present. For *these days* it seems that artists and writers are frequently playing with the tension between *these days* and *those days*, and confusing and domesticating biblical texts. In 'Intimate Supper', the British poet Peter Redgrove shrinks Genesis 1 down to the dimensions of a bachelor flat and a dinner table: the creator makes the light shine from the firmament of the ceiling, the winds blow through the hoover, he spins the shiny taps in the bathroom, wallows like Leviathan in the bath water, lays the table, walks in the garden, waits.[338] In similarly diminished scenarios, the Israeli poet Yehuda Amichai reduces the 'light of another world' to the light of the fridge; he asks to see God, but like a modern-day Moses, only gets to see the sole of his shoes; he reverses Genesis 3.9 so that 'this time God is hiding/And man shouts where are you?' – all the time declaring his desire to 'confuse the Bible', to re-sort it for a world where 'good and evil' are 'on the table before me like salt and pepper/The shakers so alike'.[339] The dominant sense in so many biblical poems is that the Bible – like all over-familiar celebrities – no longer has control over the dissemination of its own image, that it is part of the 'semiotic repertoire' of culture – familiar, part of us, available to us, but on our terms. And again and again the meaning that emerges is that the language of transcendence is no longer meaningful, that, to borrow the words of Yeats, the circus animals have deserted, the 'ladder's gone', and we must 'lie down where all the ladders start/In the foul rag and bone shop

---

[337] For a discussion of the sense of loss and disenchantment that accompanies the adulthood of secularisation, see P. Berger, *The Sacred Canopy* (Garden City, N.Y.: Doubleday, 1967); D. Wiebe, *The Irony of Theology and the Nature of Religious Thought* (Montreal: McGill-Queen's Press, 1991).

[338] P. Redgrove, 'Intimate Supper', in M. Roberts (ed.), *The Faber Book of Modern Verse* (London: Faber and Faber, 1982; 4th edn rev. P. Porter), p. 399. The poem is also discussed by Clines, *The Bible and the Modern World*, pp. 46–7.

[339] The first three twisted allusions (to the fridge, to Moses, and to Genesis 3.9) are all taken from the poem *Vehi tehillateka*, 'And this is Your Glory' (the title of which is a play on a poem of praise on Yom Kippur). The translation I am using is that of Glenda Abramson (in G. Abramson, 'Amichai's God', *Prooftexts* 4 (1984), pp. 111–26 (115–16)). The salt-shaker allusion comes from 'I Want to Confuse the Bible', in Y. Amichai, *A Life of Poetry 1948–1994* (trans. B. and B. Harshav; New York: HarperCollins, 1994), pp. 459–60.

of the heart'.[340] The language applied to divine love shrinks to the dimensions of human love (unidealised, sometimes sordid, full of vacillations and agonies), and the Bible, realising that the key trope of the time is mundane, drops its cosmic idioms, makes itself small enough to creep into flats and fridges and bathrooms, and starts talking about littleness,' death, the vulnerability of human skin, and about cancers and hospital beds. In Israeli culture, this sense of the shrinking of grandeur has an extra dimension because, in a tension that poets like Pagis and Amichai are naturally keen to exploit, a sense of bathos is built into the language in the contrast between biblical Hebrew (where *hashmal* refers to the numinous aura that surrounds the divine; and *tikkun* refers to the repair of the individual, repentance) and modern Hebrew (where *hashmal* means electricity, and *tikkun* means fixing, in the manner of a repair-man or motor mechanic).[341]

A Jonah who plays his text like a smoke-filled comedy club, who sinks like a stone and dies in a neat hospital of cancer, a fish that lies on the shore like a beached-up carcass, and a God who shrinks to a twittering bird and clenches his fingers awkwardly are symptomatic of a larger diminution, a larger sense that, in the West at least, the biblical lights are going out, and the *hashmal* is being put on a one-way dimmer switch. But what is so fascinating is that this demise, this loss of faith in the biblical, is not so much leading to an exodus of biblical images from Western culture but *is being expressed within the framework and language of biblical texts*. Mankowitz, Barnes, Rosen, Pagis, and Herbert are not throwing the book of Jonah overboard, but are *using the book of Jonah to talk about its own inadequacy, demise, even uselessness*. Even in poems when Jonah is dying, even when the fish is stripped down to a skeleton, when the book is being traumatised by footage from Birkenau or Auschwitz, the book is still surviving, still living on, still miraculously over-living the message of its own death.

But I'm coming out of my office in Biblical Studies and wandering down the corridor again. For, while secularisation is studied by theologians and philosophers of religion, it is not currently included

---

[340] W. B. Yeats, 'The Circus Animals' Desertion', in D. Albright (ed.), *W. B. Yeats: The Poems* (London: J. M. Dent and Sons, 1991), pp. 394–5.

[341] For a discussion of the reworking of biblical motifs in Israeli culture and literature, see D. C. Jacobson, *Does David Still Play Before You? Israeli Poetry and the Bible* (Detroit: Wayne State University Press, 1997).

within the curriculum of Biblical Studies.[342] A recent introduction to the Philosophy of Religion concludes with a section on the future of religion, expansively defined as something that 'emerges out of the anguish and turbulence of modern life, the apparent hollowness of the human condition' and that explores Dennis Potter's *Brimstone and Treacle* under the rubric of religion and philosophy.[343] But you will not find such discussions in introductions to biblical studies, which generally give the impression of operating for a select, already-Christian clientele. If this book is an argument for closing the gap between Biblical Studies and Jewish Studies, it is also an argument for expanding our definitions of the 'religious', not only so that Hebrew Bible texts are not necessarily assumed to fall within the belief structures of Christianity (or indeed Judaism), but so that we can pay attention to all mutations of the biblical in Culture, including those that the Mainstream may well regard as monstrous or deviant. By circumscribing the discipline and protecting it, Biblical Studies may well be closing its eyes to one of vibrant uses of the 'biblical' in Western culture: a use that, as a reflection of the paradoxical post-Christian times in which we live, animates biblical texts precisely by questioning their relevance.

This tour of the Backwaters began with a discussion of the 'disembowelled rationalism' and the disciplinary logic of the Mainstream, and it ends, in a sense, in the same place. For while Pusey and the scholars deal with the challenge by remaking the book of Jonah in modernity/science's image, and contemporary sceptics play, relentlessly, with a sense of discrepancy between a credulous *then* and a knowing *now*, both groups operate under the thoroughly modern conviction that we live in times that have shed a pre-modern attachment to miracle, magic, and the fantastic. Even the most playful and seemingly 'postmodern' of popular Backwater readings exploit the contrast between a hard-faced, knowing present, and a naïve age of faith, and so share with Durkheim a fundamental sense of teleology and progress. And if postmodernism is defined, as Vattimo claims, by the 'demythologisation of demytho-

---

[342] This may be confusing for those not familiar with the discipline, who might reasonably assume that Theology and Biblical Studies are the same subject. But the fact is that Biblical Studies and Theology have long since parted company and separated to different ends of the corridor – leading to a whole series of papers, from both sides of the split, lamenting the split and considering the possibility of a reunion.

[343] Clack and Clack, *The Philosophy of Religion*, pp. 169–89 (188).

logisation',[344] then most of these readings are profoundly modern in that they work in the tension between myth and demythologisation. The *cani cacharis* and a Jonah who sinks like a stone have more in common than they might think: indeed, it may well be, as Max Weber and Peter Berger have argued, that one is the inevitable consequence and flipside of the other. For, insofar as one represents the 'shrinkage in the scope of the sacred'[345] that attends modern Christianity (particularly Protestantism), and the other shows how that shrinkage ultimately turns against itself, they demonstrate, across the microcosm of the book of Jonah, how modern 'Western religious tradition' by definition 'carries the seeds of secularisation [and mutiny] within it'.[346]

In the final chapter, which comes by way of dessert, I imagine what the book of Jonah might look like if it were refracted back through Paul Auster, the *Gawain*-poet, and the rabbis, rather than Luther and Michaelis as its exclusive disseminators and heirs; and I question the fundamental assumption, shared by secular and Christian writers alike, that the book is by definition a biblical book to which all our preconceptions about the biblical necessarily apply. Even as I ask, *what if* Jonah is a piece of what-iffery, a story, an experiment with words, rather than a carefully honed piece of polemic, I imagine an author who is capable of the same quizzicality and subtlety as a contemporary author (so going against the grain of an association between the ancient and the simple, which is about as pervasive as the belief that our generation invented sex). Admittedly a proto-Marxist or existentialist biblical author is as historically inconceivable as an author who reads Heinrich Heine, or Voltaire on 'the Jews', but then assumptions that a biblical book must be ordered, that it must be faith-affirming and must have a singular purpose may be similarly anachronistic. For what the Backwaters do, above all, is show how ancient writers like the *Gawain*-poet and the rabbis are sophisticated word-handlers, and quizzical question-turners, and so give me ways of imagining the book of Jonah as something other than the work of a polemicist, or preacher, or anti-Jewish proto-Christian.

[344] Vattimo, *The Transparent Society*, p. 42.
[345] Berger, *The Social Reality of Religion*, p. 117.
[346] *Ibid.*, p. 116.

Regurgitating Jonah

How does newness come into the world? How is it born? Of what fusions, translations, conjoinings, is it made?[1]

There's another rendering now, but still one text. All sorts of [wo]men in one kind of world you see [Stubbs in *Moby Dick*].[2]

We should read the Bible one more time. To interpret it, of course, but also to let it carve out a space for our interpretative delirium.[3]

I. OF 'HOT CHESTNUTS', 'FLUID PUDDINGS' AND 'PLOTS THAT DO NOT SHELTER US': SOME RUMINATIONS ON THE SALVIFIC PROPERTIES OF THE BIBLE AND LITERATURE

According to the bill of fare laid out in the introduction, this chapter is advertised, fairly unappetisingly, as a regurgitation; rather more appetisingly, as a hash, a jambalaya (a recombination of older more piquant, marginal readings); and, most appetisingly of all, as a perennial biblical chestnut, puréed and served up, Terence Conran fashion, with char-grilled peppers and *pommes de terre*. The sheer volume of interpretation that we have waded through to get here punctures two myths: the myth that (to use Northrop Frye's culinary metaphor) meanings are extracted from texts, like plums from a pie,[4] and the myth that each reader uncovers a newly discovered meaning

---

[1] S. Rushdie, *The Satanic Verses* (Dover, Del.: The Consortium, 1988), p. 8.

[2] H. Melville, *Moby Dick* (Ware, Herts.: Wordsworth, 1992), p. 444.

[3] J. Kristeva, *New Maladies of the Soul* (trans. R. Guberman; New York: Columbia University Press, 1995), cited (without reference) in D. Nolan Fewell, 'Imagination, Method and Murder: Un/Framing the Face of Post-Exilic Israel', in T. K. Beal and D. M. Gunn (eds.), *Reading Bibles, Writing Bodies: Identity and the Book* (London: Routledge, 1997), pp. 132–52 (132).

[4] The saying that meanings cannot be extracted from texts by Jack Horner-like, self-satisfied readers belongs to Northrop Frye (*Anatomy of Criticism* (Princeton: Princeton University Press, 1957), p. 18).

(the margins of my edition of Jonah are now so densely scrawled with the serving suggestions of two millennia of reading that it is impossible to maintain the illusion of a pristine reading or the never-before-been-said). Like medieval manuscripts in which disagreeing disputants poke at the text with spears and barbs, or in which mischievous textual hands pull missing verses into place,[5] my edition comes pre-crammed with words and images that pull at, poke at, query the text: it comes flanked by vivid illustrations (Jonah 'huddling in the hurrock', winds wrestling, fish huddling at the bottom of the sea) and with questions scrawled in indelible ink (*'Did Jonah want judgement or did he want consistency?'* (Rosen), and 'Why *does* it seem a victory to [God]/Thus to destroy his prophet more than all the others?' [the *Gawain*-Poet]). Insofar as this reading is 'new', its newness comes from fusions, conjoinings and regurgitations, and from allowing Backwater readings to come home to the text and to settle in and put their feet up as naturally as if they had always had the right to be there.

While I do not want to get too waylaid in theoretical[6] discussions (I have other fish to fry), I want at least to gesture to the influences that spill over into this chapter since, there being no such thing as an 'innocent reading', I am at least obliged to 'say what reading [I think] I am guilty of'.[7] Lurking not very surreptitiously in the background is an awareness that reading is always an act of 'benign distortion'[8] (distributing the text's emphases, marking the *points*, joining them in a meaningful shape),[9] and that distortion and regular

[5] I'm thinking particularly of a late twelfth-century manuscript in which Augustine is pictured aggressively thrusting a spear at a patristic commentary that misquotes him, and a thirteenth-century English Book of Hours in which tiny marginal construction workers correct errors in the text by winching missing verses into place. (The illustrations, with discussion, can be found in M. Camille, *Images on the Edge: The Margins of Medieval Art* (London: Reaktion Books, 1995). pp. 21–4.)

[6] I don't mean to use 'theory' in a negative sense, so supporting the myth that it is possible to circumvent the need for theory by occupying the zone of common sense. All readers have their theories of reading, and as Eagleton comments, 'hostility to theory usually means an opposition to other people's theories and an oblivion of one's own' (T. Eagleton, *Literary Theory: An Introduction* (Minneapolis: University of Minnesota Press, 1983), p. viii).

[7] So L. Althusser and E. Balibar, *Reading Capital* (trans. B. Brewster; London: Verso, 1970), p. 14.

[8] F. Kermode, *The Genesis of Secrecy: On the Interpretation of Narrative* (Cambridge, Mass.: Harvard University Press, 1980), p. 5.

[9] One of the milder reading theories is that of Wolfgang Iser, who argues that the text provides certain key points, or 'stars', and that the reader effectively joins the dots in different ways to make different constellations (see W. Iser, 'The Reading Process: A Phenomenological Approach', in D. Lodge (ed.), *Modern Criticism and Theory: A Reader* (London: Longman, 1988),

mutation is intrinsic to textual survival. Though such self-conscious-
ness is, certainly in the field of biblical studies, usually pigeon-holed
under the heading of 'reader-response',[10] it is not simply the patent
of Messrs Fish and Iser: the consciousness of a certain (joking/
nostalgic/healthy?) dissonance between text and interpretation can
be traced as least as far back as the midrashim, and, far from being a
late twentieth-century discovery, the rather banal truism about
different eyes seeing from different perspectives makes itself felt in
the 'Dubloon' passage in *Moby Dick*.[11] This reading participates both
in the *general* awareness of the creative will involved in interpretation
and in the distinctly contemporary twists that post-structuralists and
reader-response critics give to that awareness: it believes that
'authors' are a necessary (but always in some sense artificial)
'principle of thrift in the proliferation of meaning';[12] that readers, as

pp. 212–28). Having waded our way through the interpretations of chapter 1 and 2, we may
be more inclined to take the view of Stanley Fish that 'the stars (or points) in a literary text
are not fixed' and 'are just as variable as the lines that join them' (S. Fish, 'Why No One's
Afraid of Wolfgang Iser', *Diacritics* 11 (1981), pp. 2–13 (7)).

[10] Though it may come as a surprise to literary specialists operating outside the discipline,
reader-response is still considered a fairly hot topic here in Biblical Studies. As Stephen
Moore wryly observes, there appears to be something of a 'time-warp factor' in operation
that 'enables reader-response critics to seem like an exotic new species of scholar to their
biblical colleagues long after the last reader-response critic in the far distant galaxy that is
literary studies has gratefully closed her book, and then her eyes, and slipped into the
slumber from which there is no awakening' (S. D. Moore, 'Que(e)rying Paul: Preliminary
Questions', in D. J. A. Clines and S. D. Moore (eds.), *Auguries: The Jubilee Volume of the Sheffield
Department of Biblical Studies* (Sheffield: Sheffield Academic Press, 1998), pp. 250–74 (251)).

[11] In 'The Dubloon' (chapter 99 of Moby Dick) a single coin functions 'like a magician's glass'
mirroring to every 'reader' of the coin 'his own mysterious self' (Melville, *Moby Dick*,
p. 441). As Stubbs comments (in the line that I plundered as a headquote) there are different
'renderings' but just one text. Melville is by no means the only author to anticipate the
truisms of reader-response: compare the observations of another nineteenth-century
(French) writer that it is 'childish' to 'believe in reality' since 'our eyes, our ears, our sense of
smell, of taste, differing from one person to another, create as many truths as there are men
[*sic*] upon earth' so that 'each one, therefore forms for himself an illusion of the world' (Guy
de Maupassant, cited in and trans. H. James, 'Guy de Maupassant' (1888), in L. Edel (ed.),
The House of Fiction: Essays on the Novel by Henry James (London: Rupert Hart-Davis, 1957),
p. 28).

[12] M. Foucault, 'What is an Author?', in P. Rabinow (ed.), *The Foucault Reader* (Harmondsworth: Penguin, 1984), pp. 101–20 (118). Foucault writes: 'How can one reduce the great
peril, the great danger with which fiction threatens our world? The answer is: one can
reduce it with the author. The author allows a limitation of the cancerous and dangerous
proliferation of significations within a world where one is thrifty not only with one's
resources and riches, but also with one's discourses and significations . . . We are
accustomed . . . to saying that the author is the genial creator of a work in which he
deposits, with infinite wealth and generosity, an inexhaustible world of significations . . . In
fact, if we are accustomed to presenting the author as a genius, as a perpetual surging of
invention, it is because, in reality, we make him function in exactly the opposite fashion'
(pp. 118–19). At this point I find myself thinking again of the fabulously insightful Proto-

well as texts, are always 'in contexts';[13] and that the projection of 'intention' is inevitably caught up with one's own intentions and designs on the text. Though it speaks of the author/the writer, it is wary of our tendency to deflect the plentitude of the text into the figure of the author (so creating a ludicrously over-fattened Mr Creosote[14] figure) and it works on the assumption that 'The writer's thought does not control his language from without' but that 'the writer is himself a new kind of idiom constructing itself'.[15] I won't constantly be drawing attention to the items on this postmodern creed and I won't be inserting over-anxious qualifications like 'the author (as I have constructed him)' or 'the text (as I have constructed it)' because these stuttering parentheses will make the chapter tediously anxious and self-qualifying. But I do take it as read that personal 'reading neuroses'[16] and ticks and twitches of the *Zeitgeist* will inevitably haunt this reading – betraying far more than the symptoms of interpretative community membership.

As I take the biblical text and self-consciously weave it in with strands from Melville, Auster, Camus, Barnes, and the Rabbis, I am also participating in theories of intertextuality: the premise that 'as texts are read by individual readers and reading communities who enter into conversation with them, they are woven or rewritten out of the threads of innumerable other texts'.[17] This reading works on

---

Aufklärer of the Mainstream, whose genius is precisely to pare down the book of Jonah to a single, infinitely repeatable point.

13 S. Fish, 'Normal Circumstances, Literal Language, Direct Speech Acts, the Ordinary, the Everyday, the Obvious, What Goes Without Saying, and Other Special Cases', *Critical Inquiry* 4 (1978), pp. 625–44 (637).

14 Those who don't recognise the name will certainly remember the scene in the Monty Python film *The Meaning of Life*, in which an already immense customer eats his way through an entire restaurant menu and finally, literally, explodes after eating 'one, wafer-thin mint' too many.

15 M. Merleau-Ponty, 'An Unpublished Text', trans. A. B. Ballery, in J. M. Edie (ed.), *The Primacy of Perception* (Evanston: Northwestern University Press, 1964), pp. 8–9, cited in J. Derrida, *Writing and Difference* (trans. A. Bass; London: Routledge, 1990), p. 11.

16 S. D. Moore, *Literary Criticism and the Gospels: The Theoretical Challenge* (New Haven and London: Yale University Press, 1989), p. 144.

17 G. Aichele and G. A. Philips, 'Introduction: Exegesis, Eisegesis, Intergesis', in Aichele and Philips (eds.), *Intertextuality and the Bible* (*Semeia* 69/70; Atlanta: Scholar's Press, 1995), pp. 7–18 (8). Inevitably there are problems for the reader applying intertextual theory to ancient texts (like the Bible or midrash) where we want to go on talking about the conscious greediness of the texts, and their appetite for digesting and transforming specific sources. Theories of intertextuality are often interpreted as claiming that all texts are by definition interconnected, that any text can legitimately be said to be in, or relevant to, another text, and that it is no longer possible to make empirical claims such as 'This book clearly cites

the assumption that a text is not so much an island as a 'mosaic of quotations',[18] that texts are always porous to other texts, and that they 'acquire meaning to the extent that they are situated in relation to other texts in a web of mutual interference and illumination'.[19] Again the assumptions are distinctly contemporary, but not exclusively so: the cloth metaphor mimics Julia Kristeva's and Roland Barthes's metaphors of text as 'tissue' and 'fabric' on the one hand, and the rabbinic motif of text as flax, and interpretation as stringing, on the other. The emphasis is postmodern but the general principle more pervasive: in fact the image of texts/tradition as a synchronic language is one that maps extremely well onto midrash, biblical texts, and the book of Jonah, where the 'frontiers of a book are never clear-cut' and texts regenerate themselves by 'extend[ing] beyond [their] last full stop' to 'other books, other texts, other sentences'.[20]

'My' reading, then, participates in newer poststructuralist theories of interpretation: it places itself on the postmodern side of the postmodernist/modernist divide.[21] And yet what increasingly strikes me is not so much the expected sense of rupture, but how much new stories and vocabularies of reading *share* with more traditional scholarly reading stories. As Jonathan Culler rightly points out, readers will always go on projecting the co-protagonist of 'text',[22] and readers who have 'come out' in their readerliness and who speak cavalierly of the much-trumpeted 'death of the author' still find themselves talking of the personality of the author, or (in a slightly more dissipated, and so more comfortable way) of the personality and *agency* of the text. But although we may have expanded the range of the stories of reading that can be told, there

---

texts a, b, and c.' But following Daniel Boyarin (who takes his cue from Jonathan Culler) I find that the most useful way to adapt intertextuality in this kind of context is as a means of seeing tradition as a language, or semiotic repertoire: the text still participates in a specific network of texts but the network is read synchronically rather than diachronically (see D. Boyarin, *Intertextuality and the Reading of Midrash*, pp. 28, 135 n. 2).

[18] J. Kristeva, *Semiotike: Recherches pour une sémanalyse* (Collections Tel Quel; Paris: Le Seuil, 1969), p. 146.

[19] Aichele and Philips, 'Introduction: Exegesis, Eisegesis, Intergesis', p. 8.

[20] M. Foucault, *The Archaeology of Knowledge* (trans. A. M. Sheridan Smith; London: Tavistock, 1972), p. 25.

[21] Of course the divide is not simply a divide and the relation is one of continuity *and* rupture.

[22] As Culler argues, the story of the struggle between the reader and the text will always haunt the pages of reader-response criticism, not only because it is a better adventure story, full of 'dramatic encounters, moments of deception and reversals of fortune', but because reader-response critics, like their opponents, are acutely aware that 'the reader who creates everything learns nothing' (J. Culler, *On Deconstruction: Theory and Criticism after Structuralism* (London: Routledge, 1993), p. 72).

are still a very limited number of stories of reading and a limited number of associated critic-positions. Texts tend to fall into key categories: the text that succumbs to analysis and yields its latent secrets, the text that tricks the reader and refuses captivation, or the text that engages the reader in a mutual battle of wits, in which both dodge and outmanoeuvre one another. The critic, similarly, tends to play a limited range of parts as the master-analyst (the fisher of the text's secrets and the dredger of the text's deeper meanings); the worshipper before the text's richness or density (the smitten pursuer of textual mysteries); or the deposed critic-god delighting in the surplus of the text that always eludes her (chuckling, like the deposed divine author in *Baba Metzia* 59a–b, 'My child[-text] ha[s] defeated me'[23]). The bottom line seems to be that all readers are always involved, in some sense, in textual management: we cannot let meaning ricochet in all directions, for that way interpretative vertigo and bad reviews lie. We feel the compulsion to bring the text into a manageable whole, albeit a whole that may question the sense of a whole, and integrate it through a co-ordinating (and often too predictable) postmodern thematic of 'white space', dispersal, fragmentation, and occultation. Whether we are finding new deconstructive loopholes or positing the new really real essence of the text, it seems that we still cannot escape from that most fundamental story of reading – the sense that we are giving the text a new and richer identity. I know of several recent readings of biblical texts that question their morality and their ideology/theology but have yet to read one that claims that the text is, in fact, less interesting or rich than previous readers have claimed. And as readers go on upping the ante, the critical institution becomes the staple of the text's memetic survival, constantly recreating a richer, fatter, more satisfied and satisfying text.

These stories of reading are far too strong for a single reader to resist. As I craft my own reading of Jonah, I find myself constantly drawn to the time-honoured image of critic-as-worshipper before the text's richness, or as smitten pursuer of textual mysteries. Though elsewhere I have criticised the way in which literary readings of the Bible seem so instinctively to settle into hyperbole, as if perceived moral value should somehow be deflected into aesthetic

---

[23] This passage is discussed in chapter 2, p. 102 n. 40.

value,[24] I instinctively find myself, in Jonah's case, bending the knee in the position if not of worshipper then of 'convert' (albeit not in a religious sense). I want the story of reading that I tell to encompass my own story of coming to Biblical Studies from English Literature, on what at first felt like a temporary foray, and then staying submerged 'in' Hebrew Bible because books like Jonah, Qoheleth, Genesis, Lamentations, Job (in fact even the more orthodox texts, like the 'proper' Prophets) both exceeded and countered my expectations of biblical literature. Like Gabriel Josipovici, I want to tell the story of discovering a text that is 'quirkier, funnier, quieter than I expected';[25] like Harold Bloom I see myself 'taking the varnish off'[26] a text which has been coated by centuries of polemic (or to return to my own metaphor, stripping off the polemical limpets that have so tenaciously clung to the text). When a specialist in American literature says that *Moby Dick* is richer than Jonah or Job because of the 'depths of the waters in which Melville fished',[27] I agree with him – the book of Jonah *is* no *Moby Dick* – and approaching the text like this, via the Backwaters, is like returning to a rather drear January reality, after the last millennial firecracker has popped, in that we are liable to feel the absence of comic tours around the fish's intestines, and the rich metaphorical world of conjuror-deities and wrestling winds. But at the same time it's also true that the book of Jonah languishes in the straitjacket of 'primitive narrative' (and even worse, primitive religious narrative) which, as Tzevetan Todorov and Robert Alter have argued, is often a kind of mental mirage, or alter-ego projected by modern parochialism.[28] What both the Backwaters and the Mainstream have in common is a tendency to downplay this

---

[24] For a critique of the idea that the Good Book should by definition be a good book, see Y. M. Sherwood, 'Prophetic Scatology: Prophecy and the Art of Sensation', in S. D. Moore (ed.), *In Search of the Present: The Bible Through Cultural Studies* (*Semeia* 82; Atlanta: Scholar's Press, 2000), and Y. M. Sherwood, 'Darke Texts Need Notes: Reassessing Prophetic Poetry' (unpublished paper presented to the Society for Old Testament Study annual meeting, University of Glasgow, July 1999).

[25] G. Josipovici, *The Book of God: A Response to the Bible* (New Haven: Yale University Press, 1988), p. x. (I assume that by 'quieter' he means less morally booming.)

[26] H. Bloom, *The Book of J* (London: Faber, 1991), p. 44.

[27] L. Buell, '*Moby-Dick* as Sacred Text', in R. H. Brodhead (ed.), *New Essays on Moby Dick* (Cambridge: Cambridge University Press, 1986), pp. 53–72 (53).

[28] See R. Alter, *The Art of Biblical Narrative* (New York: Basic Books, 1981), p. 21; T. Todorov, *The Poetics of Prose* (trans. R. Howard; Ithaca: New York, 1977), pp. 53–65. See also Alter's comments on the perception that 'religious narratives' will be 'moral' and 'didactic', and will not, by definition, 'indulge in all this fancy footwork of multiple ironies that we moderns so love' (*The Art of Biblical Narrative*, p. 18).

book's cleverness and detail, either by applying forces that are too centripetal, too restraining, or by playing off a naïve and simple past against an infinitely more-knowing present. And the reason that both see the text in too reductive terms is because they are languishing under essentially the same preconceptions about a biblical/sacred – and a literary – text.

For if reading is always 'reading as', or bringing a text 'into relation with a type of discourse or model which is always, in some sense, natural and legible',[29] the book of Jonah has been distorted by reading it as a biblical text, a religious text, and a work of literature, according to pervasive cultural definitions of those terms. A deeply ingrained cultural sense of the Bible as the 'Word of God', or at the very least a homogeneous canon, means that we expect that separate textual voices will be gathered into a single consciousness (it is no accident that, when trying to think of the ultimate example of the 'monologic', Bakhtin comes up with 'evangelical and biblical' discourse).[30] This book, of all books, is expected to process life into a gigantic metanarrative, to frame the world in a Great, all-encompassing Code,[31] and in this sense it coheres with broader definitions of religion as establishing serenity, countering chaos and anomie, and imposing meaningful order upon reality. Those who see religions/the Bible as a 'wish-fulfilment' projection, as Freud did,[32] and those who see religions/the Bible as repositories of truth, are united in the belief that these structures bring order to human life, and that their role is to provide security and to fulfil the fundamental desire for certainty, stability, and self-protection.

This drive to order is also reflected in definitions of that more secular human signifying practice – literature. Not only does the Western novel, according to one popular definition, arise from a loss of faith in 'providential plots' and an all-embracing 'sacred master-

---

[29] S. Rimon-Kenan, *Narrative Fiction: Contemporary Poetics* (London and New York: Routledge, 1994), p. 123.

[30] M. Bakhtin, *Problems of Dostoevsky's Poetics* (ed. and trans. C. Emerson, introduction by W. C. Booth; Minneapolis: University of Minnesota Press, 1984), p. 281. (The quotation comes, in fact, from the appendix: a collection of three fragments which appeared in the 1929 edition of *Problems*, but were removed by Bakhtin from the 1963 edition.)

[31] See N. Frye, *The Great Code* (London: Routledge and Kegan Paul, 1982).

[32] Freud famously described religious beliefs as 'illusions, fulfilments of the strongest and most urgent wishes of mankind' (S. Freud, 'The Future of an Illusion', in *Civilization, Society and Religion* (Penguin: Harmondsworth, 1985), p. 212).

plot',[33] but introductions to the narrative habitually describe the author (or the text) as a gigantic tidying, ordering presence – a kind of secular deflection of the divine author. From Paul Ricoeur to Frank Kermode and Peter Brooks, understandings of the novel are still deeply influenced by Aristotelian principles and by an under-girding belief that good fiction will stress unity, consistency, and logical coherence, and that it will be mimetic in a therapeutic sense, by 'binding and finishing off the confused luxuriance of real nature'.[34] The novel is habitually seen as a life-processor or life-packaging machine, celebrating the triumph of 'concordance' over 'discordance', 'explanation' over confusion,[35] and emphasising 'the *compatible* nature of circumstance by attaching narrated events together with a kind of logical "paste"'.[36] Fiction is habitually described as a secular displacement of salvation: the form of a novel consoles,[37] an ending resolves, 'good' novels offer security and 'Fiction provides a structure within which our lives can be under-stood.'[38] As the author posits a world structured from creation to revelation, he/she offers plot as an ordering force that wrests meaning from human temporality[39] or offers escape from the sense that 'our life is a tale without a plot or a hero, made out of desolation and glass, out of the feverish babble of constant digressions'.[40] Though the association of meaning and order is typically associated with the Structuralists and the Formalists[41] – with their Chinese-

---

[33] P. Brooks, *Reading for the Plot: Design and Intention in Narrative* (Cambridge, Mass.: Harvard University Press, 1992), p. 6.

[34] J. Henry Newman, 'Poetry, with Reference to Aristotle's Poetics', in *Essays Critical and Historical* (2 vols.; London: 1887), vol. I, p. 9.

[35] P. Ricoeur, *Time and Narrative* (3 vols.; trans. J. McLaughlin and D. Pellauer; Chicago: Chicago University Press, 1984), vol. II, pp. 31, 148. (As Ricoeur explains, 'A narrative that fails to explain is less than narrative' (p. 148).)

[36] R. Barthes, *S/Z* (trans. R. Miller; London: Blackwell, 1990; 1st edn 1973), p. 156.

[37] F. Kermode, *The Sense of an Ending: Studies in the Theory of Fiction* (Oxford: Oxford University Press, 1967), p. 151.

[38] S. McCracken, *Pulp: Reading Popular Fiction* (Manchester: Manchester University Press, 1998), p. 2.

[39] Brooks, *Reading for the Plot*, p. 19.

[40] The phrase, from the Russian writer Osip Mandelstam's *The Egyptian Stamp* (1928), is quoted by M. Berman, *All That is Solid Melts into Air: The Experience of Modernity* (New York: Simon and Schuster, 1982), p. 174.

[41] Structuralism derives from Ferdinand de Saussure's *Course in General Linguistics* (1915): a revolutionary attempt to describe the permanent deep structures of language and to treat language as a system, a *Gestaltenheit*, or unified field, in which each individual entity can only be understood as part of a larger structure of relationships. Broadly speaking, its concerns overlap with those of Russian Formalism, an attempt to produce holistic descriptions of literature based on quasi-scientific laws. The key practitioners are Claude Lévi-Strauss, the

menu-like[42] inventories of the functions of the folk-tale, their grammars of the mind, their Greimas Squares and their bold declarations that 'if we look at all the intellectual undertakings of mankind [*sic*], as far as they have been recorded all over the world, the common denominator is always to introduce some kind of order'[43] – Claude Lévi-Strauss and co. are only at the extreme end of an extremely pervasive definition. Narratives work, the deep cultural truism claims, by offering a cushioning blanket of *meaningfulness*: as Paul Auster puts it, we look at 'a mad person in the world' and say nothing because there is nothing that we can say, but we look at *Don Quixote* and say something like 'Don Quixote is consciousness gone haywire in the realm of the imaginary.'[44] The definitions generated in English Literature come extremely close to those generated by Religious/Biblical Studies: literature works by providing a sense of 'grandeur', truth, 'significance',[45] and by giving us the reassurance of a controlling God-like presence, a 'conscious mind behind the words on the page'.[46]

But what Biblical Studies and English Literature also currently have in common is a growing sense that security, coherence, and univocality may tell us more about the world of the definers than the texts under scrutiny. This change in perception can clearly be felt in Biblical Studies: at a basic level come the introduction-class clichés that 'the Bible' is Greek *ta biblia*, 'the book*s*', that Ezekiel and Jeremiah were not on commission from Hodder and Stoughton and were not working to a set remit, and that reading the Bible is like reading 'Gibbon's *Decline and Fall of the Roman Empire*, the collected poems of T. S. Eliot, . . . *Hamlet*, . . . Holinshed's Chronicle, . . . *Pilgrim's Progress* and the *Sixteen Satires* of Juvenal'.[47] At a more

---

anthropologist who famously applied Saussure's linguistic system to the study of myth; Vladimir Propp, who produced a formalist grammar or 'morphology' of the folktale (a catalogue of the actions and functions that all fairy-tales obey), and A. J. Greimas, who mapped Propp's functions on an axiomatic grid, known as the 'Greimas' or 'Semiotic Square'. (An excellent analysis of structuralism's concerns and obsessions can be found in T. Hawkes, *Structuralism and Semiotics* (New Accents; London: Routledge, 1989).)

[42] E. L. Greenstein, 'Reading Strategies and the Story of Ruth', in A. Bach (ed.), *Women in the Hebrew Bible: A Reader* (London and New York: Routledge, 1999), pp. 211–31 (221).

[43] C. Lévi-Strauss, *Myth and Meaning* (London: Routledge, 1978), p. 12.

[44] P. Auster, *The Invention of Solitude* (London: Faber and Faber, 1982), p. 147.

[45] *Ibid.*, p. 147.

[46] *Ibid.*, p. 146.

[47] J. Goldingay, *Theological Diversity and the Authority of the Old Testament* (Michigan: Eerdmans, 1987), p. 15. Although it is important to stress the ideological diversity of biblical literature, it is also important to stress that 'centripetal' ideological forces certainly prevail. And

sophisticated level comes a growing recognition that many biblical memes have survived by *shifting* genre (or by 'jumping ship') and that, in some cases, what began as relatively secular stories or stories about national identity or tribal one-upmanship, have been pre-served beyond any reasonable life-expectancy because they have been reinterpreted as divinely authored authoritative religious litera-ture.[48] The last twenty years, and particularly the last decade, of biblical scholarship have seen the theologically less congenial books (such as Lamentations or the Wisdom books) coming out of the closet, bringing with them a sense of traditional biblical complaints inverted (as the *people* challenge *God*), and confronting the reader with a deity who makes life crooked, who wraps himself in clouds so that no prayers can pass through, or who 'answers' Job's suffering with a parade of freak animals that seem (mis)designed to demon-strate the baffling 'dysteleology' of creation.[49] Increasingly, biblical scholars are beginning to engage with the radical implications of a tradition that strives towards monotheism but that has no Satan/ devil figure to fall back on – a tradition in which God, potentially, will be as diverse as life itself – metaphorically mutating into a

---

though there is scepticism in the Hebrew Bible (for example in Qoheleth) that scepticism is never a-theistic, since it was impossible for biblical writers to conceive of belief in God as a choice.

[48] So K. L. Noll, 'Is There a Text in this Tradition? Readers' Response and the Taming of Samuel's God', *Journal for the Study of the Old Testament* 83 (1999), pp. 31–51 (51). Noll's argument, that the books of Samuel were primarily written for entertainment purposes but were subsequently tamed as religious literature, draws on Daniel Dennett's *Darwin's Dangerous Idea* (London: Allen Lane, 1995), and so nicely complements our earlier discussion of the memetic survival of biblical texts. Noll writes: 'A cultural artefact is subject to a blind process of replication and descent that has little to do with its designer's intention. What survives is that which happens to thrive in a given environment, whether it was designed for that environment or not' (p. 51). Noll's argument, although a highly original and radical reading of Samuel, is in a sense not too dissimilar to earlier historical studies of other biblical literature. For example, a typical form-critical analysis of the Ancestress in Danger narrative (Genesis 12, 20, and 26), shows how an originally secular story celebrating the cunning of the ancestors and the beauty of the ancestors' wives, mutates before the reader's very eyes to become progressively more moral and pious (see for example K. Koch, *The Growth of Biblical Tradition* (London: A. & C. Black, 1969)).

[49] See Ecclesiastes 7.13; Lamentations 3.43–44; and Job 38–41, where God presents the eagle, whose young suck on blood, the ostrich, who lays her eggs on the ground where they get trodden on, the wild ass, the wild ox, and the hippopotamus (*Behemoth*) – creation not so much 'All Things Bright and Beautiful' as 'All Things Ill-shaped and Untameable'. As Rudolf Otto puts it, the circus parade of freak animals presents the 'mysterious' as 'monstrous' and intimates the 'wellnigh demonic and wholly incomprehensible character of the eternal creative power' (R. Otto 'The Element of the Mysterious', in N. N. Glazter (ed.), *The Dimensions of Job: A Study and Selected Readings* (New York: Schocken, 1969), pp. 225–8 (228)).

wound, rot in the nation's joists, she-bear and sleeper and 'living question mark'[50] as well as assuming his more familiar and reassuring guises as shield, protector, warrior, and good shepherd. The fractures or multiplicity in God are reflected in the fractures and fissures of the Book: the Bible is full of 'struggling contradictions';[51] it is comprised of books made from different textual 'fabrics' that refuse to take the same theological 'dye';[52] and a recent (Christian) theology of the Old Testament draws on Bakhtinian models to describe centripetal and centrifugal ideological/theological forces, 'testimonies' and 'counter-testimonies'.[53] An increasing appreciation of the range of biblical voices is accompanied by a sense of how voices within the Bible's covers modify, challenge and even subvert one another: Michael Fishbane has shown that 'inner-biblical interpretation' is not always about biblical voices reinforcing one another in an intertextual support group,[54] and André Lacoque has recently argued that the love poetry of the Song of Songs uses the religious idioms of the Hebrew Bible as a *language*, which it then goes on to parody and subvert.[55]

This image of biblical narratives using one another as a language and quoting one another with a whole range of intonational quotation marks (from the mocking to the pious, the gently modifying

---

[50] The image of a God with many faces, or as a multi-faceted mirror, is a rabbinic idea (see *Pesikta Kahana* 109b–110a), but one that can easily find ample biblical prooftexts. For images of God as wound, she-bear, and sleeper see Hosea 5.12, 13.8, and Psalm 44.23. For a popular literary analysis of the many faces of God in the Hebrew Bible and the description of God as a 'living question mark' see J. Miles, *God: A Biography* (London and New York: Simon and Schuster, 1995), p. 87.

[51] W. Eichrodt, *Theology of the Old Testament* I (trans. J. A. Baker; London: SCM, 1961), p. 490.

[52] M. Calloway, 'Canonical Criticism', in S. L. McKenzie and S. R. Haynes (eds.), *To Each Its Own Meaning: An Introduction to Biblical Criticisms and Their Application* (Louisville: Westminster/John Knox, 1993), pp. 121–34 (122).

[53] W. Brueggeman, *Theology of the Old Testament: Testimony, Dispute, Advocacy* (Minneapolis: Fortress, 1997).

[54] See M. Fishbane, *Biblical Interpretation in Ancient Israel* (Oxford: Clarendon Press, 1989). As the term suggests, 'inner-biblical interpretation' refers to the exegesis and re-application of biblical texts that goes on within the Bible's covers. Fishbane sees inner-biblical interpretation as proto-midrashic, giving *aggadic* and *halakhic* reworkings of biblical texts, drawing on already extant tradition as on a living language. To take a couple of examples, Jeremiah 3.1 is a rhetorical-metaphorical re-application of the divorce regulations in Deuteronomy 24.1–4, and the seventy weeks of years in Daniel 9.4 are an eschatological reinterpretation of the seventy years of exile in Jeremiah 29.10 (cf. 25.11–12). Crucially, Fishbane's study shows that biblical texts consolidate, defend, and spiritualise earlier traditions, as might be expected, but that they also parody, radically alter and rework them (compare for example Psalm 8.4 and Job 7.17–20).

[55] A. Lacocque, *Romance She Wrote: A Hermeneutical Essay on Song of Songs* (Harrisburg, Pa.: Trinity Press International, 1998).

to the radically reconstruing), is mirrored in a wider sense of cacophony, untidiness, and the defiance of structure in certain maverick biblical texts. Roland Barthes's famous essay 'Wrestling with the Angel'[56] shows how 'Greimas Squares' go pear-shaped and how the Proppian file cards begin to get mixed up when they are applied to a strange biblical narrative like Genesis 32.22–32: as God sends Jacob across the River Jabbok, then wrestles him and seeks to destroy him, the 'Originator of the Quest' turns 'Opponent' and God becomes a curiously double character, like Bertilac in *Sir Gawain and the Green Knight.* Similar intuitions of something sub- or post-structuralist are being felt at the macro-level of canonical meta-narrative. The 'Great Code'[57] is beginning to crumble; the Great Binding is coming unglued – as Regina Schwartz puts it: 'If we can sometimes discern the impulse towards metanarrative in the Bible . . . it surfaces only to be stubbornly subverted by conflicting stories', and in this sense 'biblical narratives are far more compatible with the understanding of postmodernism distilled by Lyotard as incred-ulity towards metanarratives than they are with modern biblical scholarship'.[58] As Schwartz adds, provocatively, 'If the biblical narratives cannot be accurately labelled "postmodern", it is only because they cannot exhibit credulity towards [Christian, Jewish, scholarly] metanarratives that await later periods to be imagined and still later ones to be critiqued.'[59]

Back in English Literature the idea of narrative as a smoothing, ordering, consoling life-processor is also beginning to collapse. Questioning the way in which studies of the narrative have been constrained by Aristotelian models of reading, by the organic wholes of New Criticism, and by the conventions of the nineteenth-century realist novel, Andrew Gibson explores a counter-tradition of writing from *Don Quixote* and *Tristram Shandy* through to *Ulysses* and *The*

---

[56] R. Barthes, 'Wrestling with the Angel: Textual Analysis of Genesis 32.22–32', in R. Barthes, *The Semiotic Challenge* (Berkeley: University of California Press, 1994), pp. 246–60 (although the Hebrew Bible scholar in me feels compelled to point out that the angel is not an angel but a 'messenger'). The essay is succinctly digested and summarised by J. Barton, *Reading the Old Testament: Method in Biblical Study* (London: Darton, Longman, and Todd, 1984), pp. 118–19, and it is Barton who makes the comparison between the God of Genesis 32 and Bertilac/The Green Knight.

[57] Again this is an allusion to Northrop Frye's *The Great Code*.

[58] R. M. Schwartz, 'Adultery in the House of David: The Metanarrative of Biblical Scholarship and the Narratives of the Bible', in Bach, *Women in the Hebrew Bible*, pp. 335–50 (335).

[59] Schwartz, 'Adultery in the House of David', p. 335.

Unnameable – works that refuse to provide a sense of 'a superior presence and single logic [that] controls the work',[60] that abound in what E. M. Forster called 'dents and grooves and lumps and spikes', and that (to pinch Forster's comments on *Tristram Shandy*) seem to be presided over by a god called 'Muddle' who holds the universe as if it were a 'hot chestnut'.[61] Crucially, Gibson is not just dealing in post- or late modernist narratives – narratives that deliberately and ostentatiously flaunt the conventions of realism and unity – but, like Regina Schwartz, he is implicitly questioning an unthinking contemporary reflex by which we tend to put 'form', 'design', 'purpose', 'determinacy' in the *modern* column, and 'antiform', 'chance', 'dispersal', 'indeterminacy' in the *postmodern* column,[62] as if the struggle between containment and ambivalence, security and insecurity had always typically taken place between the late 1700s and the twentieth century.[63] As many postmodern thinkers foreground,[64] and as the history of Jonah interpretation seems to confirm, the competition between centring and dispersal, centrifugal and centripetal, monologic and dialogic is by no means a purely contemporary phenomenon, and in this sense the 'modern' and 'postmodern' are simply contemporary ways of making sense of the ways that we make sense, or 'abstract idealisations of mutually incoherent aspects of the single life-process'.[65] A similar point is made in Michael Roemer's *Telling*

---

[60] A. Gibson, *Reading Narrative Discourse: Studies in the Novel from Cervantes to Beckett* (London: Macmillan, 1990), p. 8.

[61] E. M. Forster, *Aspects of the Novel* (New York: Harcourt Brace, 1954), p. 164.

[62] See, for example, Ihab Hassan's famous columns distributing the opposing qualities of modernism and postmodernism, in I. Hassan, 'Towards a Concept of Postmodernism', in T. Docherty (ed.), *Postmodernism: A Reader* (Hemel Hempstead: Harvester Wheatsheaf, 1993), pp. 146–56 (152).

[63] Of course I am not denying that modernism and postmodernism have very specific features that link them inextricably to specific moments in time. I am merely pointing out that, certainly in biblical studies, there is a tendency to condense the two terms and to read them as ciphers for cohesion and dispersal respectively. Rather than simply putting forward a quizzical reading of Jonah that will in some quarters be labelled (and dismissed?) as a postmodern reading, a whimsical contemporary aberration, I want to stake my own claim in the historical possibility of 'the text'. For it is by no means certain that a biblical text would be ordering, or indeed orthodox – in fact the evidence seems strong that ordering and 'orthodoxising' tendencies may well be retrospective projections of a modern scholarly present.

[64] For example, foregrounding his suspicion of the original and the pure, Jacques Derrida writes 'There is much of the ancient in what I have said. Everything perhaps. It is to Heraclitus that I refer myself in the last instance' (J. Derrida, 'The Original Discussion', cited in Moore, *Literary Criticism and the Gospels*, p. 143).

[65] Z. Bauman, *Mortality, Immortality and Other Life Strategies* (Cambridge: Polity Press, 1992), p. 11.

Stories (a fabulous book, crouching behind a rather bland title), in which he argues – not unlike Gibson – that the God called Muddle, Coincidence, Chance presides over the plot of traditional as well as contemporary narrative. In a discussion that orbits around bullet-point proclamations such as 'story does not make order out of chaos',[66] 'story is an encounter with the incomprehensible',[67] and 'unlike other structures, plot does not shelter us',[68] Roemer claims that plot approximates the 'impact of chance on our existence'[69] and that plot is 'an analogue of fate'.[70] Like Henry James, he argues, we are prone to think of plot as 'a box of fixed dimensions and inelastic material, into which a mass of precious things are stacked away';[71] we tend to believe that the role of art is to process 'clumsy life'[72] and to stimulate our 'desire for perfection';[73] and we dismiss novels that 'leak' too much 'arbitrariness' as 'large baggy monsters', or 'fluid puddings'.[74] But such projections of story are 'hostage to an unacknowledged Positivism'.[75] In narrative as in philosophy we prefer the idealist notion of an Idea or 'interior design' as anterior to, and subserviently expressed by, the work,[76] and we gravitate instinctively towards a masterful all-controlling, all-processing, all-

---

[66] M. Roemer, *Telling Stories: Postmodernism and the Invalidation of Traditional Narrative* (Lanham, Md.: Rowman and Littlefield, 1995), p. 43.

[67] *Ibid.*, p. 49.   [68] *Ibid.*, p. 46.   [69] *Ibid.*, p. 64.   [70] *Ibid.*, p. 59.

[71] H. James, 'Mr. Tennyson's Drama', *Galaxy* 20 (September 1875), pp. 396–7, cited in S. B. Dougherty, *The Literary Criticism: Henry James* (Athens: Ohio University Press, 1981), p. 129.

[72] H. James, cited in R. P. Blackmur, 'Introduction to James', *The Art of the Novel: Critical Prefaces by Henry James* (Boston: Northeastern University Press, 1984), p. xxiv.

[73] H. James, *The Art of Fiction and Other Essays* (New York: Oxford University Press, 1948), p. 28.

[74] H. James, letter to Hugh Walpole, 19 May 1912, in P. Lubbock (ed.), *The Letters of Henry James* (New York: Charles Schribner's Sons, 1920), vol. II, p. 237. James is referring to Tolstoy and Dostoevsky (interestingly the same author that Bakhtin selects as the prime case of dialogism is for James the prime example of leakage and flabbiness). James pronounces: 'Tolstoy and Dostoevsky are fluid puddings, though not tasteless, because the amount of their own minds and souls in solution in the broth gives it a savour and flavour . . . But there are all sorts of things to be said of them, and in particular that we see how great a vice is in their lack of composition, their defiance of economy and architecture . . . There is nothing so deplorable as a work of art with a *leak* in its interest.'

[75] Roemer, *Telling Stories*, p. 44.

[76] So J. Derrida, *Writing and Difference* (trans. A. Bass; London: Routledge, 1990), p. 11. Although philosophers can occasionally be caught confessing that words sometimes seem to tug thought in their wake (Augustine, for example, counts himself as one of the number of those who write as they learn and learn as they write (Augustine, *Letters* 143.2 = PL xxxiii, p. 585), and Maurice Merleau-Ponty observes how 'My own word can take me by surprise, and teach me what I think' ('Problèmes actuels de la phénoménologie', in *Actes du colloque internationale de phénoménologie*, Paris: 1952, p. 97; cited in J. Derrida, *Writing and Difference*, p. 11)), Derrida shows how resistance to the idea that thought is somehow led by language runs deep in the Western philosophical/academic tradition. His aim is to show how philosophy works like literature, where language runs on a looser leash – but as

perfecting author as a projection of the Enlightenment image of the crusading, conquering, self. Culturally, we are fundamentally programmed to resist any suggestion that the order of plot may be one that 'play(s) havoc' with our fantasies of order,[77] or that story is a 'safe arena' where 'we can afford to face our vulnerability and helplessness'.[78]

It seems superfluous by now to point out that Mainstream packagings of Jonah fall, without exception, into this idealist, strictly purposeful and ordered narrative zone. The canonised readings seem to be designed precisely to counter our vulnerability and helplessness by dissociating 'us' from the unfortunate character at odds with his God/his plot, and supersessionist rhetoric is a way of reinforcing this Secure Self and Vulnerable/Rejected Other dichotomy. The emergent, ebullient, vindicated self is reflected in the image of the Author – strong on genius and preacherly intentionality, strategically setting every word in place. Operating on the premise that 'poetical analysis cannot admit of *superfluous* action . . . without raising questions as to the *competence* of the literary artist', the biblical scholar H. C. Brichto sees the book of Jonah as a 'masterpiece of rhetoric' in which 'every word is in place and every sentence'.[79] The two major literary studies of Jonah in existence stress symmetry, patterning, order, and deal in tables, diagrams, charts – consigning those bits that do not seem to cohere to a perfect logical scheme to a brief spate of 'symmetrophobia'.[80] As the narrative leads the xeno-

---

narratologies and classical stories of stories demonstrate, literature is prone to be governed just as tightly as philosophy.

[77] Roemer, *Telling Stories*, p. 44.

[78] *Ibid.*, p. 86.

[79] H. C. Brichto, *Toward a Grammar of Biblical Poetics: Tales of the Prophets* (New York: Oxford University Press, 1992), pp. 63, 8.

[80] The studies I am referring to are: J. Magonet, *Form and Meaning: Studies in the Literary Techniques of the Book of Jonah* (Sheffield: Almond Press, 1983); and P. Trible, *Rhetorical Criticism: Context and Method in the Book of Jonah* (Minneapolis: Fortress, 1994); see also Trible, 'Studies in the Book of Jonah' (PhD diss., Columbia University; Ann Arbor, Mich.: University Microfilms International, 1963; order no. 65–7479). Trible argues convincingly for patterns and structures, even as she confesses that the text sometimes exhibits 'symmetrophobia', but she is forced into an elaborate and not very convincing scheme to defend how 4.10–11 'works' logically and rhetorically (see *Rhetorical Criticism*, pp. 117, 218–23). Magonet's study also stresses symmetry and patterning in the book of Jonah, and has been compared to structuralist approaches in its orientation. I am not, incidentally, disputing that structures and patterns can be found in the book, nor that such structures are significant (I myself go on to eke considerable significance from the fact that Yhwh and Jonah have exactly thirty-nine words each in the final chapter). But I am more interested in the compulsion that forces Trible to place elaborate schematic templates on parts of the

phobic reader out of post-exilic chaos and nationalism to the perfection of a 'more excellent way'[81] so the book represents structured, comely art that stimulates our 'desire for perfection'. The writer thinks like an *Aufklärer* and writes like an *Aufklärer*: he controls what he writes and so demonstrates the power of mind over brute matter.

But the tide is turning in Jonah interpretation – away from images of satisfaction, neat polemics, and the *composure* of Jonah-as-composition. As if to demonstrate how commentary – the verse-by-verse analysis of the text – can sometimes be *biblical scholarship*'s way of watching over the general from the vantage point of the particular,[82] Jack Sasson threatens to topple his own (mostly Mainstream) metanarrative when he points to the 'weakness of God's logic' and argues that God's final words to Jonah in 4.10–11 are by no means 'simple and natural', and could easily be read as a 'trifle too trite'.[83] And whereas earlier readings of Jonah acknowledge the 'strangeness' of the book as an awkward surplus to normalising interpretations, more recent scholarly readings (egged on by broader definitions of the biblical), are beginning to bring that strangeness to articulation. A new generation of Mainstream readers, clutching their expanded interpretative licences, are effectively revitalising (albeit not self-consciously)[84] the themes and questions of the rabbis, Abravanel, Melville, and the *Gawain*-Poet. Alan Cooper sees the book as 'presenting a critique and a denial of univocal meaning and the

---

text that seem more shapeless, as if structure and order and economy (as for Brichto) are the only way to literary legitimation.

[81] Cf. Paul's words to the Corinthians about the superiority of love in 1 Corinthians 12.31.

[82] Compare the discussion of Jewish readings of Jonah, and Aronowicz's and Levinas's comments on the intrinsic features of Talmudic reading in chapter 2, p. 99, n 29. My point, of course, is that pursuing everything that is possible in a question is not an exclusively Jewish preoccupation.

[83] J. Sasson, *Jonah* (Anchor Bible Commentary; New York: Doubleday, 1990), pp. 319, 349. Ultimately, however, Sasson feels compelled to convert seeming divine whimsicality into more acceptable divine inscrutability: 'God refuses to rehearse the vocabulary of mercy with which Jonah is armed and deliberately trivialises the causes that swayed him to pardon Nineveh's crime. As in Job, the relevant lesson is about the incapacity of mortals to understand, let alone to judge, their God' (p. 351). (Compare the comments on Cooper's reading below.)

[84] Alan Cooper's 'In Praise of Divine Caprice: The Significance of the Book of Jonah' (in P. R. Davies and D. J. A. Clines (eds.), *Among the Prophets: Language, Image and Structure in the Prophetic Writings* (Sheffield: Sheffield Academic Press, 1993), pp. 144–63) is very much the exception here, for his reading, drawing on insights from Abravanel, is an excellent example of how contemporary readings can be animated by (and reanimate) ancient readings.

ideology of univocal meaning found in common sense';[85] Kenneth
Craig argues that the book is too polyphonic to be straightforwardly
polemical;[86] H. Gese complicates the meaning of the book by
foregrounding the association between Nineveh and Assyria;[87]
Abraham Cohen and C. A. Keller complicate it by commanding
empathy with Jonah;[88] Serge Frolov reads the book of Jonah as the
'story of the sacrifice of its main protagonist' (that the protagonist is
thereby compelled to resist);[89] and Walter Crouch argues that Yhwh
manipulates Jonah into a position of 'self-negation' from which
death seems to be the only escape.[90] The image of a pincer-like plot
that works against the interests of its protagonist is reflected in a
larger sense of something misshapen and unresolved. Baruch
Halpern and Richard Friedman have argued that the book indulges
in compulsive paranomasia that generates 'baroque' (that is, misshapen) effects,[91] and Walter Crouch (among others) focuses on the
irresolution of the ending, claiming that 'Not only is Jonah's death-
wish denied within the body of the text of his story but he is left

---

[85] A. Cooper, 'In Praise of Divine Caprice', p. 145 (quoting S. Stewart, *Nonsense: Aspects of Intertextuality in Folklore and Literature* (Baltimore: Johns Hopkins University Press, 1980), p. 77).

[86] K. M. Craig, *A Poetics of Jonah: Art in the Service of Ideology* (Macon, Ga.: Mercer University Press, 1999).

[87] H. Gese, 'Jona ben Ammitai und das Jonabuch', *Theologische Beiträge* 16 (1985), pp. 256–64.

[88] A. D. Cohen, 'The Tragedy of Jonah', *Judaism* 21 (1972), pp. 164–75; C. A. Keller, 'Jonas. Le portrait d'un prophète', *Theologische Zeitschrift* 21 (1965), pp. 329–40.

[89] S. Frolov, 'Returning the Ticket: God and His Prophet in the Book of Jonah', *Journal for the Study of the Old Testament* 86 (1991), pp. 85–105 (97). (The title is taken from Ivan Karamazov's speech in *The Brothers Karamazov* where he famously 'most respectfully' returns the ticket to God, because he finds that any world constructed on 'unavenged tears' – even of one tiny creature – unbearable.) I am grateful to Serge Frolov for letting me see a copy of the paper prior to publication.

[90] W. B. Crouch, 'To Question an End, to End a Question: Opening the Closure of the Book of Jonah', *Journal for the Study of the Old Testament* 62 (1994), pp. 101–12 (106).

[91] B. Halpern and R. Friedman, 'Composition and Paranomasia in the Book of Jonah', *Hebrew Annual Review* 4 (1980), pp. 79–92. Halpern and Friedman describe the book of Jonah as a 'rich, almost baroque sampler of paranomastic techniques' (p. 80), constructed through 'the art of sound and language' (p. 87), and fashioned from the 'protean use of the word' (p. 82). At the same time they clearly feel compelled to fit their observations into a more orthodox literary model based on purpose, design, structure, and to rehabilitate the narrative as *almost* baroque, but in fact well shaped and thematically integrated. The authors are at pains to show how 'apparently fortuitous frolics' have 'intentional correlatives' (p. 85), and how, 'though some of the plays, while clever, seem thematically inconsequential' (p. 83), the dominant force in the text is not wordplay but 'thematic integration' (p. 80). Ultimately they argue that 'the author's artifice creates a bulwark on which the book's thematic structures lean' (p. 87) and the book's message, held up by the solid girders of pun, is the idea of Jonah the reluctant pupil, who will not learn 'the proper posture towards Yhwh' (p. 89).

hanging, his narrative thread untied and unravelling' as Jonah and the reader are denied a meaningful exit.[92] The book that was once a simple lesson about a dissident with 'slouched hat and guilty eye, skulking from his God'[93] now begins to sidle shiftily towards the stranger books in the canon. Thomas Thompson makes a double act of Jonah and Qoheleth;[94] Thomas Bolin sees the sailors' slogan 'You are Yhwh, you do what you want' (Jonah 1.15) as an appropriate caption for the book, and argues that, like Job and Qoheleth, Jonah emphasises the 'precarious nature of human existence' and 'the pain of an existence under the rule of an omnipotent but inscrutable deity'.[95]

The changing personality of the text and its increased tendencies towards pessimism and capriciousness inevitably has a knock-on effect for the projections of the Author (essentially the book in personified form) and for his larger alter-ego – the God behind the text. Both mutate into anything but comforting and all-tidying presences. John Miles, Arnold Band, and John Dominic Crossan introduce the image of an author who may be impishly, parodically at odds with the tradition,[96] and Etan Levine echoed by Walter Crouch and André and Pierre-Emmanuel Lacoque conceive of an Author who may not, necessarily, be a ventriloquist's dummy for God.[97] Alan Cooper describes the God of Jonah as 'uncanny and

---

[92] Crouch, 'To Question an End', p. 101.

[93] Melville, *Moby Dick*, p. 43.

[94] Thompson talks of 'those great agnostics, the implied authors of Ecclesiastes and Jonah' (T. L. Thompson, 'Why Talk about the Past? The Bible as Epic and Historiography' (unpublished paper presented to the Society for Biblical Literature annual meeting)). I am grateful to Thomas Thompson for sending me a copy of the paper.

[95] T. M. Bolin, *Freedom Beyond Forgiveness: The Book of Jonah Re-Examined* (Sheffield: Sheffield Academic Press, 1997), pp. 178, 185. All too aware of centripetal disciplinary forces that work to keep maverick biblical voices to a minimum, Bolin adds that he hopes that Jonah (or indeed, by implication his own work) will not be confined to a disciplinary ghetto, in 'quarantine' with these overtly odd biblical texts (Bolin, *Freedom Beyond Forgiveness*, p. 185).

[96] J. R. Miles, 'Laughing at the Bible: Jonah as Parody', in Y. T. Radday and A. Brenner (eds.), *On Humour and the Comic in the Hebrew Bible* (Sheffield: The Almond Press, 1990), pp. 203–15; A. J. Band, 'Swallowing Jonah: The Eclipse of Parody', *Prooftexts* 10 (1990), pp. 177–95; J. D. Crossan: 'Jonah is a parabolic lampoon, a parody directed at the very heart of the Bible. It converts into paradox the prophetic traditions themselves' ('Parable, Allegory and Paradox', in D. Patte (ed.), *Semiology and Parables* (Pittsburgh: Pickwick Press, 1976), pp. 247–81 (251)).

[97] Levine is the first to introduce the idea (at least in modern biblical scholarship) that the perspective of God and the Author might not be synonymous (see E. Levine, 'Jonah as a Philosophical Book', *Zeitschrift für die alttestamentliche Wissenschaft* 96 (1984), pp. 235–45, discussed in chapter 2, p. 123). Compare Crouch's observation (in passing) that 'The narrator *does not agree with Yahweh* as to the nature of the main conflict' (pp. 105–6, my italics), and André and Pierre-Emmanuel Lacocques' observation that 'God is right and

inexplicable' and 'capricious'[98] and Phyllis Trible deems the presentation of the deity as 'as chilling as it is comforting', and suggests that the 'sovereignty, freedom, retribution, vindictiveness, violence, repentance, mercy and pity [of the God of Jonah] sound the disjunctions . . . at the core of Israel's God'.[99] If one of the earliest interpretative reflexes is to emphasise God's reliability and protection – if the apocryphal book 3 Maccabees highlights how the divine Father 'watch[ed] over' Jonah when he was 'wasting away in the belly of a huge, sea-born monster' and 'restor[ed] [him] unharmed to all his family' (3 Maccabees 6.8) – recent interpreters suggest that such readings domesticate both God and God's plot. Gradually they edge towards an image of a narrative that, to use Roemer's phrase, 'does not shelter us', and that protects neither Jonah, nor the reader, from the 'incomprehensible' impact of 'chance'.[100] Admittedly there is a tendency to take divine/textual 'caprice' and dilute it in the not very mysterious mystery of a God who is so much bigger and more surprising than we ever could have thought;[101] admittedly there is a tendency for readers to subsume 'baroque' or 'polyphonic' textual effects under a Mainstream lesson that declares its presence in eighteen point type.[102] And a certain elasticity of the 'biblical' is accompanied by a rigid concept of the literary: here in the ghetto of Biblical Studies we are still working with a mental image of text as a word-search puzzle that can be ringed and solved, or as a box

---

Jonah is right, though their respective stances are mutually exclusive. Who can decide between them?' (A. Lacocque and P.-E. Lacocque, *The Jonah Complex* (Atlanta: Scholar's Press, 1981), p. 99).

[98] A. Cooper, 'In Praise of Divine Caprice', p. 150.

[99] P. Trible, 'Divine Incongruities in the Book of Jonah', in T. Linafelt and T. K. Beal (eds.), *God in the Fray: A Tribute to Walter Brueggemann* (Minneapolis: Fortress, 1998), pp. 198–208 (206, 208).

[100] Roemer, *Telling Stories*, pp. 46, 49, 64.

[101] Although he reads Jonah as a manifesto of divine 'caprice', Cooper goes on to recuperate and normalise that 'caprice' as a 'free and gracious act of God's love' (A. Cooper, 'In Praise of Divine Caprice', p. 144). He allows a mere sentence to the potentially 'dark side' of caprice and 'the view that God's destructive wrath might be just as arbitrary and unconstrained' (p. 162). The paradox is that God's amazing grace is one of the least amazing forms of amazingness, so much a part of the cultural and theological furniture that its amazingness is effectively neutralised. Thus rational culture and theology domesticate the unknowability of God into a knowable truism, and so drains it of all potential agnosticism.

[102] Halpern and Friedman are quick to show how seemingly inconsequential linguistic 'frolics' support the 'bulwark' of plot, and though Craig asserts that the book of Jonah is too 'polyphonic' to transmit a clear monologic lesson, he nevertheless receives one, loud and clear (see Halpern and Friedman, 'Composition and Paranomasia', pp. 85, 87; and Craig, *A Poetics of Jonah*).

stacked with precious things, all co-ordinated by an author who imitates the foreplanning and prescience of (the secure and protecting kind of) God.

Now while the image of Jonah as a puzzle is an idea I can relate to, I tend to think, more like Barnes, Eagleton, and the rabbis, in terms of Mensa puzzles, rotatable aporiae, and Rubik's cubes (watch now as I shift into a different reading position, moving from 'worshipper-before-the-text's-infinite-richness' to 'reader-outwitted-by-the-text'). Four years ago the book cast its spell over me, offering itself, as it has to so many readers, as a crackable code, a smiling invitation to join the Iserian dots and solve this, the most simple, GCSE-level and cartoonish of the prophetic texts. Several crumpled and binned readings later I can say, from experience, that cooking up this text – as a whole – is rather like trying to make a recipe from flour, sugar, currants, molasses, and anchovy paste: if the whole is not to be spoilt then some textual ingredients must be left discreetly under the counter. Whatever thematic drawstrings I use to pull the text together, I seem always to be left with loose threads hanging: if I try to read the book as a tractate on mercy, then I have to deal with the peculiarly mathematical turn that 'mercy' takes in Yhwh's final statement/account, and I need to explain why mercy is problematised by the prophet in Jonah 4.2; if I try to skew the book towards the comic and exploit the sackcloth-wearing cattle or the comedy of the 'aqua-psalm'[103] then I have to bury Jonah's death-wishes (which tend to leak into the comedy, like an oil slick, and turn it black); and I have to explain why, as Kenneth Craig points out, in this particular/peculiar biblical book every human character feels the imminence of death.[104] However I try and answer this text, I end up multiplying the book's eleven question marks[105] (and changing rhetorical question marks to real question marks); however I try and *account* for this text I finish up with a sum that parallels Yhwh's strange calculation (Jonah 4.11) in its strange un-accountabilty. Ultimately I am left with the image of a box, crammed with curious objects, to which the overall key is missing. Like a collection of curios

---

[103] By the 'aqua-psalm' I mean Jonah's psalm (2.1–10), which is basically a compilation and literalisation of the most watery idioms in the book of Psalms. For a fuller discussion of the 'aqua-psalm', see pp. 255–8.

[104] Craig, *A Poetics of Jonah*, p. 139.

[105] The question marks only exist in the English edition, of course, but are implied by the Hebrew.

or surreal memorabilia, this text-box comes packed with a *qiqayon* plant, an east wind, an early rising worm, cattle (dressed in sack-cloth), an aqua-psalm, and a big fish; tombola-like, it is crammed with numerous allusions to other scraps of biblical tradition. Like his namesake in the *Pirke de Rabbi Eliezer*, Jonah seems to be sending postcards – or interpretative clues – home from a whistle-stop tour of the canon, and the book appears to be a greedy consumer of other 'biblical' texts.[106] Read in the broader context of the Hebrew Bible, the book of Jonah looks rather like a performance put on by a low-budget 'rep' company, scouring the attic of the canon for existing props, to be dusted down and re-used, and looking in the backstage storehouse for fragments of existing scripts: it takes 'old' texts and makes them 'new', like the Passion account in the Gospel of Matthew.[107] The recycling is evident at the level of *character* (Jonah ben Ammitai has a walk-on bit part in the book of 2 Kings),[108] at the

---

[106] The case for the rampant intertextuality of the book of Jonah (though not in that idiom) was first made by A. Feuillet in 'Les sources du livre de Jonas', *Revue Biblique* 54 (1947), pp. 161–86. The word 'biblical' appears in inverted commas because the author of Jonah, while inhabiting a certain cumulation of tradition, was writing before the 'canon', with its edges and limits, was established. (These inverted commas can be taken as read whenever I refer to the book of Jonah's use of the 'canon' or other 'biblical' texts. Though the terms are convenient shorthand, I by no means intend to imply the image of an author with a written canon spread out over his desk.)

[107] The Passion narrative in the gospel of Matthew – in many ways the quintessential example of the Bible's tendency to digest 'Old' texts, and make them 'New' – is appropriately described by Frank Kermode as a 'seminary of (Old Testament and Apocryphal) narrative germs', transplanted onto New Testament soil (Kermode, *The Genesis of Secrecy*, p. 86). To take just a fragment of that narrative – Judas's betrayal and subsequent hanging – as an example, the thirty pieces of silver are on loan from Zechariah (Matthew 27.9; cf. Zechariah 11.12); the idea of the 'potter' and the 'field' are imported from two different corners of the book of Jeremiah (Jeremiah 18 and 32; cf. Matthew 27.9–10); and the rope with which Judas hangs himself may have been suggested by the story of Achitophel (2 Samuel 17.23). However, while Matthew and the author of Jonah both cobble together narratives from existing items (rope, coins, fields; Tarshish-bound-ships, psalms, prophets-under-plants), they take radically different stances towards the recycled texts. In Matthew, the Old texts are there to legitimate the New, and the emphasis is firmly on fulfilment, teleology; in Jonah the older texts are there to be parodied and defamiliarised – in fact, to be subjected to all the intonational quotation marks that the book of Jonah will itself be subjected to during the course of its popular interpretative history.

[108] See 2 Kings 14.25. Mainstream interpreters have claimed (rather spuriously) that Jonah ben Ammitai was selected for his eminently criticisable nationalist tendencies, since his main claim to fame is that he 'restored the borders of Israel from Lebohamath as far as the Sea of the Arabah, according to the word of the Lord', but there is no reason why we cannot turn the argument over and imagine an audience/author who would identity with Jonah in his desire to protect and secure the nation. It is also possible that Jonah is selected because he comes with little complicating biography attached, and therefore gives great scope for a story about a figure from the past. As Jack Sasson notes, 'It is reasonable to suppose that Israel's storytellers and bards launched a greater number of accounts

level of *props* (the 'ship going to Tarshish' has also sailed through
Ezekiel 27 and Psalm 28); at the level of *action* (the tableau of Jonah
under his *qiqayon* wishing that he could die imitates the prophet
Elijah sitting under his broom tree (see 1 Kings 19)); and at the level
of *script* (Jonah's hymn from the fish's belly is a medley of quotations
from the Psalms, the King of Nineveh and the sailors regurgitate
words from Jeremiah, and Jonah inverts a familiar creed in Jonah
4.2).

The text, then, spills over with an embarrassment of hermeneutic
riches: it comes packed with all kinds of weird and wonderful objects
on which to extemporise in whatever botanical-meteorological-
moral-psychological-theological idiom might take one's fancy, and it
comes crammed with all kinds of tantalising allusions crying out not
just to be simply ticked off, Bingo-hall fashion ('Ezekiel 27, Psalm 28,
and ['Two Fat Ladies'] Psalm 88'), but to be interpreted and
analysed as to their 'destructive-constructive' (or digestive-regurgi-
tating) relationships to the 'language in which [they are] situated'.[109]
The problems are that the sheer proliferation of detail defies
'principles of thrift'[110] and modest textual economies, and that it is
hard to escape a sense that no single point is big enough to constitute
a textual centre, and that each, ultimately, may be a vastly over-
grown 'red herring'. (The fact that the theme of the absent centre
runs throughout the history of Jonah interpretation – from the
medieval Jewish commentator Kimhi's theory that what we have of
Jonah is but an extract of a more complete book that is now lost to
us,[111] to Serge Frolov's 'The author of the book has a message to
convey – but it is never formulated'[112] – suggests that the image of

<hr />

regarding the patriarchs, kings and prophets than is preserved for us in Hebrew Scripture.
Some of these tales may have found a place eventually in the Apocrypha, Pseudepigrapha,
and in midrashic literature; no doubt many more are now lost to us' (Sasson, *Jonah*, p. 27).
The book of Jonah is such a story about a prophet, a way of 'prolonging scriptural speech
through the exegetical imagination' (M. Fishbane, *The Exegetical Imagination: On Jewish
Thought and Theology* (Cambridge, Mass.: Harvard University Press, 1998), p. 2).

[109] J. Kristeva, *Semiotike* (cited in and trans. Aichele and Philips, 'Exegesis, Eisegesis,
Intergesis', p. 10).

[110] Foucault, 'What is an Author?', p. 118. Exactly the same problem is posed by the text's
greedy ingestion of other biblical texts. To summarise Kristeva, the more intertexts you
include in your 'mosaic' of 'textual surfaces' the more likely you are to jeopardise a '*point* (a
fixed meaning)' (see J. Kristeva, *Desire in Language: A Semiotic Approach to Literature and Art*
(trans. T. Gora, A. Jardine, and L. S. Roudiez; ed. L. S. Roudiez; New York: Columbia
University Press, 1980), p. 65; her italics).

[111] Cited in E. J. Bickerman, *Four Strange Books of the Bible: Jonah, Daniel, Qoheleth, Esther* (New
York: Schocken Books, 1967), p. 61.

[112] Frolov, 'Returning the Ticket', p. 85.

the infinitely rich but centreless text does not come down to – even though it coheres well with – the postmodern *Zeitgeist*. Even the Mainstream, with its tendency to base interpretation around a *single* amplified moment/quotation/image, or to make the text function by *bringing in a key from outside*,[113] seems to betray a feeling that it is impossible to navigate a single coherent course through the book as a whole, and that readings work best when they work by import, or by suspending themselves from a *single*, infinitely strengthened, narrative thread.)

This reading of Jonah is undertaken in the experimental spirit of the sailors' 'perhaps' (Jonah 1.15), the King of Nineveh's 'who knows?' (3.9) and the general spirit of 'what iffery' that pervades the biblical text. Pushing at our rather stolid and congealed definitions of 'the Bible' and 'literature', it asks *what if* in reading Jonah we were constrained neither by the assumption that a biblical/religious text would, by definition, promote the comforting image of a divine carer who 'watches over Jonah [and us]' and 'restores him unharmed' (3 Maccabees 6.8), nor by a parallel model of narrative as life-processor, or antidote to the 'confused luxuriance of real nature'.[114] While I have no intention of creating my author in the image of a Marxist atheist, a proto Left Bank Paris intellectual, or a shoulder-shrugging Mankowitz/Jackie Mason figure, I believe that the image of the protagonist at odds with his plot – performed so iconically, but not exclusively, in existentialist and Yiddish literature – maps persuasively onto the book (and the regularity with which the pincer-like plot appears in older Backwater and even recent Mainstream interpretation suggests that I am 'inclining after a [considerable] majority'[115] in this respect). My premise is that the as yet vaguely defined 'strangeness' of the book derives from a lack of closure and

---

[113] The keys brought in from outside include the life of Christ, the agonies of Christian conversion and the xenophobic audience imported from Ezra–Nehemiah, and the prioritised moments are the expulsion from the fish-tomb, the fuming prophet, the prophet's sufferings in the fish-belly, and the storm-tossed ship (of state). This is not to say that treatments of other biblical texts do not prioritise one scene/moment over others: think, for example, of the apple exchange in Eden, or the way in which the prostitute–prophet marriage in Hosea 1–3 eclipses the rest of the book. But whereas in these cases the same fragment of text is prioritised because of its theological/cultural freight, or because it poses a distinctive problem, in the idiosyncratic case of Jonah the prioritised portion of text changes and the one thing that is constant is that the fragment controls the whole.

[114] Newman, *Essays*, p. 9.

[115] The phrase 'to incline after the majority' is one of the structuring principles of Talmudic debate to which even God must submit himself (see the discussion of *Baba Metzia* 59a–b, in chapter 2, p. 102, n. 40).

of enclosure – from a feeling that Jonah and the reader are held neither within a stable and univocal narrative framework, nor within an environment peacefully circumscribed by the predictability of tradition and the guaranteeability of God.

This is also a scavenging reading – one that, *like the book of Jonah*, makes newness by fusion, conjoinings, and transpositions, and that reads as if popular and Jewish interpreters also were the text's legitimate disseminators and heirs. Footnotes, which mark the points of leakage, show where I soak up now familiar motifs from the Backwaters, and where I also mop up observations from the scholarly Mainstream. At this point something of a confession is in order: if, by concentrating on certain limiting Mainstream readings I have so far tended to depict 'them' (the scholars, the biblical commentators) as bumbling stooges, rather like the unimaginative police officers who act as a foil for the maverick detective-genius in 1970s cop shows, if the emergent subtext of this book is that the professional paid readers have served the text poorly, and that the truly subtle readers are the unpaid, the unprofessionals, this is crassly cartoonish and polemically skewed. The truth is that the Mainstream is already mutinying against itself,[116] and edging towards Jewish/Popular readings – so much so that having set myself up for a superhuman vault across the abyss between Backwaters and Mainstream, I find myself in the less heroic role of reinforcing the fragile rope-bridge already slung between the two.

But even as it pushes the recent, hesitant observations of Mainstream readers (all the time hoping that our expanding sense of Bible and literature may possibly stretch to bear them), this reading puts itself on a collision course with the pervasively positivist environment of the discipline of Biblical Studies – an environment so very different to the environment of English Literature, where my own brain incubated. Jonah criticism is peppered with condemnations of

---

[116] For example, as if to demonstrate that scepticism towards metanarratives is not an exclusively postmodern phenomenon, Jack Sasson uses the centrelessness of the text to explode a universalistic–particularistic framework: 'God's opinion of Nineveh', he observes, 'shifts from strongly condemnatory [Jonah 1.3] to barely contemptuous [4.11]', and the 'boundless love of God' that is allegedly the 'book's central idea' is 'nowhere clearly stated' (Sasson, *Jonah*, p. 25). And Alfred Jepsen and Thomas Bolin criticise the totalising personification of the post-exilic period as a 'creative fiction', so anticipating their Foucault-/Hayden White-reading colleagues (see A. Jepsen, 'Anmerkungen zum Buche Jona: Beiträge zur Theologie des Alten Testaments', in H. Stoebe (ed.), *Wort-Gebot-Gelaube: Theologie des Alten Testaments* (Zürich: Zwingli-Verlag, 1970), pp. 297–305 (304), and Bolin, *Freedom*, p. 39).

other scholars' 'loose' uses of language,[117] with tight generic definitions, and with strident reinforcements of the 'indispensable guardrail'[118] of context, even though that context can only be loosely and imaginatively defined. And even as it studies the textual 'influences' – or inflowings – into the book, it sets up filters and dams to control those influences, giving strict specifications about how deep and how wide the intertextual echoes of the book can *legitimately* go. Generally speaking, the book is only permitted to swallow texts that are not problematic for its (theo)logical constitution and that uphold principles of mutual exclusion:[119] the emergent image is of a book that 'cites' intertexts thesis-fashion, with clear pedagogic intentions (albeit no footnotes). Such an environment inevitably inhibits alternative reading possibilities, and makes them nervous about voicing themselves.

[117] So John Day concludes that 'unless we are using language very loosely, it does not seem appropriate to call Jonah a parable *in sensu stricto*' (J. Day, 'Problems in the Interpretation of the Book of Jonah', in A. S. van der Woude (ed.), *In Quest of the Past: Studies in Israelite Religion, Literature and Prophetism* (Kinderhook, N.Y.: E. J. Brill, USA, 1990), pp. 32–47 (38)).

[118] The phrase belongs to Jacques Derrida, *Of Grammatology* (trans. Gayatri Spivak; Baltimore: Johns Hopkins University Press, 1974), p. 158. Undergirding the bulk of biblical scholarship is the assumption that 'the intellectual positions of the period to which it is assigned ought to clarify the text', and 'the text should inform us about the period in which it was created' (Sasson, *Jonah*, p. 27). But given that Jonah falls, unhelpfully, somewhere between the fifth and third centuries BCE – a period about which we know very little – it suggests that as long as the legitimacy of readings rests on a provable symbiosis between text and context, then no reading of Jonah can ever be fully legitimate (perhaps 'Jonah the Jew' has lingered because no reasonable substitute can be found). On a related issue, S. Schumann has questioned the assumption that the book must originate in corporate 'intellectual positions' (a kind of intellectual corporate personality): could it not have originated as 'a murmur or a question . . . not to be found in a group of people, but in the solitude of an individual'? (Schumann, 'Jona und die Weisheit: Das Prophetische Wort in einer zweideutigen Wirklichkeit', *Theologische Zeitschrift* 45 (1989), pp. 73–80 (80); cited in and trans. Bolin, *Freedom*, p. 40).

[119] So, for example, critics tend to ignore the way in which the 'overthrow' of Nineveh echoes more troubling resonances of the Sodom and Gomorrah story (resonances that emphasise God's sulphurous anger, and his proven predilection for taking the side of justice rather than mercy), and they work on the basis that, if the text is alluding to Assyrian exile, it cannot also be imbibing images of the Babylonian exile, because such inconsistency would make the text 'confusing' (so Day, 'Problems in the Interpretation of the Book of Jonah', p. 37). They also tend to gloss the admitted inner-biblical conversations in a way that reinforces the denigration of Jonah: thus the Elijah allusion makes Jonah appear even 'more foolish and petty' and reinforces the disciplinary effect, because Jonah has 'Elijah's despondency without Elijah's excuse' (see Band, 'Swallowing Jonah', p. 187; S. R. Driver, *Introduction to the Literature of the Old Testament* (New York: Charles Schribner's Sons, 1920), p. 325). For a broader discussion of how ideological constraints are imposed on the 'dialogic, polyvocal dynamics' of biblical texts, see T. K. Beal, 'Ideology and Intertextuality: Surplus of Meaning and Controlling the Means of Production', in D. Nolan Fewell (ed.), *Reading Between Texts: Intertextuality and the Hebrew Bible* (Louisville: Westminster/John Knox, 1992), pp. 27–39.

Hesitantly, my reading gathers courage, clears its throat, and begins to speak. Cowed by the heavy disciplinary atmosphere that surrounds it, it anxiously 'suggests' (rather than 'claims' or 'asserts' or 'maintains' or 'contends', in the bolder, more assertive idioms of the academic) that the biblical book of Jonah works less like a thesis and more like a 'riff', a self-conscious story: a 'story that spins itself out of itself, propelled by . . . the imagination', a story that 'can go anyplace and take off into the stratosphere', a story in which 'language takes off like a sudden gust of swallows, observations collide and procreate a joke, words jump around like fireflies . . .'[120] And it tentatively counters generic strictures by suggesting something of a *mongrel* text (neither purely comedy, nor tragedy, nor midrash, nor parable – in fact not purely anything), and a text that stymies established generic mechanisms. Nervously pushing the author-as-*Aufklärer* to one side, it replaces him with the persona of the author-as-writer, who views language (as does Paul Auster)[121] as 'an infinitely complex organism', a living body of 'cells and sinews, corpuscles and bones, digits and fluids', or who proto-midrashi-cally[122] turns and turns words like the rabbis investigating the

---

[120] The description of the 'riff' is pilfered from the story-teller and journalist, Eva Hoffman (see E. Hoffman, *Lost in Translation: Life in a New Language* (London: Minerva, 1989), pp. 218–19).

[121] Auster, *The Invention of Solitude*, p. 160. The Backwaters not only supply much of the content of my reading, but suggest analogies for how the text is doing things with words. It is not difficult to imagine a conversation between the book of Jonah and Paul Auster, who digests the book of Jonah as part of his own cultural memory tour. Auster sees language as 'a network of rhymes, assonances and overlapping meanings' which 'function[ ] as a kind of bridge that join[ ] opposite and contrasting aspects of the world with each other': 'Room and tomb. Tomb and womb, womb and room. Breath and death', he muses, 'Or the fact that the letters of the word "live" can be rearranged to spell out the word "evil" . . .' (Auster, *The Invention of Solitude*, p. 160). In a similar vein the author of Jonah plays with the root הפך (*hfk*), turn over (= overturn/destroy) and turn round (= bring to repentance), blessing and curse, his own (Hebrew) play on 'living' and being evil.

[122] Again it suggests something about the discipline of Biblical Studies that one cannot describe Jonah as loosely 'midrashic' without arguing that Jonah is a midrash in *sensu stricto*, and naming the one *singular* text that Jonah is a midrash 'on'. So, for example K. Budde argued that the book was a midrash on 2 Kings 14.25 (K. Budde, 'Vermutungen zum "Midrasch des Buches der Könige"', *Zeitschrift für die alttestamentliche Wissenschaft* 11 (1892), pp. 37–81); L. H. Brockington argued that Jonah was a midrash on Jeremiah 18.8 ('Jonah', in M. Black and H. H. Rowley (eds.), *Peake's Commentary on the Bible* (London: Van Nostrand Reinhold, 1962), pp. 627–9 (627)); and Phyllis Trible argued that Jonah was a midrash on Exodus 34.6 (*Studies in the Book of Jonah*, p. 432). The reverse reflex is to refute the argument that Jonah is a midrash on the basis that no text is alluded to more than once, and so the postulation of midrash, and the cancellation of the claim goes, rather fruitlessly, full circle. I suggest that instead of sticking to tight generic criteria for midrash (even while marginalising Midrash and Talmud within the context of Old Testament/ Hebrew Bible studies) biblical scholars may discover a great deal about the features of Old

topsytypical resonances of רג (*dag*; fish [*m*]) and דגה (*dagah*; fish [*f*]). And moving away from the idea of Jonah-as-thesis, responsibly citing its sources, it suggests that the book participates in the '*fluidity* of Israel's theological [and cultural] diction',[123] that different connotations and displacements wash into and out of the book (as in a midrash or a dream), and that the book uses the pool of memory as a linguistic 'semiotic repertoire'.[124] My book of Jonah is marked by an emphatically 'loose' use of words, and by a style that rhetoricians would term *transumptive/metaleptic*;[125] its strangeness derives at least in part from the fact that it is directed less by the desire to make a point, or by the logic of cause and effect, than by the pull of memory and the feel of words on the tongue. Thus as 'content' and 'style' form their inevitable pact, images of mutability, chance, caprice, fragility, vulnerability, and the 'plot [that] does not shelter us'[126] mimic the mutability of the book's construction.

And so my book of Jonah squats awkwardly, as my own book about Jonah does, on the margins of the academic, and both have a certain fluidity and protean quality in common. As I am easily led by the lure of language (weaving my way through Mainstreams and Backwaters, through digestive tracts, underbellies, and cultural carcasses, and themes of spinning, weaving, consuming, digesting, and regurgitation), so my 'loose' text is lured by the punning link between east winds and pre-emptive fleeing, heat and salvation, innocent blood and *qiqayon* plants and vomiting and so on and so on *ad nauseam*.[127] And as the author of Jonah unashamedly inflates his

Testament language that do not translate so easily into thesis-speak, by exploring the way the midrashists turn and handle words. Crucially I am not arguing that Jonah is in any way identical to, say, the *Pirke de Rabbi Eliezer* or *Midrash Jonah* (both of which, by their difference, demonstrate the breadth of the genre 'midrash'), but that the book of Jonah shows certain affinities with midrashic style.

123 Sasson, *Jonah*, p. 23. (Sasson's observation, together with his allusion to the way in which lines and phrases '*shuffle*' between different (biblical) texts and . . . authors' (*Jonah*, p. 164) shows how recent discussions of Bible and midrash are edging closer to intertextual theory, by moving towards the image of an open – perhaps even unpoliceable – thoroughfare between texts.)

124 D. Boyarin, *Intertextuality and the Reading of Midrash*, p. 28.

125 Transumption and metalepsis, according to Quintillian, are modes of displacement, troping on a trope, playing on sound, scenes, or any other element of the text in a chain of association and dispersion. The terms were recently revived by John Hollander in *The Figure of Echo: A Mode of Allusion in Milton and After* (Berkeley: University of California Press, 1981) and were introduced to Hebrew Bible studies by P. D. Miscall, 'Isaiah: New Heavens, New Earth, New Book', in Fewell (ed.), *Reading Between Texts*, pp. 41–56.

126 Roemer, *Telling Stories*, p. 46.

127 Inevitably this raises the question to what extent the author is a narcissistic projection of

narrative, so I, all too aware that I am trying to whip up interest for
the biblical when the crowds are in decline, announce my text like a
Victorian music-hall host, under five headings:
   Skewed beginnings (Jonah 1.1–3)
   Turbulent plots and shivering ships (Jonah 1.4–16)
   The fish and the aqua-psalm (Jonah 1.17–2.10)
   Cattle in sackcloth and mis-hung backcloths – in Nineveh–
      Jerusalem (Jonah 3.1–10)
   Awkward surpluses, sediments, and residues (Jonah 4.1–11)
and take the reader on a tour of what I consider to be the most
clever, puzzling, and even freakish narrative elements: the amazing
shivering ships of Tarshish, the seaweed-draped prophet and his
'aqua-psalm', the fabulously revolving word הפך (*hfk*), and the
mysterious lingering 'evil' that refuses to vanish, like the Cheshire
cat's smile. My reading is not so much a commentary as a series of
meditations on the difficulty of 'pointing' the narrative;[128] and at the
same time an attempt to mark the points – the sites of interest – that
puncture any clichéd, simplistic projections of the 'biblical'. It is not
so much an attempt to hazard a new Really Real and Universally
Accepted Reading of the book of Jonah, for professional legitimation, but to throw those strict principles of legitimation into
question. This reading reads as if imaginative chains of association,
the fusions between past and present, and the exaggeration and
stretching that has been so much a part of the book's survival were
an intrinsic part of the interpretative act: as if reading were a
self-conscious prolongation – and fattening – of the scriptural
imagination. It reads Jonah on the basis that 'words are plastic
objects with which we can do all kinds of things', and so produces a
text that is less a tightly structured text-box and more a 'fluid
pudding'. Our textual *dessert*, then, will be the consistency of
blancmange.

---

the reader, and to what extent the author is a projection of my (would-be) writer self.
Inevitably there is some kind of pact between us, but insofar as my author writes as I write
and thinks (associatively) as I think, he is an interesting counterpart to the proto-Christian
Author-Academic of the Mainstream, whose chief motivation seems to be to make single
points with clarity, and to use story as a pretty shell, to house the kernel of a thesis.

[128] By the difficulties of 'pointing the narrative' I mean the difficulty of marking the text's
points and weighting them with significance (I am also playing here on the way in which
the Hebrew text was originally *unpointed*, that is written without vowels). For a more
conventionally 'commentating' treatment of the text see Y. M. Sherwood, *Jonah* (The
Blackwell Bible Commentaries; Oxford: Blackwell, forthcoming).

2. REGURGITATING JONAH

Skewed beginnings: Jonah 1.1–3

You are [the narrator], you do as you please. [Jonah 1.14, adapted]

For its first eleven words in Hebrew or seventeen in English, the book of Jonah unfolds according to the precise formula of all prophetic books: the word of the Lord 'comes' to the prophet, that word is propulsive ('Arise go') and it directs the prophet to 'cry out against evil'. The monkey-wrench in the system – and one that will have a profoundly disruptive effect on the words and meaning-calculations that follow – is that in this *particular* case the object of Yhwh's attentions is the 'great city' of Nineveh, capital of Assyria. The command makes Jonah an awkward remainder within the Hebrew Bible[129] and in the Book of the Twelve, where Nahum (whose name means *comfort*) proclaims God as refuge, stronghold and protector and exalts in the dissolution of the 'bloody [turned watery] city' (Nahum 1.7; 2.8; 3.1) and Zephaniah gloatingly predicts the crumbling of Nineveh's walls and Nineveh's 'security' – imagining a lone raven shrieking from a sill, the passers-by hissing and shaking their fists, and the wild animals crawling through the ruins of this once proud signifier (Zephaniah 2.13–15). Moreover, it seems significant to me that *in only one other instance is a Hebrew prophet sent to a foreign King, and in that instance the mission is explicitly self-destructive*: Elisha is commissioned by God to anoint Hazael king over Syria, and does so weeping because (as he tells Hazael), 'I know the evil that you will do to the people of Israel; you will set fire to their fortresses, and you will slay their young men with the sword, and dash in pieces their little ones and rip up their women with child' (2 Kings 8.12).[130]

The fact that God's word comes in on such a skewed trajectory

---

[129] The typical metaphorical/historical role of Assyria in the context of the Hebrew Bible (as rod of God's anger, swarm of killer bees, genital razor, ravaging lion, and so on) is detailed in chapter 2, pp. 124–5.

[130] The only critic, to my knowledge, who even acknowledges that this is the only other example is Kenneth Craig (see K. M. Craig, 'Jonah and the Reading Process', *Journal for the Study of the Old Testament* 47 (1990) pp. 103–14 (p. 109)). But given that the book of Jonah alludes verbatim to Elijah's despair under the broom tree in 1 Kings 19, and that this scene just precedes God's commission to Elijah to anoint Hazael (which is then carried over into the Elisha-cycle), the two narratives seem to be provocatively contingent.

means that the narrative will develop outside the secure parameters of tradition and outside the realms of generic security control. Anomaly breeds anomaly and the adjusted climate of the beginning turns this book into a curious, mutant biblical species. The curious environment of its genesis encourages the growth of idiosyncratic narrative features, each of which deserves to be outlined in more detail, since they lie at the heart of the strangeness of the text. The book becomes:

1. a story that foregrounds its storyness
2. a story with a kamikaze plot
3. a story in which resistance plays an above-average role
4. a story in which familiar genre mechanisms malfunction
5. a story that (by accident or design) takes the audience through the discomforting experience of seeing one's self on the periphery of the world.

1. *This is a story that foregrounds its storyness*, a story in which the author parades his God-like omnipotence – his power to take the narrative in whatever direction he pleases. Rather like the tale of Queen Elizabeth II's meeting with Idi Amin, or Hitler's rendezvous with the Windsors, and other bizarre virtual histories detailed in Nik Cohn and Guy Peellaert's *Twentieth Century Dreams*,[131] the story of Jonah's mission to Nineveh will by definition develop in a zone of comic infeasibility and will take place in the zone of the 'Once upon a never time' where 'it happened and it never did'.[132] An audience encountering this text some time after the fifth century BCE (i.e. well after the Babylonian exile and the destruction of Nineveh in 612) would appreciate that the walls of Nineveh were being rebuilt for story purposes, and would know (like *Yerushalmi* and the Targum) that since 'overthrow' in its literal sense prevailed, the story of God's compassion on Nineveh was at most a temporary blip on the surface of a more prevailing and well-known reality. I suspect that we are not the only knowing readers to deduce that Job is a 'philosophical fable', that the 'fantastically exaggerated' Jonah inhabits a zone of sub- (or better supra-) reality, and that biblical narratives exhibit a 'whole spectrum of relations to history'[133] – even taking up the role of 'virtual history' in this *particular* case.

[131] N. Cohn and G. Peellaert, *Twentieth Century Dreams* (London: Secker and Warburg, 1999).
[132] Rushdie, *The Satanic Verses*, p. 35.
[133] Alter, *The Art of Biblical Narrative*, pp. 24, 33. I find it interesting that Alter selects as his most overtly a-historical narratives Job and the 'fantastically exaggerated' Jonah, even though

Certainly it is hard to imagine an audience who would miss the sheer abundance of clues. Everything is talked up with the air of pub-raconteur: the adjective 'big' (גדול, *gadol*) is added lavishly to almost every noun (the fish is big, the city is big, the wind is big); 'yeast' is applied prodigiously (carnival fashion) to reality (*qiqayon* plants grow like triffids, a fish hears and responds to instructions); and verbs are stretched to excess (Yhwh does not send the storm but *hurls* it [1.4], the worm does not nibble at the plant but *smites* it [4.7])[134] – the worm and the plant, like God and Jonah, are engaged in warfare and the reader can almost see the words 'Pow', 'Biff', and 'Arghh' writ large over the text. Similarly in good story-fashion, the text lurches between antipodes in a way prone to bring on sea-sickness: Jonah is told to go East and he goes West; he feels a great pleasure then a great displeasure (4.6–8); and the whole narrative hinges on the reversal of a word. As one strange premise necessitates and legitimates another, the author exploits the freedom of an environment where from now on, literally anything can happen: in the strangely counter-intuitive world that is the book of Jonah, a prophet can run away from God; the Assyrians, epitome of wicked-ness can be inspired by a five-word oracle and repent in dust and ashes; God's חסד (*hesed*; loving-kindness/mercy) can be described as a curse (4.2); and Yhwh, when asked to explain his forgiveness of Nineveh, can shun the 'natural' explanation in favour of a 'trite'[135] argument that seems to focus inordinately on the size on Nineveh and its livestock holdings. The plot can go anywhere, do anything, and the accumulation of 'who knowses' and 'perhapses' (1.6; 3.9) acts as wry commentary on the infinite possibility, and 'miraculous' caprice, of its development.

2. *This is a story that runs a kamikaze course*: a plot diving with its protagonist (and his nation) towards self-annihilation; a plot that certainly cannot be understood according to conventional definitions of 'consoling by form', or attaching events together with a kind of logical 'paste'.[136] Like Jacob's struggle with the messenger of God in

he summarises Jonah (rather blandly) as a 'parabolic illustration of the prophetic calling and of God's universality' (p. 33).

[134] The Hebrew verb is נכה (*nakah*). On the idea of the warrior worm, cf. T. L. Wilt, 'Jonah: A Battle of Shifting Alliances', in Davies and Clines, *Among the Prophets*, pp. 164–81.

[135] Sasson, *Jonah*, p. 319.

[136] Barthes, *S/Z*, p. 156. Incidentally, the image of Jonah caught in, or perhaps even sacrificed by, his pincer-like plot resonates with one interpretation of his name. Jonah's name (יונה (*yonah*)) means dove and 'dove' can signify: (1) a bird that moans and laments (Nahum 2.7;

Genesis 32, the plot of Jonah may *seem* to conform to the regular folk-tale, but as soon as the structuralist set squares and rulers and templates are laid on it, they instantly pull out of shape. Reduced to its bare bones and expressed in (loosely and playfully adapted) Proppian terminology, the plot of Jonah will be, effectively:

1. Hero is sent on anti-Quest (absolutely opposed to his own interests).
2. Hero flees the Quest, but is redirected back on course by the Quest-giver.
3. The Quest is completed and the Hero is so depressed that he asks to die.
4. The Quest-giver spends an additional chapter dealing with the Hero's residual depression and justifying the plot he set.

Not only is such a narrative about as *unheimlich* as a fairy-tale in which the woodcutter frees the wolf, shoots the grandmother, and marries Red Riding Hood, or in which the prince must complete a quest to turn his princess back into a frog,[137] but it will also lead, inevitably, to the spectacle of a hero trying to wriggle free from the lines of a narrative, to go down off the bottom of the page or to exit left to Tarshish, off-page-West (1.3).[138] In fact Mainstream dichoto-

Isaiah 38.14; 59.11); (2) a bird that flees far away from the terrors of death and that hurries to find refuge and shelter from the wind (Psalm 55.6–8); and (3) a bird that is offered as sacrifice (Leviticus 1.14; 5.7, 11; 12.8; 14.22, 30; 15.14, 29; Numbers 6.10) or as a sacrificial guilt offering (Leviticus 5.8; 12.8; 14.22; 15.15, 30; Numbers 6.11). The Mainstream has midrashically 'riffed' on meaning (1): thus Jonah is 'more like a hawk than a dove' and is a selfish bird who 'feathers his own nest' (A. Lacocque and P.-E. Lacocque, *Jonah: A Psycho-Religious Approach to the Prophet* (Columbia: University of South Carolina Press, 1990), p. 31; P. Trudinger, 'Jonah: A Post-Exilic Verbal Cartoon?', *The Downside Review* (April 1989), pp. 142–3 (143)). But a parallel and opposite 'riff' might make something of the fact that a man whose own life/reputation is put in danger by his plot has a name synonymous with a creature of sacrifice. (For a development of this idea, see Frolov, 'Returning the Ticket', p. 97.)

137 The analogy is derived from John Barton's typically lucid and entertaining description of the Proppian folk-tale in Barton, *Reading the Old Testament*, p. 116.

138 It is less interesting to try to geographically position Tarshish (suggestions include Phoenicia, Etruria in Italy, Sardinia, Tartessos in Spain) than to locate the connotations of Tarshish in the Hebrew Bible. According to Isaiah 66.19, the people of Tarshish have neither 'heard of [Yhwh's] fame [n]or seen his glory': perhaps then Jonah is grasping at textual straws to find himself a Yhwh-free place. Jack Sasson argues that its significance may be that it is a place just off the edge of the real or the known: 'Although it was not an invented place (as are Eldorado or Shangrila) Tarshish seems always to lie just beyond the geographic knowledge of those who try to pinpoint its location' (Sasson, *Jonah*, p. 79). James Ackerman sees Tarshish as a place laden with connotations of 'luxury, desire, delight' and positioned 'at the ends of the earth', and C. H. Gordon argues that 'whatever the original identification of Tarshish may have been, in literature and popular imagination it became a distant paradise' (J. S. Ackerman, 'Jonah', in R. Alter and

mies between universalism–xenophobia or 'the Christian' and 'the Jew' – or readings of Jonah as anti-hero – may (among other things) be a way of retrieving the text by forcing it to make good binary sense.

3. *This will be a story in which resistance plays an above-average role.* As every good student of Aristotelian narrative knows, plots work by finding a 'complication' to 'resolve': in the case of *Little Red Riding Hood*, the tale of how the distinctively dressed little girl took a basket of goodies to granny and how granny was grateful is lifted from banality to 'narrative' only when it has a lupine antagonist to overcome. But by way of contrast the book of Jonah stacks up a whole range of resistant forces (the fleeing prophet, the frantically rowing and protesting sailors) far in excess of the requirements of the plot; it allows those forces to elicit our sympathy in a way that Little Red Riding Hood's slavering wolf does not; and it allows those forces to linger up to and beyond the point where we expect them to be satisfied, pacified, and resolved. Inevitably this raises the question of whether these 'complications' *are* simply complications – in the sense of the servile lackeys of the plot mechanism – or whether they in fact play a much larger, independent role. Whether we think that Jonah represents (lawyer-like) a *principle* (such as that under certain circumstances 'forgiving the guilty is identical to punishing the innocent');[139] or whether we think that he is representing something less cerebral than a principle (perhaps something as visceral and simple as the interests of Israel, and the desire for God's protection, or the desire to resist self-annihilation as defeated nation or false prophet), the fact that we can think of so many ways to gloss his resistance suggests that this may be a complication with *significance* and *rationale*.

4. *It will be a story in which a deviant Word ('Arise and go – to Nineveh') has a knock-on effect, causing familiar genre mechanisms to variously malfunction.* This is clear right from the beginning when, like an unknown reagent in a common chemical reaction, the phrase 'to Nineveh' sends the prophetic tradition reeling in previously unheard-of directions. Typically, prophetic narratives conform to a distinct spatial pattern: a prophet stands 'in the presence of Yhwh' and receives

F. Kermode (eds.), *The Literary Guide to the Bible* (London: Fontana, 1989), pp. 234–43 (235); C. H. Gordon, 'Tarshish', in *The Interpreter's Dictionary of the Bible* IV (New York and Nashville: Abingdon, 1962), pp. 517–18).

139 E. Levine, 'Jonah as a Philosophical Book', p. 243.

instructions to proclaim God's word to Israelites/Judaeans who have gone 'away from the presence of Yhwh' towards other gods and the other nations. But in Jonah's case, the prophet is sent to the other nations (in fact one of the most iconically Israel-annihilating of the other nations), Israel/Judah disappear from the frame entirely, and the prophet does not stand 'in the presence of Yhwh' but shows a desperate twice-repeated wish to get 'away from the presence of the Lord.'[140] *Usually* Yhwh's word is the perfect sovereign performative, where to 'utter is to create the effect uttered':[141] the God who says let there be light, and light 'is', commands Elijah to 'Arise go to Zarapheth' and Elijah 'arises and goes', tells Jeremiah to 'Arise and go to the Euphrates and hide' and Jeremiah arises and hides,[142] and tells Jonah to 'Arise and go to Nineveh', and Jonah arises – to flee.[143] *Normally* prophets protest their inability to speak – Moses protests that he is not a 'man of words' (Exodus 4.10); Jeremiah fears that he 'does not know how to speak' (Jeremiah 1.6); Isaiah insists that his words are unworthy, his lips unclean (Isaiah 6.5) – but Jonah in contrast, comically literalises the prophetic protest as he scuttles off, in the opposite direction, *without saying a word*. The convention of prophetic resistance is derailed from its normal generic function (to illustrate the humility and wordlessness of man, and the awesome power of God) and tipped over into actual comic dissension from the task. Already we encounter the textual tendency to invert biblical tradition and to take it too literally, at its word – already we enter the zone of deviant 'intonational quotation marks'.

5. *It will be a story that – whether consciously or simply as an accident of the book's first premise – takes its audience through the discomforting experience of seeing one's self at the periphery of the world.* Most of the Hebrew Bible is profoundly Israel-centric – meaning that the vacillations of history are internally explained, that God blesses and curses in response to the nation's obedience and disobedience, *and that in this sense the nation*

---

[140] The double repetition of the phrase 'away from the presence of the Lord' in 1.3 is an example of free indirect discourse, reiterating Jonah's sole obsessive purpose, giving the reader a brief proleptic glimpse into the character's mind.

[141] Judith Butler cites the God who proclaims 'Let there be light' as the perfect example of the sovereign speaking subject (see J. Butler, *Excitable Speech: A Politics of the Performative* (New York and London: Routledge, 1997), p. 32).

[142] A similar point is made by Trible, *Rhetorical Criticism*, pp. 127–8.

[143] The Hebrew version retains the element of surprise a little longer (if indeed we could ever imagine ourselves in the position of reading the text for the first time). In the English translation, the game is given away by the 'But' in 'But Jonah rose to flee', but in Hebrew the word translated 'But' can also be read as 'and'.

has control over its fate. The other nations, for all their strength, are accessories in an internally directed master-plot: Assyria, the razor hired from beyond the river (Isaiah 7.20) is hired because of Israel's sin; Babylon is similarly used as a tool of God's wrath, to rinse out the unclean bowl of Judah (2 Kings 21.13); and, in a passage that quite literally performs the conscription of the Other as accessory in the narrative of the Self, Pharaoh's heart is hardened, and the Egyptians bombarded with plagues, boils, frogs, and lice (merely) *so that the Israelites may tell 'in the hearing of their sons and their sons' sons, how Yhwh made sport of the Egyptians'* (Exodus 10.2). Again the difference of Jonah is clear: a story, even a comic or self-consciously unreal story, where Nineveh is at the centre of the universe and where God acts primarily in response to Assyrian actions, will move, like Qoheleth, towards the vulnerable Self, the Self without control over one's fate, the Self no longer held secure in internally governable theological accounting systems. (To read this book as a simple tractate on universalism is to deny how much the Self longs and needs to be at the centre, even in so-called 'universalistic' discourse.[144])

To summarise, the book of Jonah, uniquely, will be a book at odds with 'reality', with the canon, with genre and tradition, with its protagonist, and with its audience, who will feel themselves propelled to the periphery of the world. As we progress – through the storm scene and the *unheimlich* world of Nineveh-Jerusalem, to the exacerbated tensions of the book's ending – these features will make the narrative idiosyncratically turbulent.

Turbulent plots and shivering ships: Jonah 1.4–16

The surface of the storm scene is appropriately agitated, as the tension between the pull of the divine current, and the human

---

[144] This is, of course, amply demonstrated by the Christian 'universalists' of the Mainstream, who base their 'universalism' on the cloning of the Self and the denigration of the Jewish Other. Similarly, the Hebrew Bible even in the so-called (and over-hyped) 'universalistic' passages tends to keep Jerusalem very much at the centre and avoid the absolute geographical/theological dissipation that universalism (if we could think such a thing) would actually entail. As Harry Orlinsky points out, the Hebrew Bible tends to be nationalistic-universal rather than internationalistic – a point that makes the idea that Jonah is in fact a tractate on universalism, claiming that God should be as centred in Nineveh as he is in Israel, even more untenable. (For a full discussion, see H. Orlinsky, 'Nationalism-Universalism and Internationalism in Ancient Israel', in H. T. Frank and W. L. Reed (eds.), *Translating and Understanding the Old Testament: Essays in Honor of H. G. May* (New York: Abingdon, 1970), pp. 206–36.)

counter-current, is visually whipped up in the image of the storm. That Jonah is determined to resist, and to prolong this resistance beyond mere token complication, is obvious: in 1.12 he does not say 'Turn around and row to Nineveh' but 'Take me up and throw me into the sea', as if to indicate that the only way that he will go along with the current of this plot is as a floating corpse.[145] But far more curious is the way in which Jonah's dissidence is mirrored in, and reinforced by, the subplot of the sailors who, as soon as they have identified the story that they have stumbled into,[146] also try to resist (or row against) the plot. Thus they reinforce the accumulating sense of strangeness, for what kind of plot is it that repels all its participants, and what kind of plot is it that the participants 'complicate' with such commitment that they seem to generate reams of viable counter-narrative in the process?

For mechanical plot purposes, the sailors need only to function as mere plot-accessories, put there to facilitate Jonah's escape and then to throw him overboard (whereupon that more famous plot-carrier, the fish, will take over) – and the plot would go much more swimmingly if they simply went with the flow, uttering banal lines such as 'You are indeed an evil prophet and deserve to be thrown overboard.'[147] But instead the sailors refuse simply to submit to the

---

[145] However 1.12 is interpreted it troubles the calm surface of the narrative. For interpretations of the verse as Jonah's death-wish see S. D. F. Goitein, 'Some Observations on Jonah', *Journal of the Palestine Oriental Society* 17 (1937), pp. 63–77 (68); L. C. Allen, *The Books of Joel, Obadiah, Jonah and Micah* (London: Hodder and Stoughton, 1976), p. 211; Lacocque and Lacocque, *The Jonah Complex*, p. 47; J. Limburg, *Jonah* (Old Testament Library; London: SCM, 1993), p. 55; and H. W. Wolff, who observes how Jonah is 'seeking refuge from [the Lord] in death' and sees 'no essential difference between the plea in 1.12 and the plea in 4.3, 8' (H. W. Wolff, *Obadiah and Jonah: A Commentary* (trans. M. Kohl; Hermeneia; Minneapolis: Augsburg, 1988), p. 118). Alternatively (or in addition) the instruction can be read as a way of 'saving the life of the heathen sailors and passengers on the ship' (J. D. Smart, 'The Book of Jonah: Introduction and Exegesis', in G. A. Buttrick, T. S. Kepler, H. G. May, *et al.* (eds.), *The Interpreter's Bible* VI (Nashville: Abingdon, 1956), pp. 883–4) – but to read this way is to undermine the picture of Jonah as selfish xenophobe and to release all kinds of counter-observations into the narrative. Thus Gunn and Fewell note that '[Jonah's] character takes on a new hue: this man is willing to die to save others', and, even more radically, Meir Sternberg argues that the book of Jonah 'starts by opposing a compassionate Jonah to a wrathful God' (D. M. Gunn and D. Nolan Fewell, *Narrative in the Hebrew Bible* (Oxford: Oxford University Press, 1993), p. 131; M. Sternberg, *The Poetics of Biblical Narrative: Ideological Literature and the Drama of Reading* (Bloomington: Indiana University Press, 1987), p. 56).

[146] Cf. Gunn and Fewell: 'The fearful sailors attempt to find what plot they have stumbled into' (*Narrative in the Hebrew Bible*, p. 130).

[147] It should also be noted, against projections of the sailors' piety, that the sailors emphatically do *not* utter faith-filled lines such as 'You are God and you know what is best.'

inexorable divine current, and 'row strenuously', or literally *dig*[148] against the tide to take Jonah back to shore (1.13). With a supreme reluctance that the *Pirke de Rabbi Eliezer* dramatises so effectively, they express anxiety about shedding 'innocent blood' and relinquish Jonah, Pilate-like with the disclaimer 'You O Lord have done as it pleased you' (1.14) – as if to draw attention to the Quixotic and disturbing nature of God. And in fact dissidence and the suffering of the innocent are the points that they communicate most relentlessly, as they protest their role as plot-pawns, and, in a phrase that imitates the way in which the evil of Nineveh latches limpet-like onto Jonah,[149] ask why this unsolicited evil (רעה, *ra'ah*) has somehow transferred itself to *them* (1.7, 8).

Caught between the devil and the deep blue sea – between Jonah's death and their own – the sailors imitate the Catch Twenty-Two situation in which the prophet finds himself, caught somewhere between the futility and compulsion of resistance to God. At the same time their frantic digging/rowing efforts indicate the force and futility with which the human protagonists, Canute-like, try to turn the tide of the divine current: 'The men rowed hard to bring the ship back to shore, *but they could not*' (Jonah 1.13). But even as the futilely 'digging' sailors represent the puny muscles of man up against the impressive biceps of the massive sea and storm God, they demonstrate the power of human speech in the more equitable arena of words. Like the words of Abimelech, the foreigner, as he protests against the role into which God and Abraham have scripted him,[150] the sailors' protests cause a monstrous question to raise its head about the smooth narrative surface: 'Is Yhwh so obsessed with re-capturing one fleeing prophet that he is prepared to jeopardise and traumatise the innocent in the process?'

As if to drive the anxiety home, the sailors enact the fundamental

---

[148] The Hebrew verb is חתר (*ḥatar*): to burrow, hollow out, dig, break through. The same verb is used in Amos 9.2 to describe the burrowing activities of those who dig into Sheol, in the frantic attempt to escape from God's wrath.

[149] Not only does the 'big evil' of Nineveh dump itself, unsolicited, on Jonah's doorstep in 1.2, but even when the evil of Nineveh is cancelled out by God, it seems to linger and attach itself to the prophet. The way in which evil leaks through from 3.10 to 4.1 is discussed in more detail in the analysis of Jonah chapter 4.

[150] Unlike many other Others, who are merely pawns of Israelite rhetoric, Abimelech protests to Abraham: 'What have you done to us? . . . You have done things to me that ought not to be done', and 'What were you thinking of, that you did this thing?' (see Genesis 20.9–10). Abimelech's questions trouble the smooth running of the plot and make this one of the Hebrew Bible's few truly dialogic narratives.

human longing for security, and a very unsentimentalised and literalised 'fear of the Lord/the storm' on the part of 'baby man'. As he turns up the storm (that iconic perennial reminder of human lack of control) the narrator makes a *point* of the escalating fear of the sailors – they are afraid (1.5), they are very afraid (1.10), and they 'fear a big fear' (1.16) – *and* their fear of 'perishing' – in 1.6 the captain of the sailors hopes that Jonah's God will 'give a thought to them' that they 'do not perish', and in 1.16 the sailors beseech God that they may not 'perish' and be punished for shedding 'innocent blood'. And there is something desperately human about the way in which the gods-fearing sailors[151] open as many divine insurance policies and appeal to as many deities as possible, as if the desperate live in the realm of the perhapses, grasping at maybes like life-jackets. Their 'creed' – 'You are Yhwh, you do what you please' (1.14) – makes it clear that they cannot be conscripted as forerunners of contemporary gentile/Christian piety, and that, unlike the wor-shippers in Mapple's Seafarer's Chapel, they know nothing of those more conventional aquatic metaphors – of God as 'anchor' or as 'rock'. Their affirmation of the absolute power and caprice of God suggest that the God of Jonah may share something with Qoheleth's dark, all-powerful deity, particularly when seen from the vantage point of men who feel themselves 'snared' or trapped in tangled plot-lines 'like fish caught in an evil net' (cf. Ecclesiastes 9.12).

Like the sailors, Jonah seems to be on a quest for security, enclosure, safety as he goes down to Joppa (1.3) and down to the 'innermost parts of the ship' (ירכתי הספינה, *yarketei hasefinah* (1.6)) – an unusual phrase strangely resonant with the phrase ירכתי צפון (*yarketei tsafon*, Psalm 48.2) which is used of the refuge of Jerusalem, Mount Zion.[152] Like the actions of Gabriel Garcia Marquez's Joel Arcadia Buendia, who draws circles round himself wherever he comes to rest, Jonah's going down can be diagnosed as a poignant externalisation of the desire to protect himself and hem himself in. The sailors and Jonah – who try to save one another's lives and proclaim one another's 'innocence' – participate not only in a league

---

[151] D. Daube, 'Jonah: A Reminiscence', *Journal of Jewish Studies* 34 (1983), pp. 36–43 (37).

[152] This point is made by Ackerman, 'Jonah', p. 235. Given that Mount Zion is a symbolic figure that stresses ideas of protection and dreams of inviolability, and given that the phrase ירכתי הספינה (*yarketei hasefina*) is unique to Jonah, it is by no means too far fetched to suggest that the echo is deliberate. If we do choose to point it so, it gives a national slant to the subliminal emphasis on the search for protection that may later be picked up in the belly of the Babylon-fish.

of analogy, but a certain communality of the human, as they pitch themselves against forces so much bigger than themselves. Both, it seems, are engaged in the search for salvation, the security, the safe and sound, which does not seem to lie in the direction of God – nor indeed, God's plot.

But to read the storm scene purely as a serious meditation on the collision between divine action and human counter-action is to leave a huge remainder of the comic under the desk. For like the chowder-like *Moby Dick*, shifting between its contemplation of 'whale-balls for breakfast' and its meditations on the abyss, the storm scene lurches between a lexis of fear and blood and perishing, and scenes of comic animation and in-jokes (playing on the language of the Hebrew language and the language of Hebrew tradition). When the sailors ask Jonah's occupation (his מלאכה, *melacah*, Jonah 1.8) the question is hardly psychologically plausible: surely the question is more appropriate to a dinner party than a sea-storm and does not cohere well with their reiterated 'fear'. But the incongruity does not matter, the conceptual problems are of little account – the phrase is there because it hides a joke and because Jonah's profession as prophet/ messenger (מלאך, *malak*, Jonah 1.8) is riddlingly half-concealed. Similarly, Jonah's confession that he fears the Lord 'who made the sea and the dry land' (1.9) features because it introduces comic dissonance: alleged 'reverence' jars with flight, and this is a comically apt choice from *select-a-creed*. The brief proclamation anticipates the literalising humour of the aqua-psalm and can also be read as an attempt to cajole God through flattery: 'Might the indisputable sea-God now choose to demonstrate his sovereignty over the *dry land*?'

Our author-cartoonist also shows a tendency to *animation* (compare the 'warrior worm' who 'smites' the plant in Jonah 4.7). The sea makes the metaphorical passage between the storming and the furious: in 1.11 and 1.12 the sailors and Jonah discuss how 'the sea will calm its raging against us' (וישתק הים מעלינו, *veyishtoq hayyam me'alenu*); and in 1.15, when the sailors reluctantly fling Jonah into the sea, the sea 'curbs its fury/or ceases from its raging'.[153] The journey is so regularly and unthinkingly made in English, metaphors like the 'raging sea' or 'storming anger' are so nearly dead and buried in their coffins that an English reader, reading in translation, can virtually miss it. But the suggestion is that the calm surface of the

---

[153] This is Sasson's translation (see Sasson, *Jonah*, p. 130).

water reflects an inner psychological state – as if the sea is pacified by Jonah, as if the sacrifice of Jonah eerily acts as a kind of tranquilliser on the sea's troubled brain.[154]

But the *pièce de résistance* in this chapter is 'the ship going to Tarshish' – the first prop plundered from the tradition store-cupboard. Ships going to Tarshish are well-known structures (cf. 1 Kings 22; 2 Chronicles 20.35–7; Psalm 48; Isaiah 23; Ezekiel 27), and also something of a banana-skin of tradition, for a 'ship going to Tarshish' roughly culturally translates as 'the Titanic going out on her maiden voyage'. The analogy maps almost exactly: ships going to Tarshish are proud noble structures, carrying precious cargoes, and they are generically programmed to be 'shattered' by the 'east wind', and to promptly 'sink into the heart of the sea'.[155] The 'ship of Tarshish' should be imagined as a familiar stage prop, built on a mechanism that ensures that it will inevitably tip over – for, as inexorably as icebergs and the Titanic in Thomas Hardy's poem 'The Meeting of the Twain', storm-clouds and ships of Tarshish are

---

[154] Phyllis Trible and Jack Sasson go further and argue that the phrase וַיָּטִלוּ אֶת-הַכֵּלִים אֲשֶׁר בָּאֳנִיָּה אֶל-הַיָּם לְהָקֵל מֵעֲלֵיהֶם in 1.5 can be interpreted as the sailors attempting to appease the sea, to lighten it (and not the ship) by throwing all their vessels towards it (see Trible, *Studies*, pp. 210–11, and Sasson, *Jonah*, p. 93). Though their conclusions are similar, their means of arriving at them are different: Sasson argues that the verb טול linked with the preposition אל rather than על signifies the motivation behind the casting rather than the direction (the sailors move their things towards/at/for the sea in order to appease it). Trible argues that since the infinitive לְהָקֵל has no object, and that the previous noun is the sea, the sailors are attempting to appease the sea.

[155] I am surprised that no commentators have drawn attention to this, although Sasson does observe, somewhat relatedly, that 'Tarshish is a place that in Scripture comes to symbolise goals doomed to fail' (Sasson, *Jonah*, p. 92). Certainly ships of Tarshish seem prone to wrecking: 1 Kings 22.48 (cf. 2 Chronicles 20.35–7) reports how 'Jehoshaphat made ships of Tarshish to go to Ophir for gold; but they did not go, for the ships were wrecked at Ezion-geber'; Psalm 48 praises the God who 'by the east wind did shatter the ships of Tarshish' (with an allusiveness that suggests that the tradition is well known);and Ezekiel 27.25–6 sings a dirge over the ships of Tarshish:

> So you were filled and heavily laden in the heart of the seas.
> Your rowers have brought you out into the high seas.
> The east wind has wrecked you
> in the heart of the seas.
> Your riches, your wares, your merchandise,
> your mariners and your pilots,
> your caulkers, your dealers in merchandise
> and all your men of war who are in you,
> with all your company that is in your midst
> sink into the heart of the seas on the day of your ruin.

A related text, Isaiah 23, does not mention wreckings, but exhorts the ships of Tarshish to 'wail' for their 'stronghold is laid waste' (Isaiah 23.1, 14).

simply, fatally, meant for each other. As Jonah's early audiences, like later ones, experience the knowing familiarity of the 'well-known things happen[ing]',[156] as they watch Jonah step from the proverbial frying pan into the proverbial fire, the comedy is compounded by animation and pun. The phrase 'the ship expected itself to crack up'[157] (הָאֳנִיָּה חִשְּׁבָה לְהִשָּׁבֵר, *ha-anyah hishvar lehishavair*, Jonah 1.4) blurs the lines between physical disintegration and psychological disintegration, between breaking up, and breaking down: so the ship, fearing her wrecking, becomes literally a nervous wreck.

The open thoroughfare between the literal and the metaphorical, the animate and the inanimate, suggests something of the porousness of the book of Jonah, the way in which 'words become other words, things become other things',[158] and a two-way thoroughfare opens up, in good magic-realist fashion, between the solid *terra firma* of reality and the 'most insecure and transitory of zones, illusory, discontinuous, metamorphic'.[159] *The Satanic Verses* opens with Saladin Chamcha and Gibreel Farishta falling from the solid world of a Boeing 747 then cartwheeling through the 'soft, imperceptible' metamorphic field of air-space to the all-too-real world of 1980s London; *One Hundred Years of Solitude* oscillates between the brittle gritty world of firing squads and colonels, and a world where children are born with tails and the sky rains yellow butterflies; and the *Pirke de Rabbi Eliezer* shifts between the above-ground world of the synagogue (of Alexandria?) and a fish with pearl lighting systems who takes the prophet on underwater mystery tours. The similarly lurching book of Jonah is anchored in tangible geographical landmarks (Tarshish, Nineveh – albeit a Nineveh long since reduced to rubble); it uses a real historical character (Jonah ben Ammitai) who inhabits a world that operates by normal laws of gravity, hydrodynamics, and economics (where if you throw cargo overboard ships become more buoyant (Jonah 1.5) and where passengers are obliged

---

[156] I'm referring back to Zbigniew Herbert's 'Jonah' (in D. Curzon (ed.), *Modern Poems on the Bible: An Anthology* (Philadelphia and Jerusalem: Jewish Publication Society, 1994), pp. 257–8) discussed in chapter 2, pp. 173–5.

[157] Jack Sasson's apt translation (Sasson, *Jonah*, p. 3) captures the joke that many other translations miss: compare John Calvin's astute observation that 'the expression corresponds with the idiom in our language, *la navire cuidoit perir* (J. Calvin, *Commentaries on the Twelve Minor Prophets* (trans. J. Owen; Edinburgh: Calvin Translation Society, 1847), III, p. 32). (Incidentally, the ships of Tarshish undergo similar, but less spectacular personification in Isaiah 23.1 where they are commanded to 'wail' in response to catastrophe.)

[158] Auster, *The Invention of Solitude*, p. 136.

[159] Rushdie, *The Satanic Verses*, p. 5.

to pay their fare (Jonah 1.3)) – but it is also prone to slip into an aqueous metaphoric world, where metaphors take to the hulls of ships. The sense of fluidity and changeability is echoed in the mutations and slippages of language – as the sound of *hashav* (חשב, to think or reckon) flows into the sound of *lehishavair* (להשבר, to be broken/wrecked, 1.4) or a whole stream of action gushes garrulously out of the word root 'to go down' (ירד, *yrd*). In 1.3 Jonah goes down (וירד, *vayayred*) to Joppa; in 1.5 he goes down (ירד, *yarad*) into the hold of the ship and 'goes into a deep sleep' (וירדם, *vayayradam*); in 1.6 the captain wakes him and asks 'What are you doing *sleeper* (נרדם, *nirdam*)?'; and in 1.16 the sailors 'vow vows' (וידרו נדרים, *vayyideru nedarim*). Words planted in this chapter spread out their tentacles to the rest of the book: the phrase 'the dry land' (היבשה, *ha-yabashah*) in 1.9 and 1.13 is repeated in 2.10 and echoed in the shrivelling (וייבש, *wayivash*) of the *qiqayon* plant (4.7); and the phrase 'innocent blood' (דם נקיא, *dam naqi*) in 1.14 is written in such a way as to anticipate the vomiting of Jonah in 2.10 (from the verb קיא, *qi*, to vomit),[160] which in turn is taken up in the linguistic tendrils of the *qiqayon* plant (Jonah 4.6). Clearly this is an environment where 'words are plastic material with which one can do all kinds of things'[161] and where the narrative is directed by the plasticity of the word.

The fish and the aqua-psalm: Jonah 1.17–2.10

'How are you getting along' (*wie geht's*) the blind man asked the lame man. 'As you see' the lame man replied to the blind man.[162]

Two things are stressed about the God of Jonah: he is an irresistible force and a master of strategic planning. In 1.4 he 'hurls' the wind: the emphasis is on his brute power as Sea and Storm God in contrast to, say, the carefully storing and planning sea-God of Psalm 135.5–7 who 'releases the wind from his stockpiles'. But in 1.17 the deity shifts from *Rambo*-God to God as careful administrator/strategic planner:

---

[160] The adjective 'innocent' נקי has been transmitted as נקיא which makes it look like a word based on the root קיא – to vomit (it can be read as 'let us vomit' or 'vomited'). The chain of linkage between the *qiqayon* and 1.14 and 2.11 is pointed out by Halpern and Friedman, 'Composition and Paranomasia', p. 86.

[161] S. Freud, *Jokes and Their Relation to the Unconscious* (trans. J. Strachey; Harmondsworth: Penguin, 1994), p. 68.

[162] *Ibid.*, p. 68.

unlike the divine sea-monster-tamer of Job who draws out Leviathan with a fish-hook, puts a rope through his nose, and pierces his jaw with a hook (Job 41.1–2), the God of Jonah 'appoints' his big fish in the first of four 'appointments'.[163] The strategic planning of God is picked up by Mainstream but particularly Backwater readers: in Julian Barnes's description of God as crazed admiral, steering his blubbery gaol across the sea-map; in Jack Sasson's Barnes-like observation that God is 'like a general marshalling his troops;[164] in the *Pirke de Rabbi Eliezer*'s image of the omniscient author who created and 'arranged' the fish during the first six days of creation; and in the *Gawain*-Poet's apostrophe to God as wit- (or plot-)wielder who always has 'tricks up his sleeve'. Cumulatively, the descriptions reinforce the image of omnipotent, omni-controlling divine monarch, using his 'complete operative power over the winds and water [and the fish] of the Eastern Mediterranean',[165] and pushing his armies across the text as if it were a strategy game board.

And so the big fish is finger-flipped onto stage, right on cue, and 'swallows' Jonah – only to vomit and regurgitate him in 2.10. Curiously this is one of only a few literal uses of the terms 'swallowing' and 'vomiting' in the Hebrew Bible:[166] more typically, 'swallowing' and 'vomiting' function as idioms for vacillations of power in the Ancient Near East, and participate in a whole idiomatic lexis devoted to survival, power, control, and loss of control. When Israel is victorious, Yhwh 'swallows' their enemies (Exodus 15.12) or 'vomits' them out of the land (Leviticus 18.25–7), and conversely, when the nation is oppressed it perceives itself as swallowed up like a fig/useless vessel (Isaiah 28.4; Hosea 8.7–8), or as vomited out of the

---

[163] He will go on to appoint the *qiqayon*, then a worm, and then a wind (Jonah 4.6, 7, 8). The cumulative repetition of the verb מנה (*mnh*, to appoint) emphasises Yhwh's strategic and effortless manipulation: 'And the Lord appointed a fish' (1.17); 'and the Lord appointed a plant' (4.6); 'and the Lord appointed a worm' (4.7); 'and the Lord appointed an east wind' (4.8).

[164] Sasson, *Jonah*, p. 157.

[165] J. Barnes, *A History of the World in Ten and a Half Chapters* (London: Picador, 1989), p. 177.

[166] Again I find that Sasson has beaten me to the observation: 'Curiously enough', he writes, 'there are rare scriptural examples in which the verb בלע (*bala*) "to swallow, gulp down" speaks of human or animal ingestion of food' (Sasson, *Jonah*, p. 151). Sasson goes on to suggest rather vaguely, but nevertheless provocatively, that the fact that 'swallowing' and 'vomiting' have such deep metaphoric resonances may suggest that '[Jonah] is striving for an imaginative, even metaphoric setting' (p. 152); or maybe, adjusting his comments slightly, that Jonah's psalm is digesting and evoking these metaphoric resonances in its own literal performance of them.

land into exile (Leviticus 18.25–7).[167] The idioms reach their fullest, juiciest expression in Jeremiah 51.34 where *the Babylonian exile is embodied as an ingesting and spewing sea-monster*:

> King Nebuchadnezzar of
> Babylon has devoured me,
> he has crushed me;
> he has made me an empty vessel,
> he has swallowed me like a sea-monster;
> he has filled his belly with my delicacies,
> he has spewed me out.

The Babylonian sea-monster sucks out all the rich resonances of the image: the big nation consuming the little nation, digesting and extracting Judah's rich juices, the big nation slurping up the defeated nation's goodness, fattening itself on it, then vomiting it back as a weaker, depleted, regurgitated version of its former self. This is a powerful image of being engulfed and processed as part of an alien body-system – an image that overlaps with another digestive biblical metaphor, the mouth and belly of Sheol, and Death's voracious appetite to digest.[168] Though the connection has been dismissed out of hand by the majority of scholars,[169] I suggest that memories of the

---

[167] The most extreme development of the image comes in the book of Lamentations, where the nation depicts itself as 'swallowed' by Yhwh himself, in an act of self-defeating ingestion (Lamentations 2.2, 5).

[168] For images of Sheol swallowing the individual (an image influenced by Canaanite mythology, in which the god *Mot*, Death, swallows the god Baal like an olive) see, for example Psalm 69.15. In Isaiah 5.13–14 the mouth of Sheol, and the image itself, opens wider to describe national disaster: 'Therefore my people go into exile for want of knowledge . . . Therefore Sheol has enlarged its appetite and opened its mouth beyond measure, and the nobility of Jerusalem and her multitude go down, her throng and he who exults in her.'

[169] The way in which the connection between the book of Jonah and Jeremiah 51.34 has been argued for and promptly dismissed by scholars demonstrates how scholarship runs in the groove of certain assumptions, particularly where the use of biblical tradition by biblical authors is concerned. In 1886, Charles H. Wright argued that Jeremiah 51.34 was the key text for understanding the book of Jonah, and that the book was, in fact, an allegory in which Jonah stood for Israel, the fish for Babylon/the exile, the booth for restored Jerusalem and Nineveh for Babylon (see C. H. Wright, 'The Book of Jonah', in Wright, *Biblical Essays* (Edinburgh: T. & T. Clark, 1886), pp. 34–98). As subsequent scholars dismissed the reading of the book as a complex allegory, the refutation of Wright's argument effectively removed Jeremiah 51.34 from the accepted canon of intertexts; scholars also maintained that Jonah could not be using Jeremiah 51.34 as there is considerable variation in vocabulary (the fish (דג, *dag*) in the book of Jonah is a sea-monster (תנין, *tannin*) in Jeremiah 51). Both Wright's assumption (that if Jeremiah 51 is being used, it must be being used in a point-by-point allegory), and the assumption of Wright's critics (that only direct quotation can be taken as proof of a text's incorporation) expose erroneous limiting assumptions in the study of an author's 'use' of other biblical traditions.

swallowing and regurgitating exile-fish lurk deep in the book of Jonah's belly – which is not the same as saying that Jonah is 'about' the exile in any simple sense.[170] This impression is reinforced by the line 'I am cast out from your presence/How shall I look again on your holy temple?' (Jonah 2.4) which juts out awkwardly, island-like, from the aquatic-comic surface of the psalm, and clearly suggests images of diaspora, of an Israel disorientated and displaced from its centre. Whereas popular Backwater productions of Jonah have obsessed on fear of the corrosion of the *individual* – of being chomped, slurped, gargled, being claustrophobically closeted, and tied up screaming in the captain's cabin – the biblical original, like Jewish tradition, is haunted more by *communal* concerns and by fears of the consumption and regurgitation of the nation. Appropriately, the elements of tradition imbibed by the book of Jonah seem to have something very much to do with mutability, transience, exile, and survival, with fear of being imbibed, being consumed, perishing, surviving, and being digested.

To those familiar with the Backwaters and Underbellies, what follows after 'the Lord appoints a fish to swallow up Jonah' (1.17) is bare, skeletal and, rather literally, dry. There are no carnivalesque descriptions of Jonah 'sucked in by slimy jaws as a living feast' and living among 'half-eaten fleets' and 'digested corpses, dissolved and putrid', no fantasies of him being flung into the fish's maw 'like a

---

The principles applied are distinctly like those applied to doctoral dissertations (references must be cited clearly, and quoted directly), and there is a limiting sense of quotation: the only kind of quotation/allusion permitted is the quotation of *words* and there is no sense of the quotation of *images*.

[170] Most scholars would probably agree with Peter Ackroyd that while the book is not an 'elaborate allegory of the exile . . . it is difficult to avoid the impression that the experience of the Jewish people in exile was in part responsible for that particular representation of their true place in the purpose of God which this little book sets out' (see P. R. Ackroyd, *Exile and Restoration: A Study in Hebrew Thought of the Sixth Century BC* (Philadelphia: Westminster Press, 1968), pp. 244–5). However, as the reference to a 'true place in the purpose of God', and the allusion to the 'Jewish people' suggest, the usual tendency is to give the influence of the exile a typically Mainstream nationalistic-universalistic gloss. My own view is that the book is awash with memories of exile in a different sense – as the ultimate image of vulnerability and decentring. I take the view of Danna Nolan Fewell and David Gunn that numerous biblical texts that do not explicitly cite the exile are nevertheless haunted and structured by it (see Gunn and Fewell, *Narrative in the Hebrew Bible*, p. 157) – as Fewell provocatively observes elsewhere: 'The transition that colours the whole of the Hebrew Scriptures is the Babylonian exile. It is presupposed. It is narrated. It is forecasted. It is remembered. It is re-enacted. It is the grief, the trauma, that Israel works through again and again' (D. Nolan Fewell, 'Imagination, Method and Murder: Un/Framing the Face of Post-Exilic Israel', in Beal and Gunn, *Reading Bibles, Writing Bodies*, pp. 132–52 (135)).

mote through a minster door', no bowdlerising images of death as a 'black-out in a fish and chip shop', no water-bed kidneys, no jokes about 'going colo-rectal', no yeasty liquor, no pot-holing intestinal tour, no dripping mucus, and none of the *Gawain*-poet's viscous jokes in which Jonah describes himself as the 'gaule of the prophetes' at precisely the point where he stands knee deep in 'reeking ooze' and fish-slime. The text seems to have been vacuum-pumped of all its fabulous accretions and we are left only with a psalm, a psalm that functions as Jonah's white handkerchief,[171] a psalm that reads as an absolutely conventional borrowing from the belly of the psalm corpus even as it offends the criterion of appropriateness on which biblical scholarship operates. The (proleptic/hopeful?) thanksgiving psalm ('I called to the Lord . . . and he answered me') is temporally out of kilter with a plot-line in which Jonah is still very much in distress, and it offends basic assumptions of cohesion between what biblical scholars call the text's *Gattung* (form/genre) and its *Sitz in Leben* (or 'setting in life').[172] Whereas a large body of scholarship has devoted itself to erecting appropriate and logically inferred structures around the Psalms, and to building a sense of the surrounding life, temple, cult, and worship of Israel, this psalm locates itself in a rather unusual setting-in-life (which threatens to tip into a situation-in-death) and locates itself, perversely, within the belly of the beast.

But the fish-stomach setting, combined with Jonah's opening allusion to the שאול בטן (*beten sheol*, 'the *belly* of sheol' (2.2)),[173] is the first clue that the psalm may be making its own comic, metaphor-ising-literalising pact between itself and its *Sitz in Leben*. In fact, far from erasing the cunning metaphorical plays of *Patience*, the book pre-empts, in its own Hebrew idiom, the *Gawain*-poet's carnivalesque play between hell and a belly that 'savours like hell' and 'stinks like

---

[171] Frolov, 'Returning the Ticket', p. 94.

[172] In Biblical Studies the analysis of generic units such as psalms in the context of their original setting is known as Form Criticism, and associated most famously in the case of psalms with the name of Sigmund Mowinckel. In the case of Jonah's maverick psalm the disjunction between text and context is often solved by refuge to the familiar thesis of later additions or secondary authorship. Thus Bewer notes that this 'cannot be the prayer which Jonah prayed, or which the author of the story would have put in Jonah's mouth . . . for it does not fit the situation', and Sandmel comments that while the prayer is 'beautiful' it is 'scarcely congruous' with the prophet's position in the fish's belly (J. A. Bewer, *Critical and Exegetical Commentary on Jonah* (International Critical Commentary; Edinburgh: T. & T. Clark, 1912), p. 21; S. Sandmel, *The Hebrew Scriptures* (New York: Alfred A. Knopf, 1963), p. 495).

[173] The fact that the metaphor the 'belly of Sheol' is found nowhere else in the Hebrew Bible strongly suggests that the use of the phrase here is quite deliberate.

the very devil'. Biblical lament psalmists typically position them-selves in the depths, in pitch darkness, deep down in the Pit (Psalm 130.1–2; 88; Lamentations 3.55): Jonah simply turns the metaphors into flesh – his Pit/Sheol comes with matching blubber and fins. As an ancient equivalent of *Northern Exposure's* comic clash between the language of science/fact/*Gray's Anatomy* and the language of myth, *the book of Jonah is already inaugurating the tradition of over-actualising the tradition, of taking it too literally, to comic effect,* and so invites future readers to go on crossing the boundaries between the nether-world and the nether-regions.

Nor on closer scrutiny is the psalm as *dry* as it looks, for, like blotting paper, this little piece of writing soaks up every possible synonym for water.[174] The image of the prophet cast into the 'heart of the seas', with the 'waves and breakers closing over him' and 'the deep' and the 'floods' sloshing round him (Jonah 2.3, 5), not only places Jonah among those other metaphorically drowning/sinking lament psalmists who typically find themselves engulfed by 'waters' that 'reach up to their necks' (Psalm 69.2), but makes his psalm the most concentratedly aquatic in the whole of the Hebrew Bible corpus.[175] The aqua-imagery of the book of Psalms comes from the myth-pool of the Ancient Near East where chaos is depicted as the sea or the sea-monster – but Jonah gives the tradition a uniquely de-mythologising twist.[176] If jokes, as Freud demonstrates, often derive from allowing 'watered down' words to regain their 'full' meaning,[177] Jonah's psalm works by *rehydrating* images of water. As the context dissolves the psalm in its own aqueous solution, it gently

---

[174] The way in which Jonah's psalm gushes with 'a veritable flood of water imagery' that flows as a tributary from the Psalm corpus has recently been observed by Miles, 'Laughing at the Bible: Jonah as Parody', in Radday and Brenner, *On Humour and the Comic in the Hebrew Bible*, p. 209. Though Miles does not allude to it, the point was made much earlier by A. van Hoonaker, *Les douze Petits Prophètes* (Paris: 1908), and alluded to by Feuillet, 'Les Sources du Livre de Jonas', p. 180.

[175] As Miles observes, 'water and pit imagery can be found in four of [Jonah's psalm's] seven verses. The most concentrated water and pit imagery of the Psalter (Psalms 69 and 84) is not nearly as concentrated as that' ('Laughing at the Bible', p. 209).

[176] One of the basic axioms of biblical scholarship is that the Hebrew Bible takes up and demythologises other Ancient Near Eastern traditions. So for example, Genesis 1 is remarkably similar in many respects to the Babylonian creation epic *Enuma Elish*, but at the same time it monotheises the Babylonian myth, by transforming God's battle with the Sea-God into Elohim's taming of the waters (Genesis 1.1–2) and reducing the Sun and Moon gods into mere objects of Elohim's creation. Jonah chapter 2, I suggest, gives demythologisation a comic twist. It is effectively de-demythologisation, de-metaphorisa-tion, that turns demythologised images back into water and into flesh.

[177] Freud, *Jokes and Their Relation to the Unconscious*, p. 68.

mocks the tradition: as the psalm opens the sluice gates to a torrent of fluid 'psalmisms', the joke is that *this* pseudo-psalmist really is in danger of drowning in an all-too-tangible flood of clichés, that he is enthusiastically inhabiting and living out the stock idioms of the psalm genre, and that he is proclaiming (as the water drips down from his forehead) the Hebrew idiomatic equivalent of 'I'm sunk' or 'I'm all at sea'. (A similar effect could have been achieved if the author had caused Jonah to, say, be beaten by rods, pursued by arrows or caught in a net, and had scripted him using different lament idioms from, say, Lamentations 1.13, 2.4, or 3.1.)

Imagine 'The Ancient Mariner' being read, gurglingly, from a fish-tank, and you come close to the Pythonesque spirit of Jonah's aqua-psalm. And for those who miss the excruciating over-cohesion between *Gattung* and *Sitz-in-See* or *Sitz-in-Belly*, the author adds an additional clue. As Herman Melville tips his Dutch Reformed hymn just over the brink of absurdity with the image of deity riding 'as on a dolphin borne', so the author makes underwater imagery stick to Jonah just a little too adhesively, as the prophet-psalmist complains that 'seaweed/kelp is wrapped around/clings to my head' (2.5).[178] The image of Jonah trying to extract himself from a cloying wrap of marine plants suggests that the book of Jonah not only begins the process of comic literalisation/carnivalisation by which it will continue to survive but also anticipates some of the distinctive strategies of that process. As the Backwater tradition extracts the slightly too concrete phenomena of entrails, a prophet squatting on a kidney, or a hymn-singing fish from the book of Jonah, so the book itself draws out a clump of seaweed from a pool of aquatic psalmisms. And if we read the scrambled line 'Those who pay regard to vain idols forsake their true loyalty' (2.8) as a deliberately ridiculous concatenation of psalm phrases, a joke at the expense of superior didactic psalmists, then the book of Jonah may *just* be anticipating one use for which the Backwaters will later conscript it: as a means of deflating what they perceive as the inflated piety of the biblical.

'Deliverance belongs to the Lord!' cries Jonah, appealing to the God who (according to his description) answers, hears, and brings the נֶפֶשׁ (*nefesh*)[179] up from the pit. And sure enough, God acts

---

[178] Compare Wellhausen's laconic observation that 'Die Ausmalung des Bildes . . . ist etwas weit getrieben' (J. Wellhausen, *Die Kleinen Propheten* (Berlin: Reiner, 1898), p. 221, cited in Miles, 'Laughing at the Bible', p. 209).

[179] The נֶפֶשׁ (*nefesh*) has nothing in common with the Platonic idea of the soul: it refers as

(almost) exactly according to the description of him, and lifts the prophet up out of the Sheol-fish. God's response shows an automaticity that anticipates Jonah 3.9–10, where the King of Nineveh speculates 'Who knows, God may repent and turn from his fierce anger?', and God (the divine monarch who is also curiously *subject* to human words and actions) 'repents' and 'turns' (3.9–10). But in Jonah's case deliverance comes with an unsavoury twist, a carnivalesque disjunction in which the language of praise collides with the language of being sick. Even when the prophet comes closest to extracting a predictable response from God, God's answer lacks that clean automaticity that it has in Jonah 3.9–10: Jonah is not 'delivered', nor 'cast out' as the Septuagint hygienically puts it, but regurgitated, 'vomited' or 'spewed'.[180] Jonah reaches his dry land, but only after he has been down to the depths of the sea, through a fish's belly, and emerged vomit-stained and skin-burnt – and somehow this seems typical where Jonah's experience of God is concerned.

Cattle in sackcloth and mis-hung backcloths – in Nineveh–Jerusalem: Jonah 3.1–10

In chapter 3 the plot rewinds and begins again: Jonah 3.1–3 is a comic re-performance, or re-deflection of 1.1–3. It is not simply that the word comes to Jonah again a second time (3.1), but that the words that surround that word are in a deflecting, distorting relationship to earlier narrative words. In Jonah 1.1–3 the word comes, Jonah ducks, and (in contrast to Jeremiah and Elijah) arises – to flee: in 3.1–3 the word comes, refuses to be deflected from its performative, dogged purpose, and hurtles on to Nineveh pulling Jonah in its wake. The joke lies in the way that the potential word-carrier shifts in his response through one-hundred-and-eighty degrees, and in

---

broadly as could be imagined to the blood, life, breath, self, the emotions/appetites and the very life of a human being, to the animating forces within the body.

180 An alternative way of interpreting the vomiting of Jonah is as an expression of the fish/God/the author's verdict on Jonah and his false piety: as the 'stand-up' critic Holbert quips, 'It is no wonder that immediately after Jonah shouts "Deliverance belongs to YHWH!" the big fish throws up' (J. C. Holbert, 'Deliverance Belongs to YHWH: Satire in the Book of Jonah', in *Journal for the Study of the Old Testament* 21 (1981), pp. 59–81 (74)). Personally I find such attempts suspicious as (1) they assume a trilogy of sympathy between God, the Author and the Reader, and (2) they resist the possibility that Hebrew tradition may itself be the object of parody by converting all the humour into satire and depositing it all, squarely, on Jonah's head.

speculating why the bedraggled, seaweed-draped, vomit-stained, and traumatised prophet might take a more passive attitude to the word of God this time, in the replay.

Following the word that came in on such a strange trajectory ('Arise and Go to Nineveh') takes Jonah, as perhaps he anticipated, to the most *unheimlich* of places. As they pursue the tug of this strange inaugural word, the narrator, Jonah, and the reader emerge in a strange inverted Wonderland where the city that typically runs with blood, oozes piety;[181] where the prophetic word that usually encounters resistance glides effortlessly as through a vacuum; and where, despite the fact that Jonah goes but one day's walk into the city and utters but a five-word oracle,[182] the city instantly erupts into repentance, in a spontaneous combustion effect. The three-days-'big' city of Nineveh makes it seem as if Jonah has taken 'Drink Me' potions, the sackcloth-wearing cattle are reminiscent of madly animated Mad Hatters and Mock Turtles; we are indeed in 'Wonderland', where everything is 'passing strange'.[183] But, just as Alice's down-the-rabbit-hole world is full of pools of tears, misrecognition, and babies that turn into pigs, as well as liquids that combine the comforting flavours of 'cherry-tart, custard, pine-apple, roast turkey, coffee and hot buttered toast',[184] 'Nineveh' is a place where the world is nonsensically – and discomfortingly – re-sorted, and is more of a wish-inversion than a wish-fulfilment place.

Chapter 3 is not only replaying, at a distance, the inaugural moment from its own story but is also busy replaying, at a distance, other traditional texts. While the peculiarity of a narrative about a snow-white Assyria[185] and a prophet whose mission is ludicrously

---

[181] Some commentators (for example R. E. Clements) argue that since the book of Jonah does not stress the role of the Ninevites as 'arch-enemies and oppressors of Israel', Nineveh must have a neutral signification (R. E. Clements, 'The Purpose of the Book of Jonah' (Congress Volume Edinburgh; *Vetus Testamentum Supplement* 28; Leiden: Brill, 1975), p. 18). But not only would the bloodiness of Assyria have been simply taken for granted, but the 'violence' (חמס, *hamas*) attributed to the Ninevites in 3.8 evokes the typical 'violence' (*hamas*) of the Assyrians (cf. Isaiah 10.13–14; Nahum 2.11–12, and especially 3.1; Joel 2.12–14).

[182] The brief oracle 'Yet forty days, and Nineveh shall be overthrown' (3.4) is even briefer in Hebrew and runs to only five words.

[183] Bewer, *Critical and Exegetical Commentary on Jonah*, p. 4.

[184] L. Carroll, *Alice's Adventures in Wonderland* (London: William Heinemann, 1977), p. 9.

[185] A good example of how awkwardly pious Nineveh sits alongside the rest of tradition is supplied by the apocryphal book of Tobit. Tobit, set in exile in 'Nineveh, the land of the Assyrians' (1.3) describes the Ninevites as superlatively evil: the Ninevite King Sennacherib, returning furious from the unsuccessful siege of Jerusalem and the decimation of his armies (see Isaiah 36–9) punishes the Israelites by putting them to death

easy can be exposed by a general sampling of biblical tradition, it is only when we look at strands from the book of Jeremiah that we see, specifically, how chapter 3 crafts itself from the known world of tradition deflected/alienated from itself. Even though the book of Jonah seems liberally peppered with allusions to Jeremiah, scholars have resisted pulling at the web of connections between the books because these would threaten to destabilise the critical metastory. Not only do links with Jeremiah the good prophet jeopardise the myth of Jonah the quintessentially bad prophet,[186] but the book of Jeremiah suggests that even the 'Proper Prophets' are not strangers to the theme of *the prophet at odds with or even destroyed by his God*. In the section of the book known as Jeremiah's 'Confessions', Jeremiah is presented as *deceived/seduced/raped* by the greater force of Yhwh (Jeremiah 20.7–8);[187] as protesting that his blood-and-thunder message of 'Violence and Destruction' has set him up as a 'laughing-stock' and a 'reproach' (20.8); as legitimately longing for Yhwh's vengeance (20.12); and as seeking his own death in Job-like speeches

and leaving their dead bodies outside the city walls. The story culminates in the 'overthrow' of Nineveh, which happens according to 'that which our prophet Jonah spoke against Nineveh' in one Greek edition of the text and according to 'God's word spoken against Nineveh by Nahum' in another (Tobit 14.4). The textual evidence suggests that the Jonah reading is the earliest, but was removed because the story of Jonah – with its supremely pious Ninevites – sits so uncomfortably alongside the corpse-desecrating Assyrians of Tobit, and so reinforces our sense that the pious Ninevites of Jonah are a radical anomaly within the canon. (For a more detailed discussion of the Tobit passage, see C. A. Moore, *Tobit: A New Translation with Introduction and Commentary* (The Anchor Bible; New York: Doubleday, 1996), p. 290.)

186 As if to underline the fact that readers can only admit the intertexts that support their reading, only two interpreters, with the exception of Sasson make much of the analogy between Jonah and Jeremiah's death-wishes and Jeremiah's passages of lament. Both C. A. Keller ('Jonas. Le portrait d'un prophète', see esp. pp. 338–40) and Serge Frolov ('Returning the Ticket', p. 91, n. 30) see the equation as significant, *because their broader reading framework sees Jonah as an empathetic figure*. Generally speaking, the reluctance to make the connection between Jonah and Jeremiah is symptomatic of a general reluctance among biblical scholars to explore passages of lament and protest against God. As long as Jonah's death-wish is seen as singular, as long as intertexts are denied, centripetal canonical forces are upheld as is the conviction that such protests are abnormal.

187 The controversial text reads:

> O Lord, you have enticed me, and I was enticed;
> You have overpowered me, and you have prevailed.

The translation at least partly brings out the often sexual connotations of the verb פתה (*pth*) that hover on the border of meaning between being deceived and being sexually seduced/enticed. In this context the overpowering of the prophet arguably has connotations of rape (see J. Crenshaw, 'Seduction and Rape: the Confessions of Jeremiah', in Crenshaw, *A Whirlpool of Torment: Israelite Traditions of God as an Oppressive Presence* (Philadelphia: Fortress, 1984), pp. 31–56).

that evoke the legendary memory of Sodom and Gomorrah ('Let that man be like the cities/which the Lord *overthrew* without pity'; 20.14–16) – a memory that also percolates beneath the surface of Jonah chapter 3.[188] Thus Jeremiah not only offers provocative analogies with the life of Jonah, but awkwardly (and certainly without the invitation of the critical community) introduces the image of the prophet abused by Yhwh, the prophet whose message militates against him – an image that we have already seen anticipated in the theme of the prophets' generic resistance to the divine commission and a theme that is echoed in other prophetic texts. If prophetic personae such as Jeremiah and Ezekiel are regularly presented as wronged, damaged, starved, humiliated, and overpowered by God's word, is Jonah, then, *really* such maverick text; is the prophet *really* such a criminal biblical element, a self-incriminating disturber of the Bible's pervasive peace?[189] Or is it more that Jonah's potentially self-annihilating journey to Nineveh (as the Talmud, Eagleton, and Rashi intimate) is an exaggerated narrative instance of the self-jeopardising conflict between the human prophet and the inexorably purposeful divine word?

Despite attempts to keep contact between Jonah and Jeremiah to a minimum, most commentators acknowledge that specific templates from the book of Jeremiah lurk behind and structure Jonah chapter 3. The chapter seems to be orientated around the divine principle laid down in Jeremiah 18.7–8 (the climax of the so-called 'Parable of

---

[188] Sasson finds the comparison between Jeremiah 20.14–18 and the book of Jonah 'tantalising'. For him, the way in which the Jeremiah text 'incongruously' attaches the motif of the 'destruction of cities' to 'the fate of an individual', and the way in which it echoes Jonah's vocabulary (the root עמל (to toil) is common to Jeremiah 20.18 and Jonah 4.10) makes it 'highly evocative of Jonah's problems' (Sasson, *Jonah*, p. 284).

[189] One of the most disturbing elements of the prophetic genre is the humiliation of the prophets, the way in which they lose all self-possession, and sacrifice their dignity in what the eleventh-century Jewish philosopher Maimonides called the execution of 'crazy actions'. As Jeremiah must offer a message that turns him into a 'laughing-stock', Ezekiel, the priest-prophet, is commanded to bake a symbolic cake over human excrement (an action against which he protests because this will 'defile' him, Ezekiel 4.14), and in his submission to the prophetic message he is struck by aphonia and paralysis and literally dragged back and forth by the hair (see J. Tarlin, 'Utopia and Pornography in Ezekiel: Violence, Hope and the Shattered Male Subject', in Beal and Gunn, *Reading Bibles, Writing Bodies*, pp. 175–83). The performance of the prophetic message is tied up with what Kristeva calls self-abjection and with limit experiences of the body against which the prophet protests. Not only does Jonah imitate this experience, in that he is called to pronounce a message that militates against his interests, but Jewish and early Christian projections of a bald Jonah, or a Jonah with acid-stripped and sunburnt skin, makes him more like the proper prophets yet.

the Potter'): 'At one moment I may declare concerning a nation or a kingdom that I will pluck up and break down and destroy it, but if that nation, concerning which I have spoken, turns from its evil, I will change my mind about the disaster that I intended to bring on it.' And the majority concur that Jonah chapter 3 is in some way dependent on Jeremiah 36. Jeremiah 36 tells how Jeremiah sent a written message to the King of Judah demanding repentance, in the hope that 'their plea [would] come before the Lord, and that all of them [would] turn from their evil ways' (Jeremiah 36.3),[190] but how, rather than 'rend[ing] his garments' (36.24), the King of Judah cut up the message with a knife and threw it into the fire. The narrative is yet one more explanation for the advent of the exile: the outcome is that God subsequently punishes Judah by bringing the Babylonians to cut off the 'human beings and animals' from their city, and to reduce the 'great city' (העיר הגדולה, *ha-ir ha-gedolah*) of Jerusalem to rubble (36.29). If Jeremiah 36 suggests some anxiety about the survival of text (and the dismemberment of what is, effectively, the ur-book of Jeremiah), the text re-appears in fragmented, sliced up form in the kaleidoscopically disorientated world of Jonah. Here an inverted Jeremiah (Jonah) takes a message of destruction to the 'great city' (העיר הגדולה, *ha-ir ha-gedolah*) that is *Nineveh*, and the King of Nineveh[191] responds instantly by ordering all the 'human beings and animals' to cover themselves in sackcloth. The king's decree – 'By the decree of the King and his nobles: No human being or animal, no herd or flock, shall taste anything. They shall not feed, nor shall they drink water' (Jonah 3.7) – puns on טעם (*ta'am*, decree) and טעם (*ta'am*, to taste) and the specific injunction not 'to feed/ graze' (רעה, *ra'ah*) deliberately trails and echoes the רעה (*ra'ah*, evil) that is passed on through the text. And as the king's script plays with the language of language so it plays with the language of memory: as the king hazards 'Who knows, God may . . . return from his fierce anger, so that we do not perish' (Jonah 3.9), and tells the people to

---

190 Compare God's thoughts in this chapter: 'It may be that when the house of Judah hears of all the disasters that I intend to do to them, all of them may turn from their evil ways, so that I may forgive their iniquity and their sin' (Jeremiah 36.3).

191 Several commentators have noted the anachronism/error in the phrase 'the King of Nineveh', for the Assyrians never had kings, and they have suggested that the error is due to the author's lack of knowledge, or his desire to highlight the unreality of the narrative. A further possibility (which surprisingly no one to my knowledge has suggested) is that the title 'king' is a deliberate attempt to link Nineveh to the hypothetical kingdoms of Jeremiah 18.7–8.

'turn from their evil ways and from the violence that is in their hands', he repeats the words of Jeremiah in Jeremiah 36.7 and the words of Yhwh in Jeremiah 18.7–8 almost verbatim.[192]

If we assume that we do not have to interpret the relation between Jonah and Jeremiah within an existing (and essentially supersessionist) economy of meaning, if we assume that we do not have to flatten out the web of connections to yet another version of the *useful* axiomatic showdown between the recalcitrant Judaeans and the exemplary gentiles, then we are left with a scrambled performance of Jeremiah 36 that, in its quirky dramatic quality, anticipates something of the strangely *contemporary* drama of Jonah chapter 4. Following the deviant word ('Arise Go to Nineveh') leads to further deflection, in fact to a radical inversion, and to a comic/disturbing mis-hanging of tradition. (I find it easiest to translate the inversion into the realm of performance, if I may for a moment be permitted to 'direct' the reading more explicitly.) As Jonah exits chapter 2 and enters chapter 3, the backcloth shifts from fish's stomach/hellish interior to the 'great city of Nineveh' – that is *the great city of Jerusalem hung upside down.* And he encounters a King of Nineveh who (of all people, and all places) is, uniquely for any foreigner in the Hebrew Bible, already in possession of, and familiar with, Scripture, and speaks the words of Jeremiah in perfect accentless Hebrew (imagine the Gestapo officers on a British Second World War film speaking noble speeches in a cut-glass BBC accent).[193] The fact that the King of Nineveh already possesses and quotes Scripture undermines any

---

[192] It is an indication of how democratically knowledge of 'Scripture' is spread around in this text that the sailors also seem to be familiar with the book of Jeremiah. As they plead with Yhwh not hold them responsible for Jonah's 'innocent blood' (1.14) they echo Jeremiah's warning that if the people of Judah kill him, they will be bringing 'innocent blood' upon themselves and their city (Jeremiah 26.15).

[193] Though I am rather uncomfortable with attempts to compare Nineveh to the Berlin of the Third Reich (as if the Holocaust could so easily be conscripted, by way of an analogy) the image of the inverted British War film seems to capture the spirit of the text. It is not unusual for foreigners to speak Hebrew in biblical narrative, since these narratives are not overly concerned with principles of realism, although texts like Isaiah 36.11 or Judges 12.6 do play with different accents and different languages. But somehow the fact that the King of Nineveh speaks perfect Hebrew seems so appropriate to his role as monarch of *Jerusalem Inverted,* and it seems significant that he is the only foreign monarch who knows and quotes Scripture. Another relevant text in this context is God's message to Ezekiel in Ezekiel 3.5–6: 'For you are not sent to a people of foreign speech and a hard language, but to the house of Israel – not to many peoples of foreign speech and a hard language, whose words you cannot understand. Surely, if I sent you to such, they would listen to you.' Jonah, we could say, is a *reductio ad absurdam* of God's optimistic view of any people but his own: the Ninevites listen and repent excessively, and all 'hard language' barriers are surmounted.

interpretation of Jonah as a book about missionising, or taking the Bible to the gentiles (since insofar as anyone 'has' 'the Bible' in the world of Jonah, everyone has it) and reinforces the pervasive atmosphere of the (literally) *unheimlich*, in which home and the 'bloody city' have changed places. If previous uses of traditional resources (the capsizing ship of Tarshish, the just-add-water psalm) have suggested something of the 'Am Dram', or farcical reappropriation of tradition, here we enter the realm of defamiliarising performance, analogous to the Brechtian 'A' or Alienation-Effect.[194]

As Brechtian theatre foregrounds the artificiality, even the impossibility, of events on the stage by overturning anticipated norms, so in Jonah chapter 3 the murderous Ninevites show a marked inclination towards piety. Because the narrative is clearly set in the protected environment of the once-upon-a-never-time, cushioned by the insulating wrap of comedy, the book of Jonah can become a safe forum for spinning a counter-wish-fulfilment narrative. It is not that the book of Jonah *explicitly* asks (like, say 2 Esdras, or Habakkuk) 'Are the deeds of Babylon [or Assyria] any better? Is that why it has gained dominion over Zion?' and 'Why do you make men like the fish of the sea, so that [the Babylonian aggressor] can hook them up . . . and keep on filling and emptying [his] net, and mercilessly slaying nations for ever?' (2 Esdras 3.28; Habakkuk 1.14–17), but that a certain anxiety expresses itself in the skewed fortunes of Jonah and the Ninevites. As we enter the 'what if' environment of Nineveh–Jerusalem, it seems that the Ninevites act as the absolute antithesis of Jonah, even as the sailors function as his counter-image.

Indeed, it is virtually impossible to read Jonah chapter 3 without being struck by a sense of exaggerated disparity between Jonah's (that is Israelite/Judaean) victimisation and the enemy's good fortune and strength. Everything, it seems, goes extremely well for the Ninevites and God and life seem to be under their control. Though the king says 'Who knows (מִי יוֹדֵעַ, *mi yodaya*) God may repent and turn from his fierce anger?' (3.9), his tentative words contrast with the automaticity of God's reaction: the Ninevites turn from their evil and God turns from his, as if Nineveh and God are connected cogs in a wheel. Jonah, in contrast, finds himself in a

---

[194] For a discussion of the Brechtian *Verfremdungsaffekt* (Alienation Effect) and the way in which it is designed to bring audiences out of their 'torpor', see J. Willett, *The Theatre of Bertolt Brecht: A Study From Eight Aspects* (London: Eyre Methuen, 1977).

narrative where progression is anything but automatic, where familiar texts and scenarios appear in the most *unheimlich* of situations, and where God throws monkey-wrenches into expected generic mechanisms. The relative security/insecurity of the Ninevites/Jonah is reflected in their relationship to language and to tradition: whereas the Ninevites seem to inhabit Scripture and to be the recipients of its more simple, straightforward promises, Jonah finds himself in a distorted version of the prophetic commission, and plays the part of disaffected Jeremiah in a strangely inverted form of Jeremiah 36. And whereas the Ninevites find their 'who knowses' and their 'perhapses' fulfilled in the best of possible senses, Jonah finds himself becoming the pawn of divine omnipotence and what can only be called divine 'omnisemantics'. The image of Jonah trapped in the cleverly rigged divine word הפך (*hafak*, to overthrow) seems iconic of his confusion, and his alienation from his own pronouncement reflects his alienation from his plot. As Jonah carries the word to Nineveh, only to find that it is what Lewis Carroll termed a 'portmanteau' word, a word packed with two meanings, so הפך also simultaneously disorientates the reader and destabilises an obvious, automatic rendering of the text. Since הפך is inextricably tangled up with the legendary memory of the destruction of Sodom and Gomorrah, and since in that narrative God stands unequivocally for sulphurous *justice*, we find ourselves landed with an awkward remainder that complicates any simple assertion that God saves Ninevites because God is always merciful.[195] As Jonah, interpreting הפך, is forced away from dictionary entry **1. to destroy, to overturn** to the minor entry 2. to turn around, so the reader is

---

[195] Genesis 19, the spectacular destruction of Sodom and Gomorrah in a cloud of fire and sulphur, is preceded by a strange bartering passage between God and Abraham. Here Abraham, as mercy advocate, tries to beat God down from uncompromising justice ('Will you destroy the cities if there are fifty righteous people in them, if there are forty-five, if there are forty, if there are thirty, if there are twenty, if there are ten . . .?'). At least as one Jewish midrash reads it, the text is about Abraham warning God that he 'cannot hold the rope at both ends': that he cannot have an enduring world and practise absolute justice (so the *Pesikta de Rav Kahana* 19.3). The quasi-economic exchange, where God argues for absolute justice against the big city despite a righteous remainder, is an intriguing text to read alongside his proclamation in Jonah 4.10–11 that he spared Nineveh because of the hundred and twenty thousand unknowing (rather than innocent/righteous) people in it, and the God of absolute justice contrasts tellingly with the God of (numerically motivated?) mercy. (For an indication of how inextricably the word 'overthrow' (הפך, *hafak*) and the narrative of Sodom and Gomorrah are connected in 'biblical' tradition, see Amos 4.11 ('I overthrew some of you, as when I overthrew Sodom and Gomorrah') and Jeremiah 20.16 ('Let that man be like the cities/That the Lord overthrew without relenting').)

forced towards the complication and division of meaning, and away from a predictable automaticity of response.

And so chapter 3 prepares us for the awkward surpluses and disequilibria that haunt the final chapter, but at the same time blurs the line between the Absurd and the absurd. Despite protestations to the contrary,[196] the cattle in sackcloth 'crying mightily to God' are as alien to *Israelite* tradition as pious and exemplary Ninevites, and function as a clue for the hard-of-laughing, as chapter 3's equivalent of chapter 2's cloying seaweed. Crucially, the Assyrians are neither heroes of a new gentile-based dispensation, nor the blood-curdling roaring lions of the book of Nahum – they are comic figures who participate in an overacted drama of repentance, and who in 4.11 will be described by God as 'not knowing their right hand from their left' (or, translating loosely into a more modern idiom, their 'arse from their elbow').[197] Rather than sending chariots cracking through the streets of Nineveh as in the book of Nahum, or releasing wild beasts to scavenge through its ruins as in Zephaniah, the book of Jonah punctures the Assyrians with comedy, in a just-add-sack-cloth performance of repentance that is as funny as the just-add-water approach to the psalm. Even as it inflates the enemy it parodically deflates the enemy: there is something extremely therapeutic about the image of sackcloth-swathed Assyrians, fasting, and getting down on their knees before the Judaean God.

---

[196] A common way of legitimating the sackcloth-wearing cattle is to appeal to 'similar' Persian customs reported by Herodotus: James D. Smart asserts, learnedly, that the Persians gave animals a part in mourning, and the schoolmasterly Bewer attributes the phrase to a copyist's error *and* argues for perfectly normal Persian ritual (see Smart, 'The Book of Jonah', p. 890; Bewer, *Critical and Exegetical Commentary on Jonah*, pp. 54–5). But like quizzical pupils questioning their elders' application of the classics, John Miles points out that Herodotus, Book I, 140 only speaks of exposing the dead to cows and dogs, and John Day points out that IX, 24 only speaks of the Persians cutting the manes of their horses and mules as a sign of mourning (see Miles, 'Laughing at the Bible', p. 211; and Day, 'Problems in the Interpretation of the Book of Jonah', p. 34). The crucial points are surely that animals being used in mourning are a long way from animals actively participating in repentance, and that – even if such customs did exist – they are totally alien to Israelite tradition and culture. An ancient Judaean audience, I suggest, would have looked on the fasting cattle with the same distance that we look on the medieval practice of trying animals in court, and would have seen the personification of the cattle as just another comic addition to the raging sea, the shivering ship and the human *qiqayon* plant who/that is literally the 'son of a night' (בֶּן לַיְלָה, *ben lilah*, Jonah 4.10).

[197] The phrase, which hardly seems complimentary, is understood by past and (some present) commentators to refer to a specific Ninevite sub-group, such as children or the mentally deficient (see Sasson, *Jonah*, pp. 314–15). My own suspicion is that carnival-like, the spectacle trivialises the object of fear through parody – infantalising and diminishing the loathsome Ninevites.

Awkward surpluses, sediments, and residues: Jonah 4.1–11

Backwater and Mainstream readers concur on one point: that the strangeness that percolates through the book of Jonah spills over in chapter 4. Popular contemporary interpreters tend to reanimate the book precisely by wiring it up to anti-stories and to a very contemporary sense that 'telling stories [or at least tidy stories] has become strictly impossible'.[198] These days, the stories of Franz Kafka and Alain Robbe-Grillet seem 'credible and pertinent to us because their universe, like our own, is at variance with a rational, Positivist model', and we warm to the plays of Beckett because they are determined by forces we call Absurd.[199] In this climate, the ever-adaptable book of Jonah, and particularly the fourth chapter, is undergoing something of renaissance, not just because it ends with a question mark and that most cherished of postmodern tropes – the lacuna, or white space – but because it does not resolve the narrative so much as dissolve the narrative.

Similar readings of the fourth chapter are intimated by the Mainstream, albeit with rather less relish and hefty doses of apologetic. Scholars betray their concern – and propose some antidotes to strangeness – in articles with titles such as 'To Question an End, to End a Question',[200] and 'Did God play a Dirty Trick on Jonah at the End?'[201] Phyllis Trible diagnoses the final verses of the text as suffering from 'symmetrophobia',[202] and, as he/she enters the disordered territory of chapter 4, Jack Sasson takes the interpreter aside and warns her that the text is prone to get 'whimsical and

---

[198] A. Robbe-Grillet, 'On Several Obsolete Notions', in J. Hersey, *The Writer's Craft* (New York: Alfred A. Knopf, 1974), p. 97. Similar quotations can easily be stockpiled, suggesting that the demise of fiction or proper story represents something of a contemporary *Zeitgeist*: cf. Rilke, 'Telling Stories, really telling stories, must have happened well before my time' (*Die Aufzeichnungen des Malter Laurids Brigge* (Leipzig: Insel Verlag, 1927), vol. II, p. 23; cited in and trans. Roemer, *Telling Stories*, p. 438); Andy Warhol to his scriptwriters: 'Get rid of plot' (cited in J. Stein and G. Plimpton, *Edie: An American Biography* (New York: Alfred A. Knopf, 1982), p. 234); Donald Barthelme, 'Fragments are the only form I trust' (cited without attribution in T. Tanner, *City of Words* (New York: Harper and Row, 1971), p. 400); J. Derrida, 'I have never known how to tell a story' (*Memoirs, for Paul de Man* (trans. C. Lindsay *et al.*; New York: Columbia University Press, 1986), p. 3). For these quotations, and a discussion of how the chattering classes take the demise of fiction as read, see Roemer, *Telling Stories*, p. 179–83.

[199] Roemer, *Telling Stories*, pp. 182–3.

[200] Crouch's 'To Question an End' is subtitled 'Opening the Closure of the Book of Jonah'.

[201] D. N. Freedman, 'Did God play a Dirty Trick on Jonah at the End?', *Bible Review* 6 (1990), p. 31.

[202] Trible, *Rhetorical Criticism*, p. 117; Magonet, *Form and Meaning*.

indulgent' and 'less frontal' at this point.[203] Reinforcing the Rubik's Cube or Mensa puzzle image, Gerda Elata-Alster and Rachel Salmon describe the chapter as thematically 'odd', 'temporally inconsistent', and terminating in an interminably rotatable logical aporia;[204] and Alan Cooper feels that the ending is more a 'deconstruction and re-mystification'[205] than a resolution of what has gone before. The chapter, strangely, houses structures that seem superfluous (the hut in Jonah 4.5 that seems absolutely surplus to requirements) and that are prone to disintegration (the *qiqayon* that grows and withers in one day). It also contains elements that bring about its own destructuring, crumbling, or destructuration, and that cause interpretations to shoot up, and wither, where they lie.

As it generates surpluses, sediments, residues, and poses problems of moral/rational calculation for itself, chapter 4 demonstrates why it is so difficult to bring the book of Jonah to *account*. At a basic level, the chapter itself is a complicating remainder that prevents us from generically docketing the narrative as a simple story of 'mission set – mission resisted – mission accomplished' (at the very least the chapter shows that when it comes to a conclusion/settlement at the end of chapter 3, the book is not as sorted or as settled as it likes to think it is, and that whatever the book of Jonah means, it does not mean the same as if it came to rest at 3.10). And, as if to make the meaning of the text additionally difficult to calculate, it throws in the additional surpluses of Jonah's twice repeated death-wishes, and God's (to say the least) bizarre speech of explanation in response to the over-elaborate and seemingly vindictive plant-worm-sun *mashal*. The problem with God's summary is itself mathematical: when asked to account for his forgiveness of Nineveh, Yhwh shuns the expected explanation ('I saved the Ninevites because I love them') for:

You pity/have need of the plant, for which you did not labour, nor did you make it grow, which came into being in a night and perished in a night. And should I not pity/have need of Nineveh, that great city, in which there are more than a hundred and twenty thousand persons who do not know their right hand from their left, and also much cattle [or as Sasson translates, 'animals galore']? (Jonah 4.10–11)

---

[203] Sasson, *Jonah*, p. 268.
[204] G. Elata-Alster and R. Salmon, 'The Deconstruction of Genre in the Book of Jonah: Towards a Theological Discourse', *Journal of Literature and Theology* 3 (1989), pp. 40–60.
[205] A. Cooper, 'In Praise of Divine Caprice', p. 153.

In short, God's argument would add up if it were not about adding up, if it did not seem to rely so much on body-counts – one hundred and twenty thousand people and considerable livestock holdings. It would work so much better if it did not conjure up the troubling spectre of divine auditor, or creator-as-stock-manager, for whom size seems to matter where (pragmatic) issues of destroying and reconstructing big cities are concerned.

God's declaration – relying as it does on principles of labour and economy and the consequent ill-advisedness of 'destroy[ing] suddenly and quickly what was fashioned at God's command'[206] – suggests that he is more concerned with 'saving' in the sense of conserving resources, than with saving as salvation, and is hard to square with the more comforting image of the one-sheep-hunting, calculation-discounting New Testament 'Good Shepherd'.[207] But even if, by some deft word and number jiggling, we manage to construct some kind of *proof* that the statement is equivalent to, or at least approximates, a declaration that 'I, God, am always merciful', this in turn becomes an awkward surplus, since Jonah has already shown that he *knows* that God is 'always merciful, and repents of evil' (Jonah 4.2)). The fact that Jonah already knows about principles of mercy and is questioning them, like a quizzical theology student (see Jonah 4.2), means that the abstract principle of mercy breaks down. The awkward surplus of Jonah's counter-creed stymies any attempts to read the book as a simple mercy-touting parable.

As chapter 4 leaves us with a whole herd of cattle and the problem of how to process them into some kind of impressively 'beefy' interpretation, it foregrounds its own excessive surplus over and beyond any reasonable economics of meaning. The garrulous chapter flies in the face of conventional definitions of biblical narrative as terse and dealing out information on a need-to-know basis,[208] and leaves anyone who wishes to attempt to sort it out to sift through a great deal of 'baroque'[209] and seemingly superfluous

---

[206] Cf. 2 Esdras 8.14.

[207] See Matthew 18.1–14 ; Luke 15.1–7. Again I am reminded of Sasson's observation that God's attitude is 'barely contemptuous' towards the Ninevites that he 'saves' (Sasson, *Jonah*, p. 25).

[208] The point was famously made by Eric Auerbach in his comparison of biblical and Homeric narrative in 'Odysseus's Scar' (see E. Auerbach, *Mimesis: The Representation of Reality in Western Literature* (trans. W. Trask; Princeton: Princeton University Press, 1953), pp. 3–23).

[209] Halpern and Friedman, 'Composition and Paranomasia', p. 80.

clutter. There are the two sources of shade (one shade too many), a *qiqayon* plant (why a *qiqayon*?), an early-rising worm (is the time of his rising *significant*?), and an east wind (why not a west wind – indeed why a wind at all, since Yhwh can easily achieve the desired heating effect by applying a little sun?). When Wolf Mankowitz's Jonah looks out on a stage cluttered with a strange array of props and asks 'What's the point of all this expensive business with trees, and worms and so on?', he has a point – the answer to which is, at least partially, 'pun'.

For, more than any other chapter, chapter 4 is governed by a sense of the living body of language, of words as 'cells and sinews, corpuscles and bones, digits and fluids'[210] that, with a little coercion, fuse, form mergers, and even 'join opposite and contrasting aspects of the world with each other'.[211] Several of the text's features are generated by a 'riff' on the root קדם (*qdm*): in Jonah 4.5 Jonah sits 'to the east' (מקדם, *miqedem*) of the city to be assaulted by the 'east wind' (רוח קדים, *ruach qadim*, Jonah 4.8), and in 4.2. the author stretches the word to the outside limits of plasticity as Jonah explains why he 'fled pre-emptively' or 'fled in the beginning' (קדמתי לברח, *qidammti livroah*).[212] Jonah 4.1 and 4.9 pun on the double meaning of חרה (*ḥrh*) as 'to be angry/'to be hot': as God turns up the heat on Jonah, Jonah becomes hot/angry or, as Kenneth Craig appropriately translates, 'inflamed'.[213] The *qiqayon* plant is similarly bound up with, and undone by, pun: conceivably it is put there not because the author wants to tantalise would-be scholar botanists with whether it is a castor-bean plant or a *ricinus communis*, but because a *qiqayon* can weave its tendrils back to the verb קיא (*qi*, to vomit) in Jonah 2.10, and so can sound potentially like 'the vomiting of Jonah',[214] and can also resonate with the phrase 'innocent blood' (דם נקיא, *dam naqi*) in 1.14.[215] Jonah 4.6 explains the purpose of the *qiqayon* with a play on להציל (*lehatzil*) which means both 'to rescue' and 'to provide

210 Auster, *The Invention of Solitude*, p. 160.
211 *Ibid.*, p. 160.
212 The phrase is about as awkward in Hebrew as in the translation 'This is why I fled pre-emptively', because the verb קדם (*qdm*) needs to be stretched to its outer limits to mean something like 'pre-emptively' or 'in the beginning'. (Or as Halpern and Friedman put it, with apologetic mildness, 'Here the author reaches a bit' (Halpern and Friedman, 'Composition and Paranomasia', p. 83).)
213 See Craig, *A Poetics of Jonah*, p. 17.
214 Halpern and Friedman, 'Composition and Paranomasia', p. 86.
215 To reinforce the link with the verb קיא (*qi*) the adjective 'innocent' נקי (*naqi*) has been transmitted as נקיא (still pronounced *naqi*) which can be read as 'let us vomit' or 'vomited'.

shade'[216] (thus Jonah is to be 'shaded-saved'),[217] and Jonah 4.7
ensures that the fate of the *qiqayon* is similarly subject to language,
for its demise is bound up with the nibbling activities of the superbly
rhyming 'worm at the going up of the dawn' (תולעת בעלות השחר,
tola'at ba'alot hashakar) – a phrase that rolls round on the tongue as
liltingly as the ship-cracking האניה חשבה להשבר (*ha-anyah hishvar le
hishavair*, Jonah 1.4). If earlier chapters have raised the question of the
generative allure of language, chapter 4 seems to confirm the directive
power of the word. (I strongly suspect that if 'baboon at the rising of
the moon' rather than 'worm at the going up of the dawn' worked in
Hebrew, the *qiqayon* would have suffered a rather different fate.[218])

So chapter 4 is a linguistic *tour de force* that manages, in just eleven
verses, to fuse 'shade' and 'salvation', 'heat' and 'anger', 'east winds'
and shelters to the 'east', and 'pre-emptive' fleeing, and to echo 'the
vomiting of Jonah' in the *qiqayon* plant. But when words turn, or
slide, they take sense, characters, and moral structures with them,
and the satisfaction of wordplay can lead to the associated demoli-
tion of sense. The spirit of paranomasia in this chapter is like a
poltergeist strewing objects around the stage, generating an excess of
props over meaning, and leaving God in the awkward position of
making a meaning from those objects.[219] And though Yhwh does
the best he can with the resources at his disposal, ultimately the
ending, and the character of God, suffer from the ultimate impossibility of the task. Though God's answer is appropriately punning,
though it uses the root חוס (*hus*) 'to have pity on'/'to have need
for'[220] to link his feelings for Nineveh with Jonah's feelings for a
qiqayon plant, it also performs the conceptual inadequacy of pun, in
that חוס (*hus*) is simply not enough to span the abyss between a *qal*

---

[216] The pun is brought out in the specifications of the *qiqayon*'s function in 4.6 – 'to be a shade
for his head and to rescue him' (ראשו להציל לו - להיות צל על, *lihyot tzail al rosho lehatzil lo*).

[217] Elata-Alster and Salmon, 'The Deconstruction of Genre', p. 55.

[218] Although I concede, reluctantly, that Ancient Hebrew writers did not, on the whole, have
much access to baboons.

[219] Again the problem of agency rears its head. Many commentators agree that there is
something baroque, ill-shaped, even absurd about the plot: the question is, where the
responsibility for that absurdity lies. The story can be told in several ways: with the
director of the plot as *the author* (deliberately shrinking the God character, and making a
point about the absurdity of life); as *God* (demonstrating his 'capricious' and absolute
power to do and say whatever he pleases); or as *language*, assiduously following the logic of
sound, pulling against the logic of sense, and forcing the deity (like the reader) to make
meaning from the objects that linguistic ingenuity has supplied.

[220] Cf. the discussion of Abravanel, Wiesel and Gunn and Fewell's solutions to Yhwh's *qal ve
homer* in chapter 2, pp. 127–8.

that is very, very little and a *homer* that is very, very large. The ending leaves us with a lack of a satisfactory sum(mation), and with a divine quipper/punster who is only the flippant, shrunken shadow of his former Sea and Storm God self.

As well as the surpluses generated by the agency of pun, chapter 4 abounds in surpluses that are seemingly *invested* with meaning and that tend to set the narrative at odds with itself. The first and most significant of these surpluses is the surplus of Jonah's 'voice', which includes Jonah's silence and the [pointed?] absence of Jonah 4.12. Though Yhwh is all-controlling, his perspective is not the all-devouring consciousness that we might expect it to be (he holds the physical aces, but not the *conversational* aces),[221] and though Jonah is swallowed and finger-flipped, his voice is not 'swallowed up or dissolved'.[222] Yhwh has the power to take Jonah to Nineveh but he can't make him concede; he can make sure his word reaches its target, but he can't make Jonah swallow it.

At the very heart of the book of Jonah's reputation as a strange interloper in the biblical is the *equity* and *legitimacy* given to Jonah's voice. Jonah's words and Yhwh's words are split with mathematical precision: in a pedantic commitment to dialogism they get absolutely equal air-time, and thirty-nine words, or pieces, each.[223] The equal distribution of words in chapter 4 is far more reminiscent of the Wisdom books (particularly Job and Qoheleth) than the monologic weighting towards divine speech in the Prophets. In the Wisdom tradition, debating partners set out their words strategically, like siege barriers, or pieces on a chess-board – 'Set your words in order before me; take your stand', says Elihu to Job (Job 33.5; cf. Job 16.4) – and, as they set out their words, God and Jonah suddenly seem more like fellow-disputants (or yeshiva partners), than (gigantic) God and (baby) man, and the text that at first looked like a strategy game for one begins to change to something more like a chess board.

A strong monologic/satiric vein runs through the Hebrew Bible: it

---

[221] Julian Barnes's complaint that God holds all the cards and all the aces and trumps (Barnes, *A History of the World*, p. 176) only applies to God's physical strength.

[222] From Bakhtin's definition of the 'monologic' and the 'dialogic', in P. Morris, *The Bakhtin Reader: Selected Writings of Bakhtin, Medvedev and Voloshinov* (London: Edward Arnold, 1994), p. 93.

[223] This notable symmetry was pointed out by Keller, 'Jonas: Le portrait d'un prophète', pp. 329–40. I find this (pedantic?) balancing act intriguing, despite the fact that I am usually of the opinion that the last thing you should do with words is count them, and that rather too much word-counting goes on in Biblical Studies.

teems with a veritable *Vanity Fair* of denigrated rival gods and rival kings – with 'Pharaoh Big Noise', 'Lord Delusion', the 'Lord of the Flies', and with a panoply of caricatured opponents of Yhwh who 'speak' only in a clichéd pseudo-voice.[224] The harlot-nation in the book of Hosea lisps 'I will go after my lovers' and condemns herself from her own lips (Hosea 2.5, 11); the snarling Proverbial fools and evil men snarl 'Let us lie in wait for blood . . . and wantonly ambush the innocent' (Proverbs 2.11); and the idol-makers in Second Isaiah clownishly fall down before blocks of wood and cry 'Deliver me, for you are my God' (Isaiah 44.17). Although Hebrew narrative often has what Robert Alter terms a 'paradoxical double focus', whereby on one level of causality 'God directs, history complies; a person sins, a person suffers; Israel backslides, Israel falls', but on another level protagonists are 'rendered in ways that destabilise any monolithic systems of causation',[225] the divine voice and the divine plot ultimately prevail. Moreover, characters who find themselves in seemingly self-annihilating narratives rarely articulate any unease with (let alone dissension from) the divine plot: with a silence that trembles through centuries of interpretative history, Abraham and Isaac pass in haunting wordlessness through the narrative of Isaac's sacrifice (Genesis 22), voicing nothing apart from the occasional, compliant 'Here I am.'

Given this overwhelmingly monologic context, it is surely significant that Jonah, manifest opponent of Yhwh, is *not* scripted with robotic lines such as 'Do not save the Ninevites, because I hate them', and 'God belongs to the Hebrews alone', and that his voice is by no means a polemical extension of the divine voice of the text. It is significant that (unlike that of the harlot-nation or the Proverbial fool) Jonah's position can be given a number of cogent glosses,[226]

---

[224] So T. Jemielity, *Satire and the Hebrew Prophets* (Louisville: Westminster/John Knox Press, 1992), p. 102: 'Like a canvas by Bosch or Brueghel, the prophets' portrait of Israel teems with an obscene disfigured mob: Pharaoh Big Noise, Lord Delusion, Lord Useless – those leering down approvingly on the *Vanity Fair* of Jerusalem, the street walker, the sexually alert stallions whinnying for their neighbour's wives.'

[225] Alter, *The Art of Biblical Narrative*, pp. 125–6.

[226] To give just a few examples, Levine sees Jonah as representing the position that, under certain circumstances 'forgiving the guilty is identical to punishing the innocent' (Levine, 'Jonah as a Philosophical Book', p. 243); Frolov sees Jonah as questioning the principle of salvation of the wicked at the expense of the righteous ('Returning the Ticket', pp. 98–104); the Talmud, Abravanel, and Terry Eagleton, albeit in different ways, see him as raising the problem of self-erasure, or the uselessness of a self-invalidating message; and, even though he ultimately gives the prophet a good ticking-off, Terence Fretheim sees Jonah as raising the question of whether God's compassionate actions are just (T. E.

suggesting that Jonah is more Dostoevskyian 'idea-hero' than a cardboard cut-out figure or straw-man. Indeed, rather than parodying Jonah's 'voice' in mock quotation marks, the text seems rather to dwarf, weaken or relativise the booming, all-subsuming, all-dwarfing voice of God – as if to counteract the default reader–deity alliance. So when God asks, with the air of a 'mellow Rogerian therapist',[227] 'Do you do well to be angry/inflamed?' and 'Do you do well to be angry/inflamed for the plant?' (Jonah 4.4 and 4.9), the association of anger with the root 'to be hot', combined with the fact that God has just turned the heat of the sun up over Jonah, threatens to tip the rhetorical question over into a real question and to legitimate the answer 'yes'. Conversely, chapter 4 compounds the sense of Jonah's suffering and victimisation relative to the sanguine fortunes of the Ninevites, and makes the reader uncomfortably aware of the way in which the narrative (which Jonah has never been comfortable with, and has constantly tried to escape) now makes inroads into the prophet's body and the prophet's mind. Just as he emphasised the trauma of the sailors, so the narrator seems to make a 'point' of Jonah's physical and mental anguish – his depression/distress in Jonah 4.1, and his fainting/convulsing/incapacitation under the heat of the sun in 4.8 (as Sasson comments, it is hard not to feel sympathy for 'poor Jonah' as 'the sun fries his head').[228] And whereas an earlier Jonah 'rose – and fled' in comic subversion of expectation, or sought (rather entertainingly) to dive off the bottom of the page, now we are faced with the spectacle of a protagonist who seems seriously damaged by his narrative and who *twice asks for respite from the narrative through death* (Jonah 4.3, 8). The impression that something has gone badly wrong – at least from Jonah's perspective – is reflected in the prophet's misuse of traditional texts. Whereas the 'aqua-psalm' is a playful case of comic literalisation, and is surprisingly conventional in its sentiments, Jonah's anti-prayer 'Now take my life/soul/essence from me' (Jonah 4.4) flies (blasphemously) in the face of biblical pray-ers' constant pleas for longevity, health, many sons in the quiver of one's loins,

---

Fretheim, 'Jonah and Theodicy', *Zeitschrift für die alttestamentliche Wissenschaft* 90, pp. 227–37 (227, 234)).

[227] P. Hampl, 'In the Belly of the Whale', in C. Büchmann and C. Spiegel (eds.), *Out of the Garden: Women Writers on the Bible* (New York: Ballantine, 1995), pp. 289–301 (297).

[228] The Hebrew text reads: 'And Jonah fainted/swooned'; one Greek translation gives 'he convulsed' and another 'he was incapacitated'. For Sasson's condolences with Jonah, see *Jonah*, p. 306.

and ascent from Sheol and death.[229] Perhaps even more darkly, in Jonah 4.2, the prophet takes one of the core credal affirmations of the Hebrew Bible/Old Testament, the so-called thirteen attributes (Exodus 34.6–7) and reinflects it from a statement of praise to protest.[230] Whether Jonah is protesting (like Eagleton) that the predictability of mercy renders his actions meaningless, or is protesting (like Abravanel or Malbim) that under these peculiar narrative conditions, the application of mercy is intrinsically dangerous, he seems explicitly to be raising the problem of self-invalidation/self-jeopardisation.

Thus the 'words of Jonah that come (back) to God' reply, belatedly, analeptically, to the 'words of God that came to Jonah' (Jonah 1.1),[231] and meet them with all the conciliatory urge of an irresistible force meeting an immovable object. The text tugs us towards empathy with the prophet and so exacerbates friction, because to read with Jonah is to become increasingly allied with the prophet in his perplexed and strained relations with his text. If Robert Alter's 'doubly focused' narratives set off human plots that not only 'complement', 'reinforce' but even 'contradict' the divine

---

[229] See, for example Psalm 49.15, 'But God reclaims my life from Sheol, indeed he retrieves me', and Jonah's psalm which is at least conventional in this respect.

[230] The core passage (though by no means established as the earliest) describes Yhwh as 'merciful and gracious, slow to anger, and abounding in steadfast love and faithfulness, keeping steadfast love for thousands, forgiving iniquity and transgression and sin, but by no means forgiving the guilty'. It comes directly after the sin of the golden calf, in response to which God threatens to consume all the Israelites and commands the Levites to go through the camp and purify it by killing 3,000 people – but relents after Moses's intercession. As part of the traditional language, the creed is frequently repeated (see for example Deuteronomy 4.31; 2 Chronicles 30.9; Nehemiah 9.17, 31; Psalms 78.38; 86.5, 15; 103.8; 111.4; 112. 4; 116.5; 145.8) with different inflections and different declensions. At one end of the spectrum, Nahum 1.2–3 magnifies the clause of retribution and proclaims 'The Lord is a jealous God and avenging, the Lord is avenging and wrathful; the Lord takes vengeance on his adversaries and keeps wrath for his enemies, the Lord is slow to anger and of great might, and the Lord will by no means clear the guilty'; at the other end Joel 2.13 deletes the retribution clause and proclaims 'God is gracious and merciful, slow to anger, and abounding in steadfast love, and repents of evil'. Jonah 4.2 echoes Joel 2.13 verbatim – a fact that is usually only explored in chicken-and-eggish discussions of priority: John Day argues that Joel came first, then Jonah ('Prophecy', in D. A. Carson and H. G. M. Williamson (eds.), *It Is Written: Essays in Honour of Barnabas Lindars* (Cambridge: Cambridge University Press, 1988), pp. 39–55 (49–50)); while G. H. Cohn argues that Jonah came first then Joel (*Das Buch Jona im Lichte der biblischen Erzählkunst* (Studia Semitica Neerlandica 12; Assen: Van Gorcum, 1969), p. 99, n. 2). But surely the interesting feature here is the way in which Jonah turns adulation into implied condemnation, so suggesting that, like Nahum, the prophet would take comfort from the presence of the retribution clause.

[231] The observation is pilfered from Magonet, *Form and Meaning*, p. 107 (although, like many of the Mainstream interpreters, Magonet tends to repress Jonah's words as rebellion).

plot,[232] in Jonah's case the human counter-plot swells to the status of counter-book. The antithetical reading is not repressed, hidden, waiting to be teased out; the cause of Yhwh's opponent does not have to be imagined by the 'suspicious or irritable reader';[233] for Jonah's countertext presents itself as clearly to the reader as the main – that is Yhwh's – text.

As it presents its counter-book already gift-wrapped, rather than waiting to be disentangled, Jonah chapter 4 begins to look rather like a teach-text from *Deconstruction For Beginners*. In good deconstructive fashion it demonstrates how apparently simple premises such as Jeremiah 18.7–8 can be opened out into 'essentially interminable questioning',[234] and how there are always 'anomalies' that circulate within and 'open up the system'.[235] In addition to the awkward surplus of Jonah's voice, the text leaves us with a significant sediment or residue of 'evil'. Chapter 3 concludes with the Ninevites and Yhwh coming to a neat exchange or armistice in which the Ninevites lay down their evil, and Yhwh disarms himself of his 'evil' (רעה, *ra'ah*) and his 'fierce anger' (חרון אפו, *ḥaron appo*, from חרה, *ḥarah*, to be hot/emotionally heated/angry, Jonah 3.9–10). But Jonah 4.1 opens literally 'and it was evil to Jonah – a big evil' (יונה רעה וירע- גדולה אל, *vayera el-yonah ra'ah gedolah*), and throughout the chapter Jonah feels the pressure of divine heat, both metaphorical and actual.[236] Thus the text seems to cajole us towards the conclusion that *the evil of Nineveh is not successfully cancelled out, but is caught by the*

---

232 Alter, *The Art of Biblical Narrative*, pp. 125–6.

233 So A. Bach, *Women, Seduction and Betrayal in Biblical Narrative* (Cambridge: Cambridge University Press, 1997), pp. 21–2. The emerging tradition of 'suspicious and irritable' readings, spear-headed by feminist biblical critics, is now being more broadly applied. For my own attempt to take away the mock-inverted commas from the lisping 'prostitute' in Hosea 1–3, and to imagine how her speech might disturb the text that contains her, see Y. M. Sherwood, *The Prostitute and the Prophet: Hosea's Marriage in Literary-Theoretical Perspective* (Sheffield: Sheffield Academic Press, 1996), pp. 254–322.

234 J. Derrida, *Points . . . Interviews 1974–94* (ed. E. Weber; trans. P. Kamuf and others; Stanford: Stanford University Press, 1995), p. 239.

235 J. D. Caputo (ed.), *Deconstruction in a Nutshell: A Conversation with Jacques Derrida* (New York: Fordham University Press, 1997), p. 81.

236 The verb here is רעע (to harm, displease) which is the verbal equivalent of the noun רעה (evil). Though I have translated rather blandly to show how evil and anger are passed on, it is important to note that the phrase has many potential senses, including 'This was very displeasing to Jonah, and he was dejected/depressed.' Whereas the Mainstream has gone out on something of a semantic limb to stress Jonah's anger, and to inflate that anger in blazing, *Animated Bible* fashion, the *Septuagint* renders 4.1 as 'Jonah was terribly saddened and confused/shaken up', the Targum translates 'Jonah felt extremely bad and it affected him severely', and other versions see Jonah as 'disheartened', 'grieved', 'distressed' (see Sasson, *Jonah*, p. 275).

Hebrew prophet, that the heat and anger removed from the Ninevites transfer themselves to Jonah like a leech, a germ, or a disease.[237] And it prods us to speculate what such a transfer might mean. Perhaps the point is to show that the Jeremiah equation:

$$\text{nation turning} = \text{Yhwh's turning (Jeremiah 18.7–8)}$$

only functions if it is understood (somewhat naïvely) to hang in a contextless vacuum: for forgiving one nation and strengthening it is, by definition, cursing the nations that, historically, that nation is destined to overpower and defeat. As 2 Esdras suggests, if universalism is truly to be coupled with monotheism, the sheets of relative divine reckoning must get longer, the theological calculus more and more complex: we must exit the realm of centralised, discrete 'sin = punishment but obedience = blessing' retribution formulae and move towards more convoluted and subtle equations.[238]

As evil is cancelled out on one side of an equation and on the other, and evil still remains, as an argument splits into two columns that do not meet in a resolved sum, and as the text generates awkward remainders on a micro- and macro-level, the book of Jonah illustrates that perennial awkward aphorism that, as the character Anatole puts it in Barbara Kingsolver's *The Poisonwood Bible*, life cannot be treated as a 'mathematics problem with yourself in the centre and everything coming out equal' because (to put it simply, and the point is such a fundamentally simple one) 'when you are good, bad things can still happen. And if you are bad, you can still be lucky.'[239] The plot creates a sense of life, but not neatly

---

[237] Cf. R. P. Carroll: 'The evil of Jonah transfers itself [is transferred?] to Jonah (just as Naaman's leprosy was transferred to Gehazi in 2 Kings 5.27)' ('Jonah as a Book of Ritual Responses', in K.-D. Schunck and M. Augustin (eds.), *'Lasset uns Brücken bauen': Collected Communications to the XVth Congress of the International Organisation for the Study of the Old Testament, Cambridge, 1995* (Frankfurt: Peter Lang, 1998), pp. 261–8 (264)).

[238] In 2 Esdras, 'Ezra' asks the deity to 'weigh in the balance our iniquities and those of the inhabitants of the world; and it will be found which way the turn of the scale will incline' (2 Esdras 3.34) – the implication being that a truly just God must calibrate and weigh the relative good and evil among the nations, and will inevitably need a good system of scales. A rather similar observation is made, interestingly enough, by contemporary Old Testament theologians: R. P. Kneirim notes that in the real world, full of conflicting interests, salvation, if it is not universal, i.e. eschatological, unavoidably harms or even destroys adversaries or rivals of its recipients (R. P. Kneirim, *The Task of Old Testament Theology* (Grand Rapids: Eerdmans, 1995), pp. 316–20).

[239] B. Kingsolver, *The Poisonwood Bible* (London: Faber and Faber, 1999), p. 309. Of course the idea that the book of Jonah fractures 'mechanistic' or 'mathematical' understandings of God is something of a truism in Jonah scholarship, but all too often such observations are sublimated in the Jewish–Christian contrast, where the calculable is associated with the

processed life: it is a plot that does not shelter us, and that approximates the impact of chance (or God) on our existence.[240] Carl Jung's description of God as:

the name by which I designate all things which cross my willful path violently and recklessly, all things which upset my subjective views, plans and intentions and change the course of my life for better or worse[241]

may be an overtly anachronistic graft onto the book of Jonah, and yet (like the other anachronistic graftings of Terry Eagleton, Julian Barnes, Enrique Lihn, and Zbigniew Herbert) it is also appropriate – in a sense. For God in this text is the all-powerful counter-current and irresistible counter-wind, and Jonah is the quintessentially powerless individual buffeted by 'Goddes Wyndes' and Goddes worm, and Godde's sun.

Ultimately what haunts me about the book of Jonah – and what makes it far more than a self-imploding, puzzling, piece of 'text', hanging in detachment from all mimetic connection to 'life'[242] – is the strong sub-narrative of protection and exposure, of salvation and shade. In a seemingly superfluous action that reminds us of his (pointed?) attempts to 'go down' to Joppa and 'down' to the hold of the ship, Jonah builds himself a *sukkah*/hut to shade (or protect) himself (Jonah 4.5), and he is (pointedly?) 'exceedingly happy' over the *qiqayon*-plant which comes up over him, to shade/save him from his evil/discomfort (רעה, *ra'ah*, 4.6). But the strangely *human qiqayon* – literally '*son* of a night/perishing in a night' (Jonah 4.10)[243] – evokes those numerous biblical plants that act as metaphors for human mortality by 'flourish[ing] anew by daybreak, and at dusk, wither[ing] and dry[ing] up' (Psalms 90.5–6; 144.3–4). And when the warrior worm *smites* the source of protection it exposes Jonah's head to the '*striking*' or beating rays of the sun. Even as the *qiqayon* and worm

(calculating) Old Covenant of the Jews, and the rupturing of equations with God's new and wondrous love. Paradoxically the commentators who speak so much of the rupturing of expectations give the distinct impression that their own expectations are left very firmly in place.

[240] Roemer, *Telling Stories*, pp. 46, 64.

[241] C. G. Jung, in an interview in *Good Housekeeping* (December 1961), cited in E. F. Edinger, *Ego and Archetype: Individuation and the Religious Function of the Psyche* (New York: G. P. Putnam's, 1972), p. 101.

[242] A certain clichéd presentation of postmodern literary theory suggests a focus on text in detachment from life. This is not the case, although postmodern theory does alter our understanding of mimesis, prompting us to think less in terms of life reflected in texts or in literature imitating life, and more in terms of the creation of reality by texts.

[243] As Sasson notes, this is a 'very unusual phrase, unique to Jonah' (Sasson, *Jonah*, p. 313).

contribute little to – and even jeopardise – the book's final lesson – they reinforce a subliminal sense of the sudden changeability and fragility of life – a life that can turn on a bizarre incoming word, a few pieces of sackcloth, or the fragile arbitrariness of a pun. And Jonah's constant search for shelter (in the hold of the ship, in his hut, beneath the plant) and the fact that each shelter ultimately fails to protect him, imitates the structure of the plot: the plot that does not shelter him, the plot that expresses the desire that (to plunder more words from Jeremiah) God would become his 'refuge' and not his 'terror' (Jeremiah 17.17).[244] It is not simply that the edifice of the plot crumbles in good (overtly) deconstructive fashion, but that the way in which it fails to protect or please Jonah, or indeed the sailors, creates a sense of the fragility and insecurity of life. Insofar as he seeks for security, for salvation, for the safe-and-sound, Jonah is not the selfish Other, the Jew, so much as Everyman,[245] or baby man, living a brief life between shade/protection and the assault of smiting/striking things, between being consumed and being regurgitated, between danger and survival, exile and safety, and life and death.

3. IN CONCLUSION . . . SALVAGING JONAH: THE BOOK OF JONAH AS THE QUINTESSENTIAL STORY AND THE MOST TYPICAL OF BIBLICAL TEXTS

> If the self had not always been in doubt, there would be no stories.[246]

---

[244] At this point I'm brushing up close against Carl Jung's diagnosis of Jonah, and the 'Jonah-in-the-whale-complex' as the desire to return to the womb (see C. G. Jung, *Symbols of Transformation* (New York: Pantheon, 1956), p. 419). But we do not have to see Jonah in an explicitly psychoanalytic, foetal crouch to appreciate the quest for protection that seems to permeate the text.

[245] André and Pierre-Emmanuel Lacocque also see Jonah as something of an empathetic Everyman figure. This father and son biblical scholar-psychoanalyst partnership follows Abraham Maslow's reading of the so-called 'Jonah complex' or Jonah syndrome as 'a justified fear of being torn apart, of losing control, of being shattered and disintegrated' (A. Maslow, 'Neurosis as a Failure of Personal Growth', *Humanitas* 3 (1967), pp. 165–6, cited in Lacocque and Lacocque, *The Jonah Complex*, p. 34). Our readings cross at certain points, although Lacocque and Lacocque adhere to the idea that the book was written to counter parochialism and bigotry, and ultimately see the book as a call to pull ourselves up by our psychoanalytic bootstraps, to overcome fear, and to fulfil our vocation. I am also attempting my own rapprochement between the biblical and the non-biblical/contemporary, but in a different idiom that sees the book as far less staunchly purposeful, and less confident and triumphalistic.

[246] Roemer, *Telling Stories*, p. 134.

If we need to believe absolutely that our will is free and that our actions lead to predictable results, we had best not hear or tell stories.[247]

What if what cannot be assimilated, the absolute indigestible, played a fundamental role in the system?[248]

We started with some strong readings (Jonah *is* Jesus Christ; Jonah *is* the xenophobic Jew), and we're ending with a weak one, or at least a reading about weakness, insecurity, and mutability. My reading is inverse (or even perverse) with respect to the Mainstream, not simply because it is a photographic negative of 'Jonah the Jew', but because it flies in the face of positivistic readings. The mutability of the book's structure and the surplus of detail resists the kind of critical packaging that seeks to present the book in terms of a moderate, functional meaning-economy, and so makes the image of the critic as master-analyst of the text rather difficult to sustain. Similarly, because the book decentres the protagonist and exposes Jonah's vulnerability and powerlessness in the face of a plot/God so much bigger than himself, the narrative defies the 'positivist' image of the hero who triumphs and subordinates life – and text – to his control.

But in this respect Jonah is not a mutant narrative so much as the most *typical* traditional story,[249] and the prophet is *like* Shylock and Jason and Hansel and Gretel and Parsifal and Oedipus and Raskolnikov and Ahab and Odysseus and Hercules. For, at least according to Roemer, traditional stories possess certain intrinsic features: the plots are *preclusive* (we know how they will turn out); the heroes do not seek the action thrust upon them (and in fact are often damaged by or at odds with it); and they are frequently caught in a double bind. The Assyrians knew that Gilgamesh would fail in his quest for immortality; Shakespeare's audiences knew that Shylock would not get his pound of flesh; and Jonah's audiences knew, as we do, that Jonah ben Ammitai would have to go to Nineveh as Yhwh

---

[247] *Ibid.*, p. 35.

[248] J. Derrida, *Glas* (trans. J. P. Leavey and R. Rand; Lincoln: University of Nebraska Press, 1986), cited in Moore, *Mark and Luke in Poststructuralist Perspectives*, p. 25 (no full reference given).

[249] For Roemer, the 'traditional story' is any story that represents chaotic, insurmountable forces beyond the human protagonist, and such stories, by definition, are always in conflict with a 'positivist co-ordinate system'. Traditional stories contrast with stories like *Rambo*, *Terminator*, Goethe's *Faust*, and *Jaws* (a Positivist retelling of *Moby Dick* according to Roemer): stories that affirm the triumph of the individual and the power of human beings to change the world and purge it of evil (see *ibid.*, pp. 35, 276).

prescribed.[250] Although we tend to think that heroes 'choose to be active', when we look at traditional story we find that their 'actions are almost invariably imposed':

The Labours of Hercules, Jason's quest for the Golden Fleece, Parsifal's for the Grail, and the search undertaken by Oedipus are all obligations that must be assumed. Hansel and Gretel do not go into the forest of their own accord; they are abandoned by their parents. Hamlet may wish for the cup to pass from his lips, but he is heir to the throne and forced to act by an oath exacted by his father's ghost . . . Raskolnikov attempts to prove his freedom by killing an old woman, yet proves the opposite, and though Captain Ahab seems to have an option when *The Rachel* asks for his help he chooses the inevitable.[251]

Because the plot of traditional story is preclusive – because the hero, in fact, has little chance of influencing the narrative – 'in a formal sense, all fictive figures are imprisoned by their stories' and 'the hero of the story is a victim who does not [usually; but may in fact] see himself as one'.[252] And though we tend to think that heroes seek action, it is far more common for heroes to be propelled into a narrative that they find disturbing and even frightening, and to find themselves caught in a Catch Twenty-Two, pincer-like plot.[253] Agamemnon must choose between sacrificing his daughter or preventing the Greek fleet from sailing; Orestes and Electra must choose between killing their mother or leaving their father unavenged; the main character of the Grimm brothers' fairy-tale *Godfather Death* must choose between losing his wife, or losing his own life;[254] and Jonah (and the sailors who mimic him) must choose between futile resistance or acquiescence to a plot that looks set to culminate in self-annihilation/invalidation. As Roemer observes, the situations of such narrative heroes are frequently 'untenable', and though it is something of a cliché that the tragic hero is incapable of compromise, the truth is that he would be 'delighted to compromise if it were an option'.[255]

Seen in this rather unusual light, story becomes a way of exposing ourselves to our own powerlessness: a way of exploring (in a safe, unterrifying arena) the constraint of the human individual as he/she is trapped in an *enchaînement* of consequences, and held in a web of

---

[250] *Ibid.*, p. 3.   [251] *Ibid.*, p. 5.   [252] *Ibid.*, p. 19.

[253] *Ibid.*, pp. 6–7. As Roemer points out, even Odysseus is only trying to get home (just like Hansel and Gretel).

[254] *Ibid.*, p. 5.   [255] *Ibid.*, pp. 5–6.

connections.[256] Even sanguine tales such as *Little Red Riding Hood* and *Snow White* – stories that seem to move on inexorably towards happy ever afters – enact human helplessness in the face of ravenous wolves, the gratuitous evil of stepmothers and malevolent super-natural forces, and are pervaded by an atmosphere of human 'marginality and helplessness'.[257] Contra Aristotle, 'complication' may not simply be a necessary spanner in the plot mechanism: the forces that oppose the protagonists are often projections of our deepest fears (*what if* God allied himself with the enemy, and not with us?) and of the forces of chaos that prevent us from harnessing cause and effect to our purpose.[258] This effect is exacerbated in stories that lack a happy or satisfactory ending: with Jonah, as with Oedipus, friction is exaggerated, and the meaning of the plot seems to lie in the 'unalterability' of the plot and the tenacity of the hero's struggle against it.[259]

In fact, the book of Jonah not only conforms to the model of traditional story, but highlights and exaggerates its most distinctive traits. Its plot is *emphatically* preclusive – not only because God himself is its initiator and guarantor, but because that God is uncompromisingly all-appointing and all-controlling, and because, as if to ram the point home, 1.13 shows that resistance against the divine plot-current is absolutely futile. The undesirability of the storyline is also stressed – a God who uses pious-Assyria and Nineveh as the centre of his calculations, pushes the intractability and perverseness of life to tragi-comic extremes. Moreover, the protagonists of the book of Jonah are victims who *do* recognise themselves as such, and the sailors and the prophet constantly foreground their discomfort, their resistance, and their will-to-escape. As the narrative seems to visualise the 'depotentiation of humankind [or at least Israel] inherent in story's structure'[260] by placing the centre of narrative gravity at Nineveh, so it seems to foreground the fundamental human desire for protection and predictability, and for a plot that would ultimately 'shelter us'. And the subtexts of exile and regurgitation, protection and exposure, being swallowed but not being consumed, suggest that, like all stories, this story exists because the 'self is in doubt' and because

---

[256] *Ibid.*, p. 7.

[257] *Ibid.*, p. 49. This, however, is purged in Disney which, as Roemer argues, is 'fairy tales for positivists' (p. 276).

[258] *Ibid.*, p. 48.   [259] *Ibid.*, p. 93.   [260] *Ibid.*, p. 35.

groups have had to 'confirm and confirm themselves over and over'.[261]

And in this sense, Jonah becomes not the maverick misfit in the canon, but the most typical of biblical and prophetic texts. For the Hebrew Bible can be read as an extended meditation on questions of identity and survival, marked by an exposure to the raw vacillations of life (famine, war, disease) from which we in the twentieth-century insured and inoculated West are deeply insulated.[262] Sometimes biblical authors tell stories that, rather like the Mainstream Christian–Jew dichotomies, bolster up the Self against the Other, and bullishly talk up the little brother/nation against the bigger brother/nation; and frequently they assert a monologic interpretative framework: we suffer if we go against the will of Yhwh, and in that sense life sits comfortably within the orbit of our control. But at the same time, a considerable residue leaks out of that neat, framing meta-story, as if to point to the counter-intuitive nature of a life that is always somehow intransigent and perverse. The over-harsh punishments of the books of Exodus and Numbers, the obliteration of the Wilderness generation, the long-delayed exit to the promised land followed by a so-very-brief sojourn in the land of milk and honey, point to the recalcitrance and harshness of life, and behind life – God. And God, without a devil figure exterior to him to serve as an 'excuse' for him,[263] can himself become 'like an enemy . . . making us the offscouring and refuse of the people' (Lamentations 2.4; 3.45). Within the Hebrew Bible's covers, the laws, sacrifices, psalms and commandments that exist to mollify and control recalcitrant social and divine forces co-exist alongside an image of God who is always more than the sum of our imaginings and can do whatever he pleases (Jonah 1.14). The God who is Shield, Protector, and Calmer

---

[261] *Ibid.*, p. 134.

[262] As Peter Brown soberingly observes, the Roman Empire was 'more helplessly exposed to death than is even the most afflicted and underdeveloped country in the modern world', and presumably the same would apply to the world of the authors of the Hebrew Bible (see P. Brown, *The Body and Society; Men, Women and Sexual Renunciation* (New York: Columbia University Press, 1988), pp. 286–8).

[263] So Derrida, following Freud through *Civilisation and its Discontents*, argues that within the Christian theological economy, the devil, that is 'evil for evil's sake, diabolical evil', can serve as an 'excuse (*Entschuldigung*)' for God because 'exterior to him, as anarchic angel and dissident'. In other words, he functions similarly to the Jew, who also plays the 'analogous role of economic relief or exoneration (*die selbe ökonomisch entlastende Rolle*)'. (See J. Derrida, *Archive Fever: A Freudian Impression* (trans. E. Peronowitz; Chicago: University of Chicago Press, 1996), p. 13.)

of the Storm is also Ninevite-lover, Job-afflicter, and perverse destroyer of *qiqayon* plants – God as a gigantic and ultimately unguessable force.

This image of God as a force whose intervention scrambles expectation is nowhere clearer than in the Prophets. The prophetic books are full of pictures that graphically record the vulnerability of being human: images of writhing on too short beds with too short covers (Isaiah 28.20); of lying face down and making your back like a street for the oppressors to pass over (Isaiah 51.23); of being hooked – like fish – by Babylonian fishers (Habakkuk 1.15); of being digested as a nation and having your best delicacies sucked out (Jeremiah 51.34); of being too 'small' to endure the locusts, fires (or indeed earthquakes, Assyrians, Babylonians, and Edomites) that God brings against you (Amos 7.2, 5); and of being slopped like liquid from one container to another, while other nations are allowed to settle on the lees, and to become rich, concentrated sediment (Jeremiah 48.11). And, as I have argued elsewhere, the rhetoric of prophecy is a rhetoric of distortion, and of radical defamiliarisation, designed to represent – in the trembling of language – the irruption of the mind-bending, world-bending force that is the Otherness of Yhwh.[264] In the linguistically scrambled world of the prophets a 'basket of fruit' means 'the end: destruction and corpses' (Amos 8.1–3); God, the great I AM becomes I AM NOT (Hosea 1.9); the Syrians and Ethiopians are just *like* the Judaeans, because they have been led by God through their 'Exodus' (Amos 9.7); and God *gives* the people starvation – in the perversely distorted form of the 'gift of cleanness of teeth' (Amos 4.6). The style of prophecy is overtly transumptive/metaleptic and punning:[265] thus 'justice' (משפת, *mishpat*) shifts to 'bloodshed' (משפח, *mishpach*); 'righteousness' (צדקה, *tsedeqah*, Isaiah 5.7) to 'a cry' (צעקה, *tse'aqah*); and 'Gilgal' (גלגל), the name of a shrine, mutates into the totally unpredictable anagrammatic meaning: 'Gilgal shall surely go into exile' (הגלגל גלה יגלה, *ha-gilgal galoh yigleh*; Amos 5.5–6). As words split, mutate, and recombine, they create a splintered alien world in their image. They demon-

264 See Y. M. Sherwood, 'Of Fruit and Corpses and Wordplay Visions: Picturing Amos 8.1–3' (*Biblicon*, forthcoming), 'Darke Texts Need Notes' (unpublished paper presented to the Society for Old Testament Study annual meeting, University of Glasgow, July 1999), and 'Prophetic Scatology: Prophecy and the Art of Sensation', in S. D. Moore (ed.), *In Search of the Present: The Bible Through Cultural Studies* (*Semeia* 82; Atlanta: Scholar's Press, 2000).

265 For a discussion of the transumptive/metaleptic style of Isaiah, see Miscall, 'Isaiah: New Heavens, New Earth, New Book'.

strate how the world of prophecy becomes, in effect, a sinister, marvellous Wonderland – a world that emphatically does not shelter us – in fact, a world that is defined precisely by refusing its audiences the sanctuary of the norm, and the luxuriating comfort of the familiar.

Seen from this angle, Jonah, the outcast Prophet, the un-Prophet, begins to look strangely at home in his canonical setting. The uncanny Nineveh–Jerusalem is like Amos' 'Exodus' of the Ethiopians and the Syrians: for in Jonah as in the 'proper Prophets', tradition is a language that can be radically reinflected, or re-sorted into the most mutant, thought-provoking shapes. And just as the Prophets exploit the arbitrary connections of language, so Jonah inhabits a story spun out from (arbitrary?) associations of words, and that hinges on a word that yields its least expected definition: הפך (*hafak*) means to 'turn around/bring to repentance' as unexpectedly as Gilgal means 'exile' and a 'basket of fruit' (קיץ, *qayits*) means 'the end: destruction and corpses' (קץ, *qaits*, Amos 5.5–6; 8.1–3). Yhwh's concluding *qiqayon*–Nineveh *mashal* is, in a sense, the most typical of prophetic speeches in that it frustrates expectation, perches meaning on a pun, and pushes the riddling and encrypted tendencies of prophetic discourse to extremes.[266] The prophet who runs away from God and his inverted creeds reflects the breaking/fracturing of generic convention that is intrinsic to prophecy; and the constant collapse/inadequacy of shelter mimics the prophetic tendency to snatch away security, and to rob us of the protection of familiar words and genre conventions.

As it takes the destabilisation, uncertainty, and human power-lessness that is writ large across the 'Proper Prophets', and converts it from oracle to narrative form, the book of Jonah mutates – strangely – into the most typically counter-intuitive of prophetic texts. The Prophets set up inverted imaginative worlds, and Jonah walks through one of those worlds: as the divine word comes to the

---

[266] This point is anticipated by Gerda Elata-Alster and Rachel Salmon when they argue that God's strange concluding speech 'violates textual congruity' and so 'does God's work in the world of Scripture' ('The Deconstruction of Genre', p. 57). The implication is that divine language is defined precisely by its quality to deconstruct human language. (For the encrypted nature of prophetic speech, see for example Isaiah 6.9–10 ('Go and say to this people, "Hear and hear but do not understand; see and see, but do not perceive". Make the heart of this people fat, and their ears heavy and shut their eyes . . .'), and Isaiah 29.11 ('And the vision of all that has become to you like the words of a book that is sealed. When men give it to one who can read, saying "Read this" he says "I cannot for it is sealed').)

Prophets and ruptures accepted ways of seeing, so the skewed divine word comes in to Jonah and sets off a chain of the most strange and counter-intuitive events. Jonah can be seen as an experiment in what it would feel like to occupy the strangely defamiliarising world of prophecy – albeit a world that in this case is taken to exaggerated, comedy-insulated, extremes. Jonah is the quintessential story, and the quintessential prophetic text, in that the central character is subjected to a strange world from which no 'digging' or resistance will release him (Jonah 1.14, cf. Amos 9.2).

As I propose something of a mutable canon – where conceptual boundary lines can always be imagined otherwise, and where Jonah can take his place *among* the Prophets – I am attempting to mimic the intrinsic mutability of prophetic discourse and quite deliberately to counter bland projections of the 'biblical', both popular and academic. For popular culture and Biblical Studies alike are guilty of reducing the biblical to 'anemic generalities'[267] or a 'grandiose but frozen one-dimensional narrative in which all the varieties of discourse are levelled off',[268] and of conceiving of it as something fundamentally expectation-confirming, settled, and static. As even Roemer (all too predictably) confines biblical narrative to a special, and lesser, category because religious protagonists apparently blithely 'know and trust' the plot-forces that impel them,[269] he illustrates that deep cultural reflex that sees the Bible as a neat life-processor, a repository of self-confirming theologies, a refuge of safety and salvation. But if we take the rabbis' (and Jonah's?) advice and watch over the general from the microscopic vantage point of the particular, then we begin to uncover biblical texts that betray, unexpectedly, a sense of 'profound untidiness in the nature of

---

[267] P. Ricoeur, *Figuring the Sacred* (Minneapolis: Augsburg Fortress, 1995), p. 236. Paul Ricoeur is talking here of Christian *theology*'s tendency to reduce biblical texts to a few select abstract generalities, but the analysis of the Mainstream suggests that this is not something from which Biblical Studies is entirely immune.

[268] *Ibid.*, p. 237.

[269] Roemer, *Telling Stories*, p. 6. Using the story of the sacrifice of Isaac (rather than, say, the stories of Jonah or Job or Saul) as the quintessence of the biblical, Roemer sets 'religious stories' apart from traditional stories: 'In religious stories the heroes and heroines are obliged to act, but act in a different spirit. They are not blind to the forces that impel them, but know and trust them. They do not suffer the illusion of being free . . . and are not in conflict with themselves or their situation; they accept their fate modestly instead of trying to change it arrogantly.' Again, the point is not so much to criticise Roemer as an individual, but to point to a general cultural tendency to flatten out the Bible by synecdoche, and to take the most familiar 'part' for the more stranger, more disparate whole.

things'[270] and that force us away from the image of a Bible (smugly?) enclosed in an all-embracing patina of self-satisfied interpretative peace.

But culturally – and often professionally – the Bible remains the quintessential instance of that other time, that other place, where death was 'tame', where people 'knew and trusted' the forces that impelled them, and where people believed in big fishes and kind deities – a childhood dreamtime that is associated with various ur-times in modern/postmodern studies (for we have not shaken off the spectre of Hegel yet).[271] Such times act as a foil for an age that prides itself on its 'anxiety' and its complexity as, poisoned and exhilarated by huge drafts of knowledge, it takes in, with one brave stare into the abyss, both the death of God and the decentring/demise of man. Like the Bible, (post)modern culture has its Eden, its retrospective paradise – which is also its way of flattering itself on its fall into knowledge which is also an ascent. The irony is that in post-Enlightenment Western thought, the Bible itself has become that Eden, that religious childhood place, that sanguine, apple-scented 'herbaceous playpen'.[272]

If this book was primarily written against the Christian othering of the Jew, it is also written against the othering of the Bible as the primitive sidekick of the knowing and the complex. Without creating a Bible that anxiously proves itself by denying its belief in God[273] and so plays up to sassy secular culture, and without denying that a

---

[270] R. Alter, *The Art of Biblical Narrative*, p. 154.

[271] So Zygmunt Bauman, in his incisive study of mortality, describes a bulk 'pre-modern' era where people existed in a 'resigned yet peaceful cohabitation with "tame" death' and Roemer argues that characters in biblical narrative (like their authors presumably) universally 'know and trust' the life forces that impel them (Z. Bauman, *Mortality, Immortality and Other Life Strategies*, pp. 94, 96–7; Roemer, *Telling Stories*, p. 6). Such bulk periodisation and universalisation is unconvincing, but interestingly symptomatic, suggesting that we are still very much thinking in (Hegelian) terms of the growth to cultural adulthood, even though that adulthood is now increasingly defined not by cultural ebullience, but by a tendency to alienation/depression.

[272] This fortuitous phrase is taken from D. F. Sawyer, 'The Deconstructed Male – A Biblical Theme', paper given at The Society of Biblical Literature Annual Meeting, Boston, November 1999.

[273] However, I would want to question our assumptions about the kind of God that some of these writers 'believe in', or indeed question the assumption that that God is static and credally contained. Without wanting to claim that the God of the Hebrew Bible is something like Nietzsche's 'amoral, recklessly creating and destroying, indifferently self-realising deity', full of 'internal contradictions' (F. Nietzsche, *The Birth of Tragedy* (1872), in *The Birth of Tragedy* and *The Genealogy of Morals* (trans. F. Golffing; New York: Doubleday, 1956), p. 9) – and so scoffingly countering the Christian projection of the Old Testament God with a kind of un-God – I would want to suggest that this description comes strangely

considerable proportion of the Hebrew Bible is emphatically monologic (Christian fundamentalists capture something of the tone of
Deuteronomy when they assert that God gave the 'Ten Commandments' and not the 'Ten Suggestions'), I want to argue that the only
fair presentation of biblical literature is a variegated one, for there is
a world of difference between Deuteronomy and Qoheleth, and
between the Hebrew Bible and the New Testament, and indeed the
subsequent Christian theologies that shape the Bible's popular
cultural image. My point is on one level a crass and simple (and oh
so un-modern) one: that the intransigence, randomness, incalcul-
ability of life – indeed all the 'cankers [and irritants] of the mind'
that we consider to be symptomatically modern aliments – are
articulated in ancient stories and philosophy, in the Bible and the
'Classics'.[274] 'Life is either a medley and a tangled web or a unity
and a plan and a providence', says Marcus Aurelius;[275] life is a
tangled web and also controlled by (tangled) providence, says
Qoheleth; while the book of Lamentations quashes the image of
religion wrapping the individual in comfort/cotton wool with the
counter-image of a deity who insulates himself in clouds that no
prayer can penetrate (Lamentations 3.43–4). Already there is a
movement to show how the distinctive idioms of present dissolve
into – or find analogues in – idioms of the past: Jonathan Dollimore
argues that the crisis of the individual is less a crisis than a recurring
instability deriving from the (perennial) theological obsession with

---

close to capturing something of the darker deity who skulks in some corners of the Hebrew
Scriptures.

[274] The phrase the 'cankers of the mind' comes from Seneca 'On Tranquillity', in *The Stoic
Philosophy of Seneca: Essays and Letters* (trans. M. Hadas; New York: Doubleday, 1958), p. 104.
The comparison between the Bible and the Classics is an interesting one, since both have
been cast as the source of civilisation, and the work of unified, and untroubled, selves:
classically, for Walter Pater, the Classics express the Hellenic ideal of 'man . . . at unity
with himself' (W. Pater, *The Renaissance* (1st edn 1873; London: Macmillan, 1910), p. 222).
Such definitions set up the Bible and the Classics as the foundation and the Other of
contemporary culture: as emphatically antithetical to dissension, vulgarity, quizzicality,
doubt, chaos, anxiety, and all our modern neuroses. Of course, the idea that texts express
troubled selves/worlds (albeit unconsciously) is still a version of the expressive realist,
common-sense view of literature, but nevertheless it is a useful inversion of the myth that
High Culture/Literature reflects selves and worlds that help us to abdicate chaos for unity
and order. Incidentally, I am intrigued by how, despite being reared in the climate of
postmodern theory, I find myself instinctively relating texts to life albeit in twisted forms: I
suspect with Ihab Hassan that 'we are all . . . a little Victorian, Modern and Postmodern,
at once' (see I. Hassan, *The Postmodern Turn: Essays in Postmodern Theory and Culture*
(Columbus, Ohio: Ohio State University Press, 1987), p. 88).

[275] Marcus Aurelius, *Meditations* (trans. C. R Haines; London: William Heinemann, 1961), vol.
VI, 10.

death, loss, and failure;[276] while the contemporary 'subject' who experiences him/herself as 'subjected' finds distant cousins in those who experience their lives subjected to God(s), or to the Fates. Though this may be the hardest thing for a culture of originality and progress to concede, we still go on harping on the same old themes – vulnerability, helplessness, finitude, contingency, danger, frustration, lack, the desire for equilibrium, security, stability – and we are always involved to some degree in a process of mutation, displacement, repetition, and regurgitation.

Of course it may well be that in its sheer enthusiasm to escape the intimidation of the (post)modern, and to wriggle free of projections of the Bible as simple and naïve – the book of Jonah has rather over-eagerly imbibed Backwater strategies and interpretations. Indeed this process has been a conscious one: this overtly fattened book is just as reliant on nourishment from outside as the limpet-encrusted book of the Mainstream (although this time the reliance is overt), and my ostensible aim has been to feed it, and to watch it waddle off the interpretative stage in a much richer and more satisfied/ satisfying state. But as I have assembled this reading, I have increasingly found the image of the ancient *ingénu* waiting for modern tutelage inadequate and suspect – and not only, I think, because I have become caught up in a certain tangle of cause and effect, a Chinese box structure of text and interpretation, regression and anticipation. For crucially (and recent biblical scholarship and popular/Jewish interpretation curiously coincide at this point) this is a book that seems to be anticipating the themes and styles that will later emerge in the arena of interpretation. It is a book that is already beginning the process of compilation and stirring by which it will continue to survive, and anticipating Backwater reading strategies in the way that it processes and reworks the traditions that it imbibes. As the Backwaters take the book of Jonah and push the text to its most absurdly literalist conclusions (by revelling in the image of Jonah 'going colo-rectal', or squatting on a water-bed-like kidney), so Jonah applies similar techniques to the aqua-psalm or Sheol-belly; and as the Backwaters make the book strange to itself (by stripping the whale down to a skeleton, or getting the naïve, mercy-promoting text to digest, and choke on, the indigestible reality of the Holocaust), so Jonah submits tradition to *unheimlich* distortions and

---

[276] J. Dollimore, *Death, Desire and Loss in Western Culture* (New York: Routledge, 1998), p. xix.

inversions. Meme-like, the book seems to cue in a whole range of survivals/mutations: with its chowder-like mixtures of death-wishes and aqua-psalms and shivering ships, the book spawns comic riffs on prophets 'snoring slobberingly' *and* serious meditations on the alienation and powerlessness of the human protagonist; and by anticipating the alliterative, cartoonish, paranomastic, and associative linguistic effects through which the rabbis, Auster, and the *Gawain*-poet will go on prolonging and stretching the life of the 'Word', it seems to inaugurate and legitimate an expansive approach to interpretation. Responding to such an invitation, my self-consciously elastic reading exists primarily to provoke our definitions of the biblical, to raise questions such as 'Can we conceive of a biblical text this humorous, this canonically non-conformist, this richly story-like, this linguistically agile, this savvy, this questioning, this empathetic towards the human, this lacking in reassurance of the comfort of the divine?' – and if we cannot, then by what criterion?

As I close this book down on 30 December 1999, in a country where the Bible is no longer a leading protagonist on the cultural stage, but where images of apocalypse, sin, and fall linger and structure our very conceptions of time and self,[277] it feels almost obligatory to say something appropriately sonorous about 'the future of biblical interpretation in the twenty-first century'. My tone is more hopeful than prophetic, but my hope is that, somewhere in the interdisciplinary and wider cultural space outside the delimited field of Biblical Studies, a new kind of biblical interpretation will find its place. Such interpretation, I think, will be about allowing the Word to be stretched, as it has indeed been stretched throughout the history of interpretation; about picking at the tangled web of relations between the contemporary and the ancient and the secular and the sacred, without assuming that these categories will be antithetical; and about hurling all kinds of contemporary idioms/preoccupations – all kinds of ropes of analogy – out to the shores of the ancient text in the hope that they will form some kind of attachment and in the process rearrange and reanimate the over-familiarised text. It will be

[277] For a fascinating discussion of the way in which the book of Revelation lingers overtly and covertly in the 'psychosocial' life of the 'West', see C. Keller, *Apocalypse Now and Then* (Boston: Beacon Press, 1996). For a discussion of how the psychology of sin permeates Western culture and how the 'fall' infiltrates even postmodern stories of the death of man, see Dollimore, *Death, Desire and Loss*, pp. 43, 91.

about opening up (unexpected) routes across this great amorphous mass we call Western Culture; about tracing seemingly deviant interpretative trajectories and feeding them back into the text; about encouraging the Hebrew Bible to speak in a wider range of idioms and tongues (Jewish and Popular, as well as Christian); and about foregrounding the difficulty – and opportunity – involved in reading the Bible *these days*. It will be about opening up space to track new interpretative deliriums[278] and seeking out a certain kind of inse-curity and destabilisation, rather than assuming, like Ham in Beckett's *Endgame*: 'Ah, the old questions, the old answers – there's nothing like them.' But, at the same time, it will be a process of endless regurgitation, and rearrangement, of invoking and remaking our ancestors, so that 'heterodox, heteroclite and indeterminate withal', we 'live in one human universe and astonish one another with our assents'.[279]

---

[278] 'We should read the Bible one more time. To interpret it, of course, but also to let it carve out a space for our interpretative delirium', Kristeva, *New Maladies of the Soul*, cited in Fewell, 'Imagination, Method and Murder', in Beal and Gunn, *Reading Bibles, Writing Bodies*, p. 132.

[279] Cf. Hassan, *The Postmodern Turn*, pp. xvii, 47.

Bibliography

Abramson, G., 'Amichai's God', *Prooftexts* 4 (1984), pp. 111–26

Ackerman, J. S., 'Jonah', in R. Alter and F. Kermode (eds.), *The Literary Guide to the Bible* (London: Fontana, 1989), pp. 234–43

Ackroyd, P. R., *Exile and Restoration: A Study in Hebrew Thought of the Sixth Century BC* (Philadelphia: Westminster Press, 1968)

Adam, A. K. M., 'The Sign of Jonah: A Fish-Eye View', *Semeia* 51 (1990), pp. 177–91

Adorno, T., *Minima Moralia* (trans. E. F. N. Jephcott; London: Verso, 1999)

Aichele, G. and G. A. Philips, 'Introduction: Exegesis, Eisegesis, Intergesis', in G. Aichele and G. A. Philips (eds.), *Intertextuality and the Bible* (*Semeia* 69/70; Atlanta: Scholar's Press, 1995), pp. 7–18

Alatas, S. H., *The Myth of the Lazy Native: A Study of the Image of the Malays, Filipinos and Javanese from the Sixteenth to the Twentieth Century and Its Function in the Ideology of Colonial Capitalism* (London: Frank Cass, 1977)

Albright, D. (ed.), *W. B. Yeats: The Poems* (London: J. M. Dent and Sons, 1991)

Aleichem, S., *Tevye the Dairyman and The Railroad Stories* (trans. H. Halkin; New York: Schocken, 1987)

Allen, L. C., *The Books of Joel, Obadiah, Jonah and Micah* (London: Hodder and Stoughton, 1976)

Allen, W., *Without Feathers* (London: Sphere Books, 1980)

Alter, R., *The Art of Biblical Narrative* (New York: Basic Books, 1981)

Althusser, L., 'Ideological State Apparatuses', in *Lenin and Philosophy and Other Essays* (trans. B. Brewster; London: New Left Books, 1971), pp. 160–5

Althusser, L. and E. Balibar, *Reading Capital* (trans. B. Brewster; London: Verso, 1970)

Altizer, T. J. J. and W. Hamilton, *Radical Theology and the Death of God* (Harmondsworth: Penguin, 1968)

Amichai, Y., *A Life of Poetry 1948–1994* (trans. B. and B. Harshav; New York: HarperCollins, 1994)

Anderson, B. W., *Imagined Communities: Reflections on the Origin and Spread of Nationalism* (London and New York: Verso, 1991)

Understanding the Old Testament (Englewood Cliffs, N.J.: Prentice-Hall, 1986)

Antin, P. (ed.), *St Jerome's In Ionam* (Sources Chrétiennes 43; Paris: Les Editions du Cerf, 1956)

Armitt, L., *Theorising the Fantastic* (London: Arnold, 1996)

Aronowicz, A. (ed.), *Nine Talmudic Readings by Emmanuel Levinas* (Bloomington and Indianapolis: Indiana University Press, 1990)

Arvin, N., *Herman Melville: A Critical Biography* (New York: Carbondale, 1964; 1st edn 1950)

Ashcroft, B., G. Griffiths, and H. Tiffin, *The Empire Writes Back: Theory and Practice in Post-Colonial Literatures* (London: Routledge, 1989)

Auerbach, E., *Mimesis: The Representation of Reality in Western Literature* (trans. W. Trask; Princeton: Princeton University Press, 1953)

Augustine, *The City of God* II (trans. D. B. Zema and G. G. Walsh; The Fathers of the Church; Washington, 1952)

    On Christian Doctrine (trans. D. W. Robertson, Jr.; New York: Bobbs-Merrill, 1958)

Aurelius, Marcus, *Meditations* (trans. C. R Haines; London: William Heinemann, 1961)

Auster, P., *The Invention of Solitude* (London: Faber and Faber, 1982)

Bach, A., *Women, Seduction and Betrayal in Biblical Narrative* (Cambridge: Cambridge University Press, 1997)

Bach, A. (ed.), *Women in the Hebrew Bible: A Reader* (London and New York: Routledge, 1999)

Bachélard, G., *The Poetics of Space* (trans. M. Jolas; New York: Orion Press, 1964)

Bakhtin, M., *Problems of Dostoevsky's Poetics* (ed. and trans. C. Emerson, introduction by W. C. Booth; Minneapolis: University of Minnesota Press, 1984)

    Rabelais and His World (trans. H. Iswolsky; Bloomington: Indiana University Press, 1984)

Baldick, C., *The Social Mission of English Criticism* (Oxford: Clarendon Press, 1983)

Balibar, E., 'Racism as Universalism', in *Masses, Classes and Ideas: Studies on Politics and Philosophy Before and After Marx* (trans. J. Swenson; London and New York: Routledge, 1994), pp. 191–204

Band, A. J., 'Swallowing Jonah: The Eclipse of Parody', *Prooftexts* 10 (1990), pp. 177–95

Baranczak, S., *A Fugitive from Utopia: The Poetry of Zbigniew Herbert* (Cambridge, Mass.: Harvard University Press, 1987)

Barnes, J., *A History of the World in Ten and a Half Chapters* (London: Picador, 1989)

Barthelme, D., *Forty Stories* (London: Minerva, 1988)

Barthes, R., *S/Z* (trans. R. Miller; London: Blackwell, 1990; 1st edn 1973)

    'Wrestling with the Angel: Textual Analysis of Genesis 32.22–33', in

R. Barthes, *The Semiotic Challenge* (Berkeley: University of California Press, 1994), pp. 246–60

Barton, J., *Reading the Old Testament: Method in Biblical Study* (London: Darton, Longman, and Todd, 1984)

'Wellhausen's *Prolegomena to the History of Israel*: Influences and Effects', in D. Smith-Christopher (ed.), *Text and Experience: Towards a Cultural Exegesis of the Bible* (Sheffield: Sheffield Academic Press, 1995), pp. 316–29

Battenfield, D., 'The Source for the Hymn in Moby-Dick', *American Literature* 27 (1995), pp. 393–6

Bauer, B., *Die Religion des Alt Testament in der geschictlichen Entwickelung ihrer Principien dargestellt* (Berlin: 1838)

Bauman, Z., 'Allosemitism: Premodern, Modern, Postmodern', in B. Cheyette and L. Marcus (eds.), *Modernity, Culture and 'the Jew'* (Cambridge: Polity, 1998), pp. 143–56

Mortality, Immortality and Other Life Strategies (Cambridge: Polity Press, 1992)

Postmodern Ethics (Oxford: Blackwell, 1995)

Beal, T. K., *The Book of Hiding: Gender, Ethnicity, Annihilation and Esther* (London and New York: Routledge, 1997)

'Ideology and Intertextuality: Surplus of Meaning and Controlling the Means of Production', in D. Nolan Fewell, *Reading Between Texts*, pp. 27–39

Beal, T. K. and D. M. Gunn (eds.), *Reading Bibles, Writing Bodies: Identity and the Book* (London: Routledge, 1997)

Berger, P., *The Sacred Canopy* (Garden City, N.Y.: Doubleday, 1967)

The Social Reality of Religion (Harmondsworth: Penguin, 1973)

Berman, M., *All That is Solid Melts into Air: The Experience of Modernity* (New York: Simon and Schuster, 1982)

Berthoff, W., *The Example of Melville* (Princeton: Princeton University Press, 1962)

Bewer, J. A., *Critical and Exegetical Commentary on Jonah* (International Critical Commentary; Edinburgh: T. & T. Clark, 1912)

Bhabha, H. K., 'Joking Aside: The Idea of a Self-Critical Community', in B. Cheyette and L. Marcus (eds.), *Modernity, Culture and 'the Jew'* (Cambridge: Polity Press, 1998), pp. xv–xx

'Signs Taken for Wonders; Questions of Ambivalence and Authority under a Tree outside Delhi, May 1817', in *The Location of Culture* (London and New York : Routledge, 1994), pp. 102–22

Biale, D., *Eros and the Jews: From Biblical Israel to Contemporary America* (New York: Basic Books, 1992).

'The Philo-Semitic Face of Christian Anti-Semitism', *Tikkun* 4.3 (1989), pp. 99–102

Bickerman, E., 'Les deux erreurs du prophète Jonas', *Revue d'histoire et de philosophie religieuses* 45 (1965), pp. 232–64

Four Strange Books of the Bible: Jonah, Daniel, Qoheleth, Esther (New York: Schoken Books, 1967)

Blackmore, S., *The Meme Machine* (Oxford: Oxford University Press, 1999)

Blackmur, R. P., 'Introduction to James', *The Art of the Novel: Critical Prefaces by Henry James* (Boston: Northeastern University Press, 1984)

Bloom, H., *The Anxiety of Influence* (New York: Oxford University Press, 1973)

The Book of J (London: Faber, 1991)

A Map of Misreading (Oxford: Oxford University Press, 1990)

Boer, R., *Knockin' on Heaven's Door* (London and New York: Routledge, 1999)

Bolin, T. M., *Freedom Beyond Forgiveness: The Book of Jonah Re-Examined* (Sheffield: Sheffield Academic Press, 1997)

Booth, T. Y., 'Moby Dick: Standing Up to God', in *Nineteenth Century Fiction* 17 (1962–3), pp. 33–43

Booth, W., *The Rhetoric of Fiction* (Chicago: Chicago University Press, 1983)

Bottigheimer, R. B., *The Bible for Children: From the Age of Gutenberg to the Present* (New Haven: Yale University Press, 1996)

Bowers, R. H., *The Legend of Jonah* (The Hague: Martinus Nijhoff, 1971)

Boyarin, D., *Carnal Israel: Reading Sex in Talmudic Culture* (Berkeley: University of California Press, 1993)

Intertextuality and the Reading of Midrash (Bloomington and Indianapolis: Indiana University Press, 1990)

Boyarin, J., 'The Other Within and the Other Without', in *Storm from Paradise: The Politics of Jewish Memory* (Minneapolis: University of Minnesota Press, 1992), pp. 77–98

Storm from Paradise: The Politics of Jewish Memory (Minneapolis: University of Minnesota Press, 1992)

Brichto, H. C., *Toward a Grammar of Biblical Poetics: Tales of the Prophets* (New York: Oxford University Press, 1992)

Brockington, L. H., 'Jonah', in M. Black and H. H. Rowley (eds.), *Peake's Commentary on the Bible* (London: Van Nostrand Reinhold, 1962), pp. 627–9

Brodhead, R. H. (ed.), *New Essays on Moby Dick* (Cambridge: Cambridge University Press, 1986)

Brooks, P., *Reading for the Plot: Design and Intention in Narrative* (Cambridge, Mass.: Harvard University Press, 1992)

Brown, P., *The Body and Society: Men, Women and Sexual Renunciation* (New York: Columbia University Press, 1988)

Bruce, F. F., *The Canon of Scripture* (Glasgow: Chapter House, 1988)

Brueggeman, W., *Theology of the Old Testament: Testimony, Dispute, Advocacy* (Minneapolis: Fortress, 1997)

Budde, K., 'Vermutungen zum "Midrasch des Buches der Könige"', *Zeitschrift für die alttestamentliche Wissenschaft* 11 (1892), pp. 37–81

Buell, L., 'Moby-Dick as Sacred Text', in Brodhead, *New Essays on Moby Dick*, pp. 53–72

Burrows, M., 'The Literary Character of the Book of Jonah', in Frank and Reed, *Translating and Understanding the Old Testament*, pp. 82–105

Butler, J., *Excitable Speech: A Politics of the Performative* (New York and London: Routledge, 1997)

Calloway, M., 'Canonical Criticism', in S. L. McKenzie and S. R. Haynes (eds.), *To Each Its Own Meaning: An Introduction to Biblical Criticisms and Their Application* (Louisville: Westminster/John Knox, 1993), pp. 121–34

Calvin, J., *Commentaries on the Twelve Minor Prophets* (trans. J. Owen; Edinburgh: Calvin Translation Society, 1847)

Calvino, I., *If On a Winter's Night a Traveller* (London: Picador, 1982)

Cameron, S., *The Corporeal Self: Allegories of the Body in Melville and Hawthorne* (Baltimore and London: Johns Hopkins University Press, 1981)

Camille, M., *Images on the Edge: The Margins of Medieval Art* (London: Reaktion Books, 1995)

Camus, A., 'Jonas, ou l'artist au travail', in *L'exil et le royaume* (Paris: Gallimard, 1957), pp. 101–39; ET 'The Artist at Work', in *Exile and the Kingdom* (trans. Justin O'Brien; Harmondsworth: Penguin, 1962), pp. 83–115

The Myth of Sisyphus (trans. J. O'Brien; Hamish Hamilton: London, 1971; 1st edn 1942)

Caputo, J. D. (ed.), *Deconstruction in a Nutshell: A Conversation with Jacques Derrida* (New York: Fordham University Press, 1997)

Carroll, L., *Alice's Adventures in Wonderland* (London: William Heinemann, 1977)

Carroll, R. P., 'Cultural Encroachment and Bible Translation; Observations on Elements of Violence, Race and Class in the Production of Bibles in Translation', *Semeia* 76 (1996), pp. 39–53

'He-Bibles and She-Bibles: Reflections on the Violence done to Texts by Productions of English Translations of the Bible', *Biblical Interpretation* 4.3 (1996), pp. 257–69

'Jonah as a Book of Ritual Responses', in K.-D. Schunck and M. Augustin (eds.), '*Lasset uns Brücken bauen . . .*': *Collected Communications to the Fifteenth Congress of the International Organization for the Study of the Old Testament, Cambridge, 1995* (Frankfurt: Peter Lang, 1998), pp. 261–8

Cathcart, K. J. and R. P. Gordon, *The Targum of the Minor Prophets* (The Aramaic Bible 14; Edinburgh: T. & T. Clark, 1989)

Certeau, M. de, *The Practice of Everyday Life* (trans. S. Rendall; Berkeley: University of California Press, 1984)

Chadwick, H. (ed.), *Lessing's Theological Writings* (Stanford: 1957)

Chow, S., *The Sign of Jonah Reconsidered: A Study of its Meaning in the Gospel Traditions* (Stockholm: Almqvist and Wiksell, 1995)

Christian, C., *Jonah* (London: Macmillan, 1996)

Clack, B. and B. R. Clack, *The Philosophy of Religion: A Critical Introduction* (Cambridge: Polity 1998)

Clements, R. E., *The Purpose of the Book of Jonah* (Vetus Testamentum Supplement 28; Leiden: Brill, 1975)

Clifford, J. and G. E. Marcus (eds.), *Writing Culture: The Poetics and Politics of Ethnography* (Berkeley: University of California Press, 1984)

Clines, D. J. A., *The Bible in the Modern World* (Sheffield: Sheffield Academic Press, 1997)

Cohen, A. D., 'The Tragedy of Jonah', *Judaism* 21 (1972), pp. 164–75

Cohen, J. J. (ed.), *Monster Theory: Reading Culture* (Minneapolis: University of Minnesota Press, 1996).

Cohn, G. H., *Das Buch Jona im Lichte der biblischen Erzählkunst* (Studia Semitica Neerlandica 12; Assen: Van Gorcum, 1969)

Cohn, N., *Noah's Flood: The Genesis Story in Western Thought* (New Haven and London: Yale University Press, 1996)

Cohn, N. and G. Peellaert, *Twentieth Century Dreams* (London: Secker and Warburg, 1999)

Cooper, A., 'In Praise of Divine Caprice: The Significance of the Book of Jonah', in Davies and Clines, *Among the Prophets*, pp. 145–63

Cooper, D. E., *Existentialism: A Reconstruction* (Oxford: Blackwell, 1999)

Cox, J. N. and L. J. Reynolds, *New Historical Literary Study: Essays on Reproducing Texts, Representing History* (Princeton: Princeton University Press, 1993)

Craig, K. M., 'Jonah and the Reading Process', *Journal for the Study of the Old Testament* 47 (1990) pp. 103–14

  A Poetics of Jonah: Art in the Service of Ideology (Macon, Ga.: Mercer University Press, 1999)

Crane, H., *The Poems of Hart Crane* (ed. M. Simon; New York: Liveright, 1987)

Crenshaw, J., 'Seduction and Rape: The Confessions of Jeremiah', in J. Crenshaw, *A Whirlpool of Torment: Israelite Traditions of God as an Oppressive Presence* (Philadelphia: Fortress, 1984), pp. 31–56

Crossan, J. D., 'Parable, Allegory and Paradox', in D. Patte (ed.), *Semiology and Parables* (Pittsburgh: Pickwick Press, 1976), pp. 247–81

Crouch, W. B., 'To Question an End, to End a Question: Opening the Closure of the Book of Jonah', *Journal for the Study of the Old Testament* 62 (1994), pp. 101–12

Culler, J., *On Deconstruction: Theory and Criticism after Structuralism* (London: Routledge, 1993)

Cunningham, V., *In the Reading Gaol: Postmodernity, Texts and History* (Oxford: Blackwell, 1994)

Curzon, D. (ed.), *Modern Poems on the Bible: An Anthology* (Philadelphia and Jerusalem: Jewish Publication Society, 1994)

Daniell, D. (ed.), *Tyndale's Old Testament: Being the Pentateuch of 1530, Joshua to 2 Chronicles of 1537 and Jonah* (New Haven: Yale University Press, 1992)

Darwin, C., *On the Origin of Species: A Facsimile of the First Edition With an Introduction by Ernst Mayr* (Cambridge, Mass.: Harvard University Press, 1964)

Daube, D., 'Jonah: A Reminiscence', *Journal of Jewish Studies* 34 (1983), pp. 36–43

Davies, P. R. and D. J. A. Clines (eds.), *Among the Prophets: Language, Image and*

Structure in the Prophetic Writings (Sheffield: Sheffield Academic Press, 1993)

Dawkins, R., *The Selfish Gene* (Oxford: Oxford University Press, 1976)

Day, J., 'Problems in the Interpretation of the Book of Jonah', in A. S. van der Woude (ed.), *In Quest of the Past: Studies in Israelite Religion, Literature and Prophetism* (Kinderhook, N.Y.: E. J. Brill USA, 1990), pp. 32–47

'Prophecy', in D. A. Carson and H. G. M. Williamson (eds.), *It Is Written: Essays in Honour of Barnabas Lindars* (Cambridge: Cambridge University Press, 1988), pp. 39–55

Dennett, D., *Darwin's Dangerous Idea* (London: Allen Lane, 1995)

Derrida, J., *Archive Fever: A Freudian Impression* (trans. E. Peronowitz; Chicago: University of Chicago Press, 1996)

'Faith and Knowledge: The Two Sources of "Religion" at the Limits of Reason Alone', in J. Derrida and G. Vattimo (eds.), *Religion* (Cambridge: Polity Press, 1998), pp. 1–78

Glas (trans. J. P. Leavey and R. Rand; Lincoln, Nebr.: University of Nebraska Press, 1986)

Memoirs, for Paul de Man (trans. C. Lindsay *et al.*; New York: Columbia University Press, 1986)

Of Grammatology (trans. G. Chakravorty Spivak; Baltimore and London: Johns Hopkins University Press, 1976)

Points . . . Interviews 1974–94 (ed. E. Weber; trans. P. Kamuf and others; Stanford: Stanford University Press, 1995)

Writing and Difference (trans. A. Bass; London: Routledge, 1990)

Dollimore, J., *Death, Desire and Loss in Western Culture* (New York: Routledge, 1998)

Sexual Dissidence: Augustine to Wilde/Freud to Foucault (Oxford: Clarendon, 1991)

Dostoevsky, F., *The Brothers Karamazov* (trans. D. Margarshack; Harmondsworth: Penguin, 1964)

Dougherty, S. B., *The Literary Criticism: Henry James* (Athens: Ohio University Press, 1981)

Douglas, J. D. (ed.), *The New Bible Dictionary* (Leicester: IVP, 1962)

Doyle, J., *The Male Experience* (Dubuque, Indiana: William C. Brown, 1989)

Driver, S. R., *Introduction to the Literature of the Old Testament* (New York: Charles Schribner's Sons, 1920)

Dunwoodie, P., *Camus: L'Envers et l'endroit et L'Exil and le royaume* (London: Grant and Cutler, 1985)

Durkheim, E., *The Elementary Forms of the Religious Life* (London: Allen and Unwin, 1915)

Duval, Y.-M., *Le Livre de Jonas dans la littérature chrétienne grecque et latine: sources et influence du commentaire sur Jonas de saint Jérôme* (Paris: Etudes Augustiniennes, 1973)

Eagleton, T., 'J. L. Austin and the Book of Jonah', in R. M. Schwarz (ed.), *The Book and the Text* (Oxford: Blackwell, 1990), pp. 231–6

Literary Theory: An Introduction (Minneapolis: University of Minnesota Press, 1983)

'The Revolt of the Reader', *New Literary History* 13 (1982), pp. 439–52

Edie, J. M. (ed.), *The Primacy of Perception* (Evanston: Northwestern University Press, 1964)

Edinger, E. F., *Ego and Archetype: Individuation and the Religious Function of the Psyche* (New York: G. P. Putnam's, 1972)

Eichhorn, J. G., *Einleitung ins Alte Testament* (Leipzig: 1783)

Eichrodt, W., *Theology of the Old Testament* 1 (trans. J. A. Baker; London: SCM, 1961)

Eilberg-Schwartz, H., *The Savage in Judaism: An Anthropology of Israelite Religion and Ancient Judaism* (Bloomington: Indiana University Press, 1990)

Eisenstein, J. D. (ed.), אוצר מדרשים: *A Library of Two Hundred Minor Midrashim* II (New York: 1915)

Elata-Alster, G. and R. Salmon, 'The Deconstruction of Genre in the Book of Jonah: Towards a Theological Discourse', *Journal of Literature and Theology* 3 (1989), pp. 40–60

Emerson, C., *The First Hundred Years of Mikhail Bakhtin* (Princeton: Princeton University Press, 1997)

Exum, J. C. and S. D. Moore (eds.), *Biblical Studies / Cultural Studies: The Third Sheffield Colloquium* (Sheffield: Sheffield Academic Press, 1998)

Fabian, J., 'Presence and Representation: The Other and Anthropological Writing', *Critical Inquiry* 16 (1989), pp. 753–72

Ferro, M., *Colonization: A Global History* (London and New York: Routledge, 1997)

Feuerbach, L., *The Essence of Christianity* (trans. G. Eliot; New York: Harper and Row, 1957)

Feuillet, A., 'Les sources du livre de Jonas', *Revue Biblique* 54 (1947), pp. 161–86

Fewell, D. Nolan, 'Imagination, Method and Murder: Un/Framing the Face of Post-Exilic Israel', in Beal and Gunn, *Reading Bibles, Writing Bodies*, pp. 132–52

Fewell, D. Nolan (ed.), *Reading Between Texts: Intertextuality and the Hebrew Bible* (Louisville: Westminster/John Knox, 1992)

Fielder, L., *Love and Death in the American Novel* (New York: Stein and Day, 1975)

Fish, S., *Is There a Text in This Class?: The Authority of Interpretive Communities* (Cambridge, Mass.: Harvard University Press, 1980)

'Normal Circumstances, Literal Language, Direct Speech Acts, the Ordinary, the Everyday, the Obvious, What Goes Without Saying, and Other Special Cases', *Critical Inquiry* 4 (1978), pp. 625–44

'Why No One's Afraid of Wolfgang Iser', *Diacritics* 11 (1981), pp. 2–13

Fishbane, M., *Biblical Interpretation in Ancient Israel* (Oxford: Clarendon Press, 1989)

The Exegetical Imagination: On Jewish Thought and Theology (Cambridge, Mass.: Harvard University Press, 1998)

The Garments of Torah: Essays in Biblical Hermeneutics (Bloomington: Indiana University Press, 1992)

Forster, E. M., *Aspects of the Novel* (New York: Harcourt Brace, 1954)

Foucault, M., *The Archaeology of Knowledge* (trans. A. M. Sheridan Smith; London: Tavistock, 1972)

Discipline and Punish: The Birth of the Prison (trans. A. Sheridan; Harmondsworth: Penguin, 1991)

The History of Sexuality I: *An Introduction* (New York: Pantheon, 1978)

Madness and Civilisation: A History of Insanity in the Age of Reason (London: Tavistock, 1971)

The Order of Things: An Archaeology of the Human Sciences (New York: Vintage, 1994, 1st edn 1970)

'What is an Author?', in P. Rabinow (ed.), *The Foucault Reader* (Harmondsworth: Penguin, 1984), pp. 101–20

Fowler, D. C., *The Bible in Middle English Literature* (Seattle and London: University of Washington Press, 1984)

Fox, M. V., *Qoheleth and His Contradictions* (Sheffield: Sheffield Academic Press, 1989)

Frank, H. T. and W. L. Reed (eds.), *Translating and Understanding the Old Testament: Essays in Honour of H. G. May* (Nashville: Abingdon Press, 1970)

Franklin, H. B., *The Wake of the Gods: Melville's Mythology* (Stanford: Stanford University Press, 1963)

Freedman, D. N., 'Did God play a Dirty Trick on Jonah at the End', *Bible Review* 6 (1990), p. 31

Fretheim, T. E., 'Jonah and Theodicy', *Zeitschrift für die alttestamentliche Wissenschaft* 90 (1978), pp. 227–37

Freud, S., *Civilization and its Discontents* (trans. J. Strachey; New York: Norton, 1961)

'The Future of an Illusion', in *Civilization, Society and Religion* (Harmondsworth: Penguin, 1985)

Jokes and Their Relation to the Unconscious (trans. J. Strachey; Harmondsworth: Penguin, 1994)

Friedlander, G. (trans.), *Pirke de Rabbi Eliezer: The Chapters of R. Eliezer the Great* (New York: Sepher Hermon Press, 1981)

Friedrichsen, P., *Kritische Übersicht der Verschiedenen Ansichten von dem Buch Jonas* (Leipzig: 1841)

Frolov, S., 'Returning the Ticket: God and His Prophet in the Book of Jonah', in *Journal for the Study of the Old Testament*, 86 (1999), pp. 85–105

Frost, R., *The Complete Poems of Robert Frost* (London: Jonathan Cape, 1951)

Frye, N., *Anatomy of Criticism* (Princeton: Princeton University Press, 1967)

The Great Code (London: Routledge and Kegan Paul, 1982)

Garb, T., 'Modernity, Identity, Textuality', in Nochlin and Garb, *The Jew in the Text*, pp. 20–30

Gardiner, M. , *The Dialogics of Critique: M. M. Bakhtin and the Theory of Ideology* (London: Routledge, 1992)

Geertz, C., *The Interpretation of Cultures: Selected Essays* (London: Fontana, 1973)
'Religion as a Cultural System', in M. Banton (ed.), *Anthropological Approaches to the Study of Religion* (ASA Monographs 3; London, Tavistock, 1966)

George, T., *Theology of the Reformers* (Nashville: Broadman Press, 1988)

Gese, H., 'Jona ben Ammitai und das Jonabuch', *Theologische Beiträge* 16 (1985), pp. 256–64

Gibson, A., *Reading Narrative Discourse: Studies in the Novel from Cervantes to Beckett* (London: Macmillan, 1990)

Gibson, W., *Hieronymus Bosch* (London: Thames and Hudson, 1995)

Ginzburg, L., *The Legends of the Jews* I (Philadelphia: Jewish Publication Society, 1909–38)

Goitein, S. D. F., 'Some Observations on Jonah', *Journal of the Palestine Oriental Society* 17 (1937), pp. 63–77

Goldingay, J., *Theological Diversity and the Authority of the Old Testament* (Michigan: Eerdmans, 1987)

Golka, F. W., 'Jonaexegese und Antijudaismus', *Kirche und Israel* 1 (1986), pp. 51–61

Good, E. M., 'Jonah: The Absurdity of God', in *Irony in the Old Testament* (London: SPCK, 1965), pp. 39–55

Gordon, C. H., 'Tarshish', in *The Interpreter's Dictionary of the Bible* IV (New York and Nashville: Abingdon, 1962), pp. 517–18

Gosse, E., *Father and Son* (Harmondsworth: Penguin, 1972; 1st edn 1907)

Grafton, A., *The Footnote: A Curious History* (London: Faber and Faber, 1997)

Graham, G., 'Religion, Secularization and Modernity', *Philosophy* 67 (1992), pp. 183–97

Greenblatt, S., *Renaissance Self-Fashioning: From More to Shakespeare* (Chicago and London: University of Chicago Press, 1980)
Shakespearean Negotiations: The Circulation of Social Energy in Renaissance England (Oxford: Clarendon Press, 1988)

Greenstein, E. L., 'Reading Strategies and the Story of Ruth', in Bach, *Women in the Hebrew Bible*, pp. 211–31

Grobel, L., *The Hustons* (London: Bloomsbury, 1990)

Gross, J., *Shylock: Four Hundred Years in the Life of a Legend* (London: Vintage, 1994)

Gunkel, H., *Das Märchen im Alten Testament*, ET *The Folktale in the Old Testament* (trans. M. D. Rutter; Sheffield: Sheffield Academic Press, 1987; 1st edn 1911)
'The Prophets as Writers and Poets' (trans. J. L. Schaaf), in D. L. Petersen (ed.), *Prophecy in Israel* (Philadelphia: Fortress, 1987), pp. 22–73

Gunn, D. M., 'Colonialism and the Vagaries of Scripture: Te Kooti in Canaan (A Story of Bible and Dispossession in Aotearoa/New Zealand)', in Linafelt and Beal, *God in the Fray*, pp. 127–42

Gunn, D. M. and D. Nolan Fewell, *Narrative in the Hebrew Bible* (Oxford: Oxford University Press, 1993)

Hadas, M. (trans.), *The Stoic Philosophy of Seneca: Essays and Letters* (New York: Doubleday, 1958)

Haigh, C., *English Reformations: Religion, Politics and Society under the Tudors* (Oxford: Clarendon Press, 1993)

Halpern, B. and R. E. Friedman, 'Composition and Paranomasia in the Book of Jonah', *Hebrew Annual Review* 4 (1980), pp. 79–92

Halverson, M. (ed.), *Religious Drama* III (New York: Meridian Books, 1957)

Hampl, P., 'In the Belly of the Whale', in C. Büchmann and C. Spiegel (eds.), *Out of the Garden: Women Writers on the Bible* (New York: Ballantine, 1995), pp. 289–301

Handelman, H., *The Slayers of Moses: The Emergence of Rabbinic Interpretation in Modern Literary Theory* (Albany: State University of New York Press, 1982)

Hardy, T., *The Complete Poems* (London: Macmillan, 1974)

Hassan, I., *The Postmodern Turn: Essays in Postmodern Theory* (Columbus, Ohio: Ohio State University Press, 1987)

'Towards a Concept of Postmodernism', in T. Docherty (ed.), *Postmodernism: A Reader* (Hemel Hempstead: Harvester Wheatsheaf, 1993) pp. 146–56

Hawkes, T., *Structuralism and Semiotics* (New Accents; London: Routledge, 1989)

Hawthorn, J., *Cunning Passages: New Historicism, Cultural Materialism and Marxism in the Contemporary Literary Debate* (London: Arnold, 1996)

Hendrickson, R., *The Ocean Almanac* (London: Hutchinson)

Herbert, T. W., 'Calvinist Earthquake: Moby Dick and Religious Tradition', in Brodhead, *New Essays on Moby Dick*, pp. 109–40

Herbert, T. W., *Moby Dick and Calvinism: A World Dismantled* (New Brunswick, N.J.: Rutgers University Press, 1977)

Herodotus, *The Histories* (trans. A. de Selincourt, intro. A. R. Burn; Harmondsworth: Penguin, 1972)

Hersey, J., *The Writer's Craft* (New York: Alfred A. Knopf, 1974)

Herzberg, A., *The French Enlightenment and the Jews* (New York: 1968)

Hoffman, E., *Lost in Translation: Life in a New Language* (London: Minerva, 1989)

Holbert, J. C., 'Deliverance Belongs to YHWH!: Satire in the Book of Jonah', *Journal for the Study of the Old Testament* 21 (1981), pp. 59–81

Hollander, J., in *The Figure of Echo: A Mode of Allusion in Milton and After* (Berkeley: University of California Press, 1981)

Holquist, M. (ed.), *The Dialogic Imagination: Four Essays by Mikhail Bakhtin* (trans. C. Emerson and M. Holquist; Austin: University of Texas Press, 1994)

Holstein, J., 'Melville's Inversion of Jonah in Moby-Dick', *The Iliff Review* 35 (1978), pp. 13–19

Hoonaker, A. van, *Les douze Petits Prophètes* (Paris: 1908)

Hooper, J., 'The Confession and Protestation of John Hooper's Faith', in

C. Nevinson (ed.), *Later Writings of Bishop Hooper* (Cambridge: Cambridge University Press, 1852)

Hooper, J., *An Oversighte and Deliberacioun uppon the Holy Prophet Jonas: Made, and Uttered before the Kinges Majesty, and His Most Honorable Councell* (Lent 1550), in S. Carr (ed.), *Early Writings of John Hooper Lord Bishop of Gloucester and Worcester* (Cambridge: The Parker Society, 1843), pp. 435–558

Horkheimer, M. and T. Adorno, *Dialectic of Enlightenment* (New York: Seabury Press, 1972)

Humble-Jackson, S., *Testament: The Animated Bible* (London: Boxtree, 1996)

Hurd, M., *Jonah Man Jazz* (London: Novello, 1967)

Hutcheon L., 'Circling the Downspout of Empire', in B. Ashcroft, G. Griffiths and H. Tiffin (eds.), *The Post-Colonial Studies Reader* (London: Routledge, 1995), pp. 130–35

Hutcheon, L., *A Theory of Parody: The Teachings of Twentieth Century Art Forms* (London: Methuen, 1985)

Huxley, A., 'Jonah', in G. Grigson (ed.), *The Cherry Tree* (London: Phoenix House, 1959).

Idel, M., *Kabbalah: New Perspectives* (New Haven and London: Yale University Press, 1988)

Irenaeus, *Against Heresies* in A. Roberts and J. Donaldson (eds.), *The Anti-Nicene Fathers* I (Buffalo: The Christian Literature Publishing Company, 1885), pp. 315–567

Irigaray, L., *Speculum of the Other Woman* (trans. G. G. Gill; Ithaca: Cornell University Press, 1985)

Irwin, W. R., *The Game of the Impossible: A Rhetoric of Fantasy* (Illinois, 1976)

Iser, W., 'The Reading Process: A Phenomenological Approach', in D. Lodge (ed.), *Modern Criticism and Theory: A Reader* (London: Longman, 1988)

Jabès, E., *Livre des questions* (Paris: Gallimard, 1963)

Jackson Flanders, H. *et al.*, *People of the Covenant: An Introduction to the Old Testament* (New York: The Ronald Press, 1973)

Jacobson, D. C., *Does David Still Play Before You? Israeli Poetry and the Bible* (Detroit: Wayne State University Press, 1997)

James, H., *The Art of Fiction and Other Essays* (New York: Oxford University Press, 1948)

'Guy de Maupassant' (1888), in L. Edel (ed.), *The House of Fiction: Essays on the Novel by Henry James* (London: Rupert Hart-Davis, 1957)

'Mr. Tennyson's Drama', *Galaxy* 20 (September 1875), pp. 396–7

Jankélevitch, V., *Quelque part dans l'inachevé* (Paris: Gallimard, 1978)

Jasper, D., 'The Death of God: A Live Issue?', *Biblicon* (3 May 1998), pp. 19–26

Jellinek, A. (trans.), *Bet ha Midrash* VI (Jerusalem: Wahrman Books, 1967)

Jemielity, T., *Satire and the Hebrew Prophets* (Louisville: Westminster/John Knox Press, 1992)

Jepsen, A., 'Anmerkungen zum Buche Jona: Beiträge zur Theologie des Alten Testaments', in H. Stoebe (ed.), *Wort-Gebot-Gelaube: Theologie des Alten Testaments* (Zürich: Zwingli-Verlag, 1970), pp. 297–305

Josipovici, G., *The Book of God: A Response to the Bible* (New Haven: Yale University Press, 1988)

Joyce, J., *Finnegan's Wake* (New York: Viking, 1966)

Joyner, C. (ed.), *Down By the Riverside* (Urbana: University of Illinois Press, 1984)

Jung, C. G., *Symbols of Transformation* (New York: Pantheon, 1956)

Kaiser, O., 'Wirklichkeit, Möglichkeit und Vorurteil. Ein Beitrag zum Verständnis des Buches Jona', *Evangelische Theologie* 33 (1973), pp. 91–103

Kant, I., *What is Enlightenment?* (trans. and ed. L. W. Beck; Chicago: Chicago University Press, 1955)

Kaufmann, E., *The Religion of Israel: From its Beginnings to the Babylonian Exile* (trans. and abridged M. Greenberg; London: Allen and Unwin, 1961)

Kearney, R., *Poetics of Imagining: From Husserl to Lyotard* (London: Harper Collins, 1991)

Keller, C., *Apocalypse Now and Then* (Boston: Beacon Press, 1996)

Keller, C. A., 'Jonas. Le portrait d'un prophète', *Theologische Zeitschrift* 21 (1965), pp. 329–40

Kennedy, A. L., *Now That You're Back* (London: Vintage, 1995)

Kermode, F., *The Genesis of Secrecy: On the Interpretation of Narrative* (Cambridge, Mass.: Harvard University Press, 1980)

The Sense of an Ending: Studies in the Theory of Fiction (Oxford: Oxford University Press, 1967)

Kingsolver, B., *The Poisonwood Bible* (London: Faber and Faber, 1999)

Kneirim, R. P., *The Task of Old Testament Theology* (Grand Rapids: Eerdmans, 1995)

Knight, G. A. F., *Ruth and Jonah: Introduction and Commentary* (London: SCM, 1960)

Knipping, J. B., *Iconography of the Counter-Reformation in the Netherlands: Heaven and Earth* 1 (Nieuwkoop: B. de Graaf, 1974)

Koch, K., *The Growth of Biblical Tradition* (London: A. & C. Black, 1969)

The Prophets. II. *The Babylonian and Persian Periods* (trans. M. Kohl; London, SCM, 1983)

Krahmer, A. W., *Historische-kritische Untersuchung über das Buch Jonas* (Cassel: 1839)

Kreitzer, L. J., *The Old Testament in Fiction and Film* (Sheffield: Sheffield Academic Press, 1994)

Kristeva, J., *Desire in Language: A Semiotic Approach to Literature and Art* (trans. T. Gora, A. Jardine, and L. S. Roudiez; ed. L. S. Roudiez; New York: Columbia University Press, 1980)

Semiotike: Recherches pour une sémanalyse (Collections Tel Quel; Paris: Le Seuil, 1969)

Kugel, J. L., *The Bible As it Was* (Cambridge, Mass: Harvard University Press, 1997)

'Two Introductions to Midrash', in G. Hartman and S. Budick (eds.), *Midrash and Literature* (New York: Yale University Press, 1986), pp. 77–103

Kümmel, W. G., *Promise and Fulfilment* (London: SCM, 1957)

Kundera, M., *Testaments Betrayed: An Essay in Nine Parts* (New York: HarperCollins, 1993)

Lacocque, A., *Romance She Wrote: A Hermeneutical Essay on Song of Songs* (Harrisburg, Pa.: Trinity Press International, 1998)

Lacoque, A. and P.-E. Lacoque, *The Jonah Complex* (Atlanta: John Knox, 1981)

Jonah: A Psycho-Religious Approach to the Prophet (Columbia: University of South Carolina Press, 1990)

Lauterbach (trans.), *Mekilta de Rabbi Ishmael* (Philadelphia: Jewish Publication Society of America, 1933)

Laytner, A., *Arguing with God: A Jewish Tradition* (Northvale, N.J.: Jason Aronson, 1990)

Lehmberg, S. E., *The Latter Parliaments of Henry VIII, 1536–1547* (Cambridge: Cambridge University Press, 1977)

Lettinga, J. P., *Grammaire de l'Hebrue Biblique* (Leiden: E. J. Brill, 1980)

Levenson, J. D., *The Hebrew Bible: The Old Testament Historical Criticism* (Louisville: Westminster/John Knox, 1993)

Levinas, E., *L'Au-delà du verset* (Paris: Les Editions de Minuit, 1982)

Difficile Liberté: Essai sur le Judaïsme (Paris: Albin Michel, 1963)

Levine, A.-J., 'Diaspora as Metaphor: Bodies and Boundaries in the Book of Tobit', in J. A. Overman and R. S. MacLennan (eds.), *Diaspora Jews and Judaism: Essays in Honour of, and in Dialogue with, A. Thomas Kraabel* (Diaspora Jews and Judaism 41; Atlanta: Scholar's Press, 1992), pp. 105–17

Levine, E., *The Aramaic Version of Jonah* (New York: Sepher Hermon Press, 1981)

'Jonah as a Philosophical Book', *Zeitschrift für die alttestamentliche Wissenschaft* 96 (1984), pp. 235–45

Lévi-Strauss, C., *Myth and Meaning* (London: Routledge, 1978)

Leyda, J., *The Melville Log: A Documentary of Herman Melville* (2 vols.; New York: Cordian Press, 1969)

Limburg, J., *Jonah: A Commentary* (Old Testament Library; London: SCM, 1993)

Linafelt, T. and T. K. Beal (eds.), *God in the Fray: A Tribute to Walter Brueggemann* (Minneapolis: Fortress, 1998)

Loomba, A., *Colonialism/Postcolonialism* (London and New York: Routledge, 1998)

Lubbock, P. (ed.), *The Letters of Henry James* (2 vols.; New York: Charles Schribner's Sons, 1920)

Luther. M., 'Lectures on Jonah', in H. C. Oswald (ed.), *Minor Prophets* II: *Jonah, Habbakuk* (Luther's Works 19; Saint Louis: Concordia, 1974)

McConnell, F. (ed.), *The Bible and the Narrative Tradition* (New York: Oxford University Press, 1986)

McCracken, S., *Pulp: Reading Popular Fiction* (Manchester: Manchester University Press, 1998)

Magonet, J., *Form and Meaning: Studies in the Literary Techniques of the Book of Jonah* (Sheffield: Almond Press, 1983)

'Jonah', in D. N. Freedman (ed.), *The Anchor Bible Dictionary* (New York and London: Doubleday, 1992), pp. 936–42

Manger, I., *The Book of Paradise: The Wonderful Adventures of Shmuel-Aba Abervo* (New York: Hill and Wang, 1965; 1st edn 1939)

Manuel, E., *The Broken Staff: Judaism Through Christian Eyes* (Cambridge, Mass.: Harvard University Press, 1992)

Melville, H., *Moby Dick* (A Norton Critical Edition; ed. H. Hayford and H. Parker; New York: W. W. Norton, 1967)

Moby Dick (Ware, Hertfordshire: Wordsworth, 1992)

Michaelis, J. D., *Deutsche Übersetzung des Alten Testaments mit Anmerkungen für Ungelehrte* (Göttingen: Vanderhoeck and Ruprecht, 1782)

Middleton, A., 'The Idea of Public Poetry in the Reign of Richard II', *Speculum* 53 (1979), pp. 94–114

Miles, J., *God: A Biography* (London: Simon and Schuster, 1995)

'Laughing at the Bible: Jonah as Parody', in Y. T. Radday and A. Brenner (eds.), *On Humour and the Comic in the Hebrew Bible* (Sheffield: The Almond Press, 1990), pp. 203–15

Miscall, P. D., 'Isaiah: New Heavens, New Earth, New Book', in Fewell, *Reading Between Texts*, pp. 41–56

Mitchell, S., 'Jonah', in 'Five Parables', *Tikkun* 4.3 (May/June 1989), p. 31

Mohanty, S. P., 'Us and Them: On the Philosophical Bases of Political Criticism', *Yale Journal of Criticism* 2.2 (1989), pp. 1–32

Montefiore, C. G. and H. Loewe, *A Rabbinic Anthology* (New York: Schocken Books, 1974)

Montrose, L. A., 'Professing the Renaissance: The Poetics and Politics of Culture', in Veeser (ed.), *The New Historicism*, pp. 15–36

Moore, C. A., *Tobit: A New Translation with Introduction and Commentary* (The Anchor Bible; New York: Doubleday, 1996)

Moore, S. D., *God's Gym: Divine Male Bodies of the Bible* (New York: Routledge, 1996)

Literary Criticism and the Gospels: The Theoretical Challenge (New Haven and London: Yale University Press, 1989)

Mark and Luke in Poststructuralist Perspectives: Jesus Begins to Write (New Haven: Yale University Press, 1992)

'Que(e)rying Paul: Preliminary Questions', in D. J. A. Clines and S. D. Moore (eds.), *Auguries: The Jubilee Volume of the Sheffield Department of Biblical Studies* (Sheffield: Sheffield Academic Press, 1998), pp. 250–74

Moore, S. D. (ed.), *In Search of the Present: The Bible through Cultural Studies* (*Semeia*; Atlanta: Scholar's Press, forthcoming)

Morris, P., *The Bakhtin Reader: Selected Writings of Bakhtin, Medvedev and Voloshinov* (London: Edward Arnold, 1994)

Murphy, R. E., *The Tree of Life: An Exploration of Biblical Wisdom* (New York: Doubleday, 1990)

Nabakov, V., *Strong Opinions* (New York: McGraw-Hill, 1975)

Nadel, I. B., *Joyce and the Jews* (London: Macmillan, 1989)

Neugroschel, J. (ed.), *Yenne Velt: Great Works of Jewish Fantasy* (London: Picador, 1976)

Nevinson, C. (ed.), *Later Writings of Bishop Hooper* (Cambridge: Cambridge University Press, 1852)

Newman, J. Henry, *Essays Critical and Historical* (2 vols.; London: 1887)

Nielsen, E., 'Le message primitif du livre de Jonas', *Revue d'histoire et de philosophie religieuses* 59 (1979), pp. 499–507

Nietzsche, F., *The Anti-Christ* (trans. R. J. Hollingdale; Harmondsworth: Penguin, 1990)

   The Birth of Tragedy and The Genealogy of Morals (trans. F. Golffing; New York: Doubleday, 1956)

Nochlin, L., 'Starting with the Self: Jewish Identity and Its Representation', in Nochlin and Garb, *The Jew in the Text*, pp. 7–19

Nochlin, L. and T. Garb (eds.), *The Jew in the Text: Modernity and the Construction of Identity* (London: Thames and Hudson, 1995)

Noll, K. L., 'Is There a Text in this Tradition? Readers' Response and the Taming of Samuel's God', *Journal for the Study of the Old Testament* 83 (1999), pp. 31–51

O'Brien, J., 'On Saying "No" to a Prophet', in J. Capel Anderson and J. L. Staley (eds.), *Taking It Personally: Autobiographical Biblical Criticism* (*Semeia* 72; Atlanta: Scholar's Press, 1995), pp. 111–21

Orlinsky, H. M., 'Nationalism-Universalism and Internationalism in Ancient Israel', in Frank and Reed, *Translating and Understanding the Old Testament*, pp. 206–36

Orwell, G., 'Inside the Whale', in *Inside the Whale and Other Essays* (Harmondsworth: Penguin, 1979; 1st edn 1940), pp. 9–50

Otto, R., 'The Element of the Mysterious', in N. N. Glazter (ed.), *The Dimensions of Job: A Study and Selected Readings* (New York: Schocken, 1969), pp. 225–8

Ouaknin, M., *The Burnt Book: Reading the Talmud* (trans. L. Brown; Princeton: Princeton University Press, 1995)

Paine, T., *The Theological Works of Thomas Paine* (Boston: The Advocates of Common Sense, 1834)

Palumbo, D. (ed.), *Erotic Universe: Sexuality and Fantastic Literature* (New York: Greenwood Press, 1986)

Pater, W., *The Renaissance* (London: Macmillan, 1910, 1st edn 1873)

Paton, L. B., *The Book of Esther* (International Critical Commentary; New York: Charles Scribner's Sons, 1908)

Payne, R., 'The Prophet Jonah: Reluctant Messenger and Intercessor', *Expository Times* 100 (1988), pp. 131–4

Peake, A. S., 'Jonah', in *Peake's Commentary on the Bible* (London: Nelson and Sons, 1919), pp. 556–8

Peiper, R. (ed.), *Corpus Scriptorum Ecclesiasticorum Latinorum* XXIII (Vienna: Akademie der Wissenschaften, 1891), pp. 221–6

Perrin, N., *Rediscovering the Teaching of Jesus* (London: SCM, 1967)

Pfeiffer, R. H., *Introduction to the Old Testament* (New York: Harper and Row, 1948)

Phillips, A., 'The Cultural Cringe', in *The Australian Tradition: Studies in a Colonial Culture* (Melbourne: Cheshire, 1958)

Pippin, T., *Apocalyptic Bodies: The Biblical End of the World in Text and Image* (London and New York: Routledge, 1999)

Pippin, T. and G. Aichele (eds.), *The Monstrous and the Unspeakable: The Bible and Fantastic Literature* (Sheffield: Sheffield Academic Press, 1997)

Prior, M., *The Bible and Colonialism: A Moral Critique* (Sheffield: Sheffield Academic Press, 1997)

Pusey, E. D., 'Jonah', in *The Minor Prophets with a Commentary, Explanatory and Practical* (London: Walter Smith and Innes, 1860), pp. 247–87

Putter, A., 'Patience', in *An Introduction to the Gawain-Poet* (Harlow: Longman, 1996)

Pyper, H. S., 'The Selfish Text: The Bible and Memetics', in Exum and Moore, *Biblical Studies / Cultural Studies*, pp. 70–90

'The Triumph of the Lamb: Psalm 23, Darwin and Textual Fitness' (unpublished paper presented at the *Reading, Theory and the Bible* section of the *Society of Biblical Literature* Annual Meeting, Orlando, 21–24 November 1998)

Rad, G. von, *God at Work in Israel* (trans. J. H. Marks; Nashville: Abingdon, 1980)

Old Testament Theology II: *The Theology of Israel's Prophetic Traditions* (trans. D. M. G. Stalker; London: SCM Press, 1975))

Réau, L., *Iconographie de l'art chrétien*. Tome II. *Iconographie de la Bible*. I. *Ancien Testament* (Paris: Presses Universitaires de France, 1956)

Ricoeur, P., *Figuring the Sacred* (Minneapolis: Augsburg Fortress, 1995)

Time and Narrative (3 vols.; trans. J. McLaughlin and D. Pellauer; Chicago: Chicago University Press, 1984)

Rimon-Kenan, S., *Narrative Fiction: Contemporary Poetics* (London and New York: Routledge, 1994)

Roberts, A. and J. Donaldson (eds.), *The Anti-Nicene Fathers* I and III (Buffalo: The Christian Literature Publishing Company, 1885)

Tertullian (Ante-Nicene Christian Library 18; Edinburgh: T. & T. Clark, 1870)

Roberts, M. (ed.), *The Faber Book of Modern Verse* (London: Faber and Faber, 1982; 4th edn rev. P. Porter)

Robinet, J. B., *Considérations philosophiques sur la gradation naturelle des formes de l'être* (Paris: 1768)

Robinson, B. P., 'Jonah's Qiqayon Plant', *Zeitschrift für die alttestamentliche Wissenschaft* 97 (1985), pp. 390–403

Roemer, M., *Telling Stories: Postmodernism and the Invalidation of Traditional Narrative* (Lanham, Md.: Rowman and Littlefield, 1995)

Rosen, N., 'Justice for Jonah, or a Bible Bartleby', in D. Rosenberg (ed.), *Congregation: Contemporary Writers Read the Jewish Bible* (New York: Harcourt Brace Jovanovich, 1987), pp. 222–31

Rosenberg, J., 'Jonah and the Nakedness of Deeds', *Tikkun* 2.4 (1987), pp. 36–8

Rowley, H. H., *The Missionary Message of the Old Testament* (lectures given in 1944 to the Baptist Missionary Society; London: The Carey Press, 1948)

Royle, N. *After Derrida* (Manchester: Manchester University Press, 1995)

Rubenstein, R., *After Auschwitz: Radical Theology and Contemporary Judaism* (Indianapolis: Bobbs-Merrill, 1966)

Rudolph, W., *Joel, Amos, Obadja, Jona* (Gütersloh: Gerd Mohn, 1971)

Ruether, R. Radford and H. J. Ruether, *The Wrath of Jonah* (New York: Harper and Row, 1989)

Rushdie, S., 'Outside the Whale', in *Imaginary Homelands: Essays and Criticism 1981–1991* (London: Viking/Granta, 1991)

The Satanic Verses (Dover, Del.: The Consortium, 1988)

Said, E. W., *Culture and Imperialism* (London: Vintage, 1994)

'Orientalism Reconsidered', *Cultural Critique* 1, pp. 89–107

Orientalism: Western Conceptions of the Orient (Harmondsworth: Penguin, 1995; 1st edn 1978)

Salters, R., *Jonah and Lamentations* (Old Testament Guides; Sheffield: Sheffield Academic Press, 1994)

Sandmel, S., *The Hebrew Scriptures* (New York: Alfred A. Knopf, 1963)

Sarraut, A., *Grandeur et Servitude Coloniales* (Paris: Sagittaire, 1931)

Sasson, J., *Jonah* (The Anchor Bible; New York: Doubleday, 1990)

Sawyer, D. F., 'The Deconstructed Male – A Biblical Theme', paper given at The Society of Biblical Literature Annual Meeting, Boston, November 1999

Sawyer, J. F. A., *The Fifth Gospel: Isaiah in the History of Christianity* (Cambridge: Cambridge University Press, 1996)

Scherman, N. and M. Zlotowitz, *Jonah: A New Translation with a Commentary Anthologised from Talmudic, Midrashic and Rabbinic Sources* (Artscroll Tanakh Series; New York: Mesorah Publications, 1988)

Schleiermacher, F., *The Christian Faith* (ed. H. R. Mackintosh and J. S. Stewart; Philadelphia: Fortress, 1976; 1st edn 1830)

Schniewind, J., *Das Evangelium nach Matthäus* (Göttingen: Vanderhoeck and Ruprecht, 1950)

Scholem, G., *Major Trends in Jewish Mysticism* (New York: Schocken Books, 1974; 1st edn 1949)

Scholem, G. (ed.), *Zohar, the Book of Splendour: Basic Readings from the Kabbalah* (New York: Schocken Books, 1977; 1st edn 1949), pp. 103–6

Schwarz, H., *Reimagining the Bible: The Storytelling of the Rabbis* (Oxford: Oxford University Press, 1998)

Schwartz, R. M., 'Adultery in the House of David: The Metanarrative of Biblical Scholarship and the Narratives of the Bible', in Bach, *Women in the Hebrew Bible*, pp. 335–50

Schweitzer, A., *The Quest of the Historical Jesus: A Critical Study of its Progress from Reimarus to Wrede* (trans. W. Montgomery; London: Adam and Charles Black, 1910)

Schwerman, N., H. Goldwurm, and A. Gold, *Yom Kippur: Its Significance, Laws and Prayers* (New York: Mesorah, 1989)

Scott, Jr, N. A. *The Modern Vision of Death* (Richmond, Va.: John Knox Press, 1967)

Segovia, F. F., 'Biblical Criticism and Postcolonial Studies: Toward a Postcolonial Optic', in Sugirtharajah, *The Postcolonial Bible*, pp. 49–65

Sharpe, R. (trans.), *Adomnán's Life of St Columba* (London: 1995)

Sherwood, Y. M., '"Colonising the Old Testament" or "Representing Christian Interests Abroad"', in S. E. Porter and B. W. R. Pearson (eds.), *Christian–Jewish Relations Through the Centuries* (Sheffield: Sheffield Academic Press, 2000)

'Darke Texts Need Notes: Reassessing Prophetic Poetry' (unpublished paper presented to the Society for Old Testament Study annual meeting, University of Glasgow, July 1999)

'Of Fruit and Corpses and Wordplay Visions: Picturing Amos 8.1–3' (*Biblicon*, forthcoming)

Jonah (The Blackwell Bible Commentaries; Oxford: Blackwell, forthcoming)

'Prophetic Scatology: Prophecy and the Art of Sensation', in S. D. Moore (ed.), *In Search of the Present: The Bible Through Cultural Studies* (*Semeia* 82; Atlanta: Scholar's Press, 2000)

The Prostitute and the Prophet: Hosea's Marriage in Literary-theoretical Perspective (Sheffield: Sheffield Academic Press, 1996)

'Rocking the Boat: Jonah and the New Historicism', *Biblical Interpretation* 6.1 (1998), pp. 364–402

Simon, M. (ed.), *The Poems of Hart Crane* (New York: Liveright, 1987)

Simon, M. and P. P. Levertoff (trans.), *The Zohar* (London: Soncino Press, 1934)

Sinfield, A., *Faultlines: Cultural Materialism and the Politics of Dissident Reading* (Oxford: Clarendon Press, 1992)

Smart, J. D., 'The Book of Jonah: Introduction and Exegesis', in G. A. Buttrick, T. S. Kepler, H. G. May, *et al.* (eds.), *The Interpreter's Bible* vi (Nashville: Abingdon, 1956), pp. 883–4

Soares-Prabhu, G. M., 'Laughing at Idols: The Dark Side of Biblical Monotheism (An Indian Reading of Isa. 44.9–20)', in F. Segovia and M. Tolbert (eds.), *Reading From This Place*. II. *Social Location and Biblical Interpretation in Global Perspective* (Minneapolis: Fortress, 1995), pp. 109–31

Spearing, A. C. and J. E. Spearing (eds.), *Poetry in the Age of Chaucer* (London: Edward Arnold, 1974)

Spurr, D., *The Rhetoric of Empire: Colonial Discourse in Journalism, Travel Writing and Imperial Administration* (Durham and London: Duke University Press, 1993)

Stanbury, S., 'Space and Visual Hermeneutics in the *Gawain*-Poet', *Chaucer Review* 21 (1987), pp. 476–89

Stein, J. and G. Plimpton, *Edie: An American Biography* (New York: Alfred A. Knopf, 1982)

Stern, D., '*Imitatio Hominis*: Anthropomorphism and the Character(s) of God in Rabbinic Literature', in *Prooftexts* 12 (1992), pp. 151–74

Sternberg, M., *The Poetics of Biblical Narrative: Ideological Literature and the Drama of Reading* (Bloomington: Indiana University Press, 1987)

Stewart, W., *Nonsense: Aspects of Intertextuality in Folklore and Literature* (Baltimore: Johns Hopkins University Press, 1980)

Stone, B. (ed. and trans.), *Medieval English Verse* (Harmondsworth: Penguin, 1981)

Stone, M. E. and T. A. Bergren, *Biblical Figures Outside the Bible* (Harrisburg: Trinity Press International, 1998)

Strype, J., *Ecclesiastical Memorials* II (Oxford: Oxford University Press, 1822)

Stuart, D., *Hosea–Jonah* (Word; Waco, Tex.: Word Books, 1987)

Sugirtharajah, R. S., 'A Postcolonial Exploration of Collusion and Construction in Biblical Interpretation', in Sugirtharajah (ed.), *The Postcolonial Bible*, pp. 91–116

Sugirtharajah, R. S. (ed.), *The Postcolonial Bible* (Sheffield: Sheffield Academic Press, 1998)

Sumerfield, H., L. Ryken, and L. Eldredge, 'Jonah', in D. L. Jeffrey (ed.), *A Dictionary of Biblical Tradition in English Literature* (Grand Rapids, Mich.: Eerdmans, 1992), pp. 409–11

Szymborska, W., *View With a Grain of Sand: Selected Poems* (trans. S. Baraczak and C. Cavanagh; London: Harcourt Brace, 1995)

Tanner, T., *City of Words* (New York: Harper and Row, 1971)

Tarlin, J., 'Utopia and Pornography in Ezekiel: Violence, Hope and the Shattered Male Subject', in Beal and Gunn, *Reading Bibles, Writing Bodies*, pp. 175–83

Thackston, W. M. (trans.), *The Tales of the Prophets of al-Kisa'i* (Boston: Twayne Publishers, 1978)

Thompson, L., *Melville's Quarrel with God* (Princeton: Princeton University Press, 1952)

Thompson, T. L., 'Why Talk about the Past? The Bible as Epic and

Historiography' (unpublished paper presented to the Society for Biblical Literature annual meeting, Boston, November 1999)

Todorov, T., *The Poetics of Prose* (trans. R. Howard; Ithaca: New York, 1977)

Trible, P., 'Divine Incongruities in the Book of Jonah', in Linafelt and Beal, *God in the Fray*, pp. 198–208

Rhetorical Criticism: Context and Method in the Book of Jonah (Minneapolis: Fortress, 1994)

'Studies in the Book of Jonah' (PhD diss., Columbia University; Ann Arbor, Mich.: University Microfilms International, 1963; order no. 65–7479)

Troeltsch., E., *Protestantism and Progress: A Historical Study of the Relation of Protestantism to the Modern World* (trans. W. Montgomery; London: Williams and Norgate, 1912)

Trudinger, P., 'Jonah: A Post-Exilic Verbal Cartoon?', *The Downside Review* (April 1989), pp. 142–3

Turner, A. K., *The History of Hell* (London: Robert Hale, 1993)

Vantuone, P. (ed.), *The Pearl Poems ii: Patience and Sir Gawain and the Green Knight* (New York and London: Garland, 1984)

Vargosh, T., 'Gnostic Myths in Moby Dick', *Proceedings of the Modern Language Association* 81 (1966), pp. 272–7

Vattimo, G., *The Transparent Society* (Cambridge: Polity Press, 1992)

Veeser, H. Aram (ed.), *The New Historicism* (London: Routledge, 1989)

The New Historicism Reader (London: Routledge, 1984)

Vincent, H. P., *The Trying-Out of Moby Dick* (New York: Carbondale; 1st edn 1949)

Warner, M., *From the Beast to the Blonde: On Fairy Tales and Their Tellers* (London: Chatto and Windus, 1994)

Watson, F., *Text and Truth: Redefining Biblical Theology* (Edinburgh: T. & T. Clark, 1997)

Weber, M., 'The Social Psychology of the World Religions', in H. H. Gerth and C. W. Mills (eds.), *From Max Weber: Essays in Sociology* (London: Routledge, 1991), pp. 267–301

Wellhausen, J., *Die Kleinen Propheten* (Berlin: Reiner, 1898)

Wesker, A., *The Journalists/The Merchant/The Wedding Feast* (Harmondsworth: Penguin, 1980)

White, H., *Metahistory: The Historical Imagination in Nineteenth Century Europe* (London: Johns Hopkins Press, 1973)

Wiebe, D., *The Irony of Theology and the Nature of Religious Thought* (Montreal: McGill-Queen's Press, 1991)

Wiesel, E., *Five Biblical Portraits* (Notre Dame: University of Notre Dame Press, 1981)

A Jew Today (New York: Vintage, 1978)

Willett, J., *The Theatre of Bertolt Brecht: A Study From Eight Aspects* (London: Eyre Methuen, 1977)

Wilson, A. N., *God's Funeral* (London: John Murray, 1999)

Wilt, T. L., 'Jonah: A Battle of Shifting Alliances', in Davies and Clines (eds.), *Among the Prophets*, pp. 164–81

Winckler, H., 'Zum Buche Jona', *Altorientalische Forschungen* 2 (1900), pp. 260–5

Wistrich, R. S., *Antisemitism: The Longest Hatred* (London: Methuen, 1991)

Wolff, H. W., *Obadiah and Jonah* (Hermeneia; trans. M. Kohl; Minneapolis: Augsburg, 1988)

Wright, C. H., 'The Book of Jonah', in Wright, *Biblical Essays* (Edinburgh: T. & T. Clark, 1886), pp. 34–98

Wright, N., *Melville's Use of the Bible* (Durham, N.C.: Duke University Press, 1949)

Wünsche, A., *Aus Israels Lehrhallen* II (Hildesheim: Georg Olms, 1967)

Yinger, J. M., *The Scientific Study of Religion* (London: Routledge, 1970)

Zamora, L. Parkinson, and W. B. Faris (eds.), *Magic Realism: Theory, History, Community* (Durham, N.C. and London: Duke University Press, 1995)

Index

315

New Testament

Apocrypha and Pseudepigrapha

Made in the USA
San Bernardino, CA
11 March 2015